Katherine Dunham

KATHERINE DUNHAM

Dance and the African Diaspora

Joanna Dee Das

OXFORD
UNIVERSITY PRESS

Oxford University Press is a department of the University of Oxford. It furthers
the University's objective of excellence in research, scholarship, and education
by publishing worldwide. Oxford is a registered trade mark of Oxford University
Press in the UK and certain other countries.

Published in the United States of America by Oxford University Press
198 Madison Avenue, New York, NY 10016, United States of America.

Library of Congress Cataloging-in-Publication Data
Names: Das, Joanna Dee, author.
Title: Katherine Dunham : dance and the African diaspora / Joanna Dee Das.
Description: New York, NY : Oxford University Press, 2017.
Identifiers: LCCN 2016039505| ISBN 9780190264871 (hardback) |
ISBN 9780190264901 (oxford scholarly online)
Subjects: LCSH: Dunham, Katherine | Dancers—United States—Biography. | Women
dancers—United States—Biography. | African American dancers—Biography. |
Anthropologists—United States—Biography. | African American anthropologists—
Biography. | BISAC: BIOGRAPHY & AUTOBIOGRAPHY / Entertainment & Performing Arts. |
PERFORMING ARTS / Dance / Modern.
Classification: LCC GV1785.D82 D44 2017 | DDC 792.8092 [B]—dc23
LC record available at https://lccn.loc.gov/2016039505

9 8 7 6 5 4 3
Printed by Sheridan Books, Inc., United States of America

CONTENTS

LIST OF ILLUSTRATIONS

PREFACE AND ACKNOWLEDGMENTS

I never met Katherine Dunham, but she shaped the course of my life. At age nine, I began to take jazz dance at the Center of Creative Arts (COCA), a community arts center in University City, an "inner ring" suburb of St. Louis, Missouri. I had only a vague awareness that my teacher, Lee Nolting, doubled as the ballet mistress for the Katherine Dunham Children's Workshop across the river in East St. Louis. After taking a Dunham Technique class at age twelve with Lee's husband, Darryl Braddix, I realized that many aspects of my jazz dance training, including our arm positions during warm-ups and our body-part isolations, came from Dunham Technique. Even more influentially, Lee based the COCA dance program on Dunham's philosophy of intercultural communication through the arts. Lee insisted that COCA offer scholarship programs that drew black students from the north side of St. Louis and white students from rural areas in Missouri and Illinois.[1] I was part of an organization with a mission to create community and challenge racial segregation.

When I arrived in New York City, at age eighteen, I discovered a different dance world. My ballet and modern dance classes at college were almost exclusively white, and Dunham Technique was not a part of the curriculum. It was similarly absent from most dance studios and university dance departments across the country. I also learned that Dunham was not on the syllabi in other academic departments, even though her career was relevant to anthropology, American history, African American/Africana Studies, postcolonial studies, and cultural theory. *Katherine Dunham: Dance and the African Diaspora* began as a dissertation based on the premise that Dunham's life helps us understand artists as agents of social change. Since then, it has expanded to consider Dunham as an intellectual who shaped the field of possibilities for transnational political activism, particularly in the African diaspora.

Dunham wrote and spoke about herself prolifically, and the existing biographies depend primarily on interviews with her and materials in which she had already crafted a smooth narrative. I wanted a broader picture of her as an artist, thinker, activist, and human being. Not only did this lead me to her archive at Southern Illinois University and to the collections at the New York Public Library for the Performing Arts and the Library of Congress, but also back to my hometown. In 2009, I processed the Katherine Dunham Papers at the Missouri Historical Society, which allowed that collection to become available to the public. It contains a wealth of valuable material on Dunham's life and work after 1965. I went further afield to more than a dozen archives, including the National Archives in Maryland, the Bernard Berenson papers in Italy, and the Langston Hughes papers at Yale University, to understand the reach of her influence.

My work was not solely archival. I traveled to Haiti to gain a deeper understanding of her connections to that nation; I interviewed dozens of former Dunham dancers and students from all stages of her life, ranging from those who had danced in her company in the 1940s to those who trained with her at the Children's Workshop in the 1990s. Some who spoke with me, including Vanoye Aikens and Darryl Braddix, have since passed away, and I am deeply grateful that I had the chance to hear their stories. I also began to dance Dunham Technique again. Since 2010, I have attended the Dunham Technique Seminars held annually in the St. Louis region. In 2014, I was invited to join the certification process and have since become involved in planning the annual symposium for the Institute for Dunham Technique Certification.

My connection to the Dunham community thus began before this book and will continue long after its publication, but I never experienced what it was like to be in her presence. I hover on the border between insider and outsider. At the Certification Workshop, when we pray to Dunham and speak of her technique as one does of a religion, I both join in and mentally step away, fully in support of carrying on her important legacy but unaccustomed to a cultural tradition of ancestor veneration. I recall Dunham's own words about her experiences with Haitian Vodou: "I am there to believe or not believe, but willing to understand and to believe in the sincerity of other people in their beliefs, willing to be shown, to participate, and where the participant begins and the scientist ends, I surely could not say."[2] And while Dunham always proclaimed that her technique was for everyone, I see myself as a guest in an African diasporic cultural practice. Her importance to black dancers carries a different valence, and her aesthetic belongs within the "circle that permits and protects" of black culture—even if the boundaries of black culture are always contested and fluid.[3]

There are many people who let me into their circles so that I could do this research. I thank all of the people I interviewed, who are listed in the bibliography, as well as the dozens of people I spoke to in casual conversations. Several librarians also gave helpful assistance, including Elizabeth Aldrich at the Library of Congress, Jaime Bourassa, Molly Kodner, and Dennis Northcott at the Missouri Historical Society, and Pam Hackbart-Dean at Southern Illinois University, Carbondale. I also received financial support for this work. In my earliest stages of research, I benefited from a Jacob K. Javits Fellowship from the US government. At Columbia University, I received funding from the

Graduate School of Arts and Sciences, the Center for the Study of Ethnicity and Race, and the Center for American Studies. Stanford University and the Andrew W. Mellon Foundation supported a postdoctoral fellowship during the year I began to transform the dissertation into a book. Williams College provided much-needed funds for a research trip to Haiti. Participating in the Manuscript Review Program at the Oakley Center for the Humanities and Social Sciences at Williams provided the unparalleled opportunity to have four senior scholars read and critique the manuscript at a crucial stage.

Indeed, the book would not be possible without the people who read versions of this material. Elizabeth Blackmar, Melissa Borja, Julia Foulkes, Hilary Hallett, Ana Keilson, Tamara Mann, Minkah Makalani, Michael Neuss, Paul Scolieri, Tim Shenk, Jude Webre, and Andy Whitford commented on dissertation chapters. Casey Blake, Brent Hayes Edwards, and Natasha Lightfoot read the entire dissertation. Eric Foner and Lynn Garafola were my mentors and guides throughout, offering feedback on multiple drafts. When making the transition to a book, Davarian Baldwin, Laurent Dubois, Kate Ramsey, Janice Ross, Elizabeth Schwall, and anonymous readers commented on individual chapters. Participants at multiple Mellon seminars and conferences also gave input. Jessica Ray Herzogenrath read over half the manuscript and kept me on a writing schedule. Leslie Brown, Sandra Burton, Brenda Dixon Gottschild, Susan Manning, and an anonymous reviewer read the entire manuscript and offered invaluable suggestions. Lynn Garafola continued to be a mentor throughout, and Norm Hirschy at Oxford has been an incredible editor.

Several others made this book possible. I formed writing groups with Rashida Braggs, Corinna Campbell, Carrie Gaiser Casey, Arthi Devarajan, VaNatta Ford, Charlotte Jacobs, Mariska Kappmeier, Alexis Schaitkin, Frances Peace Sullivan, and Mason Williams. Emily Flanders provided assistance in Washington, DC, and Joshua Cohen graciously shared notes from his research in Paris. Victoria Phillips deserves a special thank you for her generosity in sharing archival materials and her home. Rebecca Alaly, Om Arora and Kavita Das, Sarah Bush and David Cormode, Divya Cherian, Kamala and Kiron Das, Stacey and Gabi Gillett, Ellie Kusner, and Matt Swagler provided housing, food, and good company. A special thank you goes to Kathy Neely and the Neely-Streit family for housing me in Carbondale during my research at Southern Illinois University. Most of all, I thank my parents, Susan and Jeffrey Dee, and my spouse, Koushik Das, for their unwavering support.

Finally, I dedicate *Katherine Dunham: Dance and the African Diaspora* to three organizations that have kept Dunham's legacy going. The Fondasyon konesans ak libète (FOKAL) in Haiti, Katherine Dunham Centers for Arts and Humanities (KDCAH) in East St. Louis, and Institute for Dunham Technique Certification (IDTC) are working to ensure that future generations learn not only about Dunham's approach to dance, but also about her dreams for a better world. Thank you.

Introduction

On October 19, 1944, Katherine Dunham was backstage preparing for the opening number of her show *Tropical Revue* when someone told her the news: her impresario Sol Hurok had once again broken his promise not to book her into any segregated venues. Inside Louisville's Memorial Auditorium the black section overflowed, while the white section contained empty seats. Outside on the sidewalk, hundreds of black Kentuckians clamored to see the glamorous dancer, who had performed there in February to much acclaim. Dunham summoned the house manager to her dressing room and threatened to cancel the performance if he did not immediately allow black patrons into the white section. In turn, the manager threatened to call the police if she did not fulfill her contract. The auditorium buzzed with nervous energy as the standard five-minute delay extended to ten, then twenty, then thirty minutes. Finally, the curtains rose to reveal women in bandeau tops and bare-chested men sitting cross-legged on the stage. The music for *Rara Tonga* began, and the performers began to undulate their arms in Dunham's interpretation of Melanesian dance. The show would go on.[1]

The decision to perform, however, was not the end of the battle. Over the course of the evening, as her company members danced their way across an imaginary landscape of the African diaspora that included North Africa, the Caribbean, Latin America, and the United States, as well as a detour to the South Pacific, Dunham hatched a plan. Unlike at her recent show at a segregated theater in Kansas City, where she had danced for a small, unresponsive crowd, the patrons in Louisville roared with enthusiasm after each number. In Kansas City, Dunham had pragmatically accepted the segregated system for the evening, then moved on to the next tour stop. In Louisville, she emerged at the end of the performance wearing a sign that a company member had stolen from a segregated train car saying "For Whites Only" attached to her backside. After bowing, she turned upstage and danced a triplet step, moving her feet quickly from side to side, causing the sign to swing back and forth from her hips for all to view.[2] When the bows finished, she read a speech in which she announced that she would not return to the theater until it integrated. Her words made national headlines, and she received fan letters from across the country applauding her stance.[3] In the meantime, she and her dancers moved on to Baltimore, where they again played to a segregated audience. This time, she raised no protest. She explained to a friend that unlike in Louisville, she had never performed in Baltimore before, and that "it is important to be known and have received your status before making any moves."[4] Furthermore, she argued, the show itself, which featured talented black dancers performing sophisticated choreography rooted in an Africanist aesthetic, made a political impact by challenging racial stereotypes. She said, with a hint of frustration, "The Negro peoples, themselves, have no conception of this magnitude of the minor battles which we continually win through our artistic attractiveness."[5]

This October 1944 moment during the *Tropical Revue* tour was neither the first nor the last time that the dancer, choreographer, anthropologist, writer, and educator Katherine Dunham would have to make difficult strategic choices about how to fight racism. As an African American celebrity whose life spanned almost the entirety of the twentieth century (1909–2006), Dunham consistently faced the expectation that she contribute to the cause of racial equality, an imperative she embraced—but on her own terms. While scholars recognize her achievements in dance and anthropology, her influence on the black freedom movement both in the United States and abroad is less well known.[6] Dunham was a cultural worker in the struggle for racial justice in the twentieth century. She contributed to its intellectual framework by stressing an international perspective and by bringing dance into the conversation about how to build a sustainable cultural foundation for political activism. Her theories did not remain in the abstract because first and foremost, she danced them. Dance does not distinguish between ideas and action; in dance, ideas *are* action.[7] She also built and ran institutions, published books and articles, and attempted to live her ideals, because for Dunham, the life and the work were one. Over several decades, from the New Negro Movement to the Popular Front to the "classic" phase of the Civil Rights Movement to the Black Power Movement, she continued to refine her ideas and practices.

Though Dunham's worldview was broadly humanistic, she articulated it through what I call a *politics of diaspora*. Diaspora has become an increasingly popular framework for understanding how people build cultural and political communities across national boundaries. The term "African diaspora" only came into use in the late 1950s, but the project of diaspora among people of African descent began decades earlier.[8] In its classic definition, a diaspora is the scattering of a people from a real or imagined homeland, often under conditions of duress. The term typically connotes feelings of exile, nostalgia, longing, and a sense of in-betweenness, as one does not feel fully at home, either in the place of origin or in one's current geographic location. Dunham was a part of a generation of intellectuals who reconceptualized diaspora as a way to forge transnational unity among people of African descent for purposes of liberation from racism and colonialism. A politics of diaspora emphasizes cultural ties but recognizes and allows space for difference. While many theorists have invoked long-standing, historical, or even blood-memory cultural connections to Africa as the foundation for diaspora, a politics of diaspora also involves the conscious refashioning of existing cultural forms and even the creation of new ones. It also resists notions of cultural purity, recognizing that identity is always shifting and subject to multiple influences.[9]

Dunham played an important role in this intellectual milieu because she challenged what Michelle M. Wright calls the "inherently masculinist and nationalist constructions of the Black subject" created by W. E. B. Du Bois, Marcus Garvey, Aimé Césaire, and the litany of other men typically invoked in the lineage of the black intellectual tradition.[10] Dunham swung the needle away from nationalism and toward diaspora as the ideological framework for black liberation. For much of her life, she also thought of Haiti, not Africa, as the center of the diaspora. She theorized Haiti as the birthplace of a new humanism, one borne from the Haitian Revolution and the dynamism of cultural exchange between France and West Africa. Her theory had its problems—one scholar calls any conception of the African diaspora without Africa at the center as "fundamentally flawed"—but its intercultural foundation reflected her belief that the project of diaspora was ultimately a project for all of humanity.[11]

Dunham furthered the project of diaspora through dance. She was not the only African American who came of age in the 1920s to use dance as a weapon in the fight for racial equality, but her training in anthropology at the University of Chicago gave her additional intellectual ammunition.[12] Historically, people of African descent have used many cultural forms, including music and poetry, to express a politics of transnational liberation. Because of the "pernicious metaphysical dualism that identifies blacks with the body and whites with the mind," however, scholars have not always recognized dance as an equal part of that cultural matrix, seeing it as too close to stereotypes about hypersexuality and primitivism to be of political use.[13] Instead of fighting against the association of blackness (and women) with the body, Dunham seized that association and turned it on its head. She argued that dance was *particularly* important to the African diasporic experience. Until the twentieth century, scholars had declared that African-descended peoples in the Americas had no history. While enslaved Africans had indeed crossed the Atlantic Ocean without physical objects from home, Dunham argued that they arrived with history and memory embedded in their bodies. In the

Western Hemisphere, they used kinesthetic memory to reconstitute community and create dance practices that blended past and present, reflecting both traditions passed down as well as innovations developed in response to new conditions. Melville Herskovits, Jean Price-Mars, and Arturo Schomburg had begun to discuss ideas of "Africanist" retentions and "acculturation" years before her work appeared, but Dunham was the most compelling intellectual to articulate dance's role in those processes.[14]

Dunham was an activist as well as an intellectual. To gain the broadest sense of her influence, this book analyzes three interrelated spheres of action: her performances, her institutions, and her personal life. Performance has been the most-studied aspect of her career. Dunham founded the first black dance company in the United States to gain national and international artistic recognition.[15] With this company, she performed on Broadway, appeared in Hollywood films, and toured six continents from the 1930s through the 1960s. On occasion, she engaged in a strategy of explicit protest dance, most notably her Popular Front dances, staged in the late 1930s, and her anti-lynching dance drama *Southland* (1950), performed in the early 1950s. Dunham's carefully theorized choreography revealed how capitalism, imperialism, and global racism intersected to create conditions of inequality and violence. The reach of this work, however, was limited. She abandoned her Popular Front choreography in 1940 when her company gained national recognition, and her company never performed *Southland* in the United States.

Instead, during her performing career Dunham primarily engaged in a strategy of what I call *aesthetics as politics*. Decisions about thematic content, movement vocabulary, dancers' body types, the arrangement of said dancers in space, and performance venues express a choreographer's commentary on the relations of power governing society.[16] Dunham's formal aesthetic choices revealed a black feminist political stance. The plotlines of many of her dances normalized black lives instead of reproducing the stereotypes of the minstrel tradition that were still prevalent during the early twentieth century. She drew upon the erotic as a source of performative power, understanding from her anthropological training that sexuality was a central component of the human experience, integral to all facets of life, including religion.[17] She was unafraid to delve into Vodou, Shango, and other Afro-Caribbean religious practices onstage. She wove together ballet, modern dance, Afro-Caribbean forms, African American vernacular traditions, and Asian movement vocabularies in her choreography, challenging high/low, modern/ethnic cultural hierarchies. The Dunham company appeared in a variety of venues ranging from nightclubs to opera houses, which similarly confounded standard assignations of cultural value. Overall, her choreography expressed freedom—the freedom to engage in Africanist, black folk aesthetics in concert dance; the freedom to embrace spirituality and divine possession in performance; the freedom to be sexual, sensual, serious, glamorous, or whatever else the plot called for;

the freedom to express joy, sorrow, and laughter in a naturalistic rather than exaggerated manner; in essence, the freedom to embrace a full humanity. Her choreography thus embodied what dance scholar André Lepecki argues is one of the central understandings of the word *political*—"the movement of freedom."[18]

African American political activists did not always see Dunham's performances as "positive representation" of the race. Her expressions of sexuality, embrace of vernacular dances, and performed rites of possession did not accord with black respectability politics of the mid-twentieth century. I adopt the approach of scholar bell hooks to move beyond "good" and "bad" ideas about racial representation.[19] In broadening the field of representation for people of African descent, particularly women, Dunham's choreography was its own form of social protest.

The building of a diasporic consciousness was another political outcome of Dunham's aesthetic choices. Her audiences were approximately 90 percent white, but she paid particular attention to the 10 percent who were people of color.[20] She offered those audiences a way to view their place in the world, not as members of an oppressed minority within a colonial nation-state (whether the United States or another), but rather as a part of a diverse global majority. Her shows followed a revue format, meaning that she strung together multiple short dance numbers that shared no consistent plot. She set her pieces in Haiti, Martinique, Trinidad, Cuba, Brazil, Northern Africa, and the United States, showcasing the variety and richness of black culture. She developed a dance technique that gave her shows an aesthetic coherence, a vision of horizontal overlap that rejected the chronological out-of-Africa model of the black revues of previous decades. She visually offered solidarity across the black world, rather than relegate certain groups to a distant or near past.[21] Her technique mirrored the creolization she witnessed in the Caribbean. It challenged notions of racial and cultural purity, instead asking dancers to embrace diaspora within their bodies.

Diaspora does not fit perfectly as a way to theorize Dunham's aesthetic. Because her career began decades before the "African diaspora" became a recognized term, she used an alternate one: *primitive*.[22] Dunham trained at the University of Chicago anthropology department in the 1930s and adopted her mentors' language. Like them, she insisted that she did not take primitive to mean inferior or unsophisticated. Instead, she valorized primitive culture as closer to nature and freed of what she considered the "restrictions of civilization," which she understood as the industrialized nations of Western Europe and the United States.[23] This thinking reinforced the perception that a distinction existed between primitive and civilized. She argued that primitive societies could reveal "universal and fundamental truths" about human nature, and thus her aesthetic, rooted in her ethnographic investigations of what she called "primitives" in the Caribbean, had universal applicability in modern dance.[24] The supposedly underlying connections among "primitive peoples" gave her the legitimacy to present dances on stage from places she had never been. Although Dunham was an anthropologist, the vast majority of her dances were not set in the locations of her ethnographic research.[25] Other black artists and intellectuals had abandoned the concept of primitivism by the mid-twentieth century, but she insisted on using it her entire life to describe her aesthetic.[26]

When judged from a twenty-first century perspective, Dunham's embrace of the primitive comes across as a major blind spot in her politics. She romanticized the term and refused to see how it rendered groups of people as inferior, even if that was not her intention. At the same time, the trope of the primitive liberated her creative voice, as it did for other modern artists of the early twentieth century.[27] She attempted to elevate the primitive, show it as modern, and use it as her tool to create diaspora on the stage.

Whether to call Dunham's aesthetic and technique "black dance" raises another set of questions about the politics of her performances. In 2015, the instructor of the history class at the Dunham Certification Workshop told participants that Dunham Technique was not black dance, but rather a universal technique that drew upon several different forms, including East Asian martial arts, Indian classical dance, and yoga.[28] The instructor had plenty of quotations to back up her characterization. In 1943, Dunham objected to publicity that called her shows Negro dance, asserting that "my own artistic accomplishments can and do cover a much broader field."[29] In the 1970s in East St. Louis, Dunham refused to make her Performing Arts Training Center a part of the African American Studies department at Southern Illinois University. As her administrator Ruth Ann Taylor wrote in a terse letter to the university president, "One has to assume that the underlying concept and philosophy of the Training Center have been misunderstood or disregarded. . . . The concept is not intended for a specific group; it transcends racial groupings."[30] Finally, at a 2003 ceremony in her honor in New York, Dunham said, "There is one thing I would like to say; I am so tired of being considered a leader of black dance. . . . This is going to cause me a lot of trouble in the so-called black world. But I don't mind."[31]

Despite Dunham's statements, she is to this day called the "matriarch" of black dance and invoked as a divine ancestor in African American dance communities.[32] In a 2014 discussion about Dunham's stated desire to become the next Isadora Duncan (a white American often considered the founder of modern dance), some participants insisted that such a comparison was wrong— even if Dunham herself made it—because she belonged in a black aesthetic tradition.[33] Given what Brenda Dixon Gottschild has called the "invisibilization" of Africanist contributions to American concert dance, there is a sense that emphasizing Dunham's fusion sensibility or universalism runs the risk of reinforcing that invisibilization.[34] Thomas DeFrantz and Anita Gonzalez argue that black performance exists "without deference to overlapping historical trajectories or perceived differences in cultural capital from an elusive Europeanist norm . . . black performance derives from its own style and sensibilities that undergird its production."[35] In an ideal world, acknowledging the European-American influences on Dunham and her broad aspirations would not make the Africanist influence deferential or subordinate. Rather, it would reaffirm that a diasporic sensibility is one that rejects purist ideas of culture.

But in a world in which an individual white male is still the presumed vessel of universalism, and racial inequality still exists, calling Dunham's work black dance is essential. Building on Carole Johnson, Takiyah Nur Amin writes, "Even the varied cultural influences that Black people have assimilated which reveal themselves in movement can be understood as Black Dance because they are filtered and distilled through the varied particular and specific racialized experiences of Black people."[36] While I do not want to make culture static, and I affirm that all of our genre categories in dance have overlapping influences, we must put down stakes somewhere. I place Dunham's in black dance, and I do so with critical awareness that she felt conflicted about such a categorization.

In addition to her performing career, Dunham built institutions, a key component of her legacy that has received less attention.[37] Institutionalization has negative connotations of fixity and conservatism, but institutions also defy cultural erasure. They make claims to historical importance, durability, and relevance. The most important institution was the Dunham company itself, which provided employment to dozens of African Americans at a time when jobs for black dancers were scarce. She trained multiple generations of black choreographers and performers. Well-known alumni of her company include Talley Beatty, Julie (Robinson) Belafonte, Janet Collins, Eartha Kitt, Claude Marchant, Charles Moore, Archie Savage, and Glory Van Scott. In 1944, she defied the segregation of the New York dance world by opening the Katherine Dunham School of Dance, not in Harlem, but in the heart of Manhattan's Broadway theater district. For a decade, it was the "in" place for New York's dancers and actors to take class. In 1967 she opened another school, the Performing Arts Training Center, in East St. Louis, Illinois. Both schools promoted cross-cultural education centered on the cultures of the African diaspora as the way to prepare students to face the "problems of living" and develop what she called "socialization and humanization through the arts."[38] In East St. Louis, Dunham also established the Institute for Intercultural Communication, a museum, and a children's workshop. She ran the East St. Louis institutions for over thirty years, only moving back to New York for health reasons in her tenth decade of life.

In addition to examining her performances and institutions, this book focuses on how Dunham attempted to *live* diaspora. Her choices reflected a politics of liberation from fixed identities. At the University of Chicago in the 1920s, she "rigidly avoided sororities and club memberships of all sorts ... I had always prided myself on thinking only of 'man' in the broadest, most inclusive usage of the term."[39] During her ethnographic research trip to Haiti in 1935–36, she took advantage of being "unplaceable" in Haiti's complex color hierarchy.[40] During her performance career, she refused to be put into specific boxes, confounding critics who could not decide if she was a "cool scientist" or a "sultry performer."[41] She was publicly heterosexual, but had multiple relationships with women. Her class politics presented a contradiction. She celebrated what she called folk culture, but spoke of herself as part of an international, intellectual elite that ought to be given latitude to shape that culture.

Most importantly, she rejected a static national identity. Through her own peripatetic lifestyle, she created connections among people around the world. In the 1930s, her ethnographic research in the Caribbean gave her a new diasporic consciousness. From the late 1940s to the 1960s, she toured the globe with her dance company, maintaining no permanent US address and instead finding a sense of home abroad. In the 1960s and 1970s, she brought drummers from Senegal to East St. Louis and students from East St. Louis to Haiti. She saw herself as a cosmopolitan—in its literal meaning of "citizen of the world"—attuned in particular to what she called "noir" sensibilities, invoking interculturalism with her choice to use the French term.[42] She believed that living in the space of diaspora, in between-ness, was the way to achieve wholeness.

Dunham's remarkable capacity for reinvention was key to her survival, but it meant that she could not always fulfill her social justice aspirations. She abandoned many projects, jumping from one realm of activity to another, such as starting a health clinic in Haiti in 1959, only to dissolve it a few months later to re-launch her performing career in Europe. Although she often used her celebrity to take public stances against racism and discrimination, her participation in more recognizable political actions, such as marches or boycotts, was limited, and she sometimes insisted that she had no interest in politics. Most biographies of Dunham shy away from addressing her record of unevenness. For example, in the other versions of this chapter's opening anecdote about the Louisville protest, there is no mention of her choices not to protest in Kansas City, Baltimore, or previously in Louisville.[43] Acknowledging the complex nature of Dunham's political engagement raises intriguing questions: How did she make her choices, and why? What do her struggles to balance artistic success, personal desires, financial stability, and social justice commitments reveal about how other African American performing artists navigated similar dilemmas?

One aspect of Dunham's complex personality did not change: her indomitable will. This trait was both the very reason for the success of her pioneering efforts and the cause of problems institutionally and interpersonally. Given the United States' historic lack of support for artists, and for black artists more specifically, Dunham had to finance her shows on her own. Her refusal to give up when faced with monetary distress kept the company afloat at a time when many other dance companies failed. Her refusal to bow to racism or sexism meant that she achieved far more than anyone thought possible. She is a prime example of how we need artists to envision futures that do not yet exist.

Artists often desire to have total control over that vision, a trait that can have its downsides. Dunham ruled over her company members with an iron fist, which bred resentment. During the 1950s, she took to calling her dancers "the insatiables." She blamed the declining morale in the company on what she considered their greed, ingratitude, and jealousy, but her unwillingness to relinquish the spotlight to younger female dancers and her controlling attitude also caused conflict.[44] Contrary to popular belief, the "Katherine Dunham Company" never officially existed. Instead, programs and advertisements billed Dunham as an individual first, putting her name in a bigger font, and then her group. Sometimes, the company was not even billed at all.[45] For the sake of simplicity, this book will use the shorthand "Dunham company" to represent the group of dancers, musicians, and singers who performed with her for thirty years.

Dunham also refused to relinquish business decisions to a qualified manager or impresario (save the four years under Sol Hurok). This need for absolute control exacerbated financial problems that led, ultimately, to the collapse of her company and her New York school. It also led to administrative dysfunction at her institutions. Instead of finding qualified personnel, she cultivated an entourage of devotees. This attribute is hardly uncommon among prominent leaders of dance companies. Serge Diaghilev, Martha Graham, and George Balanchine demanded, and received, similar adulation. Exploring this aspect of Dunham's personality helps us better understand the kind of strength it took for her to defy the odds. In a cultural context that discounted dance as a legitimate art form, women as leaders, and African Americans as intelligent or artistic, Dunham's steely resolve and faith in her own genius lay at the heart of her success.

Because the personal is always political, Dunham's relationships also enter into the story. Her husband John Pratt, who was white, created the sets and designed the costumes for her company. Pratt and Dunham inverted the normative power dynamic of the United States, in which white men stand in the foreground as the figures with power and prestige, bolstered by the labor of women in the background, particularly the labor of black women. Dunham never diminished Pratt's work, but he remained the less visible partner.[46] She carried on multiple affairs during their marriage for both emotional and pragmatic reasons. Gifts of money and jewelry from romantic partners often kept her multiple institutions afloat. In an era before the existence of non-profit foundations for the arts or major federal subsidies to artists, she used all resources available to her, including her beauty and charm.

Katherine Dunham: Dance and the African Diaspora looks at Dunham's life and work as it unfolded chronologically over the course of the twentieth century. Chapter 1, "Becoming a New Negro in Chicago," focuses on her young adulthood in Chicago, from 1928 to 1935. During this period, Dunham embraced a racial uplift ideology. In 1930, she proposed the creation of a black ballet company—something virtually unheard of at the time—and distanced herself from existing African American dance styles. She separated content from form, arguing that the substance of black experience deserved representation on the concert dance stage, but presented through European-American aesthetics. She articulated a place for dance in the New Negro Movement, expanding the movement's intellectual frameworks, and brought an African American voice to both ballet and modern dance, challenging those genres' deep racism.

Dunham's ten-month research trip to the Caribbean in 1935–36 brought about a radical transformation in her approach. Chapter 2, "Finding a Politics of Diaspora in the Caribbean," examines the process by which she came to embrace Africanist aesthetics, not only as the basis for a new art form, but also as a part of a political project. With a deeper understanding of dances from Jamaica, Martinique, Trinidad, and Haiti, she argued for the artistic merit of Afro-Caribbean dance on its own terms. She also developed a new understanding of herself in relation to others of African descent that was simultaneously cultural and political. Instead of feeling the pressure of Du Boisian "double consciousness," of always viewing oneself as both black and American and struggling to reconcile the two,[47] she instead came to appreciate identity as fluid and relational. She began to believe that liberation from racial oppression was inextricably intertwined with defining oneself as part of a global majority of people of color.

Chapter 3, "Aesthetics as Politics," discusses how and why Dunham landed on the theory of aesthetics as politics as a way to harmonize her concerns for individual artistic recognition, financial stability, and social justice. It takes into account the many factors, including the struggle to make a living during the Great Depression, the pressures she faced to represent black people, and the fact that she lived in a racist and sexist society, that shaped how she developed her voice in the four years after her return from the Caribbean in 1936. I analyze her ballet *L'Ag'Ya* (1938) and revue *Tropics and Le Jazz "Hot"* (1940) to illustrate what she achieved and what remained illegible to her audiences.

Chapters 4 and 5 examine how Dunham adopted various strategies to achieve her goals during the years in which she became a national celebrity. Chapter 4, "Race and Representation during World War II," focuses on debates about Dunham's artistic choices at a historical moment when racial representation on stage and screen took on heightened political importance. It also analyzes her offstage activism. Chapter 5, "Rehearsal for Revolution: The Dunham School," looks at the Dunham School in New York, operational from 1944 to 1954, and breaks with strict chronology in order to tell a more complete thematic story. It offers the argument that Dunham was better able to further her social justice goals through education than through performance. Although the Dunham School fell short in fulfilling some of her artistic dreams, it succeeded in desegregating the space of dance in New York and in promoting diaspora as a model for a peaceful postwar global order.

Chapter 6, "The Unofficial Ambassador of Diaspora: Performing Abroad," examines how Dunham disseminated her ideas to an international audience. Between 1947 and 1960, Dunham took her company on tour to Europe, Asia, Australia, Latin America, and Africa. Though she was denied the opportunity to be an official US cultural ambassador, in large part because of her anti-lynching ballet *Southland*, she served as an unofficial ambassador of the African diaspora. This chapter argues that in so doing, she made important contributions to the global decolonization movement. She exposed international audiences to an aesthetic of modernity rooted in Africanist cultures and forged relationships with leading black intellectuals, politicians, and artists in the countries she visited. Through actions both onstage and off, Dunham helped lay the cultural foundations of post–World War II diasporic politics.

Chapters 7 and 8 consider the question of finding home. Chapter 7, "Living Diaspora in Haiti and Senegal," overlaps chronologically with the chapters that precede and follow it. It analyzes the years Dunham spent living in those two nations as an investigation into fashioning a diasporic life. Dunham ultimately found home in the state of her birth, Illinois. In 1967, she settled in East St. Louis, where she reinvented herself as a black power activist and educator. Chapter 8, "The Radical Humanist Meets the Black Power Revolution: Dunham in East St. Louis," discusses how Dunham was an important figure in the Black Arts Movement. She founded multiple institutions in East St. Louis to put into practice her ideas about African diasporic arts education as a means of community and individual empowerment. She also created networks of artists and intellectuals to promote her philosophy on a national scale.

The epilogue examines Dunham's legacy. Her contribution to the dance world is enormous; both modern dance and jazz dance would not look the same today without her. Beyond that, however, she also demonstrated how dance could be a force for social justice. Many artists who came of age during the

1930s shared her faith in the political potential of dance, but Dunham stood apart because of her longevity in the field, her intellectual rigor, and her global, multifaceted approach. By drawing upon a vast and largely unexamined archival record to analyze the multiple spheres of her influence, *Katherine Dunham: Dance and the African Diaspora* offers an expansive portrait of Dunham as an intellectual, artist, political activist, and human being. Her story deepens our understanding of the relationship between art and politics, the dancing body as a vehicle for social change, and the African diaspora as a project to reimagine our future.

CHAPTER 1

Becoming a New Negro in Chicago

How did a quiet child from a predominantly white Chicago suburb become the New Negro Movement's leading voice on dance by the mid-1930s? Most of what we know about Dunham's early years comes from her memoir *A Touch of Innocence*. She wrote the book in 1958 during a distressing period in her life. She had just disbanded her dance company because of financial difficulties and was living in a tiny attic in Tokyo. With her husband and daughter thousands of miles away in Haiti and no performance opportunities on the near horizon, Dunham turned to writing. Her agent suggested a tell-all tale about her glamorous life as an international touring star, of hobnobbing with Evita Perón in Argentina and of riding camels with heiress Doris Duke in Egypt.[1] Dunham chose, instead, to recount the story of her childhood. She painted such a vivid portrait of loneliness and abuse in *A Touch of Innocence* that Langston Hughes commented that she had "a gift for physical detail sometimes too real for comfort."[2] The book reveals how dance became one of Dunham's tools for survival, a personal narrative that she would then theorize and apply to people of African descent more broadly.

Dunham's first major trauma was the death of her birth mother, Fanny June Williams Taylor Dunham. Fanny was somewhere between twelve and twenty years senior to her second husband, Albert Millard Dunham.[3] When they met in Chicago, Fanny was a well-educated, musically gifted divorcée and mother of five who owned property and held a prestigious job as a school principal. She was also light skinned and could pass for white, whereas Albert, a tailor, had darker skin and came from a working-class family in Tennessee. Albert fell hard for Fanny, despite their age, educational, and color differences, and they married around 1905. A son, Albert Jr., was born in 1906. Using the income from Fanny's properties, they moved out of the city to the suburb of Glen Ellyn. A daughter, Katherine, was born three years later.[4] When Fanny began to waste away from a mysterious illness soon after, the young toddler could not understand why her mother was shut off from her. Fanny's children from her previous marriage, along with their spouses and children, stayed in the house for extended periods of time, causing overcrowding and tension. Dunham became a quiet and introspective child, expressing herself verbally only to her brother.[5] Then, when she was just three-and-a-half years old, Fanny died from stomach cancer.[6] Dunham's faint memories of her mother would be supplemented over the course of her childhood by her father's stories, in which his cultured and well-spoken first wife attained the status of an ideal that Dunham sought to emulate.[7]

Albert Sr. felt unable to raise the children on his own, so he sent them to live with his sister Lulu on the South Side of Chicago. The South Side, a working-class black neighborhood, was an entirely different world from the white, middle-class suburb of Glen Ellyn. Shortly after inheriting the care of the two small children, Aunt Lulu, who had had enjoyed a steady living as a beautician, was denied a renewal of her parlor lease in a downtown department store. In her memoir, Dunham blamed her aunt's troubles on the Great Migration, the influx of African Americans from the rural South to the urban North that had caused skittish white Chicagoans to enact stricter segregation policies. To save money, Lulu and the children moved into the apartment of another relative, Clara Dunham, who had recently come to the city to make a career in theater.[8]

Despite the hardship the move represented, meeting Clara's branch of the family was an important catalyst in Dunham's life. Still too young to be in school, she spent her days watching, wide-eyed, as her aunts and uncles rehearsed for a vaudeville show, *Minnehaha*, about a half-black, half-Indian woman, based on a character from Bob Cole and J. Rosamond Johnson's hit musical comedy, *The Red Moon* (1909). The feathers and fringe of the Indian costumes entranced Dunham, as did the full-throated singing of her Aunt Clara and the vigor of the dancing. She practiced the steps to show to her brother when he got home from school. Another relative took Dunham to matinees at the Grand and Monogram Theaters, where she soaked up what she called the "residuum of the minstrel era" of "bawdy" songs, "raucous" laughter, and "the guttural rasp of the blues."[9] This period of immersion in the world of black vaudeville lasted only a few months, but it made a profound impression on the motherless four-year-old. She saw the magical world of the theater as an escape from the disorienting confusion of daily life. Even as the choreography faded from her memory, the emotional resonance of performance never left her.[10]

Another anecdote in *A Touch of Innocence* describes the connection between such experiences and Dunham's racial consciousness. At age five, she and her brother moved back in with their father, who had remarried and set up a dry-cleaning business in the Chicago suburb of Joliet, which like Glen Ellyn was almost exclusively white. Dunham grew accustomed to living in a cultural context in which her neighbors and classmates came from a different racial background. Around age twelve, however, she went on a road trip to St. Louis with her stepmother, Annette Pointdexter Dunham, and a family friend. As the trio drove down the city streets, Dunham marveled at the "poverty, ready money, moonshine, dice-rolling, poker-playing, laughter, razor melees, [and] bawdiness" of the black migrants from the South who crowded the sidewalks of Chouteau Avenue. The neighborhood residents laughed at the "foreigners" in the fancy Nash automobile who clearly did not belong.[11] Despite sharing a racial identification with the St. Louisans she encountered, Dunham described the experience as an outsider. After buying catfish from a street vendor, the Joliet women quickly left. Dunham later recalled:

> The music that drifted out from every doorway as they drove away toward the bridge followed her and struck so far down into a substance that had never stirred or made itself known before that now, at this moment, began possession by the blues, a total immersion in the baptismal font of the Race. This music would sometime[s] be her only tie to these people.[12]

Dunham had certainly heard blues music during childhood visits to vaudeville theater, so her claim that the music she heard in St. Louis awakened a racial consciousness that had "never stirred or made itself known before" feels forced. Nevertheless, the anecdote establishes a recurring theme in Dunham's life: the tension between racial identification and class distinction. Expressive culture, in this case music, had the power to create racial solidarity. At the same time, its connective threads were tenuous, as her dismissive phrase "these people" suggests. At the time she was writing *A Touch of Innocence*, Dunham saw herself as part of a global intellectual elite and wanted to ensure that her readers understood her as such. In interviews from that decade she named three white men—former University of Chicago president Robert Hutchins, psychoanalyst Erich Fromm, and art historian Bernard Berenson—as the three most important influences on her life.[13] In another memoir, written in Senegal eleven years later, she would describe herself as being at home with all people of African descent, regardless of their class background.[14] Dance became the medium through which she would navigate these contradictions of belonging and exclusion, of insider and outsider status.

Dunham did not get many opportunities to develop her love of dance in Joliet. She joined her high school's Terpsichorean Club, a dance group that emphasized what Dunham called "free-style movement" based in the teachings of Austrian-born Émile Jaques-Dalcroze and the Hungarian-born Rudolf Laban.[15] Although Dalcroze is best known for creating a system of teaching music through movement (eurythmics) and Laban for notating dance (Labanotation), both men also influenced 1920s dance pedagogy in the United

States. Dalcroze believed that the gesturing body was the best medium for expressing rhythm. He championed improvisation and, in contrast to the rote repetition model of his gymnastics-oriented peers, emphasized the harmony of mind and body, in which one mentally comprehended physical sensations in order to provide the fullest natural expressions of rhythm.[16] Laban adopted a scientific approach to dance, examining how the body utilized space, time, and energy in motion. This scientific approach did not negate mysticism. To the contrary, Laban believed in dance as a spiritual force that connected the human body to a cosmic order through a dancer's ability to translate individual concrete experience into abstract expression.[17] The teenager Dunham "waved her arms in a figure eight design to the chiming of a gong and the thumping of a tom-tom," which suggests that her teacher emphasized percussive rhythm. She also "practiced special techniques for sitting, falling, jumping, leaping, and stretching," which accorded with Dalcrozian/Laban ideas about dance as emerging from natural, everyday movement.[18]

These abstract exercises, however, bored Dunham. Instead, the "enchanted" world of ballet drew her attention and admiration. Ballet offered fantastical narratives of beautiful fairies, queens, and young maidens pursued by handsome, wealthy men; the ballerina aesthetic emphasized ethereality and grace. She also fell in love with the *hopak*, a Ukranian folk dance that offered audiences visual thrills and displays of technical virtuosity, such as kicking one's legs out from a squat position with one's arms crossed. Both ballet and the *hopak* were performed at a Terpsichorean Club recital but never introduced into the classes. Dunham resigned herself to "reconstruct[ing] in her mind's eye the vision that had appeared at the recital" to fuel her desire to keep dancing. Soon, however, even the limited Terpsichorean Club lessons came to an end when her father insisted she start working in his dry-cleaning business after school.[19]

Dunham did get one opportunity to put her choreographic imagination to work: she decided to produce a cabaret evening as a fundraiser for the family's church. She recounted the story not only in her memoir, but also for journalists throughout her career. The show revealed Dunham's early fascination with adopting exotic foreign identities. Between various numbers based in her early memories of black vaudeville, she performed a *hopak* dressed as a "Russian princess," no doubt inspired by the Terpsichorean Club recital. She also choreographed an "Oriental" dance that she "reconstructed from a picture of a Turkish maiden on the cover of a pulp magazine and her recollections of Theda Bara [a silent film star] as Salome."[20] Dunham finding choreographic inspiration in a magazine illustration mirrors the apocryphal tale of modern dancer Ruth St. Denis finding choreographic inspiration in a cigarette advertisement featuring the Egyptian goddess Isis. For both black and white women of the early twentieth century, exotic performance was a means of liberation from restrictive gender and racial identities. Turning to Orientalist ideas of Eastern spirituality gave St. Denis the "cultural capital" to legitimize solo female performance as an art form, not salacious entertainment.[21] In 1907, black dancer and choreographer Aida Overton Walker famously created the dance solo "Salome" for the musical comedy *Bandanna Land*, and she repeated the performance in 1912 at Richard Hammerstein's Victoria Theater. "Salome" was one of the most well-known modern dance pieces of the first decade of the twentieth century. By taking it on, Walker staked her claim to belong to a modern theatrical tradition, expanding the performative possibilities for black women beyond the typical vaudeville tropes.[22] Dunham's liberated cabaret performances, however, scandalized the older members of her conservative African Methodist Episcopal church. Some members of the black middle classes across America in the 1920s approved of dancing schools as a means of racial uplift, but Dunham's cabaret-style dancing did not comport with the gender or class norms of what W. E. B. Du Bois called the "Talented Tenth." Opportunities to repeat the production did not arise.[23]

The restrictions on Dunham's life went beyond the stifling of her passion for dance. She loved her stepmother Annette, and referred to her as "mother," but her relationship with her father was difficult. His controlling and abusive behavior cast a dark cloud over the household. While the family kept up the appearance of middle-class respectability, the dry-cleaning business struggled to turn a profit. Albert Sr. resented his son's intellectual interests and refused to provide financial support for his college education. He was physically abusive, beating his wife, son, and daughter. At one point, he attempted to sexually molest Dunham.[24]

Dunham's difficult childhood also taught her the complexities of racial identity in the United States. Albert Sr.'s rage, at times so destructive to his family, was crucially important to survival in other circumstances. Before Dunham's birth, he and Fanny had bought the property in Glen Ellyn and begun building a house on it. The neighbors assumed that Fanny was white and that Albert Sr. was her black employee. When it was discovered that they were married, someone threw a bomb into the front window of the new home. Albert, with "murder in his eyes," then retrieved a double-barreled shotgun and sat vigil outside every night until the painting was finished and the barn was complete. The neighbors never bothered him again. Dunham took inspiration from this story of his fearless stance against racism.[25]

Dunham also learned about color prejudice from interactions with her half-siblings. In publicity materials, she always described her birth mother as "French Canadian," though Fanny also had Native American, African, and English blood.[26] The 1900 census, taken when Fanny was married to her first husband, Henry Taylor, listed her as "black"; but the 1910 census, taken when she was married to Albert Dunham, listed her has "mulatto" (demonstrating that one's racial identification could change on a bureaucrat's whim).[27] After their mother's death, the lighter-skinned Taylor children felt and acted superior to their darker half-siblings, but at the same time, they depended on the Dunhams for financial support. Young Katherine learned to be a "cultural broker" from a childhood spent attempting to navigate the color dynamics in her own family.[28]

At school, Dunham similarly had to navigate racial codes. She and her brother attended predominantly white educational institutions, where they excelled academically and had a mixed experience socially. Albert Jr. was valedictorian of his class and socially popular. He was even elected class president senior year. But when he was nominated for class president a second time, during his first year at Joliet's junior college, a white student delivered a prepared speech in which he declared that the school would face "humiliation" if they elected a black student president, "no matter how brilliant or how likable." A debate ensued, in which Albert and his sister "saw friends turn to enemies and casual acquaintances rise to what amounted to heroism."[29] Dunham struggled to maintain deep friendships in high school, sensing the "unwritten, unspoken code" of her white classmates that prevented them from offering more than casual friendliness. After Albert Jr. left home to attend the University of Chicago, her loneliness deepened. Her school picture from senior year revealed that "she was as old then as she would ever be in her life," with a "sadness in her eyes" that "frightened her."[30] Figure 1.1, from that year, captures some of that sadness. Dunham developed a protective layer of defenses that persisted into adulthood, when as the artistic director of her company, she maintained an emotional distance from her dancers.[31] She sought to observe her own life and the world around her from an objective point of view, insisting that "detachment" was the key to understanding and insight.[32]

Dunham discovered a new world in 1928, when she joined her brother at the University of Chicago. Under his guidance, she became a part of the New Negro Movement. Also known in Chicago as the Black Chicago Renaissance, the New Negro Movement brought together black artists, intellectuals, and political activists who believed that art could challenge racial prejudice. Instead of accepting white society's degrading myths about black people, New Negroes advocated for producing art that was based on the black experience. This cultural production would in turn engender a new political order, as African Americans would develop race pride and white Americans would be forced to admit that their fellow citizens of color deserved full equality. In New York, the Harlem Renaissance phase of the New Negro Movement had flourished in the 1920s; the Black Chicago Renaissance blossomed in the 1930s.[33]

Albert Jr. laid important groundwork for the Black Chicago Renaissance in the late 1920s through his intellectual and artistic pursuits. Though still in college, he was already a brilliant philosopher who counted Alain Locke, editor of the 1925 volume *The New Negro*, among his friends. Locke, in fact, urged Albert to spend the summer of 1928 with him in Europe, traveling through

Figure 1.1 Katherine Dunham, age seventeen. Photographer unknown. Missouri History Museum, St. Louis.

the Alps.[34] In 1929 Albert invited his sister to join the Cube Theatre, a "little theater" he had co-founded with his friend Nicholas Matsoukas, son of a Greek immigrant, from the University of Chicago. A little theater movement had emerged before World War I as a venue for serious theater outside the commercial mainstream. These spaces offered opportunities for immigrants, women, bohemians, and African Americans to play dramatic roles instead of caricatures. W. E. B. Du Bois had founded the Krigwa Players Little Negro Theatre in 1926 along these lines. Krigwa plays, Du Bois explained in *The Crisis*, concerned "ordinary" black people, written by black authors, performed for black audiences in black neighborhoods. "Only in this way," he wrote, "can a real folk-play movement of American Negroes be built up."[35]

In a departure from Du Bois's all-black vision, the Cube billed itself as "an independent venture of students and artists interested in all forms of modern art" and welcomed white artists who were sympathetic to the New Negro cause.[36] In January 1929, for example, Dunham performed in *The Man Who Died at Twelve O'Clock*, a one-act play by the white southerner Paul Green.[37] Green's play, like all the plays produced at the Cube, focused on the lives of ordinary African Americans and sought to challenge existing stereotypes.

The Cube Theatre became the focus of Dunham's cultural life during her first few years in Chicago. There she met artistic and intellectual luminaries such as Locke, Langston Hughes, Rose McClendon, Frank Wilson, James T. Farrell, Studs Terkel, Canada Lee, and W. C. Handy. She developed a friendship with Mary Hunter, a white director and producer who would prove influential to Dunham's career. The experimental and interracial Cube Theatre gave Dunham hope that "black and white could certainly meet on the level of art."[38] Bertha Moseley Lewis, the organizational force behind the Masque Players, who formed the nucleus of performers at the Cube, arranged for Dunham to meet actor Paul Robeson, singer Marian Anderson, and ballet choreographer Ruth Page.[39]

Reflecting on the Cube Theatre community, Dunham wrote, "We *were* the New Negro."[40] They laughed, ate, drank, debated, fought, had love affairs, and aspired to change the world through performance. Her fellow artists helped Dunham overcome her reserve—so much so, in fact, that it caused tension between her and her brother. In a letter, apparently written after a major fight, Albert warned his sister that she was becoming "two women": one who lived in a state of "cheery quiet" and "cultural expansion," and another who had "the love for show, the self-indulgence, the suave flirtations, as well as the infernal rolling restlessness" that led her into "taking long social or emotional chances with matured men," something that made him "more miserable than you will ever know."[41] Moving out of her parents' repressive household and diving into the bohemian theater world had given Dunham a chance to discover new dimensions of her personality. She could practice performing other identities, ones more flirtatious and sexually alluring. For an older brother, however, these changes threatened the ideal vision he held of his sister.

At the same time, Dunham was devastated by changes in her brother. In September 1929, she received a shock when Albert announced that he was marrying her best friend, Frances Taylor, and moving to Massachusetts to continue his studies at Harvard. Feeling betrayed and abandoned, Dunham soon after wedded a postal worker and dancer, Jordis McCoo.[42] McCoo was a kind soul, but her brother suspected that the partnership would not fulfill his college-educated sister. Albert wrote, with more than a touch of elitism, "I adjure you to think long on the true springs of inspiration and spiritual sustenance. Does he appreciate poetry?"[43] Over the next few years, Dunham would notice her brother's sensitive spirit falter in the face of brutal realities about man's inhumanity to man. Eventually, he was committed to a mental institution. Albert's illness would be the second major trauma in Dunham life.[44]

In January 1930, with her brother away at Harvard, Dunham set out to do in dance what the Krigwa and Cube had done in theater—namely, to use an art form to challenge existing racial hierarchies. Focusing on dance was an audacious move at a time when the body, especially the black female body, was considered to have little capacity for intellectual expression. Dance had only come into its own as an art form in the United States a mere twenty or so years earlier, with the solo performances of women like Isadora Duncan and St. Denis. St. Denis and her husband, Ted Shawn, in 1915, had started one of the first schools for what was considered "art-dance" (which would soon be called modern dance) in the country. By the time Dunham joined the Cube, only a handful of people, such as Martha Graham and Doris Humphrey, had started their own modern dance companies. Ballet, though it had an established history in Russia and Europe, was also a recent phenomenon in the United States. In the nineteenth century, "ballet" in the United States had meant giant extravaganzas, such as *The Black Crook*, that emphasized spectacle and sexual titillation, not aesthetic value. Recognition of ballet as a so-called legitimate art emerged after Anna Pavlova's first appearances at the Metropolitan Opera in 1909 and, later, with the national tours of Diaghilev's Ballets Russes during World War I. By 1930, ballet schools had become popular fixtures across the country, but only a handful of professional ballet companies existed, and the majority of them were associated with operas, not independent entities.[45]

Even rarer than a dance company in 1930 was a black dance company. Black dance in the early twentieth century was usually seen on America's stages as part of larger theatrical productions, primarily minstrel shows or vaudeville. Scholars now recognize the artistic brilliance of the performers and creators involved in these productions. The shows often contained "hidden transcripts" that powerfully critiqued existing social structures, but they still overwhelmingly signified "racist humiliation and self-denigration" in the public imagination of both black and white Americans.[46] Dunham voiced a desire to start a company that both challenged those stereotypes and established dance as an art form, independent of musical comedy. Some black choreographers in New York, namely, Edna Guy and Hemsley Winfield, had also begun to think along these lines, but for the most part, the concept of a black dance company was unheard of in 1930.[47]

Dunham declared to her Cube associate Hunter that she wanted to become the next Isadora Duncan, meaning the next great innovator in the field of modern dance.[48] Hunter introduced Dunham to the ballet dancer and poet Mark Turbyfill. At a time when most white Americans thought African Americans incapable of performing ballet, Turbyfill, whose main ethos in life was "experimentation," constantly opened himself to new ideas. The walls of his bohemian Jackson Park studio were "sunshine-colored"; the ceiling, "sky-blue." He was developing a theory of the "poem-dance," in which bodies expressed linguistic ideas three-dimensionally.[49] He and Dunham rented studio space from Adolph Bolm (a former star of Diaghilev's Ballets Russes) on Chicago's upscale Michigan Avenue to start their school and train dancers to perform in the new company, which they called the Ballet Nègre. The building manager soon informed Bolm that he did not want African Americans there. Turbyfill and Dunham then opened a studio in the 57th Street artists' colony in Hyde

Park. They threw a tea party to celebrate the opening, inviting Chicago's black elite. Ballet Nègre supporters included the sculptor Richmond Barthé, musician R. Nathaniel Dett, and lawyer Edith Sampson.[50]

The tea party was a success and even received a mention in the *Chicago Bee* newspaper, but attendance at the ballet classes dropped precipitously after the move. African American parents had been willing to take their children to classes on Michigan Avenue but not to the Hyde Park artists' colony on the South Side.[51] Dropping their children off in the Loop was a status symbol and also a political statement, a challenge to white supremacist notions of who belonged on the Magnificent Mile. The Hyde Park artists' colony, a neighborhood of bohemian whites and a growing African American population, did not make the same statement.

Dunham and Turbyfill also faced resistance within the dance world. In 1930, many dancers, choreographers, critics, and audience members believed that black dancers were "natural" movers, attuned solely to rhythm and incapable of being trained. Several also argued that black bodies could not form the positions required by ballet technique. Agnes de Mille told Turbyfill that a Negro Ballet wasn't possible "physiologically."[52] She would eventually change her mind, even attempting to start a "Negro Unit" of Ballet Theatre in New York City a decade later.

In spite of these obstacles, Turbyfill and Dunham did not give up. They took their cause to the press. Turbyfill wrote an article for a new African American magazine, *Abbott's Monthly*, published by Robert Abbott, editor of the black newspaper *Chicago Defender*. With the tagline "A Magazine That's Different," *Abbott's Monthly* featured stories about celebrity love affairs and sports and was designed to appeal to a mass audience.[53] Turbyfill's article, "Shall We Present to the World a New Ballet?" was supposed to appear in the inaugural October 1930 issue, but one of the editors blocked it.[54] One might not expect the idea of a Negro ballet to be controversial with a black readership. Perhaps the editor felt that the article—written by a white author, no less—had the potential to come across as elitist and Eurocentric, rather than as celebratory of race pride or appealing to the masses. It may have also been personal. That same month, Turbyfill was summarily ordered to leave the backstage area during a black dance performance.[55] Some members of Chicago's African American cultural scene felt he was an intrusion in their world.

Turbyfill's article did appear in the next month's issue, and it contained the earliest existing written expression of Dunham's artistic philosophy, since Turbyfill quoted her at length. She laid out an argument for how ballet would help African Americans create a "classic" art:

> We are not suggesting that the darker ballerina confine herself to the ballet of Pavlova. We would merely place at her disposal the technique which would enable her to express her own individuality and the genius of her race. After

this we leave it to the tom-tom, the jungle, the heat of the sun, the depth of rivers, primal gods, bondage, the cotton fields, and even, if you will, to a recent lynching in Texas, to provide material for a school of ballet, not so much to present a historical panorama of the Negro, as to express the wealth of his heritage in plastic and geometric design. Thus we can create a genuine choreography, a dance form symbolic of a self-conscious race.[56]

For Dunham, ballet was a template, a "geometric design" that would enable African Americans to transform their cultural practices into a theatrical form. She saw value in black cultural content, but not in the existing black aesthetic forms. Dunham distinguished her project not only from black popular, social, and theatrical dance, but also from the historical pageants of Du Bois and others. She did not want to relive the past; she wanted to create art for the future. In a sense, she reversed the ethic of Pablo Picasso. Whereas he drew on West African masks as a primitivist form through which to express European modernity, Dunham drew on ballet as a geometric form through which to express black modernity. Her use of the phrase "self-conscious race" echoed Locke's 1925 essay "The New Negro," in which self-consciousness was a key to forward progress and upward mobility.[57]

In Turbyfill's article, Dunham also bluntly stated that black dance did not yet exist as an art form. She admitted that some of the magazine's African American readers would voice "objection" to her assertion but went on to say that "civilization draws a sharp distinction between an uncurbed, purely racial expression, governed solely by rhythm and emotion, and the crystalline symphony of the traditional ballet."[58] She viewed Josephine Baker as "represent[ing] the masses whose dancing is more instinctive than formal."[59] Dunham was not alone among her New Negro peers in her embrace of uplift ideology. The composers William Dawson, R. Nathaniel Dett, and Florence Price, among others, advocated the use of symphonic and other European "high art" forms to modify black music and present "the Race in heroic, idealized terms."[60] They had determined, strategically, that it was the best way to gain acceptance in a deeply racist American society. They faced criticism from younger artists in the movement, notably Langston Hughes, who was a champion of black folk expression.[61]

The artistic debate mirrored the larger debate in black Chicago between the "old" settler ideology of bourgeois respectability and the "new" settler ideology of "brash public displays of nonfunctional fashions, up-tempo rhythms, theatrical personalities, and muscular confrontations" as methods of combating white supremacy.[62] At this moment in her life, the twenty-one-year-old Dunham came down on the uplift side of the debate, though her insistence on foregrounding the "genius of her race," which for her included tom-toms and "primal gods," meant that she would not forsake blackness. Furthermore, her focus on dance was itself counter to uplift, because it did

not reject the notion of associating blackness with the body. Instead, she recu-
perated the political and intellectual possibilities of embodied expression—
though in order to do so, she felt she had to reshape black dance through
ballet technique.

Although the Ballet Nègre was Dunham's first unique contribution to the
New Negro Movement, during her career she never restricted her work to the
corporeal realm. She also created institutions and archives, something that distinguished her from other dancers of the period. The Turbyfill-Dunham ballet
school closed for lack of funds and students by the end of 1930, but within a
year Dunham had a new plan, which included the Rosenwald Foundation. The
Rosenwald Foundation, founded by the Sears, Roebuck & Company executive
Julius Rosenwald, dedicated itself to social issues, and to African American
education in particular. Starting in 1928, it granted individual fellowships
to black artists and intellectuals, including Dunham's brother Albert Jr. As
she wrote to Albert in November 1931, "I am applying to the Rosenwald for
an endowment for a school which will combine a complete institution of the
dance, from which will grow the ballet, not as a production, but as a fundamental contribution."[63] Her school would go beyond only offering dance classes.
She dreamed of housing America's first library of dance, including "records
of obscure and primitive African tribes, together with their costumes," which
would create a greater understanding of dance and the African dance more
specifically.[64] At this early moment in her career, Dunham embraced Arturo
Schomburg's commandment that black artists should seek their roots in
Africa.[65] The effort to document black cultural production, through both the
body and more traditional documentary methods, would be an important
aspect of Dunham's career.

Nursing such ambitions challenged prevailing gender expectations. In the
November 1931 letter to her brother, Dunham wrote that getting the funding
would "in all probability determine whether or not I'll be just another woman,
or an actual creator."[66] She wanted to create something new for the world,
and that meant transcending the boundaries of a middle-class black woman's life. Because of the Great Depression, the 1930s saw a backlash against
the freedoms women had gained in the previous two decades. For African
American middle-class women in particular, the ethos of respectability meant
that wives, if it were economically possible, should stay at home.[67] Dunham
expressed concerns about McCoo, who "patiently waits for the thing to crash,
so that he can settle down comfortably in a home and have a child or two and
a day job and some peace . . . . I can't make the sacrifice at this time, however,
of giving up hope for a future entirely."[68] She equated the housewife role with
a life with no future. Although McCoo was also a dancer, he seemed to have
little understanding of his wife's unorthodox desires. The marriage would not
officially end for a few more years, but the seeds of dissolution were already
in place.

Dunham did not end up applying for a Rosenwald Fellowship in 1931, but neither did she become "just another woman." Instead, she continued building on the dream she had started with Turbyfill. She choreographed for a production of Hall Johnson's musical *Run, Little Chillun*, the first African American show to appear in a theater in Chicago's Loop district, and for the *O, Sing a New Song* Pageant at the Century of Progress International Exposition at Soldier's Field.[69] She trained with Diana Huebert, a follower of Isadora Duncan's "free" dance, and studied ballet with Ruth Page. Most importantly, she started the Negro Dance Group with the Russian émigré Ludmila Speranzeva, also known as Luda Paetz.[70] Speranzeva had performed with Moscow's Kamerny Theatre and the Chauve-Souris, a Russian cabaret troupe. The Chauve-Souris presented entertaining theatrical evenings of song, dance, and comedy, with elaborate costumes and the use of pantomime.[71] Speranzeva had also trained briefly with the German modern dance pioneer Mary Wigman. Wigman emphasized the use of body in "action-modes," such as "folding-unfolding, rising-falling, pressing-pulling, bending-reaching, rotating and twisting, undulating and heaving, swinging, swaying, vibrating, and shaking," instead of in specific codified movements. She based her pedagogy in improvisation, teaching her students movement principles about weight, energy, and use of space that were modeled on those of Laban, but she uniquely emphasized individual exploration and finding ecstatic expression.[72] Dunham later reflected, "I think I must have gotten a lot of that explosive feeling, and also a freedom of sexual presentation" from Speranzeva.[73]

The press appreciated the novelty of Dunham and Speranzeva's efforts. The critics called Negro Dance Group a "ballet" company, despite the turn to modern dance aesthetics, following the common nomenclature of the period for any professional dance group. Frank Hayes of the *Chicago Daily News* called the company's December 1932 performance at the Chicago Artists' Ball "the first Negro ballet ever danced."[74] News of the show reached the *Boston Globe*, which similarly called Dunham's group the "first negro ballet."[75] The *Chicago Defender* wrote of the performance:

> The modern dancers are beginning a new era in the history of the Race dancer. As in the poetry and music of the Race, the dance has outgrown the elementary period of spontaneous expression which ignores the universal language of form and technique ... [Dunham and her dancers] shall interpret the music, moods and life phases of the Race in the expressive movements of the modern dance as it is inspired by the emotions and voices from within.[76]

The *Defender* reiterated Dunham's philosophy for creating a modern black art form: use established European high-art techniques, such as ballet and German expressionist modern dance, to convey the unique experiences of African Americans. The dance *Fantasie Nègre* was the highlight of the evening.

The title came from Florence B. Price's prize-winning composition by the same name, which Price and another accomplished African American woman musician, Margaret Bonds, played live on piano at the performance. A photograph of *Fantasie Nègre* (Figure 1.2) shows the performers in high-necked, long-sleeved, floor-length dark dresses that invoke the Martha Graham Dance Company, which in 1932 was considered the vanguard of modern dance in America. They have bare feet and serious expressions on their faces, signaling that this dance had little resemblance to the minstrelsy, vaudeville, or Cotton Club jazz that dominated black dance in the 1930s.

Although Wigman's ideas represented one strain of modern dance influencing Dunham, "interpretive" dancing, most famously exemplified by

Figure 1.2 Katherine Dunham (center) and dancers in *Fantasie Nègre*, ca. 1932. Photograph by Bertram Dorien Basabe. Missouri History Museum, St. Louis.

St. Denis, represented another that equally influenced Dunham's trajectory. Interpretive dance has had a loose definition over the years, but during the 1930s, interpretive dancers strove for artistic expression by capturing the mood or essence of cultural groups seen as exotic. Dunham learned Spanish dance from Quill Monroe, partner of flamenco dancer La Argentina, and versions of Javanese, Balinese, Spanish, and other dance forms from Vera Mirova, a Russian vaudeville and theater performer. After fleeing Russia during the 1917 Revolution, Mirova traveled throughout Asia taking dance classes and performing.[77] The interpretive dance tradition also came to Dunham through Ruth Page of the Chicago Opera Ballet. Ballet companies and schools routinely included dances from around the world in their productions.[78] Before settling down in Chicago, Page had toured the globe with Pavlova and studied dance in India, Bali, China, Japan, and Spain. She took private lessons with various masters and observed hundreds of dance classes and performances, then incorporated this material into her choreography.[79]

Reflecting this tradition, the Negro Dance Group program from 1934 included numbers entitled *Arabienne* and *Nautch* (Figure 1.3).[80] In interviews and memoirs, Dunham never mentioned feelings of discomfort about performing these dances. Was she participating in what twenty-first-century scholars call cultural appropriation? Or does the fact that interpretive dance was universally common practice in the 1930s alter our understanding? Does Dunham's position as a racial minority mitigate the claims of Orientalism that we now assign to dancers like St. Denis, or were African American performers in the 1930s complicit in perpetuating "yellowface" performance idioms that supported imperialist ideologies, as Stephanie Leigh Batiste suggests?[81] All choreographers draw on learned and observed cultural practices that mix in complicated ways with their imaginations. Mirova and Page were not considered ethnographers, but they had studied multiple dance forms abroad, and they passed that knowledge on to Dunham. Where borrowing crosses over into appropriation depends on the power dynamic between the performer and the source of her material, even if the source is never fully pure or original itself. What constitutes legitimate cultural borrowing is a shifting and politicized terrain.

Dunham's most memorable performance in 1934 was in *La Guiablesse*, Page's 1933 ballet based on a Martinican folk tale. Page had never been to Martinique; instead, her ideas for the dance were inspired by Lafcadio Hearn's travelogue *Two Years in the West Indies*. The *La Guiablesse* program notes reflected the exoticized, romanticized language of all Caribbean travelogues of this period. The setting was described as one in which "tropical heat incubates a world of awesome and vaporous beings" and "sunset explodes with quivering colors that stupefy the mind."[82] The plotline follows a more familiar path. Page drew upon tropes of nineteenth-century Romantic ballet to create the figure of the Guiablesse, a ghostly female spirit who yearns after

Figure 1.3 Katherine Dunham in *Nautch*, ca. 1935. Photograph by Bertram Dorien Basabe. Missouri History Museum, St. Louis.

"earthly love" that can never be fulfilled.[83] In Romantic ballets, ephemeral and otherworldly female creatures such as "wilis" and "sylphs" lure men away from flesh-and-blood lovers. In *La Guiablesse*, the "she-devil" entices an unwitting male up a mountain, only to reveal a "hideous face." He jumps to his death rather than face the prospect of consummating love with such a dream-turned-nightmare.[84]

The 1933 premiere as part of Chicago's Century of Progress International Exposition caused a minor scandal because of its interracial cast. Page danced the title role with a group of barely clothed black men partnering her. *La Guiablesse* conformed to an established pattern of white choreographers seeking the exotic through black bodies, but it also challenged gendered racial narratives in the United States. Films such as *Birth of a Nation* established the tropes of the black male sexual predator and the innocent white female victim. *La Guiablesse* reversed the predator and victim roles. Page played the she-devil, who with her "white deceit," "comes to separate and destroy dark-skinned lovers."[85]

In 1934, with a new commission to work on, Page turned *La Guiablesse* over to Dunham to star in and rehearse. Notably, the piece was part of the first show of the Chicago Civic Opera that was fully devoted to ballet. At a time when black ballet was almost unheard of elsewhere in the country, African American performers and aesthetics were central to Page's vision for American ballet. Dunham's performance attracted much attention from the Chicago-area critics, who called the whole piece "astonishing" and praised the dancers for moving with "ease," "grace," and "eloquence."[86] News of the positive reception reached her hometown newspaper, the *Joliet Spectator*.[87] The *Defender* did not publish a review, but noted proudly that the performance had been "repeated by popular request."[88] With music by composer William Grant Still, *La Guiablesse* solidified Dunham's place as a leader of the "black ballet" movement. In the 700-page essay "Colored Culture in Chicago," written under the auspices of the Illinois Writers Project in 1937, Katherine "Kitty" de la Chapelle pointed to *La Guiablesse* as the moment when the "modernization" of black dance occurred, not only in Chicago, but also throughout the United States.[89] Although the ballet derived from a fantastical travelogue, *La Guiablesse* nonetheless provided an opening for Dunham to showcase her dancers' abilities in the high-art setting of opera.

Dunham had only positive words for *La Guiablesse*, but she began to express concern about her lack of cultural knowledge about the African diaspora. Her dance teachers had traveled extensively in Asia and Europe, but not the Caribbean or Africa. In June 1933, she wrote to the anthropologist Melville Herskovits, of Northwestern University, asking for advice about two "African" dances she was preparing for the Negro Dance Group, telling him that his recent lecture on West African culture and presentation of "Kuntu's group" had inspired her. "Kuntu's group" referred to Duke Kwensi Kuntu and a group of male performers from the Ashanti region of Africa, who had come to Chicago in 1933 to participate in the Century of Progress International Exposition.[90] "I'd like very much to have my instructor [Speranzeva] see something really authentic," she wrote. "We are working just now on 'Bamboula' but I am not exactly satisfied ... I'm afraid that the Bamboula may have a particular significance that we are overlooking. Perhaps you can offer a suggestion or two."[91] *Bamboula* referred to a dance, named after a type of drum, practiced in New Orleans, the Virgin Islands, and elsewhere in the Caribbean.[92] Not only did the *bamboula* show the persistence of Africanist aesthetics in the Western Hemisphere, but also it demonstrated that there was diasporic communication throughout the Americas. Dunham wanted to bring a greater authenticity and sincerity of emotional expression to choreography based in Africanist aesthetics.

Herskovits declined to help. Nor did he offer any information about the *bamboula*; he simply suggested that she come to visit him at Northwestern when the fall semester began. He did compliment her work in *La Guiablesse*, writing that "the performance achieved one of the things that I feel artistic performances should do, namely, giving the 'feel' of an exotic situation without attempting a realistic presentation."[93] Ironically, the entire point of Dunham's letter had been that she wanted to move toward realism. Herskovits had hit on a point of contention that has endlessly bedeviled scholars of performance, which Dunham faced acutely throughout her career: the question of authenticity and its relationship to theatrical presentation.

Dunham's letter to Herskovits was part of a turn to anthropology as a way to find adequate expression for her artistic ideas. Unlike Mirova and Page, she had not had the opportunity to travel abroad and learn other dance forms. Studying anthropology at the University of Chicago gave her the chance to do so. Franz Boas's theory of cultural relativism and emphasis on ethnographic research had revolutionized the field at the dawn of the twentieth century. Boas taught his students, including Margaret Mead, Ruth Benedict, and Herskovits, to strip the idea of primitive society of its pejorative descriptors and define it simply as a society without a written language. He also called for a more rigorous, scientific, and empirical methodology, such as extended field research, to challenge gross generalizations about other cultures.[94]

Boas's revolutionary approach encouraged many artists in the New Negro Movement to employ ethnographic techniques from anthropology to create a modern black identity.[95] Dunham was one of them, and the University of Chicago was a particularly exciting place for her, where she could learn about the newest developments in the field. Alfred Radcliffe-Brown's theory of structural functionalism provided an important framework for the anthropology department's approach. A structural functionalist viewpoint interpreted every cultural practice as fulfilling specific functions within the larger social structure. Dance was thus fully integrated into the coherent whole of a community, not isolated in an aesthetic realm. Dunham adopted this perspective.[96]

After the poststructuralist turn in anthropology in the 1970s, such approaches were deemed suspect. As the self-described black feminist socialist anthropologist A. Lynn Bolles has admitted, she initially responded to Dunham's work with "derision," feeling that functionalism did not take into account colonialism or other power dynamics.[97] Instead, its totalizing discourse seemed to reinforce colonial visions of the nonwhite world. Furthermore, functionalism denied dance's aesthetic value in favor of utilitarian purpose. Anthropological functionalism in some ways reinforced the divisions between culture as art in supposedly civilized nations and culture as functional practice in supposedly primitive ones. In the 1930s, however, anthropology's potential to counter scientific racism, and functionalism's validation of dance as socially meaningful gave Dunham powerful tools to use in furthering her goals.

The most important anthropologist Dunham met at the University of Chicago was Robert Redfield, who became her adviser. Dunham claimed that she had been awakened to the possibilities of dance anthropology during a lecture in which Redfield argued that the Lindy Hop had African roots.[98] Redfield criticized Boas's "salvage anthropology," in which an ethnographer attempts to document the disappearing elements of a culture. Instead, Redfield called for an ethnographic practice that observed and accepted cultural change. He proposed a "folk-urban continuum" along which cultural transformations occurred.[99] Dunham would later use Redfield's folk-urban continuum to interpret her ethnographic research in the Caribbean.

Although Redfield was Dunham's adviser, Herskovits was her greatest influence. He was one of the foremost scholars of West Africa and its diaspora. His best-known book, *The Myth of the Negro Past*, argued that black people in the Americas retained African cultural practices. He pointed out the malevolence of the assumption that African Americans had kept nothing of their African heritage. This "myth," he wrote, was "one of the principal supports of race prejudice in this country."[100] Herskovits's goal in *The Myth of the Negro Past* was twofold: to document retentions of African culture and to validate the complexity and sophistication of those practices. He also put forward a theory of "acculturation," a word he used to describe how two cultures—in his case, European and African—transmitted elements to each other, creating new, creolized forms. Acculturation refuted the social-Darwinist idea that an ostensibly superior European culture obliterated African culture whenever the two came in contact.[101]

Dunham's mentors represented the most progressive wing in the field of anthropology and challenged notions of the primitive as inferior, but they still operated under the assumption that a distinction between primitive and civilized existed. Many of them invoked clichés about primitive peoples' purportedly greater connection to emotion, spirituality, nature, community, and family in order to criticize Western industrial capitalism and the artificial, inorganic culture it produced.[102] Dunham could not escape this framework. At one point, she asked Herskovits's advice about her plan to do "a comparative study of primitive dancing" that would begin with Africa and include "primitive groups of American Negroes."[103] She surely did not count herself among the "primitive groups," setting herself apart as a member of the civilized world.

David Luis-Brown argues that people of color in the interwar period often used the discourse of primitivism to critique US empire and neocolonialism, even as, contradictorily, they ended up reinforcing problematic categories and romanticized notions of primitive life. Notably, in Luis-Brown's examples, the point at which individuals fail to escape racial essentialism is the point at which they encounter black women dancing, an affective experience that results in an outpouring of stereotypes about sexuality and thoughtless abandon to instinctive rhythmic and primal drives.[104] By turning to dance, Dunham had arguably chosen the most difficult path for reframing primitivism. From another vantage point, she can be said to have audaciously struck at the heart of primitivist discourse, challenging its most fundamental precepts about black women's bodies in motion.

Dunham began to feel that the library books, lectures, professors, and dance teachers in Chicago could only take her so far in her quest. So in November 1934, she turned again to the Rosenwald Foundation, with the help of a new friend she had met through her University of Chicago intellectual circles, the psychoanalyst Erich Fromm. Fromm would become an important guide in Dunham's life, helping her to understand how the familial dynamics of her childhood had affected her. He compared her to Iphigenia, the Greek goddess who was sacrificed for the sake of her community, and introduced her to the ideas of Nietzsche. He helped her parents with rent during the dark days of the Great Depression. Later, in New York, they would become lovers.[105] Convinced of her talent, in 1934 Fromm arranged for members of the Rosenwald Foundation to attend one of her performances, who encouraged her to apply for a grant.

Dunham's application, in November 1934, proposed a two-part study to fulfill her goal of creating a thriving dance institution bolstered by anthropological research. First, she wanted to train at the School of American Ballet and the Wigman School of Modern Dance (later renamed for Hanya Holm) in New York. The second part of the grant would fund field research on "primitive rhythms," ideally in Egypt or Ethiopia. The two nations loomed large in the New Negro imagination, for they represented "great civilization[s] of antiquity" that could serve as sources of inspiration for black art.[106] Dunham argued that so-called primitive dance would serve as a "stimulus" to the art of modern dance and did not limit her definition of the primitive to Africa.[107] She also suggested that doing ethnographic research among American Indians and "island peoples" would contribute to the discovery of "fundamental and universal" principles of human movement and meaning.[108]

Like many anthropologists and artists of her generation, Dunham argued that primitive peoples could reveal the secrets of how all human beings were meant to move when stripped of the artificial layers of civilization. As Batiste points out, Dunham "repeated the problematical ideas that the culture studied was ahistorical and simple" by viewing the cultures of Africa, Native Americans, and the Pacific Islands as "preindustrial, isolated, original, simple, authentic, and basic."[109] The idea of primitive art as a "stimulus" to purportedly staid, tired, and artificial European-American art was also a well-worn, clichéd idea.[110] At the same time, Dunham had a different political objective from Picasso, Gauguin, or the other artists who used primitive elements in their art, though she did not spell this out in the Rosenwald application. By creating contemporary dance inspired by what she called "primitive" aesthetics, she could make an important contribution to the New Negro Movement's campaign to present a new, modern face of black life to the world.

The Rosenwald committee members funded Dunham only to do research in primitive rhythms and suggested that she go to the Caribbean, not to Ethiopia or Egypt. They also insisted that she first spend six months studying with Herskovits.[111] Despite their liberal politics, they seemed to believe existing stereotypes about black dancers' unsuitability for ballet or modern dance. They probably also shared the widespread belief that dance was not an intellectual pursuit, and thus that the study of primitive rhythms in the Caribbean might be permissible under the rubric of anthropology, but that training at the School of American Ballet and Wigman School was not. The die that would dramatically alter the trajectory of Dunham's career had been cast.

Herskovits, who had not previously been helpful when Dunham requested assistance, soon fell captive to her intellect and personal charm, as would countless men and women throughout her career. At the conclusion of their study together, in May 1935, he wrote a letter to the Rosenwald Foundation, stating that "her work with me has been excellent, not only from the point of view of class work and scholarship, but more importantly for the purposes of her fellowship, as regards the manner of her approach to her problem and the way in which she has grown into it."[112] Dunham had a strong sense of her mission: to learn the dances of the Caribbean in order to provide the foundation for a new dance institution, in which the rhythms of African-descended peoples would reach their highest possible artistic expression. Over the course of her seven years in Chicago, she had added a new element to the New Negro Movement with her dance companies. Now she had a chance to deepen the transnational dimension of her work.

CHAPTER 2

Finding a Politics of Diaspora in the Caribbean

I n the winter of 1935, Dunham found herself lying under a sheet in a urine-soaked nightgown, starving, freezing, and more than a little frightened. She was in the Haitian countryside, almost two thousand miles away from Chicago, undergoing the first stage of initiation into Vodou. Despite her discomfort and disorientation, she felt, for the first time, the "tie of kinship that must hold together secret societies the world over" with her eight fellow initiates.[1] She had recently learned the phrase *Nan Guinée*, "from faraway Guinea," the place Haitian priests considered the common ancestral homeland of all black people.[2] A priest told her that her brother's mental illness stemmed from a failure to appease the *loa*, or spirits, because in the United States, the cultural connections of black people to Africa had been broken.[3] Dunham had gone to the Caribbean to find choreographic inspiration. She would return with a diasporic worldview and a belief in the importance of expressive culture to black liberation.

Between June 1935 and April 1936, Dunham traveled to Jamaica, Martinique, Trinidad, and Haiti to conduct ethnographic research on dance. Instead of following the objective, observational approach of her mentors in anthropology, she dove into participation and cast a self-reflexive eye on her process, noting how her subject position as an African American woman affected her interactions with others. Based on this research, she produced some of the first written pieces of dance ethnography, starting, in 1939, with a series of articles about Martinican dance for *Esquire* magazine. In 1946, she published *Journey to Accompong*, an account of her time in Jamaica; in 1947, *Dances of Haiti*, the book version of her master's thesis; and in 1969, an ethnographic memoir of Haiti, *Island Possessed*. She also transformed her findings for the concert dance stage, a process that VèVè Clark has called Dunham's "research to performance" method.[4]

Most important, Dunham began to articulate a politics of diaspora in the Caribbean. The primary catalyst was the literal fact of travel. Traveling abroad for the first time gave Dunham the chance to *live* diaspora, to experience both the alienation of dislocation and the profound joy of discovering connection across borders. In befriending future presidents and peasants alike in the Caribbean, she created an "operative diaspora," meaning relationships and networks forged among black people living outside the continent of Africa.[5] Her friendships with politician Dumarsais Estimé and anthropologist Jean Price-Mars in Haiti were particularly important, for these men introduced her to *négritude*. A term that has historically been difficult to translate into English and whose meaning has changed depending on the decade and speaker, *négritude* can be generally understood as an assertion of pride in African origins in the face of efforts to devalue blackness. Aimé Césaire famously declared that Haiti was where *négritude* "stood up for the first time," even though the term did not come into common parlance until after Dunham's visit.[6] Even without the word, the concept of embracing Africanness, known as *indigénisme* at the time, percolated among the Haitian intellectuals who shared their ideas with Dunham. Claiming blackness instead of rejecting it would be key to forging a politics of diaspora.

The emergence of a diasporic mindset in the Caribbean was also intimately tied to Dunham's new discoveries about dance. Over ten months of research, she found not only the content she sought, but also a new approach to choreographic creation. She began to understand *why* people danced, not just how they danced. Instead of serving as raw material to insert into ballet or modern dance, Caribbean dance could offer its own aesthetic principles, both in terms of philosophical foundation and formal movement structure. Through her deepened understanding of the social, political, and aesthetic values of Caribbean dance, she developed the firm belief that connection to African cultural roots was vital to the advancement of black people throughout the Western Hemisphere.

At the same time, Dunham was not only interested in mining cultural practices to find a link to an African past. She also analyzed how current political realities were shaping modern expressions of Caribbean dance. She critiqued capitalism and imperialism, objecting strongly to the United States' nineteen-year military occupation of Haiti. She developed an incisive analysis of Haitian class dynamics, observing how racism and colonialism had created a corrosive power structure. Dunham's emphasis on understanding contemporary Caribbean cultural practices in their broader social and political contexts found its way into her choreography. When she returned stateside, in June 1936, her performances would enrich the transnational dimensions of the New Negro Movement in Chicago and alert fellow intellectuals to pay attention to the dancing body as part of their investigations into the black experience.

Dunham went to the Caribbean in June 1935 intent on searching for Africanist survivals. After all, Schomburg had exhorted African Americans to "dig up their past" as the best way to create a better future, and Herskovits had argued that documenting Africanist retentions was the best way to counter racial prejudice.[7] Dunham also simply wanted more performance material. She wrote, "Ethnology excited me very much because in every unfamiliar people or custom I saw a great possibility of establishing an exotic mood in the theater."[8] Dunham's career objective was to make these dual goals compatible, so that one did not have to choose between scientific documentation and the creation of an "exotic mood." At this moment in history, however, the two stood far apart.

Dunham felt despondent when she did not immediately find the African connections she sought. The first site of her fieldwork was the Jamaican village Accompong, whose residents were the descendants of runaway slaves, or Maroons. One day, she attended a Maroon burial and noticed that the men were digging a tunnel grave. Dunham immediately thought of African-descended peoples living in Dutch Guiana, who maintained the West African custom of digging a tunnel to prevent the body from returning to the living world with the spirit. Dunham had read that this religious ritual survived in the Americas, most likely in the writings of Herskovits. She was disappointed, however, when the Maroons shrugged and told her that they were only digging the tunnel because they had hit a rock.[9]

The second site of her fieldwork was Martinique, an island sagging under the weight of French colonialism and the exploitative sugar-cane industry. She wrote to Herskovits from Fort de France, "The people are much amalgamated . . . there is much more to be done here psychologically than artistically or anthropologically. The country is slowly decaying."[10] An anthropologist today would question Dunham's assertion that there was nothing ethnographically interesting about 1930s Martinican culture, but for her and Herskovits, finding African cultural retentions in the Americas was a vitally important political project. Such findings would also mean she could bring greater authenticity for her stage work, which she was seeking. Notwithstanding her initial disappointment, over the next three months in Martinique she learned several dances, including the *ag'ya*, *majumba*, and *beguine*, which became mainstays of her choreography.

Dunham's essay "The Negro Dance" (1941) presented a less despairing view of cultural change than her letters to Herskovits in 1935 had. The intervening years had allowed her to reflect more broadly on the significance of her research. In "The Negro Dance," Dunham discussed the evolution of black

dance forms, employing Redfield's folk-urban continuum theory. Tribal dancing, in its purportedly pure, unadulterated form, existed in Africa. Folk dancing in the Caribbean was created with exposure to "the pressure of European
culture." Urban culture was thoroughly Europeanized.[11] Dunham clearly operated under the epistemological constructs of her generation. Since the late
twentieth century, definitions of "folk" and "urban" have shifted, and notions
of a tribal cultural purity have been discredited, although the political useful-
ness of an essentialist idea of Africa has not completely disappeared.[12]

Dunham went beyond the work of her mentors by offering a more precise
explanation for cultural change in the Caribbean. African dance, she argued,
had "lost its functional validity" in the Americas.[13] Dance had a specific purpose and meaning in West African societies, but there was no point in continuing to perform the dances in exactly the same way if the religious or
social purpose no longer existed. Afro-Caribbean people created new dances,
or reworked old ones, to respond to new needs. They did not pathologically
adopt the white culture of their surroundings or buckle under oppression, but
instead developed cultural practices that created meaning for their new social
contexts. Dunham's 1941 article excised the nostalgic tone of her 1935 letters
in favor of a more analytical approach.

Dunham's thoughts on the implications of cultural transformation were
not without contradictions. In "The Negro Dance," she argued that the United
States was the country in the Western Hemisphere most likely to guarantee
the persistence of African dance traditions because of the degree to which
black music and dance lay at the heart of mainstream American culture.[14]
Most scholars, including her mentor Herskovits, argued the opposite: a
place such as a rural Haitian village offered the greatest possibility for finding a connection to Africa given its purported isolation from Western-style
modernity. Dunham did not entirely disagree. In her ethnography, *Dances of
Haiti*, published in 1947, she claimed that "the dances of peasant Haiti today
might well be those of slave Haiti in the seventeenth century" because they
had "fortunately resisted strong the impact of European culture."[15] In essence,
Dunham proffered contradictory opinions. In one publication she argued that
cultural syncretism did not destroy tradition but, rather, ensured its vitality;
in another, cultural survival depended on resistance to European forms. This
back-and-forth revealed a central tension of diaspora that Dunham would
wrestle with throughout her career—namely, the debate over how best to
ensure the continuity of Africanist cultural practices in new settings.

Dunham's awareness of the limits of cross-cultural interpretation was
also important for developing a diasporic political stance. On her fifth day in
Jamaica, she observed the "Maroon version of the quadrille," which blended
English and West African dance. She later wrote in *Journey to Accompong*, "I
began to feel that the Maroons belonged to the sultry side of the Caribbean
and that their Spanish and Indian and African ancestors must have known

passions other than warfare . . . . But perhaps it is the rum and the smoking lanterns. The unveiled hip movements of the shay-shay . . . may have done things to me which I project into the innocent Maroons."[16] Dunham's writing emphasized the sensations induced in her by the choreography and the setting, connecting her readers viscerally to her experiences. She worked on the level of what critical theorists call "affect"—the unconscious bodily responses to sensations of sight, smell, sound, touch, and taste.[17] Through her language, she simultaneously invoked, then undercut, stereotypes of Spanish and African cultures as more passionate and sensuous. She seduced the reader, but then unmasked the seduction by suggesting that her subject position as an American outsider, under the influence of alcohol, may have affected her interpretation. Redfield, Herskovits, and most other anthropologists of the 1930s did not break with the third-person voice, but Dunham found it crucial to do so as a means of exposing how national difference could lead to misunderstanding.

Dunham worked to overcome national differences by developing a sense of shared racial identification. Within days of her arrival in Haiti, a man hosting a Vodou ceremony allowed her to observe it because she "was from African descent." She wrote that "he was glad to let me be present so that I would be able to tell the brothers in America."[18] In reviewing *Journey to Accompong* in 1947, Locke wrote that Dunham's work proved beyond a doubt "the effectiveness of color as an open sesame."[19] Yet her skin color did not give her automatic entrée. Locke's implication that she had gained easy access discounted Dunham's efforts to establish trust and develop empathy. She later wrote that "perseverance" was the most important trait in her ethnographic practice.[20] She told Amy Porter of *Collier's* that "a good field technique, I found, was to establish the relationship between my ancestors and theirs . . . . They thought of me as an American, not as a Negro, until I talked to them about our common African ancestors. Then they accepted me."[21] In Trinidad, one woman with Dahomean ancestors "almost wept for joy" when Dunham began to share the knowledge of Dahomey that she had gleaned from the coursework with Herskovits.[22] She found even greater openness in Haiti when she claimed that her ancestors were Haitian, though they were not.[23] Dunham's diasporic consciousness grew from this ethnographic strategy, as she learned to establish bonds based on shared cultural origins as a means of overcoming suspicion about her national identity.

As important as her efforts at racial solidarity were Dunham's efforts to learn the dances. In fact, the two were related: her willingness to dance and her clear talent solidified the ties of diasporic affinity. In the 1930s, the role of the anthropologist was to observe another culture as objectively as possible. Before Dunham left for the Caribbean, Herskovits had arranged for her to have the most sophisticated sound and film recording equipment available. If she were to follow the Boasnian imperative to amass empirical data to disprove existing prejudices, she had to have the technology to do so. In Jamaica and Martinique she used the camera extensively, which Herskovits applauded. In Trinidad, however, after getting into trouble with a local priestess for filming a secret Shango ritual, Dunham put down the camera in order to dance. She wrote, "Unless I'm dealing with purely social affairs, I must go easy on the equipment. I've seen the difference between something staged and something real, and besides people don't like it."[24]

Performance studies scholars dispute the distinction between "staged" and "real" events. Dunham wanted to see authentic cultural performances; but, as Erving Goffman argues in *The Presentation of Self*, all social life is a performance.[25] The dance one performs for family and friends is not inherently more authentic than a dance one performs on a stage or for tourist dollars. At the same time, Dunham operated in a world in which racial prejudice often meant that black cultural performance was misunderstood and sensationalized by white tourists and travel writers. To avoid exploitation, practitioners of Caribbean religions would sometimes attempt to keep their practices hidden from prying eyes, as the Shango priestess in Trinidad did in Dunham's case. By earning people's trust, Dunham could learn dances that, while not necessarily more authentic than those staged for white tourists, displayed a wider range of expressions, movements, and emotions. She also mentioned another reason for not using the camera—"people don't like it." Her motivation was not merely to gain access to authentic rituals. She also wanted to respect the people she met and their wish for privacy.

Dunham never lost the desire to document culture in a more traditional sense; all of her future schools would house either a library or a museum. Kinesthetic memory, however, would become a vitally important way in which she passed on cultural information to her dancers and audiences. In Haiti, the last and longest stop on her ethnographic research trip, she underwent an initiation in Vodou to gain a kinesthetic understanding of possession. Herskovits worried about her participation. He wrote to Dunham, "I am a little disturbed also at the prospect of your going through the canzo ceremony and I am wondering if it would not be possible for you to attend merely as a witness."[26] In the *canzo* ritual, the second stage of a Vodou initiation, an initiate walks on hot coals or performs other physically demanding feats that symbolize the passage from life into death, and thus one's readiness to proceed to the next level. Dunham had only been in Haiti for about two months at this point. Herskovits felt that she would not be able to endure walking on coals, which stretched the physical body to limits to which she was not accustomed. Ultimately, Dunham did decide against doing the *canzo*, on the advice of a *hougan* (male priest) who said she was not adequately prepared.[27] She instead underwent the *lavé-tête* ceremony, the first stage of the Vodou initiation process.

Dunham's reaction to gaining insider status through participation changed over time. In her 1936 notes she wrote, "Because I was not a Haitian I would never really see behind that bland mask, tho I attend a thousand ceremonies, dance the yonvalou until dawn, and proclaim my African heritage heartily in the retreat of the hungfor."[28] Dunham shared an African heritage with Haitians, she danced well, and she treated the people she met with respect. Ultimately, however, she felt that someone born in the United States could not fully understand Haitian culture. She also wrote to Herskovits, "The funny part of it is that everybody says that everything that everybody else found out [about Vodou] is erroneous."[29] Clearly multiple truths existed, and any anthropologist who claimed to know the "authentic" Vodou in fact only had one limited point of view.

Dunham voiced a different perspective thirty years later in *Island Possessed*. In Haiti, she felt for the first time a sense of belonging within a specialized group: her fellow Vodou initiates. The ecstasy that she experienced while dancing in Vodou rites brought her into harmony with others and the cosmos. She wrote, "We danced . . . as I imagine dance must have been executed when body and being were more united . . . in the dance of religious ecstasy . . . man might come into his own, be freed of inferiority and guilt in face of whatever might be his divinity."[30] Rather than emphasize the differences she felt, she had learned to appreciate the connections. Her ability to recognize both the fissures of national identity and the unity of ecstatic communion in Vodou serves as a prime example of how diaspora functions.

Dunham was not the only anthropologist of her generation to develop innovative ethnographic methodologies in the Caribbean. That same year, the Rosenwald Foundation also awarded Zora Neale Hurston a grant to visit Jamaica and Haiti. Like Dunham, Hurston challenged the existing understanding of the anthropologist as objective outsider.[31] In her ethnography *Tell My Horse*, however, Hurston, unlike Dunham, never raised doubts about this insider status. Nor did Hurston acknowledge that overcoming national difference required a certain amount of intellectual and emotional labor.[32] Instead, Hurston challenged Dunham's ethnographic authority and integrity. In July 1936, she wrote to Herskovits expressing jealousy and resentment that Dunham had gone to Jamaica "carrying out the program that I had mapped out for the Rosenwald gang."[33] Hurston had studied at Barnard College under Boas and also considered Herskovits a mentor. She suspected that the Foundation board had stolen her plans and given them to Dunham; Herskovits assured her that this was not so. He wrote that he himself had planned Dunham's Jamaica visit, not the Foundation, and additionally, the two programs of study were so different that Hurston need not feel any sense of competition. Dunham studied dance; Hurston studied other cultural practices.[34]

Herskovits was overlooking something both women understood intimately: in 1930s America, there was space for only one black female anthropologist.

According to Hurston, Charles S. Johnson of Fisk University "was boasting that it wouldn't be long with me and that he was grooming Catherine [sic] Dunham for the place."[35] Herskovits also ignored the fact that both women experimented with multiple forms of ethnography. In 1932, Hurston produced *The Great Day*, a full-evening dance concert about black life in a railroad camp in Florida.[36] Even though Hurston's theatrical endeavors never achieved much success, she paid close attention to music and dance throughout her fieldwork. Dunham studied music, social customs, and religion as well as dance. Like Hurston, she had literary ambitions and published many books. There was significant overlap between the two women, who saw themselves as competing for the same funding and recognition.

Hurston's criticisms of Dunham's methodology were numerous. First, she said, Dunham had missed the major opportunity to see the danced rites of the Jamaican Maroon people by leaving Accompong before January 6, the day of the Epiphany in Christian theology. Second, Dunham paid money to see staged dances. Hurston challenged Dunham's assertion that she knew "the difference between something staged and something real." Much to village leader Colonel Rowe's chagrin, Hurston refused to see the "tourist stuff" the Maroons had purportedly performed for Dunham. Hurston wrote to Herskovits that Rowe "tried to shame me by telling me how much Miss Dunham spent. I didn't tell him I had had more experience in the field than she."[37] Third, Hurston castigated Dunham for living in Accompong for only thirty days. Such a short visit, Hurston wrote in her review of *Journey to Accompong*, "hardly affords time enough for the fieldworker to scratch the surface."[38]

Hurston's final criticism implied that Dunham lacked the depth of knowledge to represent Caribbean folklife with authority. The Boasnian imperative of extended fieldwork remained central in anthropology throughout the twentieth century. Herskovits, too, had criticized Dunham's decision to visit so many locations rather than settle down in one area. Not only did she travel to four different islands in less than a year, but she also traveled from community to community on those islands. He believed she was getting only a "superficial knowledge" of dancing because of her constant traveling and because of her choice of informants. She spent much time with Doc Reeser (Dr. S. H. Rieser), an American marine who had fallen in love with Haiti and a Haitian woman, Cécile, and stayed on after the end of the US occupation (see Figure 2.1). Herskovits suggested that she try to learn about Vodou directly from Haitians themselves, instead of through a white American intermediary.[39]

Dunham at first disagreed. She wanted to soak up as many dances as possible, and she noted that Vodou ceremonies were highly localized, depending on the individual *hougan* or *mambo* (female priest) who was leading the ritual.[40] After a month in Haiti, she changed her mind, deciding that focusing on one place would indeed help her dig deeper. She continued to rely on Doc Reeser, however, as an entrée into both *Rada-Dahomey* and *Petro* ceremonies

Figure 2.1 Katherine Dunham with Fred Allsop, Doc Reeser, and Cécile in Haiti, 1935. Photographer unknown. Missouri History Museum, St. Louis.

of the Vodou practice.[41] Recognizing that conferrals of authority correlated to length of time in the field, she always told the press that she had spent eighteen months (sometimes she claimed two years) in the Caribbean, although her fieldwork in fact had lasted between nine and ten months.[42]

Regardless of the amount of time Dunham spent in the Caribbean, what is certain is that her fieldwork in Haiti is what most profoundly influenced her politics of diaspora. She fell in love with the island, writing in her notes, "There is no way for me not to be bathed in love of it . . . . I was prepared for voodoo drums, the crowded market, the handsome mulatto—but I did not know . . . that I would climb 52 stairs, enter a pale green room of Venetian shutters, cross it to open French doors, & behold one of the real beauties of the world."[43] Dunham was not alone in feeling a connection to Haiti. Of all the Caribbean islands, it held a special place in the African American imagination in the early twentieth century. It was where enslaved people of African descent had overthrown one of the world's most powerful empires and the only place in the Western Hemisphere with black self-government. Yet the Haitian Revolution had only been a partial success. Economic sanctions and diplomatic nonrecognition isolated and suffocated the island. Corrupt misrule deepened its problems. There was a huge class divide between a rural black peasantry and an urban, mixed-race elite. After the end of French colonialism, those identified as *mulâtre*—mulatto—and those identified as *noir*—black—vied for political power, and more often than not the *mulâtre* were in command. Elements of Haitian culture connected to Africa, especially Vodou, were often repressed or banned outright.[44]

Dunham arrived on Haiti's shores only one year after the end of the United States' nineteen-year military occupation, which had further complicated the political landscape. When the United States had invaded the island in 1915, the political situation on the island was highly unstable, and many black Americans publicly supported the idea that Haiti's government needed some kind of outside intervention. Those thoughts changed after the "bloody summer" of 1919, in which white mobs attacked African Americans in over three dozen cities across the United States. Black World War I veterans had hoped that their service would catalyze the government to end segregation and discrimination; instead, it seemed that racism had only worsened as competition for jobs and housing increased. The rise of Marcus Garvey, a Jamaican immigrant who founded the Universal Negro Improvement Association and called for a global perspective on black liberation, also influenced a shift in attitude. Many African Americans came to see Haitians not as backward neighbors, but as fellow members of the race in a parallel situation of oppression.[45] In 1920, James Weldon Johnson visited Haiti to investigate the occupation and published a sweeping condemnation in *The Crisis*. Johnson challenged the false "propaganda" about Haiti's purported unfitness for self-government. He condemned the invading American marines for instituting forced labor, brutalizing peasants, and raping women. Most of all, he condemned the US government for sending southerners to Haiti, men who brought their racist ideology with them.[46] Other well-known New Negro Movement leaders followed Johnson to Haiti, including Du Bois, Locke, and Hughes.[47]

African Americans were not the only ones paying attention to Haiti in the 1920s and early 1930s. Because of the occupation, Haiti became an "object of cultural fascination" for white Americans.[48] Travelogues, such as William Seabrook's *The Magic Island* (1929), and films, such as *White Zombie* (1932), sensationalized Haitian "voodoo," portraying the religion as the black magic practices of savage, uncivilized heathens. Both as a result of this sensationalism and in reaction against it, anthropologists and folklorists developed an interest in Haiti, particularly its music and Vodou religion. Herskovits conducted ethnographic research in the Haitian village of Mirebalais in 1934; in 1937 he published a book based on his findings, *Life in a Haitian Valley*, in which he countered those stereotypical depictions.

Following in Herskovits's anthropological footsteps, but with her own unique approach and goals, Dunham investigated dance as a central component of the larger Haitian social structure. Though Dunham's methodological innovations were crucially important, it is worth noting that the more traditional approach to anthropology also served her. In the twenty-first century, scholars have roundly criticized structuralism and anthropology as a whole for its colonizing implications. They have deconstructed the idea that anthropology is a "science," seeing it instead as a subjective, dialogic experience between ethnographers and the communities they study.[49] For Dunham, however, conducting what she called "a thorough scientific field study" was important to counter debilitating myth and ignorance. Using traditional tools, such as "cameras, recording equipment, and notebooks," and bringing to bear her knowledge of dance, she documented and categorized Haitian dance forms, providing specificity and historicity. She created a chart that classified fifty-seven distinct dances of sacred, seasonal/secular, and social types, which provided the foundation for her master's thesis, "Dances of Haiti."[50] She revealed important meanings and purposes of Vodou, Mardi Gras, and the popular dance parties known as *bamboches* and related them to broader social, political, and economic questions.[51] Her research was not simply a process of self-discovery. In the American cultural imaginary of the 1930s, black dance was all too often seen as a marker of primitivism, savagery, and unbridled sexuality. Dunham's affirmation of the "scientific" approach to dance was a necessary intervention to counter such ideas.

In her most important discovery, Dunham grasped how the form of a dance related to its function. Her notes reveal her fascination with the solar plexus as the region that initiates movement. She postulated that a dancer undergoing possession by a *loa* (also spelled *lwa* or *loi*), or Vodou spirit, became one with the universe, much as a fetus is one with its mother. For example, the *yonvalou*, the dance of the *loa* Damballa, the creator of the universe, initiates from that region of the body. She wrote, "The first great active centre of human consciousness lies in the solar plexus. Have modern schools recognized this in use of dance? . . . A returning to a more primitive state—a state nearer primal nature . . . . Does conjunction with the loi act from this?"[52] Given that she had discussed Isadora Duncan with Turbyfill and Hunter in 1930, Dunham probably knew that Duncan had written in her autobiography *My Life* (1927) that the solar plexus was "the central spring of all movement, the crater of motor power, the unity from which all diversities of movements are born."[53] In fact, Dunham wrote to Turbyfill from Haiti that she was listening to Bach and thinking of Duncan.[54]

Interestingly, though both Duncan and Dunham named the solar plexus as the origin of human movement, they located it in different parts of the torso. Duncan imagined it right below the ribcage, in the diaphragm area, whereas Dunham placed it lower in the pelvic region, closer to the womb. Thus Vodou did not introduce Dunham to the centrality of the solar plexus, but relocated it and made its purpose—the *why*—clearer. The creation of life literally began in the uterus. It thus made sense why movement about the unity and connectivity of life would emanate from that region of the body. In her choreography, Dunham would attempt to make such *whys* transparent as a means to counter audience ignorance. A politics of diaspora required attention to the cultural meanings behind movement.

Dunham's observations of Haitian dance also influenced her worldview by introducing her to the fusion, hybridity, and cultural mixing of the Caribbean. First and most obvious was what she called the "sometimes opposition, sometimes intermingling of African and European culture," which she believed made Haiti "all the more fascinating."[55] Herskovits and Redfield had already noted this fusion and made it the basis for their theories of acculturation and the folk-urban continuum. But Dunham noted another layer in Haiti. At *bamboches*, musicians played instruments from throughout the Caribbean, including bongos from Cuba, a six-stringed *tres* (a type of guitar) from Puerto Rico, and rattles played in the "Jamaican style."[56] During the first few decades of the twentieth century, many Haitians migrated to other islands for work and returned with new cultural influences.[57] By the time Dunham reached Haiti, she had already visited three other islands, and thus had a greater ability to recognize their distinct contributions. Through her written and choreographic work, Dunham encompassed seemingly contradictory aspects of diasporic formation. As she classified dances and noted their specific origins in order to counter a flattening or homogenizing of the black world, she simultaneously recognized that acculturation and cultural mixing always threatened to undo the neat classificatory systems she had created.

Haiti also gave Dunham multiple object lessons in the political dimensions of culture, starting with the dances of Carnival (*Kanaval* in *Kreyòl*). Historically in both Europe and the Americas, Carnival has been the pre-Lentian period during which people break established social norms and rules. Carnival parades and festivals have created a space in which peasants and other members of lower classes can mock authority figures, embrace raucous behavior, and celebrate the inversion of power structures. In Haiti, that inversion of power also meant the flouting of the restrictions on Vodou. Dunham noted that *Kanaval* in Haiti was a "mass safety valve" for the peasants, who could for this brief period escape the repressions of the Catholic Church and the *mulâtre* elites.[58] Often, the social rebellion in Afro-Caribbean Carnival celebrations took a sexual form, typically as "transgressions in words or behaviors against sexual and gender codes" were the ones most immediately available to people in repressed groups.[59]

Dunham observed these transgressions first hand during *Kanaval*, observing in her unpublished notes that the dancers "simply exchang[e] sex in clothing . . . . As they dance they are far apart from the waist up, heads thrown up to the sky, glued together only in the violent undulation & massage of sex organs."[60] Carnival dancing celebrated what Dunham called "pure & simple sex." Men danced with men, women danced with women, some danced in groups, and all let go of the repressive mores of the Catholic Church. She wrote in her field notes, "All of the things that you have ever been curious about & suppressed, dreamed of but not thought of . . . These you do now, and find that your neighbor too had been wanting to do them."[61] The proceedings made her ponder the disjuncture between human desire and the social codes that regulated it. "Could it be," she mused, "that basically there is no male & female sex?"[62] Dunham saw in *Kanaval* the fluidity of gender roles and sexual preferences when external social norms dissolved. She never published these observations, however, most likely aware that they would contribute to a sensationalist and stereotyped view of Haitians as hypersexual.[63]

Vodou ceremonies also taught Dunham the impossibility of separating the cultural and the political in Haiti. She came to believe that Vodou was a religion so powerful that it had engendered the only successful slave revolution in the Americas. In her estimation, Vodou created bonds of solidarity among the peasants that were as strong as the blood ties of family. At first, when Dunham read about the history of Haiti, she thought Vodou sounded "like an exciting fairy tale." After living in Haiti for five months, she decided, "It is no more fairy tale . . . . It is real in the terrifying ruins of La Ferrière [the fort built during the reign of King Henri Christophe, 1805–1820] and the ghostly splendor of San[s] Souci [Christophe's palace]. In the brutality of the dance and the deadly earnest of the cock-fight."[64] The revolution was a matter of life and death, and so the danced rituals took on vital importance. The island's population had to be inspired, year after year, to fight one of the world's most powerful empires. Over a hundred years later, she observed, Haitians again needed the Vodou priests to perform a "miracle" to fight the American occupation.[65] Vodou was more than simply an opiate for the masses. It provided the strength to fight for freedom against formidable odds.

In learning about the political and social strength of Vodou, Dunham developed a critique of American perceptions of Haiti as a place of savagery. She wrote in her notes, "We, the civilized nations, sacrifice millions at the altars of wars and injustice . . . . The bodies of men are burned and dismembered by angry mobs by the spirit of a blind revenge . . . . But in these smug middle-class homes they read of Vaudun—voodoo—and shudder."[66] Dunham expressed her anger at the hypocrisy of middle-class Americans, who reacted in horror to descriptions of bloody animal sacrifices in Seabrook's *The Magic Island* but turned a blind eye to lynching in the United States and the carnage of World War I. Her sense of justice inspired her to present to the world a less sensationalized depiction of Haitian culture. While she could not recreate a multiday Vodou ceremony for the proscenium stage, her choreography would link dances to certain *loa* and present other aspects of Haitian life that refuted the stereotypes in the era's literature and zombie films.

Dunham's condemnation of the United States extended beyond its sensationalizing of Vodou. She was also highly critical of the occupation of Haiti. She wrote in her notes, "I deplore here in Haiti what the Americans have done, with the sole purpose of creating a market for the producers back home.

Wall Street again. For 19 years the Haitian was a secondary party to luxuries which had developed under a capitalistic system."[67] Capital's need for markets, she believed, was the main reason for the military occupation. Her language echoed a Leninist viewpoint on the relationship between imperialism and capitalism.[68] She revealed similar thoughts about European colonialism. Although the priests in Haiti kept Vodou alive by hiding drums and performing ceremonies in secret, "across the waters the mother tree is rotting and her roots are slowly drying in the alien soil that is suffocating them."[69] The mother tree—Africa—was "rotting" in the "alien" soil of European colonialism. Dunham's perspective on Haiti as the keeper of the flame of blackness would profoundly influence her decision not to visit sub-Saharan Africa until 1962, and then only at the behest of a producer who wanted her to gather new source material for a show.[70]

Dunham further argued that the economic and political instability caused by legacies of colonialism and imperialism psychologically affected Haitians, particularly the elites. At times, her language tipped over into broad, stereotypical generalizations. She wrote in her notes, "I find the people of this blessed country utterly, thoroly [sic], totally insane."[71] She expounded on her argument in a draft of a letter to Fisk University professor Charles Johnson, in which she claimed that elite Haitians placed "extreme premium on sex activity without love" and "extreme artificiality." These traits could be traced to two causes: "First, the tremendous influence of the white planter . . . . Second, the terrible economic and psychological evil of the American occupation."[72] Whereas other writers from the 1930s saw Haitians, particularly the peasants, as psychologically disturbed because of their belief in Vodou, Dunham traced the roots of psychological distress to French colonialism and American imperialism and focused on the elites. From her perspective, the problem with elite Haitians was not that they embraced Africa too much; it was that they did not embrace Africa enough. They had cut themselves off from their heritage and from the religion that had granted them their freedom.

Dunham's personal friendships in Haiti reaffirmed her new perspective on the importance of embracing Africa. She became romantically involved with Dumarsais Estimé, a government official who would become president of Haiti in 1946. Estimé drove her around the island, lecturing her about the need to require Haitian history to be taught in the education system so that young Haitians would learn to "take pride in themselves," unlike "deracinated" black Americans, who only learned white, European history. Dunham wrote that Estimé's call to revolutionize education "was the very beginning of the movement for black identity," a beginning at which she was present. Her perception that Haitian leaders originated this movement would shape her idea that the island nation was the center of the African diaspora. She also credited Estimé with giving her a social conscience, a way to "turn this thirst for knowledge to a way of service."[73] She, too, through her performances, could educate her audiences about black history. Her friendship with anthropologist Jean Price-Mars was similarly influential. Seven years earlier, he had published *Ainsi Parle le Oncle* (*So Spoke the Uncle*), in which he argued that studying African-based folklore, instead of constantly looking to France for cultural guidance, would create a healthier political system in Haiti. His *indigénisme* philosophy was a precursor to the *négritude* most famously expressed by Aimé Césaire and Léopold Sédar Senghor.[74]

Along with growing her racial consciousness, Dunham's experiences in Haiti sharpened her class analysis. Paul, a servant who worked in her hotel, told her about "tee monde" (*ti' moun*, probably derived from the French *petit monde,* or "little world"). Tee monde was the practice by upper-class families of bringing peasants from the country to live and work in their houses. Paul worked fifteen or more hours a day, seven days a week, for an average of one cent an hour, and had to endure both verbal and physical abuse. After talking to Paul and observing "tee monde" in action, Dunham concluded that it was a system of "slavery" and that it "shatters the last illusion of one who has come to seek freedom in the Black Republic."[75] She called the elites "traitors" of the revolution, and echoing the language of her letter to Johnson, said that they were "by all standards of the outside world, totally, completely mad."[76]

Dunham mostly contained such thoughts in her notes and private letters. Her forceful critiques of capitalism, imperialism, and colonialism acquired a less direct tone in her publications. The first piece of writing she published based on her research, it seems, was an article on Haiti for the *Chicago Daily Times*, in July 1938. She toned down the language of her notes, taking out any reference to the "tee monde" system as a form of slavery and declining to link Haiti's social problems to the American occupation. Instead, she hinted vaguely at the connections, writing that to know Haiti, "We must know far more about such complicated things as the psychological effects of imposed and subordinated culture patterns under special conditions."[77] Throughout her career, Dunham disavowed any affinity with left-wing political parties, even though her sentiments about Haiti in her notes echoed black radical thought of the 1930s and the work of people such as the Trinidadian writer and socialist C. L. R. James.[78] While she would not turn these perspectives into an explicitly political platform, they did inform her choreography. By making aesthetic choices that centered Africanist practices, Dunham challenged colonialist and imperialist aesthetic hierarchies.

Dunham published her ethnographic work, but her heart lay in choreography. All of her new knowledge about Haiti—the sacred and secular dances, the class struggles, the legacies of colonialism and imperialism—found their way into plans for a ballet, *Christophe*.[79] Christophe had been one of the primary leaders of the Haitian Revolution. In the political turmoil that followed the final victory over France, in 1804, Haiti split in two. In 1807, the northern section elected Christophe as president. He declared himself king in 1811 and instituted a deeply unpopular policy of *corvée* (forced labor). When growing unrest among the people nine years later signaled that his political demise was imminent, he committed suicide. His fears proved true when his son (and heir) was assassinated ten days later.

By choosing to embody the story of the revolution through the life of Christophe, Dunham signaled that she would be examining both the triumph and tragedy of that tumultuous period. Although the ballet was never performed, examining her detailed twenty-page scenario and her correspondence with composer Still reveals how she first imagined Haiti on the concert dance stage. Furthermore, the documents show how the story of the Haitian Revolution allowed her to theorize the relationship between culture and politics through performance. *Christophe* contains an early and potent iteration of Dunham's argument that Africanist cultural practices must lie at the center of black political movements.

The first two scenes, which take place in 1791 just prior to the start of the Haitian Revolution, set up the conflict between Europe and Africa for dominance in Haiti. Dunham represented the battle choreographically and musically. In scene 1, a French Royalist tortures Vincent Ogé and Jean-Baptiste Chavannes, two *mulâtre* leaders of the revolt against the colonial government. The black generals Toussaint L'Ouverture, Jean-Jacques Dessalines, and Christophe look on in agonized silence, unable to stop the torture but plotting revenge. In scene 2, black peasants perform a Vodou ritual. The objective, Dunham wrote, was to give the audience the sense that "whatever happens is conditioned by this tense, controlled mass . . . more like one huge overwhelming creature than a body of men and women."[80] Vodou gave the masses power; it required them to think, act, and move in unison. During her field research, Dunham had noted that one of the main functions of dance in Haiti was "social cohesion." Dance brought individuals together and made them a community.[81] The revolution, Dunham believed, derived from the unifying power of dance. Notably, in scene 2 the generals are absent, portending their future alienation from the peasants.

Scene 3 takes place at a ball given by Pauline Bonaparte, Napoleon's sister, around 1801, when the French believe that they have successfully quashed the rebellion. The French and the Haitians meet and interact in the same physical space onstage. The dancing begins with traditional European court dances, such as the minuet and the waltz. Soon the crowd fades away, leaving Pauline to dance "sensuously [and] intimately" with the handsome, powerful Christophe. The radical vision of a white woman and a black man intertwined on the dance floor symbolized Haiti's precarious position on the eve of revolution. As Pauline and Christophe begin the pavane, a stately French court dance, "the beat of the Rada drums is insinuated" into the music. Africa starts to gain control. The French officers tense, hands on swords; the black generals line up against them. The tune of the "Marseillaise," representing the French Revolution, insinuates itself into the music as well. It appears uncertain whether the rada rhythm or the Marseillaise will triumph.[82] Suddenly, a "horde of ragged slaves" descends on the palace. They turn the social world of the elites, both black and white, upside down. The drumbeat turns to the "mascaron," and instead of stately court dances, the slaves begin the "obscene" carnival dances. Dunham envisioned the stage as "a mass of writhing, ragged peasants, drunk with white rum and victory . . . a riot of movement and color."[83] Caught up in the fervor of the moment, Dessalines grabs the red, white, and blue flag of France, rips out the white part of it, and triumphantly raises the new red and blue flag of Haiti. Toussaint and Christophe join him. Although the generals take symbolic positions of power, the slaves overrun the ball. Their music and dancing emerge victorious, portending the future victory of the peasantry.

Scene 4 depicts Christophe's coronation as the king of Haiti in 1811, seven years after the end of the revolution. Dunham wrote out detailed descriptions of the stage sets and costumes to be used in the scene, displaying her thorough research into the appropriate colors, styles, and motifs of early nineteenth-century colonial attire and furnishings. Again, the representation of power struggles takes place through the music and dancing. The coronation begins with a series of European court dances. Drawing on her firsthand observations of cultural mixing in the Caribbean, Dunham envisioned a courtesan from the Spanish colony of Santo Domingo dancing a tango and a rumba. Then a peasant rushes in and throws his straw hat at Christophe's feet, begging him to admit his fellow countrymen. Christophe is angry at first, but then agrees. The beat of the drums precedes the group of peasants, who enter and perform the "Congo Paillette." Dunham called the dance "one of the stateliest, most exotic of the tribal dances. It is a very subtle, controlled dance of fecundation, men and women advancing and retreating in a steady shuffle of feet to a quick side-to-side sway of extended haunches."[84] Dunham had juxtaposed what Western culture posited as opposites. The dance was simultaneously "stately" and "exotic," both "controlled" and "a dance of fecundation." It was a sexual dance of fertility that emphasized subtlety, showing that the "primitive" was still distinct from the "civilized" by being more connected to ritual and the earth, but no less sophisticated. In "Congo Paillette," Dunham reconceived the primitive and suggested that the peasantry would triumph over the elites.

In the fifth and final scene, Christophe emerges as a "tyrant," dressed all in black, the fortress of the Citadelle Laferrière looming in the background. Despite their outward displays of power, both the man and the monument are teetering on the verge of despair. Christophe's guards, loyal Africans he purchased off slave ships, rush onstage. The bodyguards dance a "grotesque, mechanical" dance in front of the king, then "exit in march formation, their carriage and unusually high steps resembling somewhat that of the German soldier under the Kaisers." Dunham's description of the movement as "mechanical" suggests the remnants of an enslaved mentality in the supposedly free land of Haiti.

The scene shifts to a group of bare-chested workers, straining to pull a heavy object up the hill to the Citadelle. Several of the workers expire from exhaustion, as the resentment of the others seem to build. Suddenly, soldiers appear and the workers rush to join their side, turning against Christophe. His African bodyguards fight them valiantly but die. Christophe ends the ballet by falling to his knees, defeated by "his people thirsty for revenge against work." He, along with L'Ouverture and Dessalines, had failed to align with the masses and had thus missed the signs that Africa would triumph over Europe in the battle for Haiti's soul and soil.[85] The final scene reiterates the larger thesis about culture and politics that Dunham developed over the course of the first four scenes. The title character's vision for a modern Haiti, one that required extraordinary physical and mental labor to overcome the ravages of the revolution, ultimately falls short. The island had the potential become a proud, independent, black nation, a beacon for the rest of the African diaspora, but instead was riddled with coups and instability. Ultimately, she wrote, the ballet symbolizes "the tragedy of a people who have never been able to grasp the real significance of their freedom."[86]

Although not an agitprop work per se, *Christophe* raised questions about colonialism, race, class, and power. The use of music and dance to tell a complex historical and psychological story was a dramatic departure from Dunham's earlier choreography. Her previous concerts had consisted of short interpretive dance numbers, whereas *Christophe*, a lengthy, five-act ballet, had a political message to impart. She did not include rada drums or carnival dances merely to set an "exotic mood," but rather to capture the way performance could inspire political action. She articulated a thesis about embodied knowledge and its relationship to politics. The peasants' political unity expressed itself through their allegiance to Vodou and the drumming and dancing practices associated with it. Supported by this cultural power, they overthrew not only the French, but also the repressive dictator Christophe. Dunham located Christophe's political failure in his inability to break away from a French colonial mentality and embrace his African roots. For Dunham, the Haitian Revolution was not only a source of an aesthetic inspiration, but also a reminder of the importance of the arts to political movements.

Dunham initially conceived the dance in Haiti and considered collaborating with Paul Robeson to incorporate it into a film.[87] She spent three years developing the project, even sending a detailed outline to Hughes in 1938, but ultimately she faced insurmountable difficulties. John J. Trounstine (the literary agent of Countee Cullen and Richard Wright) thought the ballet was too long.[88] Still initially expressed enthusiasm about composing the music in the spring of 1936 but worried, like Trounstine, about the ballet's length and felt that five scenes would be too expensive to produce.[89] Several months later he had to back out of the project altogether because of a contractual obligation to produce film scores for Columbia Pictures. He suggested that she contact Clarence Cameron White, an African American composer who had studied Haitian music, but Dunham felt uninspired by White's compositions. Months later, in the winter of 1937, she expressed hope that Still would eventually find time to compose the music, but he never did.[90] As the years passed, other theatrical productions about the Haitian Revolution were mounted, notably Hughes's 1936 play *Emperor of Haiti* (which premiered at the Karamu House Theatre in Cleveland with the title *Troubled Island*) and two plays produced in 1938 as part of the Federal Theatre Project: the "Voodoo" *Macbeth*, directed by Orson Welles, and William DuBois's *Haiti*. These shows perhaps took the wind out of Dunham's sails, as her ambitious ballet would no longer be unique. Although *Christophe* was never performed, it remains important to understanding Dunham's theoretical contributions to the cultural politics of the African diaspora.

Reluctantly, Dunham left Haiti in April 1936. She had wanted to stay longer but had run out of funding. During the last few months on the island, she had developed a new sense of self, sharpened her critique of the social and political realities that shaped the lives of people of African descent, and found aesthetic inspiration, not only in terms of content, but also in terms of the purpose and meaning for her art. She had befriended intellectuals who theorized a diasporic black identity that would guide her future endeavors. Needless to say, her transformation spelled doom for her marriage. Jordis McCoo had predicted as much only six weeks into her trip, writing glumly, "My only regret is that now you are committed definitely and exclusively to a career above all else."[91] That career would take off rapidly in Chicago upon her return.

CHAPTER 3

Aesthetics as Politics

Dunham's heart pounded as she waited for Herskovits to pick up the phone in late December 1936. For the past two years, Herskovits had been Dunham's champion. He had trained her in anthropological research methods and provided guidance throughout her time in the Caribbean. He had convinced the Rosenwald Foundation to take the unusual step of granting her a second fellowship, arguing, "We have in her one of those rare persons who combines the finest aesthetic perceptions with an intellectual capacity of the highest order."[1] With a second grant, she could "do an enormous service in the very practical matter of race-relations by presenting [Caribbean dances] in their truest light."[2] Also with Herskovits's recommendation, Dunham had won a grant from the Rockefeller Foundation to pursue a master's degree, presumably studying with him at Northwestern.[3]

Despite this support, Dunham decided to do her graduate studies at the University of Chicago under Redfield. When she told Herskovits the news, a tense silence at the other end of the line registered her mentor's disappointment. Northwestern University, she explained to him later in a letter, was too far removed from the dance community. Furthermore, it seemed less racially tolerant than the University of Chicago.[4] Ironically, on a personal level, the situation was reversed. Herskovits had called her an intellect "of the highest order," whereas Redfield at one point wrote to the Rosenwald Foundation, "She is a better-than-average student, but with her handicaps of sex and race one would certainly hesitate to encourage her to make a career as a teacher and research worker in anthropology."[5] Dunham never said whether Redfield voiced these opinions openly to her, but she did sense a growing lack of support from him as 1937 progressed.[6] After a year of taking courses and writing a thesis, Dunham left the University of Chicago without completing her qualifying exams and thus without the master of arts degree. For the next twenty-five years, performance would be her primary focus. Questions abounded as she embarked on this path. How would she fulfill the expectation of Herskovits and others that she would help solve America's racism problem? How would she communicate her new diasporic consciousness to others? How, in the midst of the Great Depression, would she make a living? And most importantly, how would she develop an artistic vision to sustain it all?

Experimentation characterized Dunham's approach from 1936 to 1939. She choreographed some work in the pre-Caribbean interpretive dance vein she had developed; she presented fairly direct translations of the dances she had seen in the Caribbean; she followed the left-leaning political zeitgeist of late 1930s Chicago and created agitation-propaganda works that condemned fascism and lynching. By 1940, however, she had abandoned all three of these approaches in favor of "fusion": a blending of her ballet and modern dance training with Afro-Caribbean forms.[7] She rejected explicit social commentary or ethnographic realism in favor of dances with more universally appealing themes, such as love triangles, and a clear emphasis on her creativity.

In short, Dunham's aesthetics became her politics. Her new dance technique, which emphasized the creative reimagining of tradition, demanded a place for people of African descent in the realm of the modern. Her exploration of sexuality onstage defied respectability politics and gender norms. Her choreography challenged stereotypes about black dancers as "natural" and black dance as instinctive rather than choreographed. White audiences could gain a new understanding of black culture as a part of global modernity, and African American audiences could develop greater race pride.

Crucially, the race pride on display in Dunham's performances was diasporic, linked neither to a singular national identity nor to an idea of an ancient African past but to what one might think of as a web or rhizome.[8] Dunham set her dances in places throughout the black world. Her seemingly neutral aesthetic choice to format the show as a revue, a series of short dances unconnected by plot, was in fact deeply political. The revue allowed audiences to "travel" without leaving their seats, on a journey of the imagination aided by John Pratt's high-quality sets and costumes.[9] This traveling occurred in a horizontal plane, through space, rather than in a vertical plane, through time. Her black audiences could experience kinesthetic empathy on an egalitarian level, a crucial aspect to the development of a diasporic sense of transnational belonging.[10]

Dunham's aesthetics-as-politics rested on the conceptualization of the relationship between form and function that she had developed in the Caribbean. From her perspective, to present aesthetic forms without conveying their functions would be to fail to transform the audience's consciousness, as viewers would merely continue to interpret black dance as mindless entertainment. Through program notes and strong narrative structures in her choreography, Dunham attempted to communicate the function, the *so what*, of the dances she presented. At the same time, she knew that a purely educational show would bore audiences and fail to pay the bills. She seemed to have found the perfect formula in 1940 with *Tropics and Le Jazz "Hot,"* a show universally proclaimed as having that elusive blend of high art, social value, and popular appeal. Dunham succeeded in defying the constraints placed on black artists, whom white dance critics accused, on the one hand, of being derivative if they choreographed in genres deemed European-American and of lacking creativity, on the other, if they performed "Negro" dances.[11] Dunham's choreography, virtually all agreed, could neither be called derivative nor spontaneous. Challenges arose almost immediately after 1940, but in *Tropics*, Dunham's aesthetics-as-politics approach had succeeded.

Dunham's first performance after she returned from the Caribbean revealed that her artistic identity was in a state of flux. The January 1937 program, *Tropics: Impressions and Realities*, opened with the "Dance of the Portresses" from Page's *La Guiablesse*—precisely the kind of interpretive dance number that Dunham seemingly would have rejected after her ethnographic research. The program also included a piece called *Lotus Eaters*, to music by Debussy, based on a scene from Homer's *Odyssey*, and a "Tango Motif" to music by Czech composer Erwin Schulhoff. The three dances reflected her artistic approach prior to going to the Caribbean and represented the "Impressions" in the title.

Dunham's *Haitian Ceremonial Dances*, *Biguine-Biguine*, and *Carnival Dances* comprised the "Realities" portion of the program. These pieces reflected her interpretation of her field experience and could be considered performed ethnographies.[12] She aimed to present not only the form but also the original function of the dances, believing she had a mission to correct the ignorance about Vodou and about Haitian culture in general. The program notes for *Haitian Ceremonial Dances* explained the meaning and significance of the "Congo Paillette," "Zepaules," and "Yonvalou." The *yonvalou* was a dance for the *loa* Damballa, represented by a serpent, and thus the movements often imitated those of a snake.[13] The program notes for *Biguine-Bigune* and *Carnival Dances* similarly explained the dances' social contexts and identified important characters appearing onstage such as the "major-domo," meaning the leader of a Haitian *Kanaval* band.[14] Dunham adapted the dances for theatrical presentation, but she presented her choreography with the full intention of educating, as well as entertaining. She broadened the horizons of her dancers and audience members, opening them up to a thriving black world outside the United States.

Another feature of the *Tropics* program was a commitment to Popular Front politics. The Popular Front was a global political movement in the 1930s in which communists, socialists, and liberal democrats formed coalitions to counter the menacing rise of fascism. In the United States, the Popular Front developed an auxiliary wing comprising artists that Michael Denning has called the "cultural front."[15] This cultural front supported the fight for social democracy by producing agitation-propaganda (agitprop) art and by sustaining activism through inspirational songs, dances, and artwork. These artists turned to the working classes and the "folk"—generally understood as people from rural areas whose cultural expressions were imagined as untainted by commercialism or formal training—for inspiration. Though artists were certainly attuned to folk culture before the 1930s, the Communist International Party's celebration of "people's culture" at its Seventh World Congress in 1935 galvanized more widespread commitment to the masses as the subjects and objects of artistic creation.[16] In response to the Seventh World Congress, the Communist Party-affiliated National Negro Congress held its first meeting in Chicago in February 1936, when Dunham was busy cataloguing dances in Haiti. In addition to supporting the main causes of the Popular Front, delegates emphasized their support for black artists, who led the fight against "demeaning and stereotypical images in the public arts."[17] According to historian Bill Mullen, "Chicago's cultural 'renaissance' and the CPUSA's Popular Front/Negro People's Front . . . were events that were historically mutually constitutive and in many ways unthinkable in separation."[18]

In her unpublished memoir "Minefields," (which in some drafts she called "The Minefield") written in the 1980s, Dunham tried to distance herself from the Popular Front. She acknowledged that in her Chicago days she had attended parties hosted by communists and socialists, but expressed distaste for the inelegant food and "heavy-handed" racial mixing at their "dismal" gatherings. She criticized left-wing "incendiary parades and speeches," which she felt were a "camouflage for potential violence and hypocrisy." At the same time, she appreciated the "enthusiastic audience" of the political Left, which had given her support at a time when many white dancegoers did not consider black choreographers to be serious artists.[19] The fact that Dunham presented her first post-Caribbean dance concert at the Abraham Lincoln Center on Chicago's South Side was a sign of at least some level of involvement, for the center was a Popular Front institution.[20]

Dunham's choreography from these years revealed an attachment to Popular Front causes. Her *Tableaux of Spanish Earth* (1937) depicted the Spanish Civil War, fought between the Republicans, who supported the democractically elected Second Spanish Republic, and the Nationalists, who supported General Francisco Franco's attempt to overthrow the government. Dunham represented "the roots of peasant Spain" through flamenco movement, "in a fiery protest to the fascist armies of Franco."[21] Her dance group performed the work throughout 1937 and 1938. She also championed anti-fascism by appearing in benefit performances for the Medical Bureau to Aid Spanish Democracy and the Wounded Veterans of the Abraham Lincoln Brigade of Spain.[22] Dunham later recalled with pride her dedication to the

Spanish Republicans and the American volunteers who had risked their lives to fight against Franco.[23]

Dunham's *Swamp*, also from 1937, explored another Popular Front cause: anti-lynching. Anti-lynching had been a centerpiece of New Negro political movements since Ida B. Wells's campaigns of the 1890s and had become central to Popular Front battles for social democracy in the 1930s.[24] Although Dunham and her dancers never discussed *Swamp* in interviews, it seems clear from the program notes and oblique references in "Minefields" that it concerned lynching. The first scene, "Tropic Death," involved a fugitive, played by Talley Beatty, being chased by a mob. The second scene, "Blues," took place in a nightclub.[25] In Dunham's solo for this section, the musician Kokomo (who hailed, appropriately, from Kokomo, Indiana, and whom Dunham had met in a barbecue shack in Chicago) sat center stage under a spotlight. Dunham crawled around him on the floor, responding to "the pain in him [that] came from a deeper source than the violence of Indiana."[26] She repeated the "Tropic Death" section as part of the Negro Dance Evening at the Young Men's Hebrew Association (also known as the 92nd Street Y) in New York on March 7, 1937. Louis Mitchell of New York's communist newspaper, the *Daily Worker*, called it the "most successful" piece of the concert "for dramatic projection."[27]

When non-Communist critics reviewed Dunham's shows, they waxed effusively about her performed ethnographies and paid little attention to the wide diversity of her work. The *New York Amsterdam News*, a major black newspaper, reported that Dunham and her group received "prolonged applause" and calls for several encores for their presentation of a "sensational group" of Haitian dances at the Negro Dance Evening.[28] The *Chicago Daily News* critic wrote that Dunham "won new distinctions" for her Haitian ceremonial dances at the benefit for the Medical Bureau to Aid Spanish Democracy.[29] Edward Barry of the *Chicago Daily Tribune* proclaimed, "These [Haitian] dances ... were so superlatively well executed last night that they constituted for the majority of the audience nothing less than a revelation."[30] Olin Downes, the music critic of the *New York Times*, and Alan Lomax, a collector of folk music, entreated her to share her knowledge of Haitian music.[31]

Because Dunham needed to make a living, she paid close attention to what appealed to audiences and critics. The nation was still in the throes of the Great Depression, and money was tight. She had no angel benefactor, no patroness, no foundation supporting her company now that the Rosenwald money had run out. In an interview, in July 1937, about her future plans, she stated, "I suppose I shall continue my experimenting in the primitive realm, which so far has proved very successful," but she also insisted that she wanted to continue to choreograph ballet.[32] Her "I suppose I shall continue" suggested a sense of resignation, but her affirmation of the desire to perform ballet, in the face of lukewarm critical reception, meant that she was not ready to give up on that aspect of her dream. She glumly noted to composer Still in August that she felt daunted by the prospect of mounting another program at a loss, but stubbornly insisted that "ballet is the only thing" that she wanted to pursue for her dance group.[33]

As she struggled to figure out her artistic vision, Dunham drew inspiration from her graduate anthropology classes. She took a heavy course load in 1937, enrolling in Introduction to Anthropology, Physical Anthropology, The American Indian, The Family, Peoples of the Pacific, The Folk Society, and Andean Cultures.[34] Reflecting the interests of Margaret Mead and other leading anthropologists of her day, much of her coursework addressed sexuality, and her archives include class notes on the biology of reproduction, mate selection, and sex within marriage.[35] Dunham reflected on the universal, transhistorical relationship between dance and sex. In a handwritten essay from the mid-1930s, she wrote, "The dance can be said to be inherently the root of the orgy, the sexual act itself being in the nature of a dance . . . . Courtship dances are undoubtedly motivated by sex and are an almost universal practice."[36] In another section of the essay, she linked sexual and religious functions of dancing. From ancient Greece to Asia Minor to the Caribbean, many societies' "chief concerns" were fertility and agricultural growth, which then logically led to religious rituals that emphasized sexuality.[37] Dunham later reflected that her academic classes gave her confidence to adopt Speranzeva's sexual expressivity in performance.[38]

When Dunham was offered the position of dance director of Chicago's Negro Unit of the Federal Theatre Project (FTP) near the end of 1937, she finally had the financial resources to pursue her artistic desires without the constant worry of box office receipts. She also no longer had time to complete the master's degree. The FTP was under the umbrella of President Roosevelt's Works Progress Administration, which aimed to provide "meaningful work" to millions of unemployed Americans, including artists. FTP national director Hallie Flanagan believed in art as a mechanism of social change. Under her leadership, FTP plays attempted to address working-class issues and combat racial discrimination. Black FTP workers received equal pay for equal work, and all FTP performances were held in integrated theaters though there were separate Negro Units.[39] On January 27, 1938, Chicago's FTP produced its first major dance concert, *Ballet Fedré*, at the Great Northern Theatre. Unlike in New York, where the Negro Unit performed separately, this program featured Dunham's ballet *L'Ag'Ya* alongside the dances of three white choreographers.

With *L'Ag'Ya*, Dunham presented a distinct aesthetic voice and a new understanding of diasporic cultural expression. She shifted focus from ideas of authenticity and origins to interculturalism and modernism. The division between "Impressions" and "Realities" blurred. To be sure, the piece included Caribbean movements in which one could trace specific Africanist aesthetics, but she seamlessly blended these with ballet, German expressionist modernism, Russian theatrical flair from Speranzeva, and her own point of view. Such cultural mixing was a hallmark of a diasporic aesthetic. She still retained the political goal of challenging derogatory stereotypes about black communities, but moved away from educating audiences about specific cultural practices. Her desire, as she stated to journalist Frederick Orme a few months after *L'Ag'Ya*'s premiere, was "to take our dance out of the burlesque—to make of it a more dignified art."[40] The rhetoric echoed her earlier uplift mentality and signaled that the appreciation for black culture that her shows imparted would come as much from her individual artistry as it would from the intrinsic values of the dances.

Dunham had begun to conceptualize *L'Ag'Ya* in 1935 after observing the *ag'ya* dance in rural villages of Martinique. The *ag'ya* was a mix of martial arts and dance, a full-body physical battle between two men set to the rhythms of the *bélé* drum and the *'ti bwa*, or two wooden sticks. The aesthetics have a remarkable similarity to *capoeira*, the Brazilian martial arts dance, pointing to the possibility of a common origin, which Dunham speculated was Nigerian wrestling. She wrote the *ag'ya* also derived from the French *savatt*, or "fight of the feet."[41] Martinican men participated in the *ag'ya* to release pent-up aggression, settle grievances, and forge social bonds. Sometimes the battles took on serious intent, with the men wrestling on the ground and beating each other bloody. Other times, men battled in playful jest, outdoing each other not with strength but with inventiveness and wit as they improvised new movements to the rhythms. Spectators came for both entertainment and community formation. They placed bets, cheered on their favorites, and shouted out advice and support.[42]

For Dunham, the *ag'ya*'s functions translated well to a tried-and-true Western theatrical plot: male rivalry over a female love interest. She set *L'Ag'Ya* in a fictional fishing village, Vauclin, in eighteenth-century Martinique. The first scene opens by the shore with Dunham's character, a young woman named Loulouse, flirting with her lover, Alcides (in later programs, the name was shortened to Alcide). They dance a loving pas de deux, a balletic duet. Another villager, Julot, watches them jealously. He decides to venture into the jungle to get a potion, the *cambois*, from a community of zombies in order to win Loulouse's love. During the "Dance of the Zombies," Julot successfully obtains the *cambois* and returns to Vauclin. His arrival interrupts a happy scene of villagers dancing a *mazouk*, or creolized version of a French version of a Polish mazurka, and the *beguine*, a flirtatious dance. Julot douses the unsuspecting group with the *cambois*. Under the potion's spell, Loulouse begins to dance the *majumba*, a highly sexual dance of courtship that, Dunham wrote, came from "ancient Africa." Loulouse begins to shed layers of clothing as the love potion takes effect. Figure 3.1 shows Dunham in the last, transparent layer. Alcides valiantly breaks the spell, saves Loulouse from disrobing completely, and challenges Julot to a fight—the *ag'ya*—during which Alcides tragically dies.[43]

Figure 3.1 Katherine Dunham in *L'Ag'Ya*, 1938. Photographer unknown. Missouri History Museum, St. Louis.

In Dunham's 1937 performances, her *Haitian Ceremonial Dances* and other works based on ethnographic research had largely communicated not only the form, but also the function of the dances on a concert stage. In *L'Ag'Ya*, she took various Caribbean dances out of their original functional context in order to serve the Western dramatic narrative of a love triangle. Comparing Dunham's 1935 ethnographic film to an excerpt of a 1947 performance of the ballet's *ag'ya* scene is a unique opportunity to analyze how her double translation of form and function operated. The comparison comes with caveats. Even though she filmed multiple examples of the *ag'ya* in Martinique, countless variations exist. After all, the *ag'ya* was an improvisational form. Thus any assertions about what the *ag'ya* "was" in its social context are necessarily speculative and imperfect. The same goes for the ballet. On any given evening, the live performance varied. Furthermore, Dunham likely modified the choreography between the 1938 premiere in Chicago, the July 1944 restaging for her show *Tropical Revue*, and the 1947 filming.

Despite a level of unknowability about both versions, certain characteristics remain constant enough to permit analysis. In the *ag'ya* as social dance, the dancers' goal is generally to *not* interact physically. When one man spins and kicks into the air, the other drops to the ground. The men advance, retreat, and shift levels. Playful evasion is the name of the game. At the end of one ethnographic clip, a participant catches his rival's legs, and they end up tumbling to the ground, entangled in each other. They laugh at the unintended result.[44] The men pay as much attention to the drum as to each other. Sometimes they turn their bodies to the musician and groove to the beat, rocking their bodies back-and-forth in synchronous, friendly, shared communion of rhythm. At other times, they face each other, but wait for the drummer's cue to make an advance. In another clip, one man lifts his left leg in parallel behind him and bounces on his right, building up anticipation for the next move. For the most part, the dancers wear collared, button-down shirts and belted pants. Some even wear hats, displaying the virtuosity of grace with their ability to keep them in place as they kick and spin. In multiple clips, the drummer wears a tie.[45]

In the ballet, Dunham remains faithful to the *ag'ya* movements. Kicks with flexed feet, spins, and level changes mirror what she filmed in Martinique, giving her audiences a fairly accurate depiction of the movement qualities. Yet there are important differences. Alcide and Julot focus exclusively on each other; the musicians are out of sight. The purpose of male homosocial bonding dissolves as the intense rivalry takes center stage. The pace of the action accelerates. There are fewer moments of pulsing in place to wait for a change in rhythm or to deliberate the next moves. The physical interaction is also much greater. One man picks the other up, spins him around, and throws him in the air. Later, Alcide and Julot lock in an aggressive embrace and fall to the ground, where they roll over each other. The goal is to subdue, even kill, the other. Most interestingly, in the stage version, the men are bare-chested and wear short, casual pants.[46] With both this costume choice and the heightened violence and aggression, Dunham's version was much more "primitive" than the original of the "primitives" she was supposedly representing.

Dunham would eventually codify many of the movements she developed for *L'Ag'Ya* as the Dunham Technique. In addition to "taking *our* dance out of the burlesque," she told Orme that one of her other goals was to "develop a technique as important to the white man as to the Negro."[47] The stereotype that black people were natural dancers—a stereotype that persists to this day and is sometimes self-proclaimed as a point of pride[48]—led to two corollary stereotypes: first, that African Americans could not dance genres that required technical training, and second, that perfecting dances derived from black culture required natural abilities, not dedicated practice. By creating a technique based on Afro-Caribbean dance, and by insisting on its primacy in the training of all dancers, Dunham struck a blow to all three stereotypes. The codification of movement rooted in improvisation always carries risks. Taking black vernacular movements out of their original contexts removes the "circle that protects and permits" and also transforms the political and communal potential of those forms.[49] For Dunham, the political benefits of institutionalization outweighed the potential negatives.

A WPA archival photograph of the "Dance of the Zombies" section of *L'Ag'Ya* highlights the early development of the Dunham Technique. In Figure 3.2, the couple on the far left face each other with legs opened, turned out, and bent. The stance is reminiscent of a balletic second position, but with the legs wider apart, allowing the pelvis to drop lower to the ground. The dancers spread their arms out over their legs, shoulders higher than elbows, and elbows higher than wrists. Instead of curving the arms and separating the fingers, as one would do in ballet, the *L'Ag'Ya* dancers bend their elbows angularly and turn their palms down, fingers fused together.[50] The performers are in what has become "Dunham second position," a position of strength and clear, unambiguous lines.

Figure 3.2 "Dance of the Zombies" scene of *L'Ag'Ya*, 1938. Works Progress Administration/ Federal Theatre Project. Courtesy of Prints and Photographs Division, Library of Congress.

Dunham's *L'Ag'Ya* choreography and technique shaped the future not only of black dance, but also of concert dance overall. During the decade of the 1930s, artists and intellectuals called for creating uniquely American forms of art appropriate for a democratic society instead of imitating hierarchical, elitist, and increasingly fascist European culture.[51] By the mid-1930s, Martha Graham and other choreographers believed that they had found the answer: modern dance *was* American dance. It would represent the ideals of freedom and liberty that made America the most modern country in the world.[52] Figures in ballet, most notably impresario Lincoln Kirstein, shared Graham's ideals. Kirstein founded Ballet Caravan in 1936 as an attempt to create an American ballet, with American dancers, music, and themes. The American style, he wrote in *Blast at Ballet* in 1938, was "frank, open, fresh and friendly."[53] Both ballet and modern dance choreographers in the 1930s drew upon black aesthetics as part of that new Americanness, but few hired African American dancers to perform in their companies.[54]

While sharing Graham and Kirstein's desire to find new material and forms of expression, Dunham had little interest in creating a distinctly American dance. Instead, she sought to redefine who could represent universal human themes and be the face of modern embodied expression. The *majumba, mazouk*, and *ag'ya* introduced an Africanist vocabulary that fulfilled the modern dance dictum that movement express the inner emotional and psychological landscape of the modern individual. Two decades earlier, Aida Overton Walker had voiced her disappointment that American theater offered no space for black love stories because white audiences generally saw black performers as incapable of complex human emotion.[55] In contrast, the lead characters in *L'Ag'Ya* dance a tender, romantic, duet. Dunham's ballet carved out a new space in concert dance for black aesthetics and stories.

Critics loved *L'Ag'Ya*. According to Cecil Smith, music critic of the *Chicago Daily Tribune*, *Ballet Fedré*'s "first honors" went to Dunham's piece. Smith had studied music at Harvard and taught at the University of Chicago; he would go on to write one of the first histories of American musical theater, in 1950.[56] Robert Pollak, music and theater critic of the *Chicago Daily News*, wrote that "the show was clearly stolen" by Dunham's choreography.[57] The *Defender* enthusiastically endorsed Dunham as "the most outstanding Race dancer in the world today" and hyperbolically claimed that *L'Ag'Ya* was "the most thrilling theatrical experience one has ever witness[ed] of Race members."[58] The only dance critic to review the show, Ann Barzel, offered the most stereotypical comments in the national publication *Dance* (later *Dance Magazine*). She asserted that Dunham's work in modern dance was "imitative" and that *L'Ag'Ya* succeeded because the dancers "have not been trained much or tampered with," a complete misunderstanding of the training in ballet, modern dance, and Afro-Caribbean movements that *L'Ag'Ya*'s complex choreography required.[59] No critic commented on the sexually suggestive nature of the *majumba* or believed that it detracted from the artistry of the performance. Such perceptions would shift in the 1940s as American culture grew more conservative.[60]

L'Ag'Ya also had ramifications for Dunham's personal life. She had separated from McCoo soon after returning from the Caribbean. Through the FTP project she met John Pratt, a white costume and set designer who was assigned to the ballet. She invited him back to her house one evening, and, she recalled later, he "began kissing me in a way I had never been kissed before."[61] As Pratt's romantic partner, Dunham gained entrée into Chicago's North Side society. In turn, Pratt joined Dunham in South Side churches and barbecue shacks. They received hostile looks and comments on streetcars, in restaurants, and almost everywhere they went, except for the left-wing circles of the FTP, the University of Chicago, and their artistic community. Dunham recalled that "it was astonishing to the person on the street just to see us walk down the street together."[62] Dunham's romance with Pratt gave her yet another reason to identify with the Popular Front, as that community was one of the few in the metropolis that accepted and supported their interracial relationship.

Shortly after the *Ballet Fedré* performance, the FTP dissolved the dance division of the Negro Unit. Government officials gave the excuse that black performers were needed for theater projects, such as *Little Black Sambo* and *The Mikado*, but Dunham pointed out that white theater and dance productions were proceeding simultaneously without any conflict.[63] She suggested that racial motives were at play: "That thing which we as Negroes must continue to build, namely an incentive for training by having our work placed on a dignified and appreciative basis is withdrawn from them at least with, *if not because of* their unusual success, must, I feel, be made an issue of."[64] Dunham implied that the overwhelmingly positive critical response to *L'Ag'Ya*, which occurred at the expense of attention to the white *Ballet Fedré* choreographers, played a role in the dissolution of the Negro Unit's dance division.

Now Dunham had to go back to self-financing her company, which meant that audience appeal again took on urgency. A few months after the *Ballet Fedré* concert, the company performed at Chicago's Goodman Theatre, part of the Art Institute. Critics panned the dances that fell outside the bounds of "primitive" dance. Smith asserted that one "danced in the style of Martha Graham" and another in which Dunham "interpreted symbolically" a Turbyfill poem "in a modified ballet style" were "extremely weak in composition and movement."[65] His criticisms reflected the stereotype that African Americans were incapable of choreographing in the genres of ballet and modern dance. One could perhaps argue that since most white dance teachers of the time refused to accept black students, Dunham's opportunities to train in those styles were indeed limited; she had begun ballet classes late, at age nineteen, and received her modern dance training primarily from a Russian actress-dancer. The purportedly liberal Rosenwald Foundation had refused to fund study at the School of American Ballet and the Wigman School. At the same time, her training in Afro-Caribbean dance had lasted far shorter (ten months) than her years of ballet or modern training, but this fact did not seem to bother Smith. Throughout the rest of her career, Dunham faced critics who insisted that her race limited her artistic range.

A year later, acceding to critical tastes, Dunham eliminated the balletic and Graham-esque works from her repertoire. In November 1939, the company again performed at the Goodman Theatre. This time, Smith found fault with the agitprop piece *Tableaux of Spanish Earth*, which he called "phony" and "quite out of Miss Dunham's real métier," even though she had been successfully performing it for the past two years.[66] The *Chicago Dancer* critic similarly felt that it had a "superficial approach," whereas "this was never felt in the primitive numbers."[67] *Tableaux of Spanish Earth*, too, would be eliminated from performances by the end of the year.

The affirmation Dunham received for *L'Ag'Ya* gave her the confidence to continue in the direction of fusion. From 1938 to 1940, she expanded her repertoire to include the works *Peruvienne* (1938), set in the world of sixteenth-century Incas, and *Rara Tonga* (1938), set in Melanesia. She fulfilled the promise she had made in her Rosenwald application to take inspiration from a wide range of so-called primitive societies, including those of indigenous Americans and "island peoples."[68] She also choreographed new dances set in other regions of the African diaspora she had yet to visit in person, blending her ethnographic research and her interpretive dance background. One of her best-loved numbers, *Bahiana* (1939), also called *Batucada*, provides a compelling example of how she did so.

In the late 1930s, Dunham first heard the song "Batucada," by Brazilian composer Don Alfonso.[69] Entranced by the tune, she choreographed a short dance in which a woman from the Bahia region of Brazil flirts with a group of fishermen. Dunham had not yet visited Brazil. The source of her expertise, she claimed, was a "drummer boy" in her company, but the programs from the 1938–1940 concerts list only two drummers: Gaucho Vanderhans, from the Dutch Antilles, and Candido Vincenti, from Cuba.[70] Regardless of the accuracy or source of her knowledge about Brazil, Dunham created a dance that evoked the mood of the song "Batucada" and the Afro-Brazilian community that inspired it.

The curtain rises to reveal the fishermen sitting stage left singing and playing instruments such as the *calabasse*, a drum originally from Mali, and the guitar. The men also carry the instruments of their labor, such as nets and rope. A fisherman takes a rope from his shoulder and throws one end off stage right to lasso a woman from Bahia ("La Bahiana"), played by Dunham (see Figure 3.3). She emerges from the wing singing "Batucada" and slowly winds herself into the rope as she moves across the stage toward the seated men. The choreography consists of triplet steps, the gentle swaying of hips, and a few

Figure 3.3 Katherine Dunham in *Bahiana* (*Batucada*), ca. 1948. Photograph by Roger Wood, ArenaPAL Images. Jerome Robbins Dance Division, The New York Public Library for the Performing Arts, Astor, Lenox and Tilden Foundations.

contretemps, a balletic catch-step. One of the fishermen rises from his seated position to dance with Dunham. She twirls in and out of the rope, nearing her admirer then moving away. She repeats the same flirtatious coming-and-going with another potential lover, the man holding the rope. The piece ends with Dunham and the rope-man (who was often played by Vanoye Aikens) executing a lighthearted, yet precise pelvic thrust toward each other to the drum's last two beats, suggesting playfulness rather than sexual foreplay.[71] Audiences throughout the company's thirty-year performing career loved *Bahiana*, but young adults in the twenty-first century viewing it on film have a tendency to see it as misogynist and troubling. For them, the act of lassoing Dunham with a thick rope potentially equates black women with cattle and evokes the brutalities of the slave whip.[72]

Critics noticed no difference between the dances set in the islands of her ethnographic research and those like *Bahiana* that derived largely from her imagination. At the 1938 Goodman Theatre concert, Smith wrote, "An authentic rhumba from Santiago de Cuba, two Peruvian popular dances, and a bailana [*sic*] from Brazil all illustrated the success with which the dancer has assimilated the results of her study in these exotic places."[73] At this point, she had not been to Cuba, Peru, or Brazil.

Chicago dance critics also approved of a major addition to Dunham's repeat appearance at the Goodman Theatre: an Americana section rooted in African American vernacular dances. Earlier in 1939, Dunham had landed a position as dance director for *Pins and Needles*, a Broadway revue produced by the International Ladies' Garment Workers Union that often revised material based on current events. The position came through Mary Hunter, the woman who had introduced Dunham to Mark Turbyfill. While Dunham was in New York rehearsing the new numbers for *Pins and Needles*, she attended a concert commemorating black composers, which revived her interest in African American vernacular expression. She worked with theater veterans Tom Fletcher and Noble Sissle to learn Southern African American social dance steps, including the Pas Mala, Ballin' the Jack, Palmerhouse, and Cakewalk, which she then incorporated into her revue as "Plantation Dances." The November 1939 performance also included creative reworkings of urban African American social dances, in which Dunham combined what she had learned from Fletcher and Sissle and from her visits to storefront churches and barbeque shacks in Chicago. She explained in her memoirs, "If I could research and present the equivalent from other countries, I could not consider myself a conscientious field anthropologist if I neglected the rich heritage of the American Negro."[74]

The "field anthropolog[y]" Dunham conducted for her "Plantation Dances," however, was very different than what she had done in the Caribbean. In Haiti and elsewhere, Dunham had participated in sacred rituals and in social events of local communities, examining how such dances performed certain functions in society. In this case, rather than go to the American South herself, Dunham drew upon theatricalized versions of the folk. Fletcher was a well-known vaudeville and black musical theater performer; Sissle was the impressive co-creator (along with Eubie Blake) of *Shuffle Along* and other musicals. Dunham claimed that she was the first person to revive the plantation dances after "a hiatus of more than fifty years."[75] The statement was untrue. The Cakewalk and other dances had been an important component of minstrelsy, black vaudeville, black musical theater, urban competitions, and even recreational dancing throughout the early twentieth century. Her erasure of this history points to the problematic way Dunham sometimes separated herself from performers who came before her, even as she relied directly on their guidance.

When Dunham premiered *Tropics and Le Jazz "Hot"* at the Windsor Theatre in 1940, she eliminated not only the Graham-esque, ballet, and Popular Front dances that had troubled critics during the past two years but also the performed ethnographies. Gone were *Haitian Ceremonial Dances* and explanatory program notes. Almost every piece in the program showcased her new fusion aesthetic, and the revue offered the most expansive vision of diaspora thus far. Even the title *"Le Jazz "Hot"* internationalized jazz, often considered a purely American art form. Critics in New York, both black and white, proclaimed the performance a watershed moment. Walter Terry's article, "Katherine Dunham Emerges Leader of Negro Dance," crowned her as the founder of black dance an art form. Dan Burley of the *Amsterdam News* agreed. "As an independent medium of expression," Burley wrote, "the Negro dance has been established here by Miss Dunham."[76] *New York Times* dance critic John Martin called Dunham a "revelation" and her choreography "the nearest thing that has yet been shown hereabouts to the basis of a true Negro dance art."[77] Planned as a one-time afternoon show, *Tropics and Le Jazz "Hot"* ran for the next twelve Sundays.[78]

Despite the praise, the exclusive focus on Dunham as a black dancer minimized her innovations in the field more broadly as well as her desire to develop a technique that would be widely applicable to all dancers. Martin wrote, "Miss Dunham has apparently based her theory on the obvious fact so often overlooked that if the Negro is to develop an art of his own he can begin only with the seeds of that art that lie within him."[79] The assertion was off for a number of reasons. Dunham did not believe that the seeds of her dance choreography lay "within" black bodies, like some kind of genetic marker, but in the social worlds of black communities. She had told Orme in 1938 that the musicality and dancing abilities attributed to black people were "not based on any physical difference nor is it psychological; we are *sociologically* conditioned."[80] Dunham also believed that the "seeds" of a black dance company lay as equally in ballet as in folk forms. Martin expressed "distress" that Talley Beatty and Archie Savage, two male dancers in Dunham's company, had a "tendency to introduce the technique of the academic ballet." "What is there in the human mind," Martin asked, "that is so eager to reduce the rare and genuine to the standard and foreign?"[81] There was an element of homophobia to Martin's comment, since he only criticzed the male dancers performing ballet, still a highly feminized genre in the 1930s. Burley, though he wrote from an African American perspective, similarly asserted that Dunham's winning "formula" was "simply the use to fullest advantage of the natural dancing technique of the Negro instead of the copied ideas of the whites."[82] Dunham argued that the primitive was a technique that needed to be learned, no less than ballet. It would take years to convince Americans of this fact.

Burley disliked one manifestation of the "natural dancing technique of the Negro" that Dunham put on display: the dance *Bre'r Rabbit an' de Tah Baby*, which according to the program notes was set during "childhood in the American minstrel days."[83] Minstrelsy had been a staple of American musical theater for over seventy-five years, and Dunham saw no problem with including it in her show. In her "Negro Dance" article, she argued that minstrelsy "served to make the Negro newly conscious of the value of his own expression."[84] Because minstrelsy was popular primarily between the 1830s and the 1890s, her happy depiction of black life in the South seemed to gloss over slavery and the oppressive racism that followed the end of Reconstruction. Critic Margery Dana of the *Daily Worker* echoed Burley. Dana criticized the Americana numbers for mirroring Broadway's stereotypical representations of African American life. Dana especially disliked that Dunham used burnt cork—blackface—in the *Bre'r Rabbit* dance.[85]

None of the other critics mentioned the burnt cork. Dana may have lied to rouse up the leftist readers of the *Daily Worker*, but such a blatant misstatement would have violated journalistic ethics. More likely, because the *Bre'r Rabbit* ballet was in the suite of minstrel dances, other critics thought it was normal for the performers to blacken their faces. Blackface appeared in many films and shows of the 1930s and early 1940s, such as *Swing Time, Kid Millions, Babes in Arms, This Is the Army, Jazz Singer*, and both the film and stage versions of *On Your Toes*, a musical choreographed by George Balanchine. Dunham responded quickly to the critics. By the third week of the show, the title *Bre'r Rabbit an' de Tah Baby* and subtitle "Childhood in the American Minstrel Days" had disappeared in favor of *Plantation and Minstrel Dances from the Ballet Bre'r Rabbit*, which kept the choreography but changed the contextualization.[86] Presumably, the blackface disappeared as well.

Despite the issues with Bre'r Rabbit, *Tropics and Le Jazz "Hot"* was not only aesthetically significant but also politically significant in breaking down The Great White Way's racial barriers. Burley proclaimed that history would remember the moment when Dunham "conquered Broadway" and transformed audience's perceptions of black dance as an art form.[87] Although white Americans made up the majority of her audience, Harlem's artistic elite, including Hughes, Sissle, Ruth Ellington, Eslande Goode Robeson, and Richmond Barthé, had turned out for opening night in full force. Political figures came as well, including Roy O. Wilkins and Bessie Allison Buchanan, who would become the first African American woman to serve in the New York state legislature.[88]

Dunham's creative expansion beyond the islands of her ethnographic research allowed her to create a broader vision of diaspora on the stage. The revue format helped to promote that vision. Unlike earlier African American dance concerts, such as Negro Dance Evening in 1937, *Tropics* did not have a chronological narrative. The publicity flyer for the Negro Dance Evening had stated that the program started in Africa in order to show the "roots" of contemporary black dance. It continued with dances from the Caribbean, the first stop of the slave ships in the New World, and then dances from the United States, and finally, a section called "Modern Trends."[89] This type of chronology also characterized *O, Sing a New Song* (1934), the pageant in Chicago for which Dunham had contributed choreography.[90] The progress narrative implicit in these and several other performances highlighted the achievements of African Americans and relegated their contemporaries in Africa and the Caribbean to a less civilized past, even though the dances in all sections of the program were choreographed roughly at the same time. In contrast, the program notes of *Tropics and Le Jazz "Hot"* did not suggest a temporal arc or hierarchical artistic relationship between the different numbers. Nor did Dunham begin with Africa and conclude with something considered the most "modern." The first act consisted of dances set in Melanesia, southern Spain, Cuba, and Mexico; the second act was set in Peru, Brazil, and Haiti, and the third, in the United States.

In future revues, Dunham refined the three-act structure based on theatrical considerations. The first act consisted of dances intended, in her words, to "tantalize" the audience with exotic depictions of tropical cultures. The second act was a longer work that often addressed more serious themes and could be set anywhere geographically. Finally, the third act featured crowd-pleasing "Americana" numbers and often concluded with *Havana—1910*, obviously, not set in the contemporary United States, but rather in pre-World War I Cuba.[91] Dunham's African American audiences viewed a reflection of themselves onstage not as an oppressed minority within the US nation-state or as linked to greatness solely in an ancient African past, but rather as part of a vibrant, flourishing, global black culture active in the present moment.

While enabling a broader vision of diaspora, Dunham's use of material from Haiti, Jamaica, Martinique, and Trinidad to set dances in Cuba, Brazil, Peru, and Melanesia represented a slippage that the common denominator of "primitive" allowed, buttressing assumptions of homogeneity and misrepresenting specific cultural practices. Dancer Vanoye Aikens recalls that in *Bahiana*, set in Portuguese-speaking Brazil, the musicians "sang all kinds of shit, you know, and it was supposed to sound like Spanish."[92] Indeed, in the film version of *Bahiana*, one musician calls out *"baile, muchacha!,"* a Spanish phrase.[93] It is unclear whether Dunham made this linguistic substitution because she was being careless or because she thought that the cultural mixing in the Caribbean made it perfectly plausible to have Brazilian dockworkers sing in Spanish. Discussing *Peruvienne* later in her career, she said, "Most of our work has a very distinctive use of rhythm ... there is something in the workings of rhythm that everyone seems to understand. The Indian dances fit in with a primitive program most naturally."[94] While Dunham was interested in representing Caribbean history and memory, she was equally as interested in activating those repositories to create a modern identity through performance and to find universals that linked humankind together. For her, "primitive rhythms" were an underlying universal that connected people not only to each other, but also to the cosmos, giving them an integrated and coherent sense of self.

Dunham's adherence to ideas of primitivism, and her political stances, would face increasing scrutiny as she became better known in the public sphere. The success of *Tropics and Le Jazz "Hot"* led to her being cast in a feature role as Georgia Brown in the Broadway musical *Cabin in the Sky*, which Dunham co-choreographed with George Balanchine, although she did not receive creative credit.[95] What she did get was fame. Reporters increasingly wanted to interview her, and in these exchanges, she rejected any public image of herself as political. Whether because she wanted to maintain widespread appeal or because she feared that an outspoken political stance would detract from an emphasis on her artistry, she refused to take on the role of racial justice activist. Reporter Emily Herzog of the celebrity-interest magazine *WHO* wrote in May 1941, "Dunham is peculiar, as a recognized Negro artist, in that she has little dedication to the cause of her people."[96] Dunham told Herzog, "If I develop as an artist and do whatever I do well, it will be understood that I am a Negro and it will make the same thing easier for someone else .... I am not at all chauvinistic. I just like to dance."[97] Dunham felt no need to stage an explicit social message. Her identity as an artistically accomplished black woman, she believed, would change existing perceptions; racial progress would come as a result of audiences' exposure to her excellent choreography and well-trained dancers. In the coming years, her experiences with more hostile and direct forms of racism on tour would cause her to rethink her apolitical strategy.

CHAPTER 4

Race and Representation During World War II

In December 1944, Helen Vail of Windham, New York, wrote Dunham a letter brimming with disappointment. Vail had recently attended Dunham's hit show, *Tropical Revue*, and was dismayed that "sex, sex, sex," most often in "vulgar" form, had emerged as the dominant theme of the evening. In her opinion, Dunham had pandered to the worst stereotypes about black hypersexuality and promiscuity instead of committing herself to positive representation. Vail, who was white, claimed that she observed African Americans in the audience reacting as she had, with "varying expressions of hurt and shock and downright shame" on their faces. She concluded, "There are no two ways about it; you are an important member of your race . . . what you do will either help or hinder."[1]

Vail was not alone in scrutinizing Dunham's actions for evidence of her contribution to the fight for racial equality. Over the course of the early 1940s, Dunham became a national race representative. Her appearances on Broadway, in Hollywood films, and on cross-country tours, coupled with the explosion of a national black press, made her a celebrity. She was charged with representing not only her race, but also her gender, placing her at the center of debates about what constituted the proper expression of a black woman's sexuality. During World War II, her aesthetics-as-politics approach was often reduced to a highly subjective and ever-shifting litmus test: did she represent African Americans (especially women) in a positive light?

"Representation" as a concept gained prominence during World War II. The new global situation, in which the United States had a clear interest in disavowing Nazi Party rhetoric about creating a master race, provided an opening for African Americans to protest segregation and discrimination. US government officials and civic leaders preached tolerance and equality as inherently American values and thus were forced to become more responsive to pressure from civil rights organizations.[2] Once the United States officially declared war in December 1941, black political leaders called for a "Double V" campaign: victory against fascism abroad and victory against racism at home.[3] Central to the fight was the question of representation. As the war began to generate jobs for men and women from all sectors of society, the Popular Front language of economic rights gave way to a moral rhetoric about racism. While many on the political left continued to argue that racism was part of the worldwide exploitation of nonwhite peoples, a more mainstream belief emerged that racism was "aberrant Americanism."[4] The United States government explained away racism as an individualistic psychological issue that would end once ignorance abated. According to this logic, if white Americans saw racial minorities on the stage and on screen as smart, accomplished, and talented people, prejudice would eventually disappear.

For a black celebrity, the societal demand to represent the race spilled beyond the footlights and into daily life. During World War II, Dunham was a fixture not just on the arts page but also on the gossip page and the front page. Her decision to marry Pratt had ramifications for how people perceived her commitment to racial justice. She also began to take decisive action against segregation. Whereas in May 1941, she had insisted to reporters that she was not political, her experiences with intense racism on national tours and in Hollywood from 1941 to 1943 galvanized her to protest existing conditions, turning her into an activist in a more traditional sense. She was strategic with her choices, adapting her methods to new situations. Sometimes she embraced the rhetoric of integration, and at other times she spoke of the need to create a strong African diasporic community. In press interviews she explained racism as a problem of individual prejudice; in private correspondence, she noted the structural inequalities that had deeply embedded racism in American society. She was duly recognized at the time for her activism, if generally not by historians since.[5]

Offstage, Dunham's actions—such as suing a hotel for racial discrimination—were clearly understood. Onstage, what counted as activism was much more ambiguous, as she had to navigate changing contours of what constituted a positive or acceptable representation of black people, and particularly black womanhood. The sexual objectification of the black female body had been a cornerstone of anti-black racism for centuries.[6] Laden with knowledge of this history, some civil rights leaders in the early 1940s demanded conformity to middle-class gender respectability norms. Dunham also had to contend with a changing artistic climate, one in which dance critics and fellow artists who increasingly favored abstraction in concert dance began to discount her productions as purely entertainment.

For financial, political, and artistic reasons, Dunham at first refused to conform to respectability discourse or the trend toward abstraction. As someone who employed over twenty full-time dancers as well as musicians, stage managers, and administrative personnel, she did not have the range of choices that a solo performer might. Keeping dozens of people on the payroll was in itself a political act at a time when there was a dearth of jobs for black artists. Aware the bottom line, she acquiesced to Sol Hurok's demands to make the revue a more spectacular multisensorial experience. But there was also agency in Dunham's choices. Independently of Hurok, she grew bolder in bringing what she called the "folk dominions" of expression to the stage, including more explicit performances of sexuality. On a deeper level, she embraced dance as a way to express the erotic—in Audre Lorde's sense of the term—as a form of power.[7] Rather than continually recalibrate her shows to conform to what counted as positive representation "du jour," she pursued the freedom of individual artistry. She created her own complex vision of the black world on the stage, depicting a range of cultures, situations and interpersonal conflicts, and personalities from scoundrels to saints and everything in between. She rejected simple notions of good or bad images, even if her audiences could not always see past that binary model.

When Dunham did make a decisive artistic shift to appease activists and critics with her show *Carib Song* (1945), she received equal criticism. Her experience of encountering opposition at every turn was later echoed by Frantz Fanon, who recounted in his book *Black Skin, White Masks* (1952) that every tactic he had tried to combat white supremacist ideas about blackness ended in failure.[8] Nonetheless, Dunham refused to give up. Her efforts to balance competing demands have reverberated throughout the decades and into the twenty-first century, in which parallel figures such as Beyoncé have been the subject of similar controversies about the intersection of black female sexuality, the obligation to represent the race, political activism, personal artistic freedom, and commercial success.[9]

Hollywood gave Dunham her first taste of the major challenges ahead. After finishing the national tour of *Cabin in the Sky* in the spring of 1941, she and her dancers settled in Los Angeles, eager to make a splash on the silver screen. After living there for a few months, she wrote to her mother, "You've no idea how close and organized prejudice is in Hollywood, which is, after all, the controlling center of propaganda of the country . . . I know you're surprised at the alacrity with which I use racial distinctions, because formerly I'd try to avoid such knowledge. But the movie colony . . . ha[s] opened my eyes to a lot."[10] Growing up in Joliet, Dunham had attended an interracial school and participated in integrated sports and clubs. In Chicago, she circulated in the racially integrated spaces of the University of Chicago, Popular Front, and bohemian arts community. While she had certainly encountered discrimination before, the entrenched racism of Hollywood shocked her.

Dunham fought back by pushing the boundaries of racial representation in her choreography for several films. In so doing, she faced problems of translation. She had staked her approach to dance on her ability to show the relationship between form and function, but she could not control the context of her choreography to the same extent on celluloid. In moving to another art form, one which imposed its own conception of form to fit its function, her dances took on alternate meanings to support messages that Hollywood wanted to convey.

Dunham ran headlong into conflict when she was working on her first picture, *Carnival of Rhythm*, a Technicolor short produced by Warner Brothers in 1941. She had envisioned it as an "authentic" portrayal of Brazilian folk life in the Bahia region, whereas producer Martin Sobelman warned that they would have to sacrifice authenticity for a coherent storyline that would "sell."[11] Problems escalated when the Motion Picture Producers and Distributors of America, commonly known as the Hays Office after its president, Will Hays, objected to having Dunham's African American dancers portray Brazilians. Only a year before, Twentieth Century Fox had produced a hit film, *Down Argentine Way*, which featured the rising Brazilian star Carmen Miranda. Miranda, who had pale skin and European facial features, had quickly become the face of Brazil—even all of Latin America—to American moviegoing audiences. She had become part of the Hollywood arm of Roosevelt's "Good Neighbor Policy," designed to shore up support for the United States during World War II among Latin America's white middle and elite classes.[12] The Hays Office feared that portraying Brazilians as black would offend both Brazilian dignitaries and American audiences.

To fight the restrictions, Dunham invited Brazilian ambassador Dr. Carlos Martin and other Brazilian officials to watch a rehearsal for the film's dance numbers. The officials applauded Dunham's work and supported her dance company. Reluctantly, the producers let the film go forward, but the Hays Office demanded that the original title, *La Bahiana*, be changed to the geographically nonspecific *Carnival of Rhythm*. It still hoped to mitigate the potential repercussions from associating blackness with Brazil.[13] Despite these limitations, Dunham received a credit for production and choreography, a major step in Hollywood given that the choreographic contributions of black dancers had mostly gone unrecognized, as had the work of choreographers in general.[14]

Although Dunham won the battle of racial representation, she could not control all aspects of the film. She intended one number, "Adeus Terras," ("Goodbye Earth") to be a religious possession ritual. In the middle of the dance, Dunham, moved to a state of spiritual ecstasy by the drums, lowers herself to the ground. In a pushup position, she twists her hips and shoulders back and forth, then flips to face her torso and head upward, a look of rapture or possession on her face. She flips to face down again, then up and down in a rapid sequence. A divine spirit has taken her over. Dunham fully commanded her individual performance of the choreography, but compromised on its staging. The set, an open marketplace, did not suggest a sacred space. Nor did the narrator's introduction to the scene mention religion—just the "wonder of old Africa." At the end of the number, Dunham walks off into the dark with a male partner as the narrator proclaims that it is now time for "love's fulfillment." The statement suggested that the purpose of "Adeus Terras" was not spiritual, but rather heterosexual courtship.[15]

Scholar Hannah Durkin argues that "erotic readings of [Dunham's] work were unintended" in *Carnival of Rhythm*, but Dunham was quite open about the erotic dimension of her work—it was the framing that distorted it.[16] Because of her background as an anthropologist, Dunham was well aware of the ways dance connected sexual ecstasy and religious possession. She candidly explained in her letter to Sobelman that *Bahiana* was a "voluptuous number" and *Macatau* "passionate and frenzied," in which she planned to be "dressed to show a great deal of my body."[17] The problem was not that Hollywood producers forced an erotic reading of her choreography, but rather the editing of the film made it impossible for Dunham to express the integration of the erotic and the religious. The sensuous experience of possession instead became a sexual experience of foreplay.

Carnival of Rhythm received favorable reviews, including an accolade from the *Los Angeles Times*, which wrote that it was "widely acclaimed as perhaps the best short film of its type ever produced."[18] In New York, the film appeared in conjunction with a series of other dance shorts featuring the Ballet Russe de Monte Carlo, the Bolshoi Ballet, flamenco dancer Carmen Amaya, tap artist Bill Robinson, and others as part of the "first all-dance film festival" at the Fifth Avenue Playhouse. Martin deemed the festival an "important and historic" event for experimenting with the convergence of two artistic genres.[19] Thus Dunham was not only at the forefront of conversations about racial representation in Hollywood, but also part of the vanguard of dance on screen. Inspired both by Dunham's anthropological research in Haiti and this new dance-film genre, Eleanora (Maya) Deren, Dunham's administrative assistant at the time, would soon after pursue a successful career as an experimental filmmaker.[20]

While the artistic community regarded *Carnival of Rhythm* highly, Dunham's appearances in *Star Spangled Rhythm* (1942) and *Stormy Weather* (1943) gave her nationwide recognition and catapulted her to celebrity status. The latter film tells the story of Bill Robinson through song and dance, presenting a "cavalcade" of twentieth-century black theatrical history, beginning with early vaudeville.[21] Of the eight black-cast musicals during Hollywood's golden era of the mid-twentieth century, *Stormy Weather* was unique in several respects. Unlike the five that had preceded it, *Stormy Weather* took place in the urban North, not the rural South. It definitively tried to make sense of modern black experience, rather than present a mythical, nostalgic view of southern black life.[22] The shift occurred partially because the NAACP took advantage of the World War II situation to lobby for more positive representation of African Americans in film, in particular focusing on the singer Lena Horne (the female lead in *Stormy Weather*) as a vehicle to promote the NAACP's values of middle-class respectability.[23] The lobbying resulted in Twentieth Century Fox deciding to film *Stormy Weather* "straight," meaning that clichéd stereotypes of black comedy "such as proverbial laziness, crap shooting proclivities or any other of the traditionally accepted characteristics" were not used.[24]

Dunham's choreography occurs during the musical break of Horne singing the title song "Stormy Weather," a blues number first performed by Ethel Waters in Harlem's Cotton Club in 1933.[25] When the break begins, the camera pans to Dunham and her dancers standing underneath the overpass of a train, a setting that represents the urban underclass: gamblers, prostitutes, and street hustlers. Suddenly, lightning flashes and thunder rolls. Dunham looks into the sky as the scene dissolves into a dream ballet taking place on a large stage. She appears at the top of a ramp upstage left, wearing a long-sleeved, leotard top and flowing pieces of fabric as a skirt, which blow in the wind to epitomize "stormy weather." She moves her hips in a figure eight as she walks down the ramp, kicking every third step to an orchestral rendition of a blues beat. As the melody begins, she stops on a platform and performs a sequence of adagio ballet steps: she extends her leg high to the side and points her foot (a développé), does a contretemps catch-step, and circles her leg in a *rond de jambe en l'air*. A group of male dancers enter, performing athletic, balletic jumps with leg extensions and pointed toes. Women soon follow, wearing the same costumes as Dunham. The men partner them in fouetté turns and acrobatic lifts. As Dunham continues to dance to the melody in a balletic style, the blues beat returns. Several men and women sink to the ground, knees apart, and pulse their torsos rhythmically, while others stay standing, moving their hips, torsos, or shoulders in rhythm. We are in a hybrid world, in which Dunham's extended legs, pointed feet, and upright carriage, signifying European ballet, move to the melody in juxtaposition to her dancers' bodies moving to the blues.[26]

Dunham called the number an "an escapist impression" from the realities of modern black life—namely, the prostitutes and their potential customers trapped under an elevated train track.[27] Indeed, the ballet appeared as a dream sequence because it did not fit into the movie's teleological progression of black dance. As a performance (a dream ballet) within a performance (the train-tracks sequence) within a performance (Horne's song) within a performance (the movie), it was quadruple-displaced from the "reality" of the audience. Virtually no one else in the film had the room to venture so far. Even the Nicholas Brothers, with their clearly choreographed, elegant routines, fit within circumscribed notions of black dancers as tap artists.

The revolutionary aspects of Dunham's performance went largely unnoticed. The film premiered in July 1943; it was a box office success and received positive reviews for the singing and dancing. Herman Hill of the *Pittsburgh Courier*, a black newspaper, reserved his highest praise not for Dunham, but for the Nicholas Brothers. Hill wrote of the duo, "Professionally tops in their art, their performance is sensational, their precision remarkable, and their grace and aplomb almost unbelievable."[28] Other reviewers highlighted Horne's star turn or Cab Calloway's performance, both of which, like the Nicholas Brothers, fell within existing tropes of black performance. Six months earlier, Peter Suskind, a columnist for the *Norfolk Journal and Guide*, a weekly black newspaper published in Virginia, had discussed why Dunham lacked wider recognition in the black mainstream. Suskind postulated that "interpretive dance forms" were "relatively new and foreign to Negro audiences," leading many potential fans to skip her shows.[29] Although all the reviewers of *Stormy Weather* spoke positively of the dream ballet, it lay too far outside the bounds of mainstream black performance to warrant in-depth critical response.

No reviewer dedicated more than one line to Dunham and her dancers; still, the film exposed her to numerous black audiences for the first time. The fan mail in Dunham's archives from 1943 predominantly is from men who saw *Star Spangled Rhythm* or *Stormy Weather*. These letters commented not on Dunham's aesthetic innovations, but rather on her body. One fifteen-year-old boy who had seen both films concentrated his praise on her legs and announced proudly that he served as vice-president of a hundred-person Dunham fan club in Brooklyn.[30] She also quickly became a favorite pin-up girl among black troops fighting in World War II. In the publicity photographs from Twentieth Century Fox, Dunham exudes a glamorous sensuality and extends a beautifully sculpted leg into the air from the slits in her skirt (see Figure 4.1). The caption underneath a similar photograph, which appeared in the *Afro-American*, called her a "perfect figure for a pin-up girl."[31]

In addition to appearing in Hollywood films, Dunham performed in several West Coast theaters from 1941 to 1943. Her characterization of these performances in her memoirs belies her claim that her audiences, rather than she or her choreography, had changed over the course of World War II. She had arrived on the West Coast after months of touring with the all-black cast of *Cabin in the Sky*, which included several veterans of the "chitlin," or black vaudeville, circuit. Dunham noted that this experience had made her more comfortable with folk humor, which she equated with graphic, ribald sexual jokes.[32] She wrote that she made the transition from "concert" dance to "variety vaudeville" by creating new dances calculated to appeal to audiences in Los Angeles.[33] Without visual evidence, it is impossible to determine whether these numbers were more sexually suggestive than her earlier repertoire, but she affirmed that her aesthetic had shifted.

Figure 4.1 Katherine Dunham and male dancer in publicity shot for *Stormy Weather*, 1943. © Twentieth Century Fox. All rights reserved. Katherine Dunham Papers, Special Collections Research Center, Southern Illinois University Carbondale.

The West Coast also exposed Dunham to a more sexually open world. In 1941 she met Dorothy Gray, a niece of Charlie Chaplin and a former child star, who saw the company perform at the Paramount Theater in Los Angeles. Dunham felt drawn to Gray's unbridled enthusiasm and energy. Gray had had a wild childhood and an illegal marriage at age sixteen. Dunham and Gray began a love affair that was simultaneously romantic, sisterly, and maternal, for Dunham was thirty-two and Gray nineteen. Their close relationship caused Gray's mother great consternation, and she spewed racist invective to Pratt over the phone.[34] The tactic had little chance of working, as Dunham, Pratt, and Gray enjoyed taking vacations together.[35] The relationship with Gray came at a time when Dunham, who often described herself as "prudish" and puritanical, was attending parties in Los Angeles' left-wing circles that involved watching pornographic films. Dunham claimed in her memoirs that these films held no interest for her, but they formed a part of her experience.[36]

When reminiscing about her time on the West Coast, Dunham reflected on the sensuous nature of performance. She wrote in her memoirs:

> My affective self often operated on its own. As for instance certain of my "love making" numbers on stage (*C'est Lui* for nightclubs, *Batucada* for theatre) would re-enact with the audience back and forth until it was hard to know who was

making love to whom. There is nothing comparable to that tentative feeling out of each other, then the decision to belong to each other, the mounting excitement leading to climax and a gentle, in some instances disminuendo—or, as in *Barrelhouse* or *Sister Kate*, a brash victory.[37]

Despite the undeniable sexual politics of the choreography that emerged with more confidence on the West Coast, Dunham maintained the position that her choreography did not contain any explicit social message. As Honore Weld wrote in *People's World*, San Francisco's communist newspaper, in July 1942, Dunham did "not think of herself as a Negro fighting for justice for her people, but as 'the embodiment of a movement struggling for freedom.'"[38] Dunham asserted that her activism came through her body, not the specific narratives of her choreography or her offstage actions. Her willingness to step fully into the sensuality of performance expanded the possibilities for women and African Americans. She may not have choreographed dances about sharecropping or participated in Communist Party rallies, but her movement expressed the aspirations toward freedom that were at the center of the fight for equality.[39]

Weld doubted that Dunham's revues would achieve the intended effect of erasing racial prejudice. She commented, "Remembering the burning of the books and the persecution of the most brilliant minds and talents under the Nazis, one may feel that here is a forlorn hope."[40] Writing for a communist newspaper, Weld undoubtedly believed that racial prejudice was linked to class oppression and thus could not be alleviated through representation alone. Her critique spoke to a larger issue that Dunham would face when she left Hollywood and the West Coast: the limited ability of her audiences, even sometimes her African American ones, to see black dancers outside existing stereotypes. By refusing to compromise her expressive freedom, Dunham opened her body up to misreading from those who only knew how to interpret her movements through European-American paradigms and to harsh judgment from those who believed that civil rights progress could only be made through representations of the black female body that accorded with middle-class notions of respectability.

Such judgments would emerge throughout the two-year tour of *Tropical Revue*. Dunham left Hollywood in 1942 to begin developing the production. Although her film work had greatly increased her name recognition, she no longer wanted to endure the constant discrimination she faced in Tinseltown. As she wrote to her mother, "Hollywood has been very difficult . . . . I have lost many opportunities and much income by refusing to play the role of a maid. I've been so close to extinction that I've decided that if I can't do something positive, I won't do anything at all."[41] But Dunham's refusal to accept degrading film roles coupled with her inability to manage money left her impoverished by June 1942. She had made quite a large income in 1941—$50,000—but spent $52,000 on costumes, sets, lighting, publicity, and employee salaries.

She also bought designer clothes and expensive jewelry, which she felt a performer of her stature ought to wear in public.[42] Dunham dancer Lavinia Williams recalled feeling "stranded" in Hollywood. The dancers would sometimes eat only one good meal a day, costing fifteen cents, at Father Divine's, a low-budget restaurant operated by the spiritual leader Reverend M. J. Divine. On their way there for a meal, Williams and other company members would keep walking right past Father Divine's if they saw people they knew coming down the street, preferring to starve rather than undermine the image of themselves as sophisticated artists.[43]

To combat this penury and secure her company's future, Dunham decided to hire the impresario Sol Hurok to manage the *Tropical Revue* tour. She aspired to rival another of his clients, the Ballet Russe de Monte Carlo, one of the few dance companies at the time that had both artistic legitimacy and widespread commercial success.[44] Hurok had helped the Ballet Russe achieve that balance. His assistant, Gerald Goode, told Dunham that they would widen her audience base by building the show around her "most theatrical" numbers, by adding an orchestra, chorus, and other musicians to amplify the show's production values, and by creating a "provocative title." The publicity would focus on Dunham's stylized depictions of American black folk life.[45]

Dunham did not agree with Goode's final proscription. She made her point of view clear in a letter during the negotiations:

> I feel you are overlooking a broad very general appeal in stressing the American negro folk aspect of our work . . . . I have never been and do not inten[d] to begin to be limited to this phase . . . . I left New York in a negro show 'Cabin in the Sky.' Among other pictures since I have been on the west coast I made one which is all negro [*Stormy Weather*]. If I continue in this same vein I will be defeating my main purpose which is to establish the negro in the field of art as an individual.[46]

Dunham pointed to another of Hurok's clients, Marian Anderson, as a model for how she wanted to be presented. Everyone knew Anderson was black but accepted her as an opera singer, applauding her performances of German lieder as enthusiastically as her renditions of black spirituals.[47] Dunham did not deny her great interest in and commitment to material from African diasporic cultures, but limiting the artistic range of her work, she felt, would be antithetical to her mission. She wanted recognition as an individual artist. In her opinion, black theatrical entertainment to date had failed to allow performers to transcend stereotypes and achieve status as independent talents. Even when she had broken existing molds of black performance in *Stormy Weather*, she had done so as part of an all-black film, thus inevitably imposing racial boundaries.

Aside from questioning the framing of her show as "Negro folk," however, Dunham took Goode's advice. *Tropical Revue* opened on Broadway at the Martin Beck Theatre on September 19, 1943. She had previously shown eight of the show's thirteen dances in New York, in 1940, with *Tropics and Le Jazz "Hot,"* but Hurok brought in a full orchestra, the singer Bobby Capo, the Dowdy Quartet, the Leonard Ware Trio, and the Dixieland Jazz Band to add to the entertainment value of the production. *Tropical Revue* included new sets, costumes, and additional numbers from Dunham's Los Angeles "variety vaudeville" choreography. Although hiring Hurok did have the intended effect of increasing the company's box office revenue and national visibility, the success came at a cost. His publicity materials, such as the one pictured in Figure 4.2, shaped audiences' mindsets before they even entered the theater.

Figure 4.2 *Tropical Revue* publicity flier, 1944. Cover art by Al Hirschfeld. © The Al Hirschfeld Foundation. www.AlHirschfeldFoundation.org. Image from Beinecke Rare Book and Manuscript Library, Yale University.

Al Hirschfeld's caricature of Dunham emphasizes her breasts and hips, priming viewers to read her dancing as sexual titillation. Disembodied black hands pound a drum, separating the music from the human beings playing it in a further objectification of the performers. Phrases like "primitive rites!" punctuated with exclamation marks, heightened the sensationalization.

When talking to the press about *Tropical Revue*, Dunham continued to promote aesthetics-as-politics, just as she had done on the West Coast. The day before the Broadway opening, she explained to the *Amsterdam News*, "I have never gone into a direct social message. You see my work is creative and very broad and I have always felt that much more can be done by a company that works on the same standard as any other. In this way we are able to attract people who would not come if we were doing propaganda."[48] As part of her strategy to change perceptions of black culture, Dunham wanted exposure to the widest audience possible, which she believed would not happen if New Yorkers perceived her work as "propaganda." An apolitical approach in fact was a political strategy, and one that fit well with making a decent living.

As an artist, Dunham also wanted to present her choreography as representing universal human ideas. Some scholars have questioned the use of the word "universal" in relation to Dunham, suggesting that "humanist," with "a concern for the welfare and dignity of human beings, especially the marginal," is a better term.[49] Dunham did call herself a humanist, but, throughout her career, she also made reference to the universality of dance and of her choreography. Her training in anthropology had led her to believe that finding universal human truths was the goal of humanistic inquiry. She also wanted to challenge the normative idea of a white, European/European-American male as the default representation of humankind.[50] Trapped in a view of blackness as irreducibly exotic and foreign, however, many viewers of *Tropical Revue* did not learn to see Dunham's dancers as universal beings.

Dunham's most significant new addition to *Tropical Revue*, the second-act ballet *Rites de Passage*, exemplified the conflict between her universalist intentions and audience reception. She had choreographed the dance in 1941 as an embodied investigation of generalizable anthropological theories about the relationship of the individual to society. It was more than a dance; it was an argument about humanity expressed through movement. Dunham wrote that *Rites* "was used to illustrate my contention that primitive societies were more caring, more attentive to the individual passing the crises of adolescence, initiation in the men's or women's cult, courtship, mating, than in western societies."[51] She embraced the idea that primitivism had something to offer the industrialized world—namely, a greater sense of community cohesion and an understanding of how sexuality was intimately linked to other social concerns, especially fertility and religious rituals.[52]

While no footage of the original production exists, photographs from the late 1940s and a reconstruction filmed in 1980 under Dunham's direction provide some clues as to the original movements. The music by company pianist Paquita Anderson evokes Igor Stravinsky's celebrated score for *The Rite of Spring*, with dissonant chords and jarring rhythmic patterns, but further layered with Haitian drum rhythms. The men wear secured loincloths; the women wear cropped tops and fringed skirts, leaving much of their torsos bare. All three sections comment on sexuality in some aspect. The first ritual, "Fertility," concerns "marriage or mating." The second ritual, "Puberty," focuses on male circumcision as an initiation into manhood. In the third, "Death," the widow of the king fulfills a witch doctor's command to perform the "ceremonial ritual of fecundation" with the king's brother to demonstrate that the cycle of life continues.[53]

When "Fertility" begins, two women stand stage right and slowly but forcefully raise and lower their hands, as if pounding a hole into the ground for planting. A group of men sit downstage left, rolling their wrists, pulling their arms back, then thrusting them forward again in an aggressive, penetrating gesture, again suggesting implantation. More men and women enter to fill the space. Eventually, one couple takes center stage (see Figure 4.3). The other women fan out in an arc behind them. They circle their arms and contract their pelvises deeply on the first and fifth beats of every phrase, ending with their hands in front of their lower abdomens. The center couple contract their pelvises toward each other, then away. The drums start to beat faster. The male dancers approach the women, contracting their pelvises and thrusting their arms forward as they walk, while the women bend in deep plié, arms open wide, alternately pressing their right and left shoulders forward, welcoming

Figure 4.3 "Fertility" section of Katherine Dunham's *Rites de Passage*, ca. 1948. Photograph by Roger Wood, ArenaPAL Images. Jerome Robbins Dance Division, The New York Public Library for the Performing Arts, Astor, Lenox and Tilden Foundations.

the men's advance. The center couple begins to dance in unison, shifting torsos left and right synchronously, in an abstracted simulation of copulation.
The surrounding women dancers sink to the ground, sitting with knees open.
The men facing them mirror the open knees but hover slightly above them by
balancing in a first-position grande plié. All shift ribcages left and right rapidly
in unison, also abstractly representing copulation. As the music and dancing
build to a climax, the chorus of dancers begin to jump, turn, and rapidly make
figure eights with their pelvises, filling the stage with movement; the central
male protagonist flips his partner in an aerial somersault, promenades her
around in a ballet *attitude* position, and in the final moment, lifts her straight
above him, her body elongated and strong from the tips of her pointed toes to
her head, the ultimate phallic gesture.[54]

By including both ballet *attitudes* and rapid figure eight hip movements,
Dunham's climax scene characteristically fused movement genres, which
challenged a strict reading of "Fertility" as a dance of "primitive" communities only. The other two sections, "Puberty" and "Death," continued the aesthetic fusion. Musically, Dunham melded a Stravinsky-esque piano score with
Haitian drumming, again fusing European and Africanist aesthetics. The concept, title, and musical score invoked Nijinsky's landmark of ballet modernism, *The Rite of Spring* (1913). Though purportedly representing a "primitive
society," Dunham's choreography showcased the dancers as distinctly modern
beings, a modernity informed by a deeper connection to humanity's primal
needs, which could only be expressed through the body.

The Dunham company's first performance of *Rites* took place in an academic
setting, Yale University, as part of a lecture-demonstration for the Graduate
School Anthropology Club. Professor Donald Horton, who had arranged the
event, wrote, "Few of us have been so deeply stirred by any dancing as we
were by this return to simple, universal human experience."[55] Geoffrey Gorer,
another Yale anthropologist, wrote Dunham an enthusiastic letter, stating
that *Rites de Passage* was "the best and most revolutionary type of choreography which it has been my good fortune to see."[56] The dance became a part of
the company's repertoire on the West Coast, and its theatrical premiere on the
East Coast occurred as part of the opening of *Tropical Revue*.

In the context of a Broadway show publicized as sizzling and alluring, *Rites*
risked losing its connection to anthropological theory about the individual's
relationship to society, potentially appearing instead as a number about sex
danced by black performers wearing very little clothing. Dunham attempted
to mitigate this interpretation with program notes that read, "The rites dealt
with here do not concern any specific community nor any authentic series
of rituals. They were created to try and capture in abstraction the emotional
body of any primitive community and to project this intense, even fearful,
personal experience, under the important change in status and the reaction
of the society through this period."[57] In *Rites*, Dunham emphasized creativity

over authenticity and abstraction over narrative, positioning herself as a modern artist employing the trope of the primitive to explore the universal experiences of mankind.

Dunham's choreographic exploration of ritual garnered contradictory responses, nowhere more so than in Boston. After opening night, in January 1944, Boston's censor John J. Spencer banned *Rites* for being "suggestive and offensive." Elliot Norton, an influential journalist known as the "Dean" of American theater critics, agreed with the censor and said that the puberty and mating rituals were "altogether too explicit."[58] Margaret Lloyd, the dance critic of the *Christian Science Monitor* and author of *The Borzoi Book of Modern Dance* (1949), found *Tropical Revue* "boring as well as distasteful" because of its focus on "show business and sex," the latter "constantly recur[ring] as sheer animality, calculated and knowing."[59] But Lloyd, unlike Norton, felt that of all the show's numbers, *Rites* alone had "a certain dignity that commands respect" because sexuality was treated as part of religious rituals.[60]

Dunham biographer Joyce Aschenbrenner suggests that the ban of *Rites de Passage*, not *Brazilian Carnival Macumba* in which Dunham performed a striptease, or *Tropics—Shore Excursion*, in which she provocatively thrust, bumped, and circled her hips, suggests that it was Dunham's social message, rather than her violation of "public morals," that unnerved the censor.[61] In *Rites*, Dunham looked at sexual activity during puberty, mating, and death as universal human impulses, not as licentious behavior. The work proposed an alternate understanding of the human life cycle, challenging social norms to a much greater extent than a number like *Shore Excursion*, in which a black woman dancing in a flirty, suggestive way could be interpreted as reinforcing existing stereotypes. The group dynamic of *Rites* may also have disturbed the censor.[62] In *Macumba* and *Shore Excursion*, Dunham danced solo, portraying a fairly harmless individual. In *Rites*, the communal ritual overwhelmed individual expression, and this cohesive group was entirely African American. Onstage, the dancers demonstrated solidarity and resilience in the face of disruptions to the community, a symbolic act that had offstage implications during a time of increased civil rights activism.

The censorship triggered counterprotests by liberal white Bostonians. Influenced by the writings of Margaret Mead, Havelock Ellis, and the "first wave" of feminism in the 1920s, many white, middle-class liberals had developed a more open approach to sexuality. World War II had brought "unprecedented opportunities for premarital experience," especially among the white, college-educated middle class.[63] Magazines, advertisements, and other media encouraged women to increase their sexual appeal to boost the morale of America's soldiers. These changes were not universally applauded, nor did they apply equally to women of different races or classes. Fears that women were transgressing gender boundaries by working in factories, wearing trousers, and socializing in public without male chaperones led to attempts to control female sexuality.[64] Within African American communities, some objected that sexualized displays of black women supported negative racial stereotypes; others applauded depictions of female entertainers as glamorous and attractive.[65]

In protesting the censorship of *Rites de Passage*, the liberals among Boston's cultural elite argued that more explicit portrayal of sexuality did not lie outside the boundaries of art. Dunham's exploration of alternate cultural understandings of puberty and courtship resonated with audiences who were eager to embrace sexuality as a natural part of life.[66] One man wrote a letter to the editor of the *Boston Globe* in which he argued that Dunham was a "serious artist" who had performed *Rites* elsewhere without controversy. He pointed out that the censor ignored the city's burlesque houses, but was denying Bostonians the opportunity to see high quality artistic work.[67] The preeminent *Boston Herald* theater critic Elinor Hughes called the censorship an "embarrassment" to Bostonians, "far too close to outmoded Puritanism and cultural witchburning for comfort." She pointed to Dunham's college education, anthropological work, publications, awards, lectures at Yale, and performances with the San Francisco Symphony Orchestra to demonstrate the backwardness of the censor's decision, writing, "The reception met here by Miss Dunham was enough to depress and dishearten those who like to think of Boston as the home of the arts."[68]

Dunham had two choices in response to the censor's ban: perform *Rites de Passage* anyway, which would have probably resulted in her show getting canceled, or drop it from the evening, which would have let the censor win. She ingeniously did neither. The evening after the ban was announced, the audience awaited in breathless anticipation. There had not been time to print new programs, and so *Rites* was still listed in the second act. But what would viewers see? When the curtains rose, the dancers stood onstage in their costumes, motionless. The music began to play, and the dancers remained still, only shifting poses to signal the beginning of a new section. Dunham truncated the three scenes, as she felt her point would come across without going into the full eight to twelve minutes of each rite. The audience gave the performance a standing ovation, and the censor said nothing.[69] Dunham had triumphed. She had found a solution that both ensured her company's financial stability and maintained her political integrity. While the censor may have taken away the motion, her message of black unity and solidarity onstage—and potential interracial solidarity with white audiences—remained.

The debate in Boston over *Rites de Passage* echoed in milder form when Dunham toured across the country. No other city banned the dance, but regional arts critics, most of them white, disagreed with each other about *Rites*. In St. Louis, one reviewer called it "weird" and "savage," whereas another argued that it "compared in intensity, awareness and technical means with that of any dance group that's been here in the past."[70] In Chicago, many of the headlines included either the adjective "brilliant" or "torrid"—sometimes both.[71] Dunham defied easy categorization. She summoned power through not being pigeonholed.

American audiences responded enthusiastically to *Tropical Revue* and filled Hurok's coffers. By the end of the national tour, the show had revenues of over $1 million, with a top ticket price of $2.50.[72] Despite these successes—or most likely because of them—white dance critics in New York increasingly characterized Dunham's choreography as entertainment, not art. Martin, who in 1940 had proclaimed Dunham the founder of a new artistic genre, wrote in September 1943, "As an anthropologist, the gist of Miss Dunham's report seems to be that sex in the Caribbean is doing all right. She seems to have remembered certain testimony along this line that eluded her when she last appeared hereabouts, and which no doubt Hollywood has brought to her mind."[73] A year later, he wrote another review of *Tropical Revue*, stating that "serious artistry" was "conspicuously lacking" and that Dunham, "truth to tell, is not an especially distinguished choreographer."[74] Edwin Denby noted in December 1944 that the show was "lighter," and "more gaily playful" than the previous year's premiere and called her an "entertainer" rather than an artist.[75]

Their charges were racialized. Several choreographers in the early 1940s moved fluidly between the concert stage and Broadway or Hollywood, including Balanchine and Jerome Robbins, without receiving the criticism Dunham did for turning toward entertainment. Changing ideas of what counted as "high art" in modern dance also affected interpretations of her work. As the 1940s progressed, many white modern dance choreographers were moving toward an aesthetic of "mythic abstraction," which New York critics came to associate with the vanguard of the field, instead of narrative-driven dances like those of Dunham.[76] In addition, the "association of artistic legitimacy with sexlessness" was strong in modern dance in the 1940s, although a dance like Martha Graham's *Night Journey* (1947), which depicted the mother-son incest story in *Oedipus Rex*, was well-received. There was a racial double standard delineating which modes of exploring sexuality were acceptable and which were not.[77]

Pearl Primus's arrival on the dance scene also heightened the criticism of Dunham. Born in Port of Spain, Trinidad, in 1919, Primus had migrated with her family to New York when she was two years old. An excellent student, she attended prestigious Hunter College High School and Hunter College, where she majored in biology and competed in track and field events. Although she had intended to become a physician, the collusion of racism and sexism rendered a career in medicine highly difficult. Primus instead found a job in 1941 with the National Youth Administration and was assigned to its dance company as an understudy. She loved her new position and began training at the New Dance Group, a left-wing school originally founded as the Worker's Dance League in 1932.[78] In the early 1930s, the purpose of dance as conceived at New Dance Group was to stimulate audiences to think about class struggle.

By the time Primus arrived in 1941, the school had become less overtly political and more professionalized, but progressive thinking remained pervasive.[79] Primus also joined the Communist Party, furthering her commitment to the political left.

In February 1943, Primus took part in a dance concert at the 92nd Street Y in New York City and astounded the audience with her powerful dancing. Unlike Dunham, Primus put messages about social justice directly into the content of her choreography. She performed a solo, *A Man Has Just Been Lynched*, to the words of Abel Meerpol's poem of protest against lynching, "Strange Fruit." Meerpol (also known as Lewis Allan) was a Jewish schoolteacher in the Bronx who belonged to the Communist Party. In 1939, Billie Holiday had performed the poem as a song at Café Society, an interracial, progressive nightclub in downtown New York. Rendered in Holiday's haunting, powerful voice, the song became an instant hit as an indictment of racism and was later called "the beginning of the civil rights movement," though, of course, that designation overlooked earlier efforts.[80] If it did not exactly launch a new movement, the song epitomized the synergy between left-wing activism and civil rights that had been building during the decade of the 1930s.

Primus was not the first to choreograph to "Strange Fruit." In 1939, Robbins choreographed a duet for himself and Anita Alvarez at Camp Tamiment, a left-wing resort in the Poconos, and performed the piece at the 92nd Street Y in August 1939.[81] When Primus appeared on the same stage four years later, she danced her version to the spoken poem, rather than Holiday's song. She portrayed a white member of the lynch mob, reacting with grief and horror to the realization of her own participation and complicity. She rolled on the ground in anguish, arched her back, ran furiously across the stage, and hammered her fists into the ground.[82] One critic wrote that "every muscle of her body cried the agony, the hatred, the despair, the futility and the utter pain . . . . The dancer writhed, drew a vivid picture of the physical and mental torment of the ordeal. She was superb."[83] In another solo, *Hard Time Blues*, Primus explored the plight of sharecroppers. For her, dance could and should convey an explicit political message.

In February 1944, Burley directly compared Dunham and Primus in the *Amsterdam News*. Although he had written in glowing terms about Dunham only a few months earlier, in this column he focused less on his own opinions and more on those of others. Writing under the pen name Don Deleighbur, Burley reported that "the serious student of the dance" saw Dunham's *Tropical Revue* as "more akin to Minsky burlesque than to serious art," whereas Primus was the "representative of the highest attainment in our cultural approach to interpretative dancing."[84] Dunham, he said, had in 1939 seemed "well on the way" to becoming a serious artist, but the influence of Hollywood, with its emphasis on sexuality and "box office appeal," had negatively influenced Dunham's approach. Now she was "taken over by the glitter and glamour of the extravaganza" and included stripteases in her work. Primus, on the other hand, "dances and expresses therein a deep and sincere understanding of her people, of the Negro's struggles, of his frustration. She is an artist of the people."[85] The perception that Primus was more committed than Dunham to the cause of racial justice has continued into the twenty-first century.[86]

The opinions of a few cultural arbiters, however, white or black, did not represent the broader public. In February 1944, the New York Public Library named Dunham one of twelve African Americans on its Honor Roll of Race Relations of 1943 "for her success in presenting authentic dances of the Negro."[87] The Time Corporation, American Film Center, and William J. Small advertising agency all asked for her help in creating film and radio segments promoting racial tolerance. The NAACP, Department of Civil Liberties of the Elks Lodge in Washington, DC, the National Negro Congress, National Committee to Abolish the Poll Tax, numerous Harlem charities, and virtually every racial justice organization active during World War II asked her to speak or perform.[88] The Institute of Human Relations explained, "We feel that a dancing program by you would foster appreciation of and engender good feeling towards the negro more successfully than any speech by any person could do."[89]

The optimism expressed by these organizations reflected the current mainstream belief that racism was a product of individual ignorance rather than a practice deeply embedded in the nation's legal and political institutions. In the twenty-first century, most critical race theorists express skepticism that changing a person's mental attitudes can undo structural inequality of racism. Even if it could, one would be hard pressed to say that the passive act of watching a performance could single-handedly rewire a person's interpretive framework about race. At the same time, as Susan Manning points out, Dunham's performances "changed many spectators' perceptions of black bodies in motion" and thus the "social meanings of physical bodies."[90]

Although a significant number of organizations and individuals appreciated both Dunham's artistry and the political contribution she was making through her art, it was an inescapable reality that New York's cultural elites could often make or break a dancer's reputation. Aware of this fact, Dunham expressed annoyance with their changed perceptions. She said to Amy Porter of *Collier's* magazine in April 1945, "I am right now doing some of the very same dances I did for those Sunday concerts [in 1940]. Only then it was art, and now it's sex."[91]

So Dunham shifted strategies, abandoning the revue model and the sensationalist publicity campaigns that accompanied it. She bought out her contract with Hurok (a hugely expensive endeavor) and, with Hunter's help, mounted a "musical play" called *Carib Song* on Broadway.[92] Dunham played a farmer's wife in Trinidad who begins an affair with a fisherman. Upon discovering her infidelity, her husband murders her. The dramatic dance that ended the first act, *Shango*, exemplified the shift in Dunham's approach. Shango is the name of the syncretic Trinidadian religion that blends Yoruban and Catholic traditions. It is also the name of the West African Yoruban deity of thunder. During her Caribbean research trip, Dunham had witnessed a Shango possession in Trinidad, in which a man had run "down to the altar doing a queer hook step and with his hands locked behind him. He knelt in the blood from the fowl and pigeons, and kissed the ground, blood and all."[93] Dunham used the image of that poultry sacrifice at the altar as the basis for *Shango*. Only thirty seconds of film footage of the work from the 1940s exists, but a 1987 recording of the Alvin Ailey American Dance Theater performance of *Shango* gives a sense of what viewers may have experienced watching *Carib Song*.

The piece begins with villagers gathering to make an offering to the Shango deity. A priest walks in, holding a white chicken (a prop) to offer in sacrifice. One man holds a knife, another a bowl in which to catch the (imagined) blood. After slitting the chicken's throat, the man with the knife sits on a bench with the women of the village. The priest and the man with the bowl circle the stage, flicking (imagined) blood on the congregants and chanting prayers (see Figure 4.4). After receiving the blood and prayer, the congregants begin to sway and chant to the rhythm of the drums. The last congregant, the man with the knife, starts convulsing, his eyes rolling back in their sockets as he falls to the

Figure 4.4 Katherine Dunham's *Shango*, ca. 1948. © George Konig/Victoria and Albert Museum, London.

floor. He begins flicking his tongue, signaling that the Vodou *loa* Damballa has possessed him. The possessed dancer undulates his spine like a snake to propel his body forward on the floor, keeping his hands tied behind him. He eventually stands, walks to the altar, climbs up, opens his arms wide like Jesus on the cross, and is carried off the stage. The other villagers continue to express devotion through their dancing bodies, repeating a sequence of side steps and turns that leads to hypnotic exhaustion.[94] A Damballa possession would most likely not occur in Trinidad, since the deity is not a part of the Shango pantheon. Dunham told a radio interviewer that she had "hesitate[d] to do the strictly authentic in ritual" in *Shango* because she felt "a little superstitious."[95]

Unlike in *Rites de Passage*, the ritual in *Shango* relates less obviously to mating or fertility. Rather, it reveals the power of the divine in union with man. No one could accuse Dunham of depending on her physical desirability to win audiences, neither in *Shango* nor in the show overall. *Carib Song*, however, did not appease her critics. White viewers objected to her decision to situate such a serious story in the Caribbean, because it violated their cherished stereotypes about island nations. Producer Alfred Berger wrote Dunham a letter asking whether she would "change the pervading mood from a somber, brooding one, to a gay one, more in keeping with the (valid or not) popular conception of Trinidad? Send the audience away happy and not bored."[96] Lewis Nichols of the *New York Times* decried the slow pace of the show, saying, "An evening with its origins to the South should not be so slow; the heart beats faster there."[97] *Time* called it "so lethargic and sedate that it virtually libels the reputation of the tropics."[98] As Berger had predicted, white critics were upset that the show did not conform to their expectations of the Caribbean.

Black critics, while not sharing the desire to see a more sensual and lighthearted depiction of Trinidad, held conflicted opinions about the show's aesthetic merits and its political implications. Many considered *Carib Song* tedious and boring.[99] In his review for *Cleveland Call & Post*, Lou Swartz said he was tired of seeing black people portrayed as primitives. Although he admitted that the "dramatic simplicity and vitality" of the West Indies in *Carib Song* was "most stirring," he felt that the theater was an important part of "advancing the position of the Negro today in a social as well as an economic cause" and that the show had "poor race picturization."[100]

Carib Song appeared on Broadway at a time when African American leaders and journalists were increasingly critical of the representation of black life on stage and screen. The same month as the musical's premiere, September 1945, the Associated Negro Press reported that Lena Horne had backed out of playing the lead in MGM's *St. Louis Woman* because of "public and press criticism" from those who "desire to have the better side of Negro life portrayed." The article mentioned *Carib Song* as a primary example of a negative, stereotypical representation of black life that "cultural circles" were "frowning upon."[101] The show closed after only one month.

In contrast to the controversies over the merits of her onstage representations, Dunham's commitment to fighting racism in offstage arenas was
widely recognized and appreciated during World War II. Lesser-remembered
instances of this activism were her performances at military bases, where
she insisted on integrated seating—even though the military itself maintained racially segregated units.[102] She also fought against segregation in
hotels, restaurants, and theaters, as one of the many black entertainers
whom Martha Biondi calls the "unsung heroes" of the civil rights movement in the North.[103] The first flurry of newspaper articles about Dunham's
battles with hotel discrimination coincided, probably not coincidentally,
with the opening of *Tropical Revue* on Broadway in September 1943. The
politically conscious Dunham was also a savvy publicist with a show to
promote. A few days before the company arrived in New York to begin
rehearsals, the left-wing newspaper *PM* reported that the dancers did not
yet have a place to stay during the *Tropical Revue* run. Hurok had booked
rooms at the Windsor Hotel, but after learning that the company members were black, the hotel manager canceled the reservation, claiming that
other guests now had plans to stay longer than originally intended. The
Waldorf-Astoria, Astor, Algonquin, and Hotel Beverly similarly claimed
that their rooms were all booked. Managers at the Beverly suggested that
Dunham's company stay in Harlem at the Hotel Theresa, but as *PM* pointed
out, Dunham wanted rooms in midtown, close to the Martin Beck Theatre
where they were performing.[104]

   PM followed up four days later with a second article. "For the first time, I
am getting a little angry," Dunham stated. "It is gradually beginning to wear
me down. Some of the kids in the company say they'd almost rather stop dancing than go through all this over and over."[105] She told *PM* about the numerous
instances of discrimination they had faced on tour over the past two years. The
country was in the throes of World War II, fighting fascism to save democracy,
making the blatant racism even more jarring. The psychological distress of not
knowing, at each stop, whether they would find housing, a restaurant, or even
a place to get a cup of coffee created a formidable distraction making it harder
for Dunham' to concentrate on her creativity.[106] In Cincinnati, the hotel manager at the Netherlands-Plaza asked the company to move out because the
culinary workers' union was threatening to pull its employees from the hotel.
Dunham refused to leave and instead remained for two weeks. On the West
Coast, Dunham had seen signs everywhere saying, "We Do Not Serve Colored"
or "White Only." In Carmel, California, hotel managers canceled the company's reservation, leading to a frantic search for a place that would take them
in. When even the auto camp refused to take black guests, Dunham returned
to the hotel and forced them to accept the reservation. The Associated Negro
Press picked up the *PM* story. As a result, news of her battles reached readers
of the *Norfolk Journal and Guide, Atlanta Daily World, Philadelphia Tribune*, and

other black newspapers across the country.[107] "Because of the war," Dunham stated, "it would seem ridiculous if it were not so tragic."[108]

The experiences Dunham relayed in her press interviews challenged the myth that segregation was an issue only in the South or only a matter of a handful of bigoted individuals. Public school teacher Alexander Stearns wrote Dunham a letter the day after he read the second *PM* article to express his dismay about the discrimination she had experienced in Cincinnati and New York. Stearns, who was Jewish, assured her that "all right-minded Jews in particular are opposed to such anti-Negro bias," and enclosed an editorial from the Yiddish newspaper *The Day*, which used Dunham's story to decry racism. The editorial's author could not understand such discrimination, because the dominant media propaganda identified racism as "the work of the lowest, most reactionary, un-American elements of the population," and yet these prestigious midtown Manhattan hotels had denied access to Dunham's company members.[109] In purportedly liberal California and Oregon, hotels and restaurants had also refused to accommodate them. The Dunham dancers' experiences pointed to a systemic and deeply ingrained racism in American society that the mainstream press and US government tried to deny.

After the successful run of *Tropical Revue* in New York City, the company embarked on yet another cross-country tour with full awareness of the discrimination they would face. Some company members, emboldened by their success on Broadway, performed daily acts of resistance. Williams always went to the main window at any kiosk or take-out establishment to order coffee despite receiving threats of violence for refusing to stand in "Colored Only" lines. In the few cities the company toured in the South, Williams recalled overhearing black women in the bathroom muttering, "These Yankees coming down here are always ruining it for us."[110] Dunham took on larger fights. In Chicago, in June 1944, the company was appearing at the Blackstone Theater—but had been denied lodging at the Blackstone Hotel. Dunham sent a letter through the law firm of Dickerson and Cyrus, threatening to sue for racial discrimination.[111]

Dunham's most famous action against segregation occurred a few months later in Louisville, Kentucky, where following a successful performance, she read a speech to the audience stating that she would not return until the theater was desegregated (see the Introduction).[112] Not only did Dunham show savvy judgment in choosing Louisville, rather than Baltimore or Kansas City, to take her most public stand against segregation, but also she knew how to maximize the impact of her actions. She wrote to Goode, "If you were as vitally interested in these problems as you profess to be, it may be that you can use the enclosed comment for favorable publicity particularly stressing the fact that critics of Louisville in spite of this gave us glowing reviews."[113] Dunham's speech made the national news, appearing as a story in the *Negro Digest* and *PM*, among other newspapers.[114] Fans from across the country sent

Dunham letters applauding her stand. One particularly touching letter came from Norman Johnson, a fifteen-year-old boy in Evansville, Indiana. Johnson wrote, "It made me feel so happy to pick up the paper and read that you had told an audience in Louisville that you would never play there again until Colored People were allowed were allowed to sit on the main floor and enjoy the same rights that White People enjoy."[115]

Dunham's tactical choices could frustrate her company members. At one stop in California, in 1943, Hurok found an abandoned building, where the landlord "threw down dirty mattresses" for the company to sleep on, while Dunham stayed in a luxurious hotel suite, using her celebrity and affiliation with her white husband Pratt, white secretary Deren, and other white personnel to break the color barrier. When dancer Talley Beatty demanded a company meeting to address the inequality, Dunham said, "What do you expect? Give you my suite?" Beatty was fired for "questioning Mr. Hurok's and [Dunham's] integrity."[116]

Beatty had also begun to feel dissatisfied with what he felt was a lack of political, social, or artistic merit in Dunham's work. As he put it, "I was getting pretty tired of peeking up under Katherine's dresses and going 'Hey bobo!' "[117] Dunham remembered the sequence of events differently. In her memoirs, she wrote that Beatty and Janet Collins quit a few days after she had walked into a rehearsal wearing a new, expensive fur coat. In her opinion, they and many of the other dancers resented her display of wealth and luxury, not recognizing her star status or the tremendous efforts she made to keep them all housed, clothed, fed, and paid.[118] She mentioned nothing about housing inequity. Perhaps Dunham felt she deserved better accommodations because of her stature as the company's star, or perhaps she felt that breaking down the barriers of segregation could only happen slowly, first with one person rather than a full company of twenty to thirty dancers. Whatever the reason, she did not always fight the fight for her entire company.

As a celebrity, Dunham's personal life also became political, especially because she had chosen to marry Pratt. Dunham and Pratt had begun their romantic relationship in 1938, but the public only became aware of their involvement when the press reported that they had wed on July 10, 1941, during a whirlwind trip to Tijuana, Mexico, with Dorothy Gray in tow. Figure 4.5 shows the couple in Hollywood around the time of their marriage. Only later did they discover that such "border marriages" had no legal standing in the United States. After further research, they learned that California, where they were then living, and most other states in the American West banned interracial marriage. Dunham later wrote that they did not legally marry until 1950, in Las Vegas, Nevada, in order to adopt their daughter Marie-Christine. Pratt was not present; Dunham's lawyer stood in for him. Yet even these unorthodox nuptials were technically illegal (Nevada also banned interracial marriage

Figure 4.5 Katherine Dunham and John Pratt, ca. 1941, in Hollywood. Photograph by Lette Valeska. Missouri History Museum, St. Louis.

until 1959), and the Clark County registrar never recorded their marriage.[119] Quite possibly, Dunham and Pratt were never legally wed.

In the 1940s, interracial marriage was not only widely illegal but also highly stigmatized and controversial. Langston Hughes observed in the national edition of the *Chicago Defender*, in 1945, "One of the surest ways for a Negro leader to lose much of his prestige with the Negro masses is for him to marry a white woman."[120] Hughes explained the feelings of resentment whenever "prominent race men" decided to marry outside their race, which symbolized rejection or abandonment of the black community. He analyzed Gwendolyn Brooks's poem, "Ballad of Pearl May Lee," in which the protagonist feels a strange sense of exultation when a mob lynches her lover, who had cheated on her with a white woman.[121] Although Hughes did not comment on the reverse gender situation, Dunham's choice to marry a white man raised ire. One Chicago man wrote angrily that he was tired of seeing her in photographs with white men, leaving those like him with no chance.[122]

As more black entertainers, politicians, and businessmen married to white spouses gained national prominence through the rise of the black press, interracial romance made the transition from a taboo topic into a subject of public debate and celebrity gossip. The civil rights activism of World War II and calls for a racially harmonious America further raised awareness of the situation. Intellectuals such as University of Chicago professor Giuseppe Antonio Borgese optimistically and naïvely declared that interracial marriage would end the problem of racism in the United States.[123] In September 1945, *Negro Digest* editor John H. Johnson asked if Dunham or Pratt would consent to an interview about their relationship. Johnson admitted that he "may be stepping into a hornet's nest" by addressing the issue of interracial marriage, but said that he believed that such a roundtable "would contribute to a better understanding of the entire question."[124] The other prominent figures he asked included Jack Johnson, Richard Wright, Cab Calloway, and William Grant Still, men who had risen to positions of public prominence and married white women. The only other woman invited—Thyra Edwards—was a Communist Party member who had married a Jewish left-wing activist. There is no indication that Dunham participated, but later in 1945, Johnson wrote to Dunham again, asking if she would submit a short essay on the topic, "My Most Humiliating Jim Crow Experience."[125]

Dunham's reply illustrates the tension between racism as problem of individual bigotry and racism as a structural issue. By 1945, she had been refused lodging, food, coffee, and admittance to movie theaters on the basis of her race. She had been forced to sit in segregated train cars. The story she chose reflected none of those experiences. She wrote to Johnson, "To be perfectly honest, [my most humiliating Jim Crow experience] was one which involved prejudice by Negroes against guests of mine and my husband who happen not to be Negroes."[126] In the early 1940s, Dunham and Pratt went to a black nightclub in Los Angeles. The manager asked them to leave the dance floor, saying that mixed couples were not welcome. Dunham argued that they were married and allowed to dance together in white establishments in Los Angeles, to no avail. They walked out, humiliated, as the nightclub patrons watched.[127]

In explaining her reasoning to Johnson, Dunham wrote, "I am not anxious to fight in this very important struggle for equality of peoples unless it is to be done on a completely honest and rational basis . . . . I feel that if I can expose some of our own misjudgments and eradicate some of our own negative attitudes, we will at least have better equipment for the larger ill to be reckoned with."[128] Dunham emphasized that individual prejudices needed to be eradicated on the way to making systemic or structural change. Though she hinted that she saw white supremacy as the "larger ill" of society, she believed that only people who had risen above their personal prejudices could win the battle. Tactically, however, she knew that her story might rub *Negro Digest* readers the wrong way. If Johnson did not want that story, she said she would "write one of my many 'runner-up' experiences, which would certainly be more according to regulation."[129]

Johnson responded that he would be "very happy" to include her essay on the nightclub, because "one of the things that we are most proud of in our work with NEGRO DIGEST is the fact that we have independence and that we try to have the courage of our convictions. Perhaps doing the article with the slant you mention will antagonize a few people, but we do not think that is important."[130] Johnson's reply makes sense in light of Adam Green's analysis of the *Negro Digest* as a publication that strove to present diverse points of view.[131] The magazine, however, never published Dunham's story; it is unclear whether her grueling performance schedule prevented her from ever writing the piece or whether Johnson changed his mind about printing something so potentially provocative.

Dunham's affair with another white man in the 1940s had different political ramifications: it led the FBI to open a file on her. Thomas Wells (Tim) Durant, a wealthy writer and producer, developed an attraction to Dunham while watching her perform as Georgia Brown in *Cabin in the Sky* (1941) in Los Angeles. After seeing her again at Ciro's nightclub and in the film *Star Spangled Rhythm*, he decided to invite himself and his best friend, famed actor Charlie Chaplin, over to her apartment.[132] A tall, handsome, well-educated, wealthy, and congenial New Englander, Durant loved to take Dunham out to romantic dinners, nights of dancing, and vacation getaways in the woods of Maine. At the time, Pratt, who had been drafted into the army, was fighting in Europe, and the distance strained his and Dunham's relationship. At one point, Pratt wrote her from the field, "Dear, if you want to marry Tim, if that's it, just say so to yourself without torturing yourself and everyone else ... I think my chances of living through this war are very small."[133] Dunham did not leave Pratt, but she continued the romantic liaison with Durant until at least 1947 and received money from him to support her company, school, and various other ventures.[134]

The affair embroiled Dunham in the FBI investigation of Chaplin. The *Great Dictator* star had become an outspoken Soviet sympathizer after the Nazi invasion of Russia. When one of Chaplin's lovers filed a paternity lawsuit in 1943, the FBI took advantage of the legal trouble to begin persecuting him for his Communist ties. The FBI also filed an indictment against Durant, hoping to discredit Chaplin by branding his close friend as morally dissolute for having an affair with a married black woman.[135] In May 1944, Durant wrote to Dunham detailing the story he had given to the FBI, saying, "I want to refresh your memory on what took place," in order to ensure that their stories coincided. He offered several innocuous reasons for their cross-country flights and road trips together. He wrote, "I'm sorry all this has come up Katherine and I hope it won't be too disturbing. I feel it will go no further but then I didn't think I would be indicted—nor did anyone else."[136] From then on, the FBI began to track Dunham.[137]

The FBI found several reasons to suspect that Dunham supported communist activities. In the early 1940s, she gave her name, money, and time to the American Society for Russian Relief, the National Council of

Soviet-American Friendship, the Joint Anti-Fascist Refugee Committee, the International Workers Order, and the Southern Conference for Human Welfare, organizations that were all on the FBI's Communist Front list. She also supported Communist Party candidate Benjamin C. Davis in his campaign to be Harlem's representative in Congress. The FBI noted her participation in these causes and also tracked her various personal friendships with Communist Party members.[138] Although Dunham never joined the Communist Party USA, she had come of age during the Popular Front period in Chicago when left-wing political groups stood on the front lines against social injustice of all kinds. Though there were limitations to the Communist Party's dedication to anti-racism, it went much further than other political parties. For an African American interested in racial equality in the 1930s and 1940s, involvement with organizations tied to communism or socialism was practically unavoidable.[139]

In addition to her political coming-of-age in the Popular Front, Dunham expressed positive feelings toward Russia. The Toronto *Evening Telegram* reported in January 1944 that Dunham's film short *Carnival of Rhythm* had been selected "by the very choosey Russian censor Michail Kolotzoff, who only selected eight films last year . . . . It is more than a probability that she and her company will go to Russia under the exchange system of artists proposed between Russia and the United States."[140] Dunham told the *Philadelphia Tribune* a month later that black artists should look to Russia if they wanted better roles "portraying Negroes at an advantage," because all Hollywood offered were minor, stereotypical parts.[141] In 1946, Dunham's manager, Mark Marvin, sent a letter to Anatoly Gromov, press secretary for the Soviet Embassy in Washington (and, as it turns out, a KGB agent), saying that Dunham eagerly wished to tour Russia the following year and wanted Gromov's help in arranging it.[142] Around this time she told a Russian magazine, "In Russia lies the greatest possibility of Negro peoples feeling themselves a part of a larger group."[143] That African Americans needed to forge international connections was one of Dunham's primary beliefs. If African Americans saw themselves only within the context of the United States, they would feel downtrodden. By experiencing life in Russia, they could see alternate possibilities for the future.

The Dunham company never made it to Russia. Instead, Dunham decided to fight back against racial discrimination on her home turf. Although *Tropical Revue* had brought her fame and box-office success, dance critics had turned against her and did not understand her aim to "embody a movement expressing freedom." When she pivoted to *Carib Song*, a serious musical play, she encountered just as much criticism. So Dunham shifted her focus away from performance to a second front in the battle for artistic legitimacy and racial progress: the Katherine Dunham School of Dance, located in the heart of midtown Manhattan. With this institution, Dunham sought to reshape the New York dance world in her image.

CHAPTER 5

Rehearsal for Revolution

The Dunham School

B uried in Dunham's archive, between letters from civil rights organizations beseeching her to perform at their fundraisers, is a simple piece of yellowed paper. Without fanfare, the document lists the people who attended a company rehearsal at the Dunham School in New York, on January 20, 1946, which included among others George Balanchine, impresario Lincoln Kirstein, Broadway performer Joan McCracken, anthropologist and writer Harold Courlander, French anthropologist Claude Lévi-Strauss, and South African novelist Stuart Cloete.[1] Langston Hughes, Doris Duke, and performers from the Metropolitan Opera also regularly dropped by to watch rehearsals.[2] Rarely, if ever, has a dance school routinely brought together such an acclaimed, international group of artists and intellectuals. Such was the uniqueness of the Dunham School, a pedagogically, artistically, and socially revolutionary institution in the heart of the Broadway theater district, operational from 1944 to 1954. Though Dunham's spectacular revues and outspoken stances against segregation have endured more prominently in dance historical memory,[3] the daily operations at 220 West 43rd Street radically transformed how people thought about dance education and did the most among her many projects to challenge the racial status quo of the United States.

The Dunham School had a modest start. Franziska Boas, daughter of the famed anthropologist and an expert in "primitive" music and dance in her own right, joined forces with Dunham in January 1944 to open a school at 323 West 21st Street in Manhattan. The two women shared an interest in anthropology and expressed admiration for each other's work in exploring the role of dance in primitive society. They also shared a belief in using dance education as a means of anti-racist activism. Boas had started her own school in 1933, and besides the New Dance Group it was one of the few that had an interracial staff and student body.[4] But despite the seemingly natural fit, the Dunham-Boas collaboration did not last long. With Dunham constantly moving from city to city on tour with *Tropical Revue*, communication broke down, making it difficult to make decisions about class offerings, rates, and publicity. Dunham wanted to limit Boas's role to teaching one or two classes, whereas Boas wanted to be codirector of the school, an understandable demand given that she was the one in New York running the daily operations.[5] The two also had different approaches to dance pedagogy. Dunham emphasized technique, for she believed that black artists needed to disprove the racial stereotype about African Americans being natural dancers. Boas felt that technique was important, but she insisted that black students needed to develop their creativity and choreographic skills in order to succeed in the field of dance. The partnership dissolved in less than a year—though the relationship between the two women would always remain amicable—and Dunham began the search for her own space.[6]

What Dunham did next was one of the most audacious political moves of her career. In January 1945, while still on tour, she issued a press release to announce that she had purchased a $200,000 mansion at 14 East 71st Street as her private residence and the site of a future Katherine Dunham School of Dance.[7] This location was in the heart of Manhattan's Silk Stocking district on the Upper East Side, and she was staking her claim to equality among the elite. The press release noted that her new neighbors would be the Fricks, the Guggenheims, and former New York governor Herbert S. Lehman and his wife.[8] Dunham's white secretary, Eileen Hamilton, conducted the negotiations, so neither the owner, Walter S. Gubelman, nor his lawyer knew who the actual buyer was until a reporter from the *New York Herald Tribune* called to confirm the sale.[9] Duham's brilliant maneuver forced housing discrimination into the open, for any excuses made to retract the deal would clearly show racial bias.

The purchase made the front page of the *Amsterdam News* and the *Afro-American*. Abe Hill, of the former, proudly noted that Dunham "has always been in the forefront of breaking down racial prejudice" and that her purchase had "floored" New Yorkers.[10] While Ethel Waters and other wealthy black entertainers had purchased lavish homes in Harlem, no African Americans owned a residence on the Upper East Side between Park and Fifth Avenue.[11] Burley, who had previously criticized Dunham's sexually suggestive dancing, wrote a congratulatory article that appeared in three black newspapers. He saw the purchase as a bold, daring move that would accelerate desegregation. She had always been at the forefront in breaking barriers, he wrote, but "this must represent a distinct triumph: a breaking through of color lines and restrictions that others before her could have accomplished had their minds been set on doing just that." He compared Dunham to Paul Robeson, saying the two shared "tenacity of purpose," and concluded, "somewhere down the line the dream of a new world envisioned by both Katherine Dunham and Paul Robeson is bound to appear."[12]

But just two weeks after the announcement, her lawyers wrote to say that Gubelman was "greatly upset about the situation" and "most anxious that you favorably consider the suggestion that you withdraw from the deal."[13] Not satisfied with Gubelman's timid mode of persuasion, one of Dunham's potential neighbors, a plastic surgeon, filed a lawsuit in conjunction with the owners of 18 East 71st Street to prevent Dunham from moving in. The surgeon claimed that his complaint had nothing to do with race, but rather with zoning. The Upper East Side, he stated, was a residential neighborhood, and a dance school would violate zoning laws. The front page of the February 24, 1945, *Amsterdam News* ran the headline "N.Y.C. Silk Stocking 400 Attack Katherine Dunham," and condemned the racial discrimination at play, as did the national edition of the *Chicago Defender*.[14] In a triumph for Dunham, the New York Supreme Court denied the surgeon's claim, stating that Dunham's purchase was her "constitutional right."[15] The judge agreed, however, to grant a temporary injunction against her moving in.

Dunham ultimately lost the battle to keep the mansion. Probably realizing that the opposition would be so fierce and well funded that it would take years to get the school off the ground, Dunham made the pragmatic choice to back out of the sale. She explained that an investigation of the zoning laws had revealed that she could not run a school in the neighborhood without the New York State Board of Regents approval.[16] She had already made her point by negotiating to purchase the home and feeding the story to the press. She may have lost the house, but she had won the publicity war. In an exquisite irony, Dunham's potential neighbor, Mrs. Herbert Lehman, sent her a form letter during the middle of the controversy asking for her sponsorship of a new, interracial community center in the Bronx, to which Dunham graciously telegrammed her reply: "I am very happy to lend my name as sponsor to anything so worthy. Delighted at magnificent inter-racial understanding which this gift implies."[17]

Despite the intense opposition she faced to opening a school in a white neighborhood, Dunham did not retreat to Harlem. After a brief stay at Caravan Hall on 59th Street, she leased space in the Broadway theater district: 220 West 43rd Street, between Seventh and Eighth Avenues. After pouring thousands of dollars into renovations, she opened the Katherine Dunham School of Dance in September 1945. The former rehearsal space for George White's *Scandals*, a series of revues modeled after the Ziegfeld Follies, now included two large studios with mirrors and fixed barres, storage space for costumes, equipment, and instruments, dressing rooms for men and women, office space, and a library.[18] Advertisements for the school appeared in the *New York Times, Dance Magazine*, and black newspapers in multiple cities on the East Coast. The copy read, "Enrollment for the most complete EDUCATION IN DANCE: Primitive Rhythm—Percussion—Ballet—Modern—Dunham Technique."[19] Letters of inquiry soon began to flood into the school, and the evidence in Dunham's archives suggests that most came from people who had seen the ads in black newspapers.[20] Her publicity strategy had reached a broad-based dance population and at the same time gave extra encouragement to black dancers.

Because the Dunham School received GI Bill funding, it also attracted World War II veterans. Several soldiers and Women's Army Corps volunteers, who had watched Dunham's movies or seen her perform at military bases, wrote letters asking if they could enroll.[21] The school's proximity to Broadway attracted actors such as Marlon Brando, James Dean, José Ferrer, and Shelley Winters (see Figure 5.1). Brando became a particularly avid student of dance and drumming; it helped that he was in love with his Dunham Technique teacher, Julie Robinson (later Belafonte).[22] David Vaughan remembers students from the School of American Ballet flocking to the Dunham School to take Primitive Rhythms, Boogie, Dunham Technique, and other classes not offered anywhere else in the city.[23]

Figure 5.1 James Dean and Eartha Kitt in a Dunham Technique class. Photograph by Dennis Stock, Magnum Photos. The picture is dated 1955, but the Dunham School closed in 1954, and James Dean was in California from May 1954 until his death in September 1955. Most likely, this photograph was taken in 1953, when Stock took several other photos of Dean for *Life* magazine.

Given the positive feedback and enthusiasm, Dunham decided to expand course offerings and developed a certificate program. By January 1946, she had changed the name to the Dunham School of Dance and Theatre. In addition to dance and drama courses, the summer quarter brochure listed the following classes: General Anthropology, Spanish, French, Music Appreciation, General Philosophy, Playwriting, History of Drama, History of Dance, Comedy Techniques, Dance Notation, and Introductory Psychology.[24] The roster of teachers represented a racially diverse, international cohort of artists and scholars at the forefront of their disciplines. Mexican-born José Limón taught modern dance. Todd Bolender, who had danced with Ballet Caravan, Ballet Theatre, and the Ballet Russe de Monte Carlo, taught ballet. Lena Belloc taught Laban notation, a method for recording dance. Basil Matthews, a Catholic priest from Trinidad with a doctorate in sociology from Fordham University, taught philosophy. He was not the only PhD on staff. Ben Frederic Carruthers, who taught Spanish, had a PhD from the University of Havana, and the two anthropology instructors, Joyce Wyke and Alta Gusar, were pursuing PhDs at Columbia University. Henri "Papa" Augustin from Haiti taught percussion.

The intellectual and artistic energy emanating from the Dunham School must have been palpable. The *Amsterdam News* reported "unusually large student registrations" for the summer of 1946, as hundreds of children and adults signed up.[25] Most of the classes lasted an hour. The school's brochure listed sixteen elementary-level classes in Dunham Technique in 1946–47, nine classes in elementary ballet, and one class in Limón's elementary modern. The cost per course that year was $30 for a twelve-week term. Therefore the cost per class was extremely high—$2.50, or approximately $31 in 2016 dollars. Students who wanted to enroll in a certificate program were required to complete twenty-five credit hours per week and pay $350 per term, or approximately $4,333 in 2016 dollars.[26]

Despite the high tuition costs and a large student population, the school soon ran into financial trouble. The statement of income and disbursements for the week of September 21, 1946, roughly one year after the opening, shows that total expenses for the week, including salaries, maintenance, and utilities, came to $1,633. Tuition income was only $183.26, suggesting that a large number of students received financial aid in some form or another.[27] The federal government paid for several students on the GI Bill, and many students had work-study scholarships, called Student Aid.[28] Other income that week came from the school's monthly fundraising party, La Boule Blanche ($570.42), a private donation ($30), and Dunham's own money ($900), landing the school around $50 in the black—but only because of her massive personal loan.[29] When enrollment increased or a friend donated money, Dunham did not pay off debts; instead she hired more instructors and added new classes. One year out, Dunham estimated that the school was over $45,000 in debt (mostly to herself), but she was "vitally excited" by seeing her dream come to fruition.[30]

A central component of Dunham's dream was her pedagogical mission to train the whole person, or "total dancer."[31] In the mid-twentieth century, there was a division between those who followed Margaret H'Doubler's idea that dance education should aim to help students lead better lives and those who saw dance education as a means to a vocational end.[32] Most private studios took the latter path, focusing on professionalization, but Dunham envisioned her school as serving both goals—and more. She called it a "laboratory" for her ideas about education.[33] "Theatrical artists," she claimed, "are too often handicapped by lack of understanding of the development of general culture and its importance in a specific field."[34] Dancers needed to communicate *why* they performed certain movements, what social reasons and emotions drove the dancing. Only then could they hope to connect to audiences on an emotional, visceral level and create cross-cultural understanding. Students in the dance division's two-year certificate program, for example, were required to take one hour a week each of percussion, music appreciation, dance history, visual design, choreutics (a system of dance analysis developed by Rudolf Laban), anthropology, a language, and finally three elective hours, in addition to fifteen hours a week of dance technique.[35]

This multidisciplinary arts education served nonprofessional students as well. To anyone who asked, Dunham repeated a consistent message: training in the performing arts and humanities prepared students to face life's problems.[36] Too often, she felt, individuals wandered through life unaware of how the world worked and how they fit into it. They lacked understanding of humankind's basic emotional and spiritual needs. Human beings needed to connect with the divine; to communicate with others across racial, ethnic, linguistic, class, or gender differences; and to release emotional energy through music and dance. Without such social awareness and channels for catharsis, individuals were "badly equipped" for the "problems of living."[37]

Dunham believed that African Americans had a particularly difficult time breaking out of their social position in the United States. Therefore, she focused the energies of the school on the cultural practices of the African diaspora to provide an alternate framework for her black students. She wrote to Edwin Embree of the Rosenwald Foundation in 1946, "Until people, particularly minority groups, have some picture of their own placement in the general world patterns, they will not be able to extend beyond the narrow confines which are set up for them by our own education and capitalistic systems."[38] Dunham envisioned her school as the antidote to existing systems of oppression, particularly the American public education system which denied black children an accurate or complete understanding of African American contributions to history.[39] She also wrote that capitalism contributed to the oppression of minorities, one of the few hints in Dunham's archive that she sympathized with a leftist analysis of racism. Notably, Dunham insisted on helping students find their place in "the world," not "the United States." The education was diasporic, not nationalist.

This total education, with an emphasis on the African diaspora, was not only for adults. Children flocked to the school, especially to Walter Nicks's Saturday morning dance class and Papa Augustin's drumming class.[40] Figure 5.2 shows youngsters releasing their backs in an arch after bending their knees forward in a "hinge" position, a classic Dunham Technique exercise at the barre. What may appear to be a simple picture of students dancing in fact reveals how revolutionary the Dunham School was. First, the majority of the youth are African American, but not all. Most studios in New York were segregated in the 1940s, and those that were integrated were majority-white.[41] At the Dunham School, integration had blackness at the center. Second, boys as well as girls are participating, despite the stigma often attached to boys taking dance classes during the mid-twentieth century. Third, the students are at a ballet barre, a symbol of an elite art form, but executing a movement inspired by Dunham's ethnographic research in Haiti. As Elizabeth Chin has stated, the Dunham Technique was "a direct

Figure 5.2 Children in a Dunham Technique class, ca. 1946. Photograph by Arnold C. de Mille. Katherine Dunham Papers, Special Collections Research Center, Southern Illinois University, Carbondale.

challenge to the unspoken cultural and racial hierarchies of the dance studio."[42]

Promoting her technique lay at the heart of the Dunham's mission to redefine dance education. Although she would continue to change her technique over the course of several decades, the New York school was the first place that officially offered Dunham Technique classes. During these years, she established many of the exercises that are still done today. Dancer Lavinia Williams's notes indicate that that Dunham Technique classes in the 1940s began with an extensive warm-up at the ballet barre, emphasizing stretches for the leg and back.[43] Particularly novel for dance students in the 1940s was the Dunham Technique's liberated use of the spine and pelvis. While the contemporaneous Graham Technique emphasized contraction and release as a percussive, singular action, Dunham's contraction and release could either percussively isolate the pelvis or move fluidly up the entire spine. Dunham's use of the pelvis was also more three dimensional, not just contracting forward and back, but also moving side to side, on the diagonal, in a circle, or in a figure eight. After the barre warm-up, students learned movements that traveled across the studio floor on the diagonal, called Progressions. These Progressions included Caribbean dance steps, such as the *yonvalou* or *congo paillette*, which required students to learn complex rhythmic patterns. They had to lower their center of gravity by deeply bending their knees and pitching their torsos forward. They also had to learn the drumming rhythms, history, and meaning of the dance steps. Progressions also included balletic movements, such as turns with the leg in an *attitude* front (leg bent and turned out) position.[44] A Dunham dancer had to master multiple ways of moving the body.

Dunham Technique, and the Dunham School more broadly, were major influences on the development of the emerging genre of jazz dance. In Dunham Technique classes at the school, students practiced isolations, meaning that they learned to move individual body parts—head, shoulders, arms, rib cage, hips, or feet—in rhythmic patterns while keeping all other parts of the body still. Jack Cole was simultaneously teaching isolations in his Hollywood dance classes. By the 1950s, through the synergistic merging of East Coast and West Coast dancers, isolations had become a cornerstone of a jazz dance class warm up.[45] The Dunham Technique was not the only source of the development of jazz dance at the Dunham School. Instructor Marie Bryant, a former dancer with Duke Ellington's band, taught Lindy, Swing, and Boogie—black social dance precursors to jazz dance that were not typically considered "techniques" and thus not generally taught at other dance schools at the time. Their presence on the Dunham School course roster paved the way for jazz dance to become a staple of dance school curricula.[46] Peter Gennaro, future Broadway choreographer, taught Boogie at the school and took classes in Dunham Technique and primitive rhythms. His choreography for "Mambo" and other numbers in *West Side Story* (both stage and film versions) disseminated jazz dance to a broader audience and seems particularly influenced by his training at 220 West 43rd Street.[47]

The Dunham School also provided a vehicle for Dunham to retrain her company members. She was notoriously strict as a teacher and artistic director. In Figure 5.3, Dunham points intently at an unseen dancer rehearsing onstage. Even when the company was performing grueling one-night stands on tour, she (or her dancer Lenwood Morris) taught daily ballet class and held rehearsals right up to curtain time. During intermissions, she would gather the dancers onstage and give them extensive notes for improvement.[48] She aimed at the highest standards of performance and professionalism, but despite such efforts, she had received criticism for commercialism in *Tropical Revue* and primitivism in *Carib Song*. She wanted to recapture the artistic stature that she had enjoyed in 1940. She explained to writer Katharine Wolfe in December 1945, "the public has treated the [Dunham] technique too lightly."[49] She planned to present the company in a "strictly ballet performance to counterbalance the present attitude of the public toward the group."[50] To do so, she put a moratorium on performing for six months and paid her dancers full-time to train rigorously in ballet at the school.[51] Although part of Dunham's

Figure 5.3 Katherine Dunham giving corrections to her company, ca. 1950s. Photographer unknown. Missouri History Museum, St. Louis.

mission had been to show that the "primitive" rhythms of African diasporic peoples could form the basis for a dignified and rich art form, she now turned to ballet technique to prove African Americans' worth as dance artists of the highest caliber.

Ballet was enjoying a great surge in popularity and stature in the United States in the mid-1940s. Audiences flocked to performances by the Ballet Russe de Monte Carlo, Ballet International, and Ballet Theatre, which would be renamed the American Ballet Theatre in 1957. Ballet had spread to Broadway as well. The trend had begun with Balanchine in the mid-1930s and reached a groundswell in the early 1940s. Agnes de Mille received great acclaim for her balletic choreography in *Oklahoma!* (1943), and Robbins's number *Fancy Free* (1944) for the Ballet Theatre was so popular that it inspired an equally successful Broadway musical, *On the Town*. Ballet choreography was no longer considered stuffy, old fashioned, or elite; it represented a fresh artistic approach with the added bonus of popular appeal. Even Martha Graham, famous for rejecting ballet early in her career, had begun to hire dancers with ballet training.[52] Ballet was booming, and Dunham wanted to be a part of it. Through this genre, she could gain the artistic acclaim she desired without sacrificing the box office.

Dunham sought out Todd Bolender to help transform the company's image. Originally trained in modern dance, Bolender had performed with most of New York's major ballet companies of the period. Starting in the fall of 1945, he taught ballet to the Dunham company at the school. Dunham also asked him to collaborate with her on choreography to Stravinsky's "Histoire d'un Soldat" ("A Soldier's Tale"). She wanted Leonard Bernstein to conduct the New York Symphony Orchestra playing Stravinsky's score as her company danced.[53] In associating herself with Bolender, Stravinsky, Bernstein, and the New York Symphony Orchestra, she placed herself in the highest echelon of New York's performing arts world.

In addition to serving as company ballet master, Bolender defended Dunham's artistry. In 1946, the Minneapolis-based African American dancer and choreographer Eunice Brown wrote the article "An Experiment in Negro Modern Dance" for *Dance Observer*, a major dance publication, in which she dismissed Dunham's contributions to concert dance. Brown portrayed the interracial modern dance company she founded with her sister Bernice in distinct contrast to Dunham's "entertainment."[54] Bolender wrote an impassioned response to the editor of *Dance Observer*. He argued that Dunham was "the first well-known Negro concert dancer in American culture" and an artist of serious intent. He concluded, "I will leave it to your readers to decide whether a concert program based on the following music is worthy of the classification 'serious': Aaron Copland, Ravel, Mozart . . . Darius Milhaud and Igor Stravinsky."[55] Prior to 1946, Dunham's repertory contained no dances set to music by these composers. In making the turn to ballet now, she was in a way returning to her first inclinations in 1930, when she aimed to use ballet (and in 1946, its sonic parallel, classical music) as a project of racial uplift as well as a legitimizing strategy for her artistic worth.[56]

Dunham, however, could not satisfy both her critics and her producers. She wrote excitedly to Embree that the new concert program would "restore me to the good graces of the critics who were rather cross when I went into the revue field."[57] Yet no prospective investors wanted to support Dunham's ballet endeavors. The Broadway producer George Abbott wrote, "I am much more enthusiastic for the novelty features which have been incorporated in your productions, than in the straight classical ballet. I hope, however, for your sake, that I am as wrong as can be."[58] The first sign that Abbott was not wrong appeared at the Columbia "Pop" Orchestra Concert at Carnegie Hall in May 1946. As of April 9, Dunham planned to include one of the new balletic numbers, *Pink Scene*, to music by Copland. Four days later, she told the director she would do *Rara Tonga*, her Melanesian "Primitive Rhythms" standby, instead.[59] Perhaps Dunham felt insecure about showing a new piece on a stage as prestigious as Carnegie Hall, though insecurity was not her trademark. More likely, investors had been effective in discouraging her from venturing into the classical ballet realm. In a letter written to her lawyer that same month, she stated vaguely that "various production reasons" had led her to decide to return to the revue format of her previous shows.[60] Once again, she had attempted to pivot artistically but faced a wall of hostility built largely by racial discrimination.

By the time Dunham finally premiered her next Broadway show, *Bal Negre*—literally, "Negro Ball"—in November 1946, her plan to move away from primitive rhythms had fallen by the wayside.[61] Gone were ballets set to music by classical composers like Ravel or Mozart; absent was *Rites de Passage*, which in its abstraction attempted a high-art modernism through primitivism. Advertisements billed the show as "A Musical Revue of Caribbean Exotica."[62] When Mary Titus, a graduate student at Ohio State University, wrote to Dunham asking about the use of percussion in modern dance, Dunham declined to answer the question, saying, "My particular interest, as you know, is in primitive rather than modern."[63]

Bal Negre was not just a pragmatic shift to please audiences or a return to primitivism, however. It also represented a reassertion of diaspora that reflected Dunham's renewed excitement about anthropology. She found a way forward fueled by artistic inspiration, not simply in response to discrimination. In 1946, she developed an interest in Cuba, a country she had not visited on her ethnographic research trip in the 1930s, and quickly arranged a visit to the island. She recruited several new drummers on this trip. In May 1946, she sponsored "Cuban Evening" at the school, at which Hughes and the Afro-Cuban poet Eusebia Cosme read their poems, accompanied by dance and music.[64] She also fell in love with the poems and songs of Nicolás Guillén. She wrote to him that he had been the inspiration for the "Cuban Evening" benefit and asked for copies of his music.[65] Cuban drummers Luis Miranda, Candido Camero, Francisco Aguabella, Mongo Santamaría, and Armando Peraza became regulars at the Sunday afternoon company rehearsals.[66] Gilberto Valdés, a Cuban composer who specialized in Afro-Cuban music, conducted the orchestra for *Bal Negre* and wrote two new pieces of music for the show.[67]

Bal Negre presented the most explicitly Africanist dances in the Dunham repertory, including *Shango, L'Ag'Ya, Congo Paillette, Son, Rhumba,* and *Nañigo,* the latter a new Cuban dance. Robert Sylvester of the *Daily News* declared that Dunham was "at her best" in *Bal Negre,* and the mercurial Martin stated that *Bal Negre* "surpasse[d] previous shows in taste, general artistry."[68] Though the ballet numbers had fallen by the wayside, the dancers' six months of intense training had clearly paid off. Not all the critical response was positive. Ezra Goodman of *Dance Magazine* stated that Dunham was "exploiting the ethnic of a people in terms of cheap theatricalism" and "dish[ed] up an ethnic without ethic."[69] No matter what performance strategy Dunham adopted—revue, musical play, ballet, Afro-Caribbean based—someone was there to claim it was neither artistic nor socially relevant.

In her fight for artistic legitimacy, Dunham decided to start a second company, the Experimental Group, which drew its members from talented youth at the school. Several dancers, including Eartha Kitt, Walter Nicks, and Julie Robinson, would eventually join the Dunham company, and a fourth, Gennaro, would become a Tony Award–winning Broadway choreographer. Emerante de Pradines, a famed Vodou singer from Haiti, entered the group as a singer, but eventually danced many of Dunham's roles. She would go on to teach at the Yale School of Drama and at Stanford University before returning to Haiti.[70] Unlike the Dunham company, which was entirely black at the time, the Experimental Group was interracial.

In addition to developing young dancers, the Experimental Group kept up a positive public image for Dunham's institutions by performing at schools and benefit fundraisers for which it received little to no pay, gigs that the Dunham company could not afford to take. Among its many appearances, the Experimental Group danced at meetings of several chapters of the NAACP, an Anti-Discrimination Meeting of the New York Citizens Political Action Committee, a rally for the Progressive Citizens of America, and a concert at the Natural History Museum. The repertoire consisted primarily of Dunham's education-oriented Haitian choreography from the 1930s that the main company had stopped presenting in 1939, after it had become more commercially successful.[71] Antoine Bervin, Haitian member of the Pan-American Union, wrote a thank-you letter after the Experimental Group's show at Howard University in June 1947. He stated that the performance had done much for "international understanding" by bringing "a genuine aspect of our life and customs to the American people."[72]

Indeed, the Dunham School and Experimental Group were primary avenues for Dunham to continue to combat the mystification and demonization of Haiti. The school offered classes in Haitian drumming and had a room dedicated to books, newspapers, historical archival materials, and films about Haiti, which, she boasted, was the "largest [collection] in North America."[73] The monthly Boule Blanche fundraiser party emphasized Haitian music, dance, and food, which "affords an opportunity for a large number of the general public to become acquainted with Haitian folk ways."[74] Dunham awarded scholarships to Haitian students de Pradines, Mathilde Holly, and Jean-Léon Destiné. Destiné, after performing in *Bal Negre*, went on to form his own successful dance company, which toured five continents. He was considered one of the most important ambassadors of Haitian culture and was, in many ways, the father of Haitian folkloric dance.[75] Even though he had begun dancing before coming to New York, his experience at the Dunham School and the years of performing in *Bal Negre* gave him the technical training and professional experience he needed to launch an independent career.

The Experimental Group also challenged racial segregation. In late October 1947, a deluge of admonishing letters and angry telephone calls flooded the WABD (New York) and WTTG (Washington, DC) television stations. That week, the "Look upon a Star" program had featured two teenage members of the Experimental Group, Robinson and Nicks, dancing together. What exactly they danced is lost to history, but in the slightly blurry newspaper photographs taken at the time, Nicks wears loose, cropped pants, a sleeveless white shirt, and a bandana around his neck, the costume that Dunham's male dancers wore in several Cuban dances. Robinson has on a blouse and a flowy skirt that shows off her legs when caught mid-twirl, as she is in one photograph. Both are barefoot, and the background contains drums, a small tree, and wooden outdoor furniture.[76] Based on the costumes and setting, it seems likely that they performed a lighthearted, flirtatious courtship dance deriving from Caribbean social dances, a genre that lay at the heart of Dunham's oeuvre.

For the more than one hundred viewers who wrote and called in, the dance was an abomination, not because of the choreography or costumes, but because of the people dancing. Robinson was white, and Nicks was black. Television stations had earlier that fall begun to broadcast Brooklyn Dodgers games in which Jackie Robinson was a player on the field and had faced no objection. The difference was that these dancers were opposite-sex, attractive teenagers, raising the specter of miscegenation in people's minds. For the first time in American history, the call to censor depictions of racial integration officially spread to the newest communications medium: television.[77]

How the stations responded would set a precedent for how to handle such protests in the future. Television broadcasts in the United States had officially begun in 1931, but less than ten thousand households owned TV sets by the end of the 1930s. The production of television sets ceased during World War II to conserve resources for the war effort. Viewership slowly began to grow again after the war ended. Still, in 1947, only 44,000 households owned televisions, as opposed to 40 million who owned radios, and TV broadcasts could only be transmitted as far south as Washington, DC. Newspapers covering the "Look upon a Star" controversy reported that the producers responded to the protests by "dumping the objecting letters into a waste basked" [sic] and by asserting, "The prejudiced television viewer can exercise his democratic privilege of switching his dial off."[78] Instead of a parade, march, petition, or speech, Dunham had used dancing teenagers to force media executives to take a stance in favor of integration.

The incident was a highly public example of Dunham's overall mission to display American democracy in action at the Dunham School. Various publicity efforts promoted her interracial vision. One press release proclaimed that the interracial student and faculty composition "provides living proof that the races of mankind can live and create in complete harmony and understanding.... The Dunham organization takes its great success as proof that complete interracial justice must ultimately be achieved if American culture is to finally be truly democratic."[79] In a photograph from the *New York World-Telegram*, a racially mixed group of children, mostly girls, hold drums between their knees or on their laps.[80] This image also challenged gender assumptions about percussionists.

Dunham's primary strategy was to make interracial dancing—and by extension, interracial living—normal, not radical or unorthodox. She emphasized in an August 1946 interview with *Glamour* magazine that racial integration was not artificially forced upon the school:

> From the staff on down, the school is roughly half Negro and half white. The ratio is accidental, not the result of any quota system. There is no question of mutual toleration or of anything implying an effort of any kind. The racial problem simply does not exist at the school and it is an example of how easily color difficulties are solved once they are taken out of the problem class and dealt with casually on a natural basis. Miss Dunham does not wish the school to develop into anything like a political unit.[81]

By insisting that the racial integration of the school had developed naturally, Dunham distanced herself from the Communist Party gatherings of her young adulthood in Chicago, where she felt that the racial mixing was forced.[82] The statement also offered a point of distinction from the New Dance Group, an overtly left-wing dance school in Manhattan that similarly boasted an interracial student body and faculty. The Dunham School did not turn away any paying student who wished to take classes, and thus did not have a quota system per se. The application form for scholarships, however, asked for students' "complexion," which indicates that Dunham did take an interest in shaping the racial makeup of the school.[83] In more subtle ways, by placing advertisements in a diverse array of newspapers, by granting scholarships to Haitian students, and by emphasizing techniques identified with African diasporic traditions, Dunham ensured that her school would attract students from multiple backgrounds. She also ran advertisements in the *Daily Worker* that mentioned the school's course offering in Russian (an offering not mentioned in the ads placed in any other paper), which signaled her savvy sense of advertising.[84]

Dunham's interracial model also reflected the cosmopolitan ethos of the immediate postwar period, epitomized by the founding of the United Nations. A Dunham School prospectus from 1946 reported that the students and staff "work together in harmony; a reflection of the cooperation now stirring in the world at large."[85] People from across the globe came to study at the school. The French government wanted to send students from its colonies in Africa and the Caribbean, and a number of newspapers ran a feature article about a Swiss woman who had moved to New York to take dance classes with Dunham.[86] The US government granted the Dunham School permission to enroll students on nonimmigrant visas. Cuban, Palestinian, Haitian, and Irish students took classes from teachers who hailed from Haiti, Trinidad, Mexico, Austria, and elsewhere.[87]

These internationalist and interracial leanings aroused the suspicion of the federal government. Since the incident with Durant in 1944, the FBI had continued to monitor Dunham's activities. In addition to noting her Russian and Communist Party connections, the FBI documented Dunham's relationship with the Council on African Affairs (CAA), which the agency deemed a Communist Front organization.[88] Max Yergan, along with singer and activist Paul Robeson and others, had founded the CAA in 1937 as the International Committee on African Affairs. It initially focused on teaching Americans about Africa and supporting Africans to come to the United States to further their education. The organization was renamed the Council on African Affairs in 1942, and it became more politicized. The CAA advocated decolonization in Africa and lobbied the US government to support the continent's economic and social development. Although the CAA was founded by black radicals, it attracted widespread support from black liberals and middle-class organizations during World War II, primarily because the war provided an opening to legitimize anticolonial activism. In his 1941 State of the Union address, President Roosevelt had proclaimed "Four Freedoms" that peoples "everywhere in the world" had the right to enjoy.[89] The declaration gave anticolonialism a new currency. The instability created by World War II further created opportunities to advocate independence. In the early to mid-1940s, the predominant political vision among African Americans emphasized people of color as a global majority demanding freedom.[90]

Dunham, who had long stressed diasporic connections, fit in easily with this movement. In September 1945, she established a $2,000 scholarship through the American Council on African Education to send an African student to an American university for four years, demonstrating her and the CAA's mutual interests.[91] A month later, she received an invitation from Robeson to hear him talk about his travels abroad. Dunham replied that she would be glad to attend if she could come late, as she was "terribly interested in [the] world situation as affects our own circumstances here."[92] Although she never made it to the meeting, she donated money to the CAA to support Robeson's vocal opposition to "the sharpened campaign against minorities and the related problems of colonial peoples." Her company performed a "spirited dance" at the CAA's "Freedom for Africa" rally at Madison Square Garden in July 1946. A newspaper photo shows Dunham in the audience standing between Robeson and Congressman Hugh De Lacy, a former Communist Party member.[93]

Though Dunham was not one of the leaders of the decolonization movement of the 1940s, she provided cultural support for the CAA's political project. Her years of experience forging diasporic cultural connections through anthropology, education, publications, and performance provided a way to create political unity. She said to a Russian magazine, "Many Negroes don't know that there are people in South America and in the West Indies who are like them. [My company] has created a much larger horizon for them. By showing people (and my own company) that they belong to a world scheme, it has made them less frustrated I am sure."[94]

Dunham's role as cultural ambassador extended to the social sphere. From April to June 1945, the United Nations Conference on International Organization met in San Francisco to write the charter for the United Nations, a document that, in theory, would govern international relations in the postwar era. In May, Dunham gave a party for the Haitian delegates that black journalists described as "one of the most scintillating cocktail affairs, with all of the celebrities 'worth knowing' present," and "a stunner of a cocktail party."[95] White journalists and entertainers attended as well.[96] If Dunham was not in the back rooms hammering out policy, she created a space for interracial and international sociality, contributing, in her own small way, to the faith that an international political entity could work.

Her support of Robeson, the CAA, decolonization, and interracial mixing at her school challenged the cold warriors' nationalistic vision of the United States. US government officials also linked communism and sexual deviance.[97] The fact that many homosexual dancers and supporters congregated at the Dunham School and enjoyed her monthly Boule Blanche parties raised the suspicions of the FBI, as did the mere fact of black and white citizens commingling. The parties brought together artists, intellectuals, and wealthy donors of many ethnicities to dance and drink into the wee hours of the morning. More informally, the energy and excitement generated in a Dunham Technique class meant that students would keep drumming and dancing after class officially ended. The drums were "always" going, no matter what time of day or night.[98] One FBI informant telegraphed, "You'd be gee-whizzed at the after-hour orgies that take place thrice weekly at one of the town's most famous interpretive dance studios (Katherin [sic] Dunham's . . .)."[99]

Overall, the vision of the Dunham School increasingly clashed with the vision of the US government as the optimism at the end of World War II turned into the fear and suspicion of the Cold War. Although Dunham never directly engaged in communist or socialist political organizing, government officials during the Cold War began to treat any racially progressive activity as suspicious. In April 1947, less than two years after officially opening the school, Dunham left the country, taking her company on a tour of Mexico. She would not permanently return to the United States for another twenty years. Although no direct evidence proves that Dunham left for political reasons, her departure occurred the year that the House Un-American Activities Committee (HUAC) began its investigations of the writers known as the Hollywood Ten.

After Dunham left, the school's financial problems grew. Tuition barely covered one-tenth of the cost of running the school. With a new international tour to finance, she could no longer spend thousands of dollars a month from her personal bank account to support it. Instead, she borrowed money from wealthy friends. By May 1948, the school owed tobacco heiress Doris Duke $30,000.[100] Besides the monthly Boule Blanche fundraiser, no formal mechanism existed for soliciting private donations. It is unclear why Dunham asked Duke for loans, not outright gifts, or why Duke never offered her contributions as donations. The school had no "angels" in the African American community or in New York City generally to underwrite its operations.

Personnel problems plagued the school in Dunham's absence. She was unable to keep a director for more than a year. Dorathi Bock Pierre, former editor of *Educational Dance* magazine, resigned soon after Dunham left for Mexico in April 1947. Pierre's successor, Bertrand Yeaton, lasted less than a year, as did the next director, Verne Van Bynum. The faculty disliked Van Bynum intensely, especially because their pay was delinquent.[101] Under the next director, Elsie Du Truielle, appointed in 1949, faculty salaries still were delinquent, which led to lowered morale.[102] Du Truielle was a socialite who lacked training in finance or management. She quit in May 1950, citing the impossibility of fulfilling Dunham's vision without Dunham's presence. Administrators and faculty battled for control, each claiming to know more about what their absentee leader's wishes were.[103]

An additional problem was that teenagers were handling most of the daily operations. Students on Student Aid had to work a certain number of hours of work a week in exchange for classes. In theory, high school students were the perfect work-study candidates. They were at the right age to train intensively for professional careers but lacked the funds to pay for such training, and they generally did not have outside jobs. Work-study students mopped the floors, cleaned the mirrors, operated the elevators, answered phones, and filed registrations. Yet teenagers had competing priorities. One work-study student missed afternoons at the school when she had too much homework. Another begged to be excused from work because her mother needed help packing a suitcase for a trip. Older work-study students left when paid performing opportunities arose or when they decided they needed a full-time job to survive.[104] The workforce was in constant flux.

In October 1948, Dunham despaired over the poor administration and felt embarrassed by what she saw as her institution's declining reputation. She lamented that "no-one would take my advice and close the School." She hoped that her former manager Dale Wasserman would step in, "so that at least if nothing can be done about finances, the disgraceful disciplinary and moral reputation of the School might be governed to a degree."[105] Perhaps the FBI informant had not been too far off about the parties in the studio after late-night classes. Without Dunham's oversight, the difficulty of running an institution with dozens of staff members, hundreds of students, and a bewildering array of divisions and programs (a dance division, drama division, cultural studies program, certificate program, scholarship program, work-study program, Boule Blanche fundraisers, Experimental Group, film series, and more) was overwhelming. The company was always Dunham's first priority and, as she said, "Just to keep the company going morally and artistically represents a full time task for me."[106] When she and her dancers were living in New York, Dunham had integrated the operations of the company and the school, for the latter provided a home base for the former. Once she was abroad, she had too many other pressing problems to handle.

The students, not privy to the behind-the-scenes financial problems and personnel conflicts that mounted in Dunham's absence, received excellent training and flourished. Arthur Mitchell, who began taking Karel Shook's ballet class at the school in 1951, remembers that "it was the place to go" for the "in people" of the theater and dance scene.[107] Michelle Newton was a scholarship student from 1949 to 1952. She already spent much of the day dancing at the High School of Performing Arts, and every evening she danced more at the Dunham School. She loved "primitive dancing" and took classes in Dunham Technique, Brazilian-Haitian dance, Afro-Cuban dance, Boogie, ballet, and makeup application.[108] The young Ural Wilson wrote to dance director Syvilla Fort in May 1949 to say that he had learned "more than I thought possible" at the Dunham School and now felt the desire to express himself through dance even more deeply. He asked if it would be possible to receive another scholarship to continue his training. He did, and Wilson became one of Dunham's most devoted company members, and eventually a teacher at her Performing Arts Training Center in East St. Louis.

Glory Van Scott remembers the excitement in the air when she first walked through the doors in the early 1950s. Van Scott had trained at the Graham School, where the Graham company dancers formed a tight circle apart from the students. In contrast, the Dunham dancers, when on break from their international tours, engaged with the students and encouraged them. Youngsters in the dressing room would keep practicing steps from the classes that had just ended, unwilling to let the excitement and infectious energy abate. Van Scott remembers feeling "things pulsating and vibrating and being *alive* . . . you are learning all of this history and anthropology and dancing your heart out until the point where the walls used to turn colors with people who really loved it and danced it. It was awesome."[109] Van Scott would go on to join the Dunham company, perform on Broadway, and earn a PhD degree.

Despite the excellent artistic and life training the school provided, it could not continue to function without proper funding or administration. Dunham spent a total of two months in New York City during the four years from 1949 to 1953, and the school fell down the list of her priorities. A final blow came when Dunham had a disagreement with Fort, the supervisor of the dance division and a beloved teacher. In January 1954, Fort opened a studio with her husband Buddy Phillips, one block away on 44th Street, and most students followed her.[110] The Dunham School closed one month later.

The Dunham School's influence in the dance world continued for decades after it closed. Its presence in the heart of Broadway's theater district had altered the geographic and symbolic space of the Great White Way. When Dunham had first offered "Negro" dance classes in 1930s Chicago, black parents had refused to send their children, seeing Africanist cultural practices as backward and shameful. By 1954, not only African American children, but also students from around the world took classes in Dunham Technique and African diasporic dance forms at the school as part of the foundation of a proper education in the art of dance. The school trained an entire generation of performers. Beatty, who taught at the school in its early years, filled the ranks of his company with Dunham School students.[111] Mitchell joined the New York City Ballet in 1955 as only the second African American company member. He co-founded the Dance Theatre of Harlem in 1969 with Shook, his former ballet teacher at the Dunham School. Destiné went on to run a world-renowned dance company. Countless others had successful careers on Broadway, in Hollywood films, and in dance companies across the country. The Dunham School's influence also extended beyond the dance world. Students who entered its doors received a message of racial equality and international peace built on cross-cultural understanding, which they took with them into all areas of their lives. Through the school, Dunham's contributions to fighting segregation, promoting racial tolerance, and advocating peaceful internationalism were integral to the civil rights movement during and immediately after World War II.

CHAPTER 6

The Unofficial Ambassador of Diaspora

Performing Abroad

On December 9, 1950, the curtains of the Santiago Municipal Theatre in Chile opened for the second act of Dunham's revue. Onstage, a chorus of black dancers stood in a bucolic Southern landscape. The world premiere of the dance drama *Southland* began with the chorus asking, rhetorically, "Is it true what they say about Dixie? Does the sun really shine all the time?"[1] Pratt's scenery, featuring a graceful plantation mansion and a giant magnolia tree, seemed to indicate that it did. The drama that unfolds onstage, however, soon troubles the idyllic setting. A white woman falsely accuses a black field hand of raping her, stirring up an imaginary mob of white townspeople, who hang the man from the magnolia tree. Mourners then carry the lynched body through a nightclub, where the black patrons respond with dances of violence, sorrow, and bewilderment.[2] Sandwiched between two acts of rather lighthearted fare, *Southland* stunned the Chilean audience and shocked even those who knew the choreographer well. For years, Dunham had insisted that she had "never gone into a direct social message."[3] Seemingly out of the blue, she had decided to premiere a dance drama about lynching.

Since leaving the United States three years earlier, Dunham had been struggling with a dilemma faced by almost all African Americans performing abroad during this time of decolonization: did she represent the United States, or did she represent people of African descent fighting for freedom? Dunham had always rejected such binary thinking, yet at no point did W. E. B. Du Bois's idea of "two-ness,—an American, a Negro; two souls, two thoughts, two unreconciled strivings"[4] resonate more strongly than during the company's international tours between 1947 and 1960. Although she considered herself a loyal American, as the Cold War deepened, Dunham felt increasingly dismayed by the United States' racism and jingoism, a dismay that ultimately resulted in *Southland*. At a time when the US government viewed any anti-racist activism as tantamount to Communist subversion,[5] Dunham's daring had consequences. The State Department took action to suppress *Southland* and refused her company funding and official support for several years. Unlike Josephine Baker, however, her shows in Latin America were not canceled; unlike W. E. B. Du Bois or Paul Robeson, her passport was not revoked.[6] She made strategic decisions that enabled her to keep touring, eventually reaching six continents. Denied the opportunity to represent the United States as an official goodwill ambassador, she created a role for herself as an unofficial ambassador of the African diaspora.

This ambassadorship came at a crucial historical moment. In the wake of World War II, Europe's empires began to crumble. New nations searched not only for new political arrangements, but also for new cultural identities, freed from Eurocentric hierarchies. Dunham's choreography was a cultural argument for the creation of a diasporic sensibility. Dances such as *Southland* and *Tango* (1954) explicitly condemned repressive and violent political regimes, but just as importantly, her seemingly banal dances, such as *Veracruzana* (1949) encouraged artists in decolonizing states to embrace their Africanist and indigenous cultures. When they were not performing, she and her dancers participated in *candomblé* rituals in Brazil, drumming circles with African immigrants in London, and social gatherings in Haiti, building solidarities across national boundaries. Onstage and off, Dunham contributed to the vision of a new world order that challenged both colonialist and cold warrior ideologies.

Dunham's initiation of cross-cultural exchanges began in April 1947 in Mexico, the company's first stop on its international odyssey. There was a growing interest in both modern dance and folk dance in Mexico, but no group like Dunham's that combined the two. The company performed to sold-out houses in the capital for seven months, receiving accolades from President Miguel Alemán Valdés and members of the press.[7] Her dancers offered classes to locals, who were inspired not only by Dunham's aesthetic, but also by her methodology of ethnographic research. One student, Ana Mérida, who had trained with modern dancers Anna Sokolow and Waldeen von Falkenstein, ended up performing with the Dunham company. A few months later, Mérida co-founded the Academia de la Danza Mexicana, which was dedicated to the "recovery, revalorization, and diffusion of Mexican artistic expression" while "linking tradition with new artistic currents."[8] The exchange went both ways. On a side trip to a coastal town in the state of Veracruz, Dunham convinced some of the local residents to teach her *bamba*, a social dance with distinct African influences. Dancer Vanoye Aikens remembers spending "weeks" learning folk dances from elderly Mexican men in Mexico City.[9] Dunham choreographed the dance *Veracruzana* based on this folk material, though of course reworked through her characteristic fusion aesthetic. It was a number that would stay in her repertory for most of her international touring career.

Like most of Dunham's dances, *Veracruzana* stuck to a fairly superficial plotline: an unwitting husband leaves for work, and his beautiful wife carries on an affair with a local cad. The politics lay in its presentation of disparaged and hidden Africanist cultural practices as high art. By intermingling the *bamba* with ballet and modern dance movements, Dunham offered a vision for concert dance that included Africanist aesthetics. She outfitted the piece with elaborate costumes (see Figure 6.1) and set pieces, signaling that her work

Figure 6.1 Katherine Dunham in *Veracruzana*, ca. 1949. Photograph by Studio Iris, Paris. Missouri History Museum, St. Louis.

had production values on par with any top theatrical presentation. Finally, by claiming the right to dance and sing the *bamba*, the predominantly black Dunham dancers reminded their audiences of the African presence in Mexico, a presence often suppressed or ignored.[10] Overall, *Veracruzana* affirmed both the modernity and humanity of people of African descent and transmitted that message to its audiences.

After Mexico, the Dunham company toured Europe, where dances such as *Veracruzana* captivated audiences all over the continent. The show's London manager gushed, "In my many years of show business I cannot recall any better notices for any London show premiere."[11] Several London critics compared the impact of the troupe to that of Diaghilev's Ballets Russes, and the *Chicago Daily News* reported, "La Dunham is sweeping Europe in a way that tops even Isadora Duncan."[12] The comparisons to the company that had revolutionized ballet and to the woman often considered the founder of modern dance implied that the Dunham company represented a watershed moment in dance history.

Dunham's success gave her entrée to Europe's intellectual and social elite. In London, she befriended David Astor, a member of the wealthy Astor family and publisher of *The Observer*.[13] In Paris, she had a love affair with Serge Tolstoy, grandson of the famed writer Leo Tolstoy, and through him met several members of European royalty. She danced the night away with playboy Prince Ali Khan (then married to Rita Hayworth), sparking rumors of a romantic liaison in the American press. Khan gave her a large diamond necklace that she would later pawn to keep the company financially afloat.[14] One baroness introduced Dunham to the acclaimed art historian Bernard Berenson, an American expatriate living in a villa, I Tatti, in Tuscany. Berenson, eighty-three, and Dunham, forty, began an intense love affair of the mind, sharing thoughts about art, culture, beauty, and the meaning of life. They felt aligned in their wish for a more humane world. Berenson and Dunham's written correspondence from 1948 to 1959 provided the basis for her unpublished memoirs, "Love Letters from I Tatti" and had a profound influence on her lifelong self-perception as belonging to an international elite, rather than to an American or black nationalist one.[15]

Dunham's work also resonated with ordinary Europeans. Gauging reception is a notoriously difficult task, but fan letters in her archives attest to the fact that at least some audience members understood that her aesthetic revolution had political implications. Antonio Sant'Angelo from Milan, Italy, wrote that the show was "certainly useful to attract all the sympathies and to raise in estimation for your race, according to a right and holy idea of justice."[16] After seeing *Caribbean Rhapsody*, A. Wolters of Amsterdam similarly wrote, "I hope you [are] fully aware of the great apostleship of your work. . . . Herewith you can tell the world of the beauty, the fairness, the nobleness of the coloured, especially of the negro soul."[17] While romanticized and racially stereotyped in their own way, such statements revealed an optimism that Dunham's embodied representations could challenge colonialist depictions of black bodies.[18]

Nowhere did the show's political implications resonate more strongly than in Paris, where Dunham opened on November 25, 1948. Paris was home to African and Caribbean intellectuals who in the 1930s had formulated the philosophy of *négritude*.[19] Césaire attributed a political and historical ethos to the term, in which *négritude* signified a shared reality of colonialism, enslavement, oppression, and resistance to those forces. Senghor adopted a more essentialist vision of *négritude* as an expression of the black soul. In 1939, he famously wrote, "emotion is Negro, as reason is Hellenic" in his essay "What the Black Man Contributes."[20] Senghor dreamed of a "civilization of the universal," a peaceful future to which all peoples contributed. Black Africans, he claimed, would contribute rhythm and a harmonious sense of being in the world to the *métissage* (mixture) of this new civilization. Not surprisingly, his ideas were met with a storm of criticism for reinforcing racial stereotypes.[21]

Dunham was the dancer and choreographer for whom *négritude* intellectuals had been waiting. Throughout the 1930s and 1940s, *négritude* had primarily found expression in written form. Senghor sometimes referenced sculpture and painting, but dance did not yet have a place in the *négritude* vision. The dominant representation of black dance in Paris was Josephine Baker, whose 1925 *Revue nègre* gave audiences a version of black vernacular dance based in the improvised, rhythmic aesthetic of jazz. Although recent scholarship suggests that Baker had more control over her choreography than she claimed publicly, for Paris audiences, her performances remained the essence of primitive spontaneity, a spontaneity that held out hope for "saving" European civilization from itself.[22] Her willingness to embrace ideas of the primitive savage did not fit the *négritude* vision.

But if these intellectuals did not welcome Baker, most Parisians idolized her. Given their tremendous love for the Black Venus, it is not surprising that the French public went wild for Dunham. After the November 1948 opening of *Rhapsodie Caraïbe*, reporters hid in the dancers' dressing rooms, hoping to snatch a quote or a photo. Dunham wrote to a friend, "I must get away as I am absolutely not equal to the demands of press and public. I have never seen such people in my life!"[23] When the company returned the following year, the opening night audience was a veritable Who's Who of Paris, including the ambassadors of the United States, Brazil, Mexico, Austria, and Haiti; intellectuals Georges Duhamel, Maurice Garçon, André Maurois, and Senghor; writers Andre Breton and Jean-Paul Sartre; painter Paul Colin, and dozens of other well-known actors, playwrights, composers, fashion designers, politicians, and "personalities," including several members of French royalty.[24]

Parisian critics saw Dunham's work as a sea change in black dance aesthetics, declaring that Baker had only shown the primitive side of black dance, whereas Dunham expertly fused the primitive with the sublime. René Dumesnil, dance critic for Le Monde, interpreted the Dunham aesthetic as a study in contrasts: "the sudden, hysterical, frenzied movements in appearance, but expertly controlled ... bestiality, yes, but so intelligent and directed that one admires it and surrenders to the sorcery."[25] Dinah Abragam of Le Combat, a left-leaning newspaper, similarly felt that Dunham's dancers "not only possess, in all their integrity, the ancestral instincts of their race, but also discipline these instincts in the service of the highest art ... and add to it technical achievement."[26] For these critics, Dunham combined the best of the primitive and the civilized, the instinctual and the technical, revolutionizing the art of dance in the process. Their interpretation of fusion rendered blackness eternally primitive, instinctual, ancestral, and even "bestial," needing Dunham's genius guiding hand to transform it an entity someplace between African and European, in a league all its own.

An important review in the journal Presence Africaine gives us a sense of how Dunham's work reverberated among the négritude thinkers. Founded in 1947 by Alioune Diop, the journal gave the négritude movement a "permanent voice to propagate its ideas."[27] Presence Africaine's editors refrained from taking an explicit anticolonial stance, preferring to focus instead on integrating "African originality" and cultural practices into Senghor's "civilization of the universal."[28] Paul Niger, a Paris-based poet and political activist originally from Guadaloupe, wrote the review of Dunham's Rhapsodie Caraïbe for the journal's sixth issue. It was the first article, or even substantive mention, of dance in Présence Africaine's brief history, and therefore set an important precedent for how embodied performance would be included in the project of building an African diaspora in the post–World War II era.

Niger's review walked the fine line between race pride and race essentialism. Like the white French critics, he claimed that Baker showcased only primitivism, whereas Dunham's performance offered a "real synthesis" of "classicism and negro dance, which has been agreed upon as purely physical, muscular and rhythmic." Niger's subtle choice of words—saying that black dance "has been agreed upon" rather than "is" purely physical and rhythmic—pointed to his unwillingness to fully stereotype black culture. Ultimately, however, he joined the chorus of voices that equated blackness with the healthy tonic of simplicity and pre-industrialism: "Katherine Dunham launches us towards new understanding for those who want to know or find the essential rhythm of the black man ... the deep rhythm of man stripped of the trappings of mechanistic materialism and the hectic pace of life."[29]

The recourse to racial essentialism continued in Niger's descriptions of the specific dances. He wrote that some numbers showcased the "simple beauty [and] rhythm" of the "pure state" of black people. One of these was Bahiana, which, he argued, revealed the joy and holistic integrity of a black community through the "great communion that gushes from the sweet music of muscle and movement." Other dances, such as *Blues*, set in urban Chicago, exposed the "crushed, deformed, [and] disfigured" lives of black people struggling to survive in a racist city, "with its ridiculousness, its meanness and despair."[30] Niger reinforced stereotypical notions of blackness for an important political end. His analysis clearly painted *Rhapsodie Caraïbe* as exposing the stark difference between black communities living in freedom and those living under white supremacy.

Niger also saw in *Rhapsodie Caraïbe* a utopian promise of diasporic harmony. The show, he argued, revealed "the profound unity of feelings, rhythms, and sources of the black soul." Importantly, this black soul was not purely African or Francophone. "We feel Africa and America intimately intertwined," wrote Niger. Dunham's "precise and cordial intelligence about the habits and history of the black race" constructed a new vision of diaspora "with a kind of love and pride." Her emphasis on the "Latinized negro," in particular, exposed the Francophone Africans in Paris to lesser-known areas of the diaspora.[31] Niger and the other editors of *Présence Africaine* sought proof of black unity across lines of language and nation, and Dunham's revue exhibited that unity.

As Niger's review indicated, Dunham's shows had an important impact on Africans living in Europe. In London, Ghanaian percussionists came onstage between matinee and evening performances to exchange rhythms with Dunham's Haitian, Brazilian, and Cuban drummers, building a diasporic cultural sensibility.[32] T. R. Makonnen, secretary of the Pan-African Federation in London, called Dunham's potent combination of artistry and intellect "perfection" and essential to the cause of promoting African culture around the world.[33] Senghor claimed that Dunham's *Rhapsodie Caraïbe* caused a "cultural revolution" among African students in Paris, who were awakened to the idea of using their own dance forms in the anticolonial struggle.[34]

And what did Dunham think about the interpretations of her work as a fusion of African rhythm and European refinement? In an interview with London's *Leader* magazine, in June 1948, she insisted that "dancing need not be racial." Instead, "a young Englishman could dance my way" if he had been "brought up to drum rhythms."[35] She stressed that aesthetic development was sociological, not biological, a departure from both *négritude* and the dominant European mentality. Later that year, she explained to a London radio program, "As an anthropologist, I became interested in taking things which look loose—abandoned—natural primitive movements—and presenting them as a technique as highly developed as Russian Ballet."[36] Dunham challenged the notion that "primitive" dance lacked technique. She put Caribbean dance on an equal level with the most classical of dance forms: ballet. She continued, "I felt that this feeling for fundamentals in mood and physical expression that the West Indians had, this correctness of function . . . could become useful in our own theatre."[37] Her dances represented a fusion sensibility, but not a fusion of low and high, primitive and civilized, or other such hierarchical distinctions, as the word "fusion" often implies. Instead, Africanist aesthetics of the Caribbean already contained within them an integrated coherence of emotion, thought, and physicality, which could provide the basis for a new approach to performance.

Dunham's dance *Afrique* (1949) also challenged existing conceptions about her fusion aesthetic. She choreographed the dance during the company's stay at a casino in Monte Carlo in early 1949, and it served as the opening number for virtually all of her revues between 1949 and 1960. She insisted that the dance had "authentic material" and "African movements" in it, even though she had not yet visited Africa when she choreographed it.[38] Although her drummers at least had engaged in cultural exchange with African musicians in London, the choreography suggests that *Afrique* was more of a diasporic pastiche, borne out of Dunham's ethnographic research in the Caribbean and her creativity.

The dance concerns a day in the life of an imaginary village somewhere in Africa, though the title indicates that it is in a French-speaking region, a place, as described in the program notes, where "The ladies are lovely / And the men are handsome and strong."[39] These lines simultaneously challenged depictions of Africa as a savage continent and reinforced the most clichéd of gender stereotypes. Programs a decade later, in 1959, say that the dance took place in the Congo.[40] The notes called the music a "Native Air" composed by her Spanish-speaking Cuban drummers, Julio Mendez and La Rosa Estrada. Eventually, the Portuguese-speaking Brazilian composer Bernardo Noriega orchestrated a score that included trumpet, piano, and other instruments.[41] Before the dancers even appeared on the stage, the overture signaled a cultural blending with only tenuous connections to Francophone Africa.

The eight-minute dance begins when a group of women enter downstage and mime scooping water into pots from an imaginary stream. Behind a bamboo curtain, a "witch-doctor," in a costume made entirely of straw, whirls in a circle. Three men enter, jumping, leaping, and turning in a virtuosic, masculine manner. Then the bamboo curtain lifts and "the lighting is full and bright—the setting is hot and sunny." Three women walk downstage, arms around each other's waists, doing head circles in unison to the right and left as someone sings, "lei-lei-lei-lei-lei-lei-lei," syllables not referring to any particular language. The women stop downstage left and gently swing their hips right and left as they sink to the ground and rise back up. Meanwhile, another group of women enter and dance in a circle to a *bamba* tune. Eventually, all seven women start dancing together. They keep a step-touch rhythm with their feet as they create swooping curves with their arms.[42]

Next, a trumpet signals the entrance of the queen (see Figure 6.2), from upstage left, seated on a platform carried by four men. She makes sinuous snakelike movements with her arms as the men bring her center stage. When she steps off the platform, she starts shaking her hips with subtle, small, rapid

Figure 6.2 Katherine Dunham in *Afrique*, ca. 1949. Photograph by Roger Wood, ArenaPAL Images. Jerome Robbins Dance Division, The New York Public Library for the Performing Arts, Astor, Lenox and Tilden Foundations.

movements, much like those made by a belly dancer, as the music hints at a North African or Middle Eastern sound. We are no longer in the Congo. The aesthetic quality of the queen's movements differs sharply from the larger-scale hip and full-body movements of the other female dancers. The men surround her and perform virtuosic jumps as she articulates her arms in a curving, S-shaped snake pattern. After another short solo, consisting mostly of arm and head movements, she walks elegantly back onto the platform and is carried offstage, after which the curtain closes.[43] The characters—women who carry pots, men who display warrior-like virility, a witch-doctor, and a queen—are generic archetypes.

Dunham offered one oblique explanation for the generic and stereotyped images, in a 1949 interview with R. Goupillières of Radiodiffusion Français. When Goupillières asked, "Why, since virtually all of your show takes place in the Caribbean or Latin America, have you included Africa [with *Afrique*]?" she responded, "In these islands, the blacks who were transported during the colonial period felt in times of joy or sorrow of the land of their ancestors, and that is why the opening of the show is titled 'Afrique.'"[44] The dance rendered an imagined ancestral home of Western Hemispheric black communities. Authenticity and specificity mattered little, for Dunham intended the audience to read the dance as the nostalgic imaginings of the people and communities depicted in the rest of the program, not as the literal ancient past. The dance could also be read as a call for diasporic unity. In 1959, programs noted that Dunham dedicated *Afrique* to "the free state of Ghana," a former British colony. The dance celebrated an idealized image of a unified Africa across linguistic or national boundaries.

Later in life, Dunham offered another interpretation for *Afrique*, one that virtually nobody comprehended in the late 1940s. Her production notes from the late 1970s stated, "There is a satirical intention."[45] Dunham went into further detail about what she meant by "satirical" in a 1987 interview with dance critic Jennifer Dunning. Her inspiration, she stated, came from watching what she considered mediocre performances that African choreographers staged for Parisian audiences during her first visit in 1948. These shows, she felt, lacked theatricality and flair. Rather than reproduce their earnest attempts at authenticity, she created *Afrique* "almost tongue-in-cheek."[46] Dunham insinuated that she intentionally invoked clichéd gender stereotypes and characters as a way to poke fun at her fellow choreographers and the thirst for authenticity among audiences. The satirical meaning was lost on the dancers. Van Scott, who joined the company for the 1959 European tour, "absolutely loved" performing *Afrique* and called it "magnificent." The choreography, she felt, encouraged synergy and connection among the dancers. Van Scott recalled, "It's not just I'm doing some step. That's not it. Your *soul* is involved in this. It was unreal."[47] For her, the meaning of *Afrique* lay in the world of black unity it created onstage.

Whether meant to portray an idealized diasporic world or to parody extant notions of "African" dance, *Afrique* faced several detractors after it premiered in Dunham's second iteration of *Rhapsodie Caraïbe* at the Théâtre de Paris on October 19, 1949. Dinah Maggie, *Le Combat*'s most important dance critic, declared that Dunham's "first mistake" was to choreograph new numbers like *Afrique*, because "she could certainly not draw new inspirations from her European tour."[48] Maggie and others had understood Dunham's fusion to be of authentic African movements with Western techniques; the fact that Dunham created a number set in Africa while at a casino in Monaco challenged that perspective.

Nor did all African audience members in Paris appreciate the liberties Dunham took with *Afrique*. Keita Fodéba was a law student from Guinea who had founded Le Théâtre Africain de Keita Fodéba in Paris in 1948. When asked in a radio interview in November 1949 (one month after *Afrique*'s premiere) if his troupe was similar to Dunham's, Fodéba responded, "No no no. Ours has nothing to do with Katherine Dunham ... it is absolutely authentic."[49] To differentiate himself, Fodéba emphasized his authentic Africanness. The repetition of "no" implies that he took great pains to distance himself from the theatrical nature of Dunham's revues. Ironically, it was Fodéba's very claim to absolute authenticity that she challenged through her *Afrique* satire. For her, diaspora necessarily required a creative reimagining of African aesthetics, but taking liberty with such aesthetics could be seen as anathema to the efforts of Fodéba and other African students, for whom the continent was not an imaginary homeland, but rather a real place.

Despite his public rejection of Dunham's aesthetic, Fodéba wrote her a letter only six weeks after the interview to ask for advice about directing a dance company.[50] Clearly, her show had made a strong impression, and not an entirely negative one. Two years later, Fodéba would change the name of his company from Le Théâtre Africain to Les Ballets Africains. In 1957, he would write an article in *Presence Africaine* in which he argued that it was impossible to have absolute authenticity in stage presentation.[51] His philosophy reflected a softening of opposition to her theatricalized visions. After Guinea achieved independence in 1958, Fodéba accepted president Sekou Touré's invitation to relocate the company to Conarky and become the National Ballet of Guinea.[52]

Dunham's renown in Paris also led to an important change in her private life: she and Pratt adopted a child. In December 1948, an unmarried Frenchwoman wrote to Dunham asking for money to help send her young daughter, Marie-Christine, to nursery school. Marie-Christine's father was black, and therefore the woman's family and friends had rejected her. She turned to Dunham because "my baby is of the same race of yours, and I know by many people that you are very kind."[53] Dunham invited the woman and Marie-Christine to visit her backstage. Over the next year, Dunham and Pratt became very emotionally attached to the child and asked to adopt her; Marie-Christine's mother, who loved her daughter deeply, faced an ultimatum from her new fiancé: him or her mixed-race daughter. In May 1950, the adoption was finalized.[54] Marie-Christine would spend her childhood shuttling between boarding school and accompanying her parents on tour.

Dunham's newfound stature among Europe's intellectual and political elite also gave her a voice in a broad public arena, and she used it to challenge racism. In November 1949, she told the Paris communist newspaper *L'Humanité* that in the United States, she and her company "suffer racial prejudice unceasingly. Tired and hungry, I have been turned out of a restaurant, a theater, with the advice that I look for an authorized establishment for 'my kind.'"[55] Dunham gave an interview to the Italian Communist newspaper *Unità* a few months later voicing similar criticisms.[56] The US State Department monitored her statements, but took no actions against her.[57] Instead, they feted her. US ambassadors invited her to cocktail parties in Paris, held teas in her honor in Rome, and threw soirées for the entire company in Stockholm. In Belgium, the American ambassador arranged a gala performance with the queen in attendance.[58] These demonstrations of public support, of course, served US interests by presenting American diplomats as enlightened nonracists who supported free speech.

Dunham also spoke out against nationalism. In March 1950, she issued a statement of support on the Italian radio for a man named Garry Davis, who had recently renounced his US citizenship to declare himself a "citizen of the world." She asserted that Davis was "a symbol of action for all people who feel that human beings have the right of equality."[59] She later mused privately to Berenson that she and Davis shared the desire to distance themselves from "this terrible thing that is happening to people's souls" in the United States, which was increasingly becoming defined by Cold War jingoism.[60] Dunham felt drawn to alternate modes of forming community. In her 1969 ethnographic memoir *Island Possessed*, she called it a "noir" sensibility, rooted in a feeling of solidarity with others of African descent but extending to people of color more broadly.[61] One could also describe this feeling as diasporic or even internationalist. Such a sentiment of resistance to the hegemonic Cold War order ran as the palpable undercurrent of her seemingly apolitical choreography.

In Latin America—where the company toured after leaving Europe in early 1950—Dunham transformed her spoken resistance into more explicit and dramatic action, most notably with the premiere of her anti-lynching dance drama, *Southland*, in Chile. In 1980, Dunham wrote that the inspiration for *Southland* came from the murder of Emmett Till, a tragedy now considered a major catalyst in the "classic" phase of the civil rights movement.[62] In the 1987 interview with Dunning, Dunham repeated that Till's violent end in August 1955 weighed upon her until she found a way to channel those emotions into choreographing the dance drama.[63] Yet the dance's premiere in December 1950 occurred five years *before* the teenager's death.

Instead, Dunham's impetus for *Southland* emerged out of her left-leaning roots in the New Negro and Popular Front movements, roots that she and others downplayed during the Cold War. During the height of agitation-propaganda work in the late 1930s, she had choreographed *Swamp*, a dance about lynching, but let it disappear from her repertoire.[64] Constance Valis Hill reports that Dunham had researched records of lynching at the Tuskegee Institute, which she would have only had the chance to do before leaving the country in 1947.[65] Thus the theme had been swirling in her mind for years. Why, then, did it finally appear onstage at the end of 1950, long after the trend of performing agitation-propaganda choreography had dissipated? Throughout her career, Dunham had drawn explicit connections between racism at home and racial oppression abroad. It is thus no accident that the immediate catalyst for *Southland*'s creation was not an experience with discrimination in the United States, but in Brazil.

In July 1950, the Dunham company reached São Paolo, the first stop on its Latin American tour. Upon her arrival, Dunham discovered that her reservation at the city's leading hotel—the Esplanada—had been canceled. When Pratt went to find out why, the hotel manager told him that they did not accept black guests. Dunham decided to file a lawsuit and called Gilberto Freyre, the esteemed scholar of Brazilian race relations whose work she considered influential to her own thoughts about race.[66] Freyre gave Dunham the name of a trusted lawyer and assured her that he would help publicize her fight against the hotel. Within forty-eight hours, the incident made front-page headlines in all of Brazil's major newspapers, and the residents of São Paolo protested in the streets.[67] The news traveled to North America, where *Time*, the *New York Times*, and several major African American newspapers reported on the events.[68] Freyre, also a member of Brazil's Chamber of Deputies, co-sponsored a bill that made it a penal offense to discriminate on the basis of race. Brazil's legislature passed Law No. 1390 against racial discrimination within a year.[69] Many Brazilians at the time prided themselves on their country's supposed lack of racial discrimination, but the Esplanada's treatment of Dunham shattered that myth. Through her lawsuit, she demonstrated solidarity with black people in Brazil and gave legitimacy to the Afro-Brazilians who had already begun to realize that the color-blind nationalist rhetoric rang false.

After São Paolo, the company went to Rio de Janeiro, where Dunham explored the favelas, or slums, where many of the city's black residents lived. She described in a letter to Berenson the pools of human and animal feces in which children played, the shock of constantly seeing men fondling their genitals in public or passed out drunk, and the generally decrepit state of the favelas.[70] Dunham later wrote in her memoirs that the simmering potential for violence in Rio reminded her of the situation among the urban black poor of the United States.[71] She also instructed Berenson to read Freyre—the scholar who had sponsored the antidiscrimination law—because he offered "some explanation" for the degradation she described in her letter.[72] In his book *The Masters and the Slaves*, Freyre wrote that "what appears to be the influence of race is purely and simply that of the slave, of the social system of slavery."[73] He argued that sexual excess, violence, and ignorance in Brazilian slums came not from the residents' race, but rather from the conditions of slavery that affected Brazil's social structure to the present day. Such reasoning fit Dunham's sociological understanding of human behavior and would become the underlying thesis of the second act of *Southland*.

Dunham's experiences in Brazil, therefore, were the tipping point toward taking a more explicit stance choreographically. On the next tour stop, in Argentina, she began to create and rehearse *Southland*. She was always a strategic activist, taking risks from positions of relative security. For the past three years, she had received positive audience response and backing from national governments in Europe and South America. Argentina's president Juan

Perón and his powerful wife, Evita, enthusiastically supported the company, though a competition developed between Evita and Dunham in the glamour department (see Figure 6.3).[74] She was also more financially stable, for she had received a commission from the National Symphony in Chile to create a new work. She now had the money to hire an Argentine composer, Dino di Stefano, who wrote a score that combined Southern African American songs with European symphonic music.[75] Dunham decided to premiere *Southland* during the next tour stop, Santiago de Chile.

Dunham waited until the last days of the Santiago run to stage the dance drama, building up audience and press enthusiasm for the company's work first. The company received glowing reviews after opening night, on November 24, 1950, with critics writing, "without doubt, [it is] the most original, novel, and attractive show that the Chilean public has seen in years."[76] On December 5, the newspaper *El Mercurio* ran a startling announcement: Dunham would premiere a new dance the following afternoon, described only by the tantalizing quote: "The person who truly loves his country is equally capable of seeing the good and the bad in it, and upon discovering the bad, should denounce it at the cost of his liberty and life."[77] The dramatic statement, in which Dunham expressed a willingness to die for the cause of protesting injustice, alerted readers to the high stakes of this performance. She also carefully positioned

Figure 6.3 Katherine Dunham with Evita and Juan Perón in Argentina, 1950. Photograph taken by the Subsecretaria de Informaciones, Dirección general de prensa, division fotografía, Argentina. Missouri History Museum, St. Louis.

herself as a patriot to dampen the accusations of anti-Americanism that would likely erupt.

And erupt they did, as Dunham had landed herself in the combustible matrix of Cold War politics and civil rights. Instead of performing *Southland* the next day as promised, Dunham delayed the premiere by three days. While the newspapers reported that "technical difficulties" had caused the change,[78] more likely the US embassy's reaction put a halt to the proceedings. According to a cable, sent December 12, 1950, from the embassy to the State Department, Assistant Cultural Affairs Officer Richard Cushing called Dunham and Pratt to a meeting on December 6 upon hearing about *Southland*. In the meeting, Cushing pressured them to take the dance drama off the program, arguing that it "clearly follows communist line propaganda and serves to create ill feeling toward the United States." Dunham tried to persuade him that she desired to make American democracy stronger, not undermine it, explaining, "[I am] really interested in a solution of the problem and this is my way to do it." A State Department official questioned Dunham's logic, scribbling in the margins of the embassy cable, "What are South Americans to do about [lynching]?"[79]

Why, indeed, had Dunham decided to present her solution to America's racial violence problem in Chile, rather than in the United States? Her reasoning, she told Cushing, was that the piece happened to be ready and she felt the compelling artistic urge to go forward.[80] Yet Dunham also made a political and personal choice. She knew that racial discrimination and Cold War politics were entwined globally. In Europe, the left-wing press had taken a great interest in her views on racial discrimination. In Brazil, her experiences fighting discrimination had made national headlines in the United States. Her stance in Chile against lynching, she probably reasoned, would have repercussions beyond South America. Also, lynching in a sense was not the sole subject. It was a dramatic way to tell a broader story about racial violence and its effects, a story that would resonate across cultures.

Because Dunham performed under a private contract, rather than with government sponsorship, the US embassy could not cancel the concert. Taking extralegal measures to stop the ballet would likely have generated even greater anti-American propaganda, especially since the Chilean newspapers continued to build anticipation for the work.[81] On December 9, the second-to-last night of the company's run, American diplomats, with full foreknowledge of what was about to appear onstage, sat uncomfortably in the audience next to Chileans. Dunham read a prologue in which she stated that *Southland* did not represent all of America, or even the entire South. Lynching, however, was still a real problem, and thus she felt obligated to speak out about it. Then the dance drama unfolded in the darkened hall, causing tears and shock among audience members.[82]

No original film of the performance exists, but tapes from a 1981 rehearsal of Dunham teaching *Southland* to her students in East St. Louis give a sense of the choreography. In the first scene, a group of male field hands enter, dragging imaginary burlap sacks of cotton. The field hands reach center stage, stop, jump over their bags into a perfect ballet second position, execute double pirouettes, and launch into a Charleston. They continue performing high-energy, technically difficult movements such as hitch-kicks, leaps, and turns. Next, a group of women enter from stage left to form a circle with the men in preparation for a square dance. They perform Southern African American vernacular steps, such as the Palmerhouse, Patting Juba, Pas Mala, and Falling Off a Log. The scene of the black couples dancing together suggests a happy world, insulated from white society. As the music shifts, all the couples drift offstage except for one pair, who begin a romantic, balletic pas de deux with several lifts, leg extensions with pointed feet, and intertwined limbs.[83]

These dances appeared in Dunham revues of the 1940s as part of the *Plantation and Minstrel Dances*, in which the black social world remained jubilant and self-contained. In *Southland*, however, the scene quickly darkens with the intrusion of a white couple who tumble out from under the magnolia tree. In Chile, Julie Robinson, the only white dancer in Dunham's company, played the female role, and Lenwood Morris, a light-skinned African American dancer, donned whiteface and a red wig to play the male character.[84] The couple's lovemaking quickly turns into abuse. The man, thinking that his lover is making fun of his sexual shortcomings, beats her unconscious and flees. A black field hand enters and instinctively reaches out to see if the battered woman needs help. She awakes at his touch. Feeling shame and anger, she points a finger at him and shouts, "Nigger!" This one word hangs in the air, a portent of the hanging to come.

The rape accusation stirs up an imaginary mass of white townspeople. As a symbol of unseen mob's growing anger, the white woman dances a habanera, a sensuous Cuban dance done to a syncopated rhythm, often vocalized as "*Da*, ka *ka* kan, *da*, ka *ka* kan."[85] W. C. Handy referred to the habanera as "the call of the blood," a description that suggests the irresistible, even primal, pull forward in the scene's action toward its violent conclusion.[86] She finishes her solo by wrapping her hair around her neck like a noose, pulling herself up as high on her toes as possible (see Figure 6.4). The mob heeds her embodied suggestion. At the end of the scene, the field hand swings down from the tree, hanging from his neck by a rope, as a vocalist sings "Strange Fruit." Dunham knew, from Billie Holiday's success, that this song had a powerful impact on listeners.[87] Even if the Chilean audience members did not understand the English lyrics, the embassy officials certainly did.

The second scene, "Basin Street Blues," takes place in a nightclub, the setting for several Dunham dances, including *Barrelhouse* (1939). Again, the context of *Southland* creates a mood different from that of her other nightclub

Figure 6.4 Julie Robinson in *Southland*, 1953. Photographer unknown. Courtesy of Julie Robinson Belafonte, from her personal collection.

dances, which often include moments of humor. In *Southland*, no comedy offsets the tragedy. As the lights come up, a blind beggar—an allusion to Tiresias, the sightless prophet of ancient Greek myth—enters the café. The dancers sit around, listlessly, waiting for something to happen. Soon, the chorus enters carrying the shrouded corpse of the lynched field hand. The dancers react viscerally: a woman bursts into tears, a man stabs a knife violently into the floor, a couple clings to each other in a slow grind, and another pair stumbles awkwardly. Only the blind beggar, Dunham later wrote, "sees the true fact" of what the lynching represents, for "the rest feel but cannot define" how this violence has affected them.[88] The scene showcased the ramifications of racial violence for a community, whether that was a small town in the United States or a favela in Brazil.

Cushing demanded another meeting after the performance and accused Dunham of anti-Americanism. He brought up two additional issues to buttress his claim. First, the Chilean communist newspaper *Democracia* had recently reported that she had signed the Stockholm Appeal, a communist document, a charge she denied.[89] Cushing then read a quote attributed to her in Santiago's *Pro Arte* newspaper: "The American is a simple, unaffected man in a country dominated by a sort of dangerous infantilism, made more dangerous by a devilish power of the dollar ... He is only interested in what glitters."[90] Dunham used similar language to criticize American capitalism in private letters to Berenson, but she insisted to Cushing that the journalist had misrepresented her ideas to write an article filled with "hysteria and raceism [*sic*]."[91]

The embassy took action to blunt *Southland*'s impact. The cable to Washington stated, "Santiago newspapers have carried laudatory stories about the two-week Dunham engagement, but failed to make specific mention about 'Southland.'"[92] The comment was blatantly untrue. Prior to the premiere of *Southland*, all of Santiago's newspapers had prominently discussed the dance. On December 10, the day after its premiere, no paper mentioned it.[93] Clearly, someone from the embassy had sent the press an explicit message not to report on it further, for such an anticipated work would normally have received some response. A Communist journalist met secretly with Dunham to confirm that indeed, the embassy had censored newspaper mentions of *Southland*.[94]

Experiencing the embassy's power to affect publicity, Dunham agreed to let the United States Information Service (USIS) publish refutations of her purportedly pro-Communist actions in Santiago's three major newspapers. In them, Dunham denied that she had signed the Stockholm Appeal, condemned the *Pro Arte* article, and softened her stance on *Southland*. The concluding paragraph read, "She would like to explain that this thing [lynching] isn't common in the United States, that it occurs very rarely, and that it has diminished considerably over the course of time."[95] Ironically, the American embassy undermined its own censorship by discussing the dance drama prominently in the local newspapers. Even publicity aimed at damage control extended the life of *Southland* beyond its two performances.

The attempts to suppress the dance spread beyond Chile. The cable recommended direct action "toward elimination of the dance from Dunham's repertoire," and copies were sent to eleven other US embassies in Latin America.[96] For the rest of the Latin American tour, however, the US embassies did not need to exert pressure; Dunham removed *Southland* from the repertoire on her own. She knew any other course would affect not only her own career, but also the livelihood of her dancers, musicians, singers, and staff members on her payroll. The company that she had spent decades building could crumble if it were denied international touring opportunities. Apparently, Dunham also stopped giving interviews to communist newspapers.[97] She never again mentioned the Stockholm Appeal, the *Pro Arte* article, or her USIS-published retractions at any point in her life. Instead, Dunham's January 24, 1951 letter to Berenson compared her experiences in Argentina to those in her current tour stop of Lima, Peru, as if the three weeks in Chile had never happened.[98] She dedicated only one sentence to Chile in her 1980 memoirs: "Our next stop [on our Latin American tour] was Santiago in Chile of which I remember little."[99] She had no desire to give anyone a reason to conflate her danced protest with Communist Party activism. Only in 1987, when Alvin Ailey's decision to stage an evening of Dunham's choreography revived public interest in her career, did she begin to talk more openly about *Southland*. Even then, she omitted most of the details about the events surrounding the performance in Chile, focusing instead on the 1953 performance in Paris.[100]

Despite the hostility she faced in Chile and a cold shoulder she received from the American embassy in Argentina during a vacation there, the rest of the US embassies in Latin America embraced Dunham. After all, she was one of the only cultural weapons the United States had on the continent to fight Communist claims about America's racism and cultural vacuity. Before Dwight D. Eisenhower established the President's Special Emergency Fund in 1954, no formal funding mechanism existed for sending artists abroad. The federal government did support some cultural tours in the 1940s and early 1950s, but mostly to Western Europe.[101] In Lima, Peru, the company's next tour stop, the US embassy's public affairs officer ensured that all its interactions with Dunham served "to discredit propaganda emanating from certain quarters here about racial discrimination in the United States."[102] He arranged for the ambassador and several embassy officers and their wives to sit in public boxes at the opening-night performance. The public affairs officer hosted a reception for the company at his home, as did the ambassador and a cultural assistant. The US embassy in Haiti also showed no reservation in accepting Dunham when she and the company arrived a few months later. The ambassador assisted her with publicity and ticket sales, and invited the company to a reception at the embassy on July 4 (see Figure 6.5). The embassy's public affairs officer wrote a positive report to the State Department, stating that "Dunham's visit had a good effect on American-Haitian relations, and she received outstanding personal recognition and attention."[103] The ambassador told Dunham's stepmother, Annette, that the company "had done more to bring people together than any person or thing had done during his residence here," as people across Haiti's color spectrum attended her shows and mingled at the after-parties.[104]

Figure 6.5 Katherine Dunham with a US diplomat and a Haitian senator at a US embassy party in Port-au-Prince, July 4, 1951. Photographer unknown. Missouri History Museum, St. Louis.

Just as importantly, the embassies' political need to support Dunham meant that she was able to continue the diasporic ambassadorship that she had initiated with African leaders in Europe. The Lima officer reported that her company participated in cultural exchange with local Afro-Peruvian dancers and musicians, including Rosita Ríos, the "matriarch of the local negro community."[105] Seeing Dunham's show directly inspired siblings Victoria and Nicomedes Santa Cruz to lead an "Afro-Peruvian" arts movement. Previously, black Peruvians had not identified themselves as part of an African diaspora. Nicomedes asserted that Dunham's 1951 show in Lima was "the first positive publicly staged demonstration of blackness in Peru." Inspired by Dunham's ethnographic methods, he and his sister began to research Afro-Peruvian folklore as the basis for new choreography that resulted in "an unprecedented public staging of blackness that emphasized racial difference and Black pride."[106] Rex Nettleford wrote that seeing her company perform in Kingston, Jamaica as a teenager in 1951 had a significant impact on him. It reaffirmed that "the likes of us had something to say for ourselves in our music and our dance."[107] Eleven years later, he founded the National Dance Theatre Company of Jamaica. Like other Caribbean nations following World War II, Jamaica desired both modernization and greater independence from European colonial domination.[108] The Dunham company epitomized the combination of the two and thus legitimized Nettleford's aspirations. In Haiti, in 1951, President Magloire was so impressed with the company's performances that he began the process of founding the Haitian Academy of Folklore and Classic Dance.[109]

Although State Department support rested on the unspoken assumption that *Southland* would not reappear, Dunham decided to mount it again during her return European tour. In January 1952, she had learned she had achieved her life-long dream of becoming pregnant, though "there was not the remotest possibility" that Pratt was the father. She fretted about revealing her infidelity, but Pratt welcomed the news with joy. His reaction, Dunham stated, was the "sort of shining beauty of spirit that has kept us together."[110] The joy was short-lived, for she miscarried in London. She blamed the miscarriage on the economic need to maintain a heavy performing schedule, but the fact that she was forty-three with a history of infertility probably had much to do with the pregnancy's failure. In a testament to her "the show must go on" mentality, born from economic insecurity, Dunham was relieved to find out that King George V had died the same day as her unborn child—thus closing London's theaters for three days and giving her time to recover in the hospital without missing a performance.[111] Despite the tremendous personal loss, Dunham told Berenson that the experience of being pregnant gave her the "supreme satisfaction" that she could "exist apart from this institution [the company]."[112] Perhaps this knowledge gave her the courage to mount *Southland* once again. Taking a risk that could result in the company's downfall seemed less devastating than before.

A few months later, an upsetting experience in Italy further motivated Dunham to revive *Southland*. The American military had established bases along the coast of Italy after World War II, bases that remain operational in the twenty-first century. In a letter to Berenson, Dunham called the outposts a "plague of American occupation," whose inhabitants spread insidious ideas about racial inferiority. She felt "especially enraged" when a sailor from South Carolina insulted one of the men of the company and wrote, "I feel an impulse to keep *some* part free from the plague."[113] As dancer Robinson later stated, Dunham and the company were relatively naïve about racism that existed in Europe, instead seeing the United States as the primary source.[114] Dunham told Berenson, "I plan to do our ballet *Southland*" because "part of my feeling of incapacity and creative immobility comes from not saying what I want to say."[115]

Given what had happened in Chile, Dunham pre-emptively approached the US embassy in Paris to discuss the dance drama. She later offered two different versions of what happened. In a letter to Berenson, dated February 1, 1953, Dunham wrote that the cultural attaché had "very warmly recommended that I have no reserve[ation]s."[116] When she had gone to Berenson's Tuscan villa to discuss *Southland* a month earlier, he had heartily disapproved of the dance, warning, "All of the communists in Western Europe will take it up ... A mad resentment will be roused against you in the United States. It may end by driving you to seek refuge in Russia."[117] His disapprobation had caused her to weep the entire way back to Florence. Perhaps to win back his approval, she insisted in this February letter that the American government was on board.[118] In an interview with Constance Valis Hill in 1993 about the same meeting, Dunham presented herself as a strong-willed activist who defied political repression. She recalled that the attaché told her, "We know that you wouldn't do anything to upset the American position in the rest of the world," intimating that she should not perform the piece. She added, "He wouldn't go any farther. So I did it."[119] In this later account, Dunham resisted the attaché's clear insinuation that she should not perform *Southland*.

Whether Dunham received an explicit green light or not, on January 9, 1953, *Southland* opened in Paris. While the choreography remained the same as before, Dunham made an important change to the framing. In Santiago, the spoken prologue had focused exclusively on America's lynching problem. In Paris, by contrast, it stated: "'Southland' is a comment on violence and its attendant guilt ... The ballet is directed ... toward the conscience not of one nation, but of all human beings who are not yet aware of the destructive dangers of hatred."[120] Dunham knew her audience. In Paris, debates over colonialism were at the forefront of the public discussion. Making a connection between lynching in the United States and racial violence against African colonial subjects (though she couched such a connection in more generic language) gave the dance drama even greater resonance. Robinson's friend Nazir, who was Pakistani, wrote her that it was "a very opportune moment for such a performance, as the French repression in Tunis and Morocco is at its peak."[121]

Virtually every French newspaper wrote a review of *Southland*, and news of the performances spread to Germany and the United States.[122] The dance drama received mixed responses, with some critics wishing Dunham would return to her lighthearted *Rhapsodie Caraïbe* days and others commending her courage and artistry.[123] The American embassy offered no comment. Even though the performance generated tremendous publicity without causing any official blowback, Dunham removed *Southland* from the program after six weeks. As she and her former dancers told Hill in 1993, its emotional toll was too great.[124] *Southland* disrupted the interracial solidarity between Robinson, the company's sole white dancer, and the others. Robinson was inseparable from her fellow dancers Dolores Harper, Jacqueline Walcott, and Frances Taylor. The four women were collectively known as "The Sadies."[125] In *Southland*, though, Dunham forced Robinson to shout "Nigger!" and instigate the lynching of an innocent black man. One night after rehearsal in Argentina, Robinson overheard Harper saying to the other Sadies, "Nobody would say [nigger] that way if they didn't really mean it."[126] Robinson burst into tears and fled to the lobby of the hotel, where dancer Lenwood Morris consoled her and urged her to fulfill her artistic duty to perform the role.[127] Robinson and the Sadies reconciled quickly, but the specter of racism had indelibly strained the familial bonds of the company.

Regardless of her dancers' distress, Dunham felt positive about performing *Southland* in Paris. She wrote to Berenson in February 1953, "I know also that this has done more good for the American government than perhaps even they know .... It has proven to the world ... that freedom of speech still remains one of our basic principles."[128] Dunham may have been correct in surmising that the American cultural attaché in Paris was sympathetic to her cause; Washington, however, did not view *Southland* as good diplomacy. Three weeks into the Paris run of *Southland*, the State Department made an inquiry with the FBI, which suggests that it was seeking ways to discredit her. The FBI responded, "No investigation has been conducted by the FBI concerning Katherine Dunham," and merely mentioned a few ties she had to Communist Front organizations in the 1940s.[129] Although the FBI had spoken to her in connection to Durant and tracked activities at the Dunham School, apparently such efforts did not merit official status of a full investigation. The State Department's query seemed to stop there. They would not persecute Dunham, but official support would no longer be as readily forthcoming.

Even without *Southland*, Dunham's repertoire continued to animate and inspire audiences in Latin America in 1954; Mexico in 1955; Asia, Australia, and the Pacific Islands from 1956 to 1958; and Europe from 1959 to 1960. The Dunham company's success occurred as opposition to Cold War politics increased, conditioning a receptive audience to her vision. In 1955, representatives from twenty-nine Asian and African nations met in Bandung, Indonesia. Bound together by the common experience of colonialism, these representatives called for decolonization and the formation of economic and political alignments among the countries represented at the conference. They sought a new world order apart from the bipolar dominance of the United States or the USSR.[130] Such a new world order required new thinking about culture. In 1956, *Presence Africaine* sponsored the International Conference of Thinkers and Writers in Paris to insist upon the "centrality of the cultural" in the debates over how to create independent nations, since "after all, economic debates often relied on cultural stereotypes that needed to be expunged."[131] In 1957, Ghana achieved independence from Great Britain. New president Kwame Nkrumah called for the liberation of the entire continent and the creation of a pan-African solidarity based on an "African personality," in other words, complete liberation from white supremacist ideas about race and culture.[132]

Dunham's shows provided a model for the transnational alliances that these leaders wished to see in the world, and for a much wider audience than those present at international conferences. After all, the cost of admission to a theater was cheaper than a plane ticket to Paris or Bandung. At the same time, the working masses were not a part of Dunham's social circles or her audiences. Tickets were affordable for middle classes, but they were too expensive for the working poor. She still operated in a realm in which highly educated thinkers, artists, and politicians saw themselves as determining the future. In 1959, Sarah Maldoror wrote on behalf of the Patronage Committee of the Théâtre Populaire Africain that they "were extremely happy" to attend Dunham's revue once again in Paris and that "we hope that one day, within the domain of theatre, we will attain the high quality of your show." Maldoror then invited her to join the committee, which included well-known intellectuals and artists from throughout the diaspora, including Fodéba, Senghor, Césaire, Nicolás Guillén, and Richard Wright.[133] Dunham was seen as one of the cosmopolitan elites who could forge cultural unity in the post–World War II period.

Dunham's piece *Tango*, performed in 1954 in Argentina, reveals the complexity of her class allegiances. Dunham thought of *Tango* as a protest dance against political repression. In the years since the company's performances in Buenos Aires in 1950, her Argentine friend Pepita Cano had died after falling from a balcony. Dunham suspected foul play by the Peronist government, even though Cano was a society woman with few political interests. Dunham acknowledged that the anti-Peronist "aristocracy" formed her social circle in Buenos Aires, and the stories of Cano's death came from them.[134] During her return visit in 1954, she not only felt frustrated and saddened by the loss of her friend, but also sensed growing tension, restlessness, and potential for violence in the streets of Buenos Aires. She decided to express this mood choreographically in *Tango*.

The dance interweaves Osvaldo Pugliese's classic tango music with ominous beats of a military drum. The number opens with side booms shining directly on Dunham's face, "dramatically set in an unforgiving expression of anger" (see Figure 6.6). Wearing all black, and placed against a dark brown backdrop, she and a male partner dance a "hard" tango, with hands slapping shoes and heels stomping. The man "hits her with his knee so that she opens hers" and while such a gesture suggests "sexual motivation," it also "refer[s]

Figure 6.6 Katherine Dunham in *Tango*, 1954. Photographer unknown. Missouri History Museum, St. Louis.

to the clashing of two people ideologically." The piece "ends on a harsh, sharp note of defiance" against the Perón government.[135]

According to Dunham, Argentines appreciated her anti-Peronist gesture. When the curtains closed on *Tango* on opening night, the audience gave the company a massive standing ovation.[136] Research by Eugenia Cadús, however, reveals that most Argentines did not interpret *Tango* as a protest against Perón, but rather as the opposite: "an affirmation of Peronism's values."[137] Perón embraced the democratization of culture and celebrated the working masses. In that vein, Dunham staged the tango, a popular social dance originally created by Afro-Argentines and immigrants, as high art. She dressed the male dancers in open shirts, characteristic of the descamisados, the working masses who supported Peronism. One Argentine reviewer wrote that "the popular nature of Katherine Dunham means liberation."[138] Ironically, Dunham's dance did create solidarity with the Argentine people—just not for the reasons she envisioned.

Despite the Dunham company's continued success, like many (if not all) dance companies, it was facing financial problems. The costs of transporting sets, costumes, dancers, and other personnel across international borders mounted. Difficulties in converting currency and fighting double taxation exacerbated the money woes.[139] In 1954, a potential source of financial support came in the form of the President's Special Emergency Fund, a government program sponsoring American artists abroad as cultural ambassadors. Because the State Department lacked artistic expertise, advisory panels in dance, music, and drama were formed under the auspices of the American National Theatre and Academy (ANTA) to consider applications and send recommendations to the State Department. Dunham's company never received a Special Emergency Fund grant, even though she herself would receive one as an individual in 1965.

Dunham asserted that *Southland* was the sole reason her company did not get funding from the State Department, but other issues also contributed. First, she struggled to find the time to submit an application. In September 1955, the dance panel minutes note, "We should try to approach [Dunham] again," suggesting that they had reached out to her and received no response.[140] As the artistic director, sole choreographer, lead dancer, and business manager of a large company, Dunham had no time or energy to do what she admitted in 1956 to a friend was necessary: "We could arrange quite easily for a certain amount of subsidy through the State Department. These things have to be worked on . . . I honestly have not had time to make up the proper letters for such subsidy."[141] As another friend pointed out two years later in 1958, "I don't think that you can honestly say that you have either cultivated or worked at any of kind [sic] of friendliness to the press or to the State . . . You have identified yourself as an European artist for the past ten years."[142] Her failure to apply to the dance panel for several years and her refusal to play the political game largely precluded her ability to receive sponsorship for the first four years of the fund.

When Dunham finally communicated with the panel in 1958 to request sponsorship, the concerns the panel raised were not about her politics. Instead, they questioned her artistry. Research by Clare Croft and Penny Von Eschen has shown that racialized assumptions about what constituted high art stood in Dunham's way. During the Cold War, the United States aggressively sought to present itself as the nation most capable of leading the modern world. The State Department, guided by the dance panel, sponsored artists like Martha Graham whose work fit its particular idea of modernism. As Croft has argued, the "key" to mid-twentieth-century American modernism was abstraction, art that was seemingly universal and stripped of specific cultural referents. Because such abstract universalism simultaneously registered as American, the United States could proclaim that its culture—and thus, its political system, economic system, and hegemony over the rest of the globe—was good for everyone.[143]

Dunham refused to cede the terrains of universalism or modernity to white America. As she had written in 1941, "Every person who has a germ of artistry seeks to recreate and present an impression of universal human experience."[144] She communicated her version of universalism through culturally specific practices most often rooted outside of the United States. Her choreography, titles, costumes, sets, and music explicitly referenced other locations in the African diaspora. Even the bodies that constituted the company did not conform to a nationalist vision. A full 50 percent of her dancers, singers, and musicians were not US citizens.[145] As she had said in her 1948 interview in London, the Caribbean was the source of her aesthetic modernism. She challenged America's perception of itself as the modernist vanguard and of its white citizens as the only ones capable of representing universal human experience. The panel questioned whether Dunham's diasporic vision could adequately represent the United States. One member complained that her work was "not typical" of the "American scene," and thus should not receive sponsorship.[146]

Despite the panel's concerns, and Dunham's refusal to adhere to a narrow vision of Americanism, panel members finally did conclude that she was a "great American artist" and at their May 1959 meeting, approved her for a tour of Africa.[147] The State Department, however, never finalized the tour. Its obstinate refusal to support Dunham caused conflict with American foreign service members throughout the 1950s, who wanted to use Dunham's popularity to increase pro-American sentiment. In 1956, the US embassy in Canberra, Australia, observing Dunham's success, had begged the State Department to fund the company on a tour throughout Southeast Asia. The State Department rejected Canberra's request for money, stating, "During 1940's Dunham affiliated with certain organizations later listed by [HUAC] . . . no record since then . . . . Reports received from field uniformly [sic] excellent . . . it is suggested Embassy, in discretion give nominal endorsement and extend appropriate courtesies."[148] Saying that Dunham had "no record" since the 1940s and that the reports from the field were unilaterally "excellent" was strange because her performances of *Southland* had set off alarm bells across South America in 1950 and prompted the State Department to initiate a query with the FBI in 1953. The State Department's final recommendation to provide "nominal" support suggests that the memory of *Southland* did linger. Despite acknowledging that Dunham was an excellent artist, the State Department may have feared that she would again speak her mind about racial discrimination. Official backing would thus imply the US government's tacit agreement with her political views.

They need not have worried. Dunham's public statements about American racism had softened since her interviews with communist newspapers in 1950. When a Singapore newspaper in 1957 asked for her opinion on the civil rights movement in the United States, she replied, "In the North there is no resentment . . . . But in the South, responsible for the importation of the Negro as a slave, it is a guilt complex . . . . There are only a few diehards who want to start another civil war . . . . I do not believe this agitation will last more than a couple of years."[149] By declaring that racism was a psychological problem relegated to an aberrant few in a specific geographic region, Dunham reaffirmed the US propaganda that racism was not institutionalized in the nation's political and economic systems. Such adherence to the party line ensured that the State Department would not take steps to shut down her tours.

Even with Dunham's more moderate stance, the State Department held firm against granting her funding. In May 1960, the US embassy in Vienna reported that Dunham's show was an "unqualified critical success" but that attendance was moderate because of "inadequate promotion" on the part of American officials. The situation was "potentially embarrassing," given that Dunham was an "articulate and positive exponent [of the] position of Negroes in American Life" who therefore deserved official support. The embassy suggested that that the "Department explore possibility [of] Emergency President Fund assistance."[150] The State Department stood firm, replying, "Dunham performances should not *repeat not* be under US government sponsorship."[151] Despite the negative reply, the USIS office in Vienna, in coordination with the USIS office in Bonn, Germany, arranged for Dunham's company to have a television engagement. They did what they could for her, but her company dissolved in June 1960 due to lack of funds.

It was in part the very success of the company abroad from 1947 to 1960 that foiled Dunham's last attempt to revive the company in 1962. In challenging Eurocentric ideals of high art, Dunham opened up space for newly decolonized countries, and other nations with large nonwhite populations, to make claims for self-representation on the international stage. This opening meant, in a sense, that these groups no longer necessarily wanted or needed her to represent them. While dance scholar Anthony Shay has concluded that the Moiseyev Folk Dance Company from Russia was the most influential model for the national dance companies that emerged in the 1950s, the Dunham company most prominently put an Africanist aesthetic front and center for global audiences, paving the way for international acceptance of "folkloric" ensembles from predominantly nonwhite nations. Like Dunham, the artistic directors of these companies emphasized that the dances were based in ethnographic research; unlike Dunham, they claimed a national identity as a marker of authenticity.[152]

When Dunham decided to stage a comeback revue, *Bamboche!*, in New York in October 1962 after a seven-year hiatus from Broadway, the reviews were lukewarm at best. *Bamboche!* followed her standard three-act template of a journey across the African diaspora. Allen Hughes, a dance critic for the *New York Times*, noted that "nowadays we are so accustomed to seeing ethnic dances in relatively pure styles that they look a bit strange when hoked [sic] up with the trappings, manners, and general hullabaloo of the music hall and nightclub."[153] Les Ballets Africains du Guinea had electrified New York

City during their 1959 tour, and other ensembles like the Ballet Folklórico de Mexico had also begun to perform in the United States that year.[154] African American critics also voiced dissatisfaction with Dunham's revue model. Jesse Walker of the *Amsterdam News* felt that the juxtaposition of vigorous Brazilian dancing with African American gospel songs was in "extremely bad taste."[155] Instead of the planned nine-month national tour, the show closed after only a few weeks in San Francisco and New York, effectively ending the company.[156] Dunham mused to a friend, "I have gradually grown to feel that the 'correct' museum-piece authenticity of the transplants is less important than the alive presentation of the ethnic flux that is going on in our time . . . resulting in the sort of mélange that was the point of 'Bamboche' . . . a point that I'm sorry to say a number of the critics seemed to have missed."[157] Dunham had served as an unofficial ambassador for the African diaspora for more than a decade. She had directly inspired black artists in Peru, Senegal, Guinea, Haiti, and Jamaica to form their own dance companies and indirectly inspired dozens of others. Now they wanted to represent themselves. To continue to promote her diasporic vision, Dunham had to transition from performance to other spheres of influence and action.

CHAPTER 7

Living Diaspora in Haiti and Senegal

Two years into the company's international tours, Dunham began to feel the existential burden of rootlessness. Her clothes, papers, and material objects were in storage facilities on multiple continents, facilities that occasionally sent her letters threatening to throw away her belongings if she did not pay her overdue bills. Endless one-night stands in cities and towns across the globe meant living out of a suitcase—a luxurious Louis Vuitton trunk, to be sure, but a symbol of the itinerant life nonetheless. She wrote to Dorothy Gray in July 1949, "I have such a strong desire to feel roots somewhere and now it has become practically an absolute necessity for any feeling of security and peace."[1] When Dunham decided to find a place to call home, she did not hunt for an apartment in New York City, America's dance capital, or in Chicago, close to her family. Instead she turned to the island where she had experienced spiritual awakening and a deep sense of belonging: Haiti.

There is no better way to understand what it is like to live diaspora than to look at Dunham in Haiti. A central tension of diaspora is the disjuncture between the symbolic uses of a place and the lived experiences of people in that location. From its revolution to the present day, Haiti has loomed large as both metaphor and symbol for a variety of causes.[2] But Dunham did not simply "use" Haiti from afar to further her artistic ideals; she tried to live out her ideals in and through Haiti. Though this chapter spans the 1940s through the 1990s, it focuses in particular on the early 1960s, when Dunham lived in Port-au-Prince full time. Many African American intellectuals of that era lived abroad because of racism and Cold War anticommunism in the United States. As had W. E. B. Du Bois, Richard Wright, and others, Dunham experienced the difficulties of trying to construct a diasporic life in a world organized into nation-states. Perhaps more so than any other moment in the twentieth century, the early 1960s—which witnessed the end of formal colonialism in much of Africa—were years particularly rife with debates about prioritizing national sovereignty or transnational solidarities.[3] Adding a further layer of complication, Dunham attempted to transition from performing artist to development specialist during these years. The latter was a role for which she had little training and few skills. She advocated for cultural tourism as an economic and political boon to the island. Her ideas sometimes clashed with what local officials and citizens wanted; at other times, her simple presence as a foreigner, regardless of her best intentions or actions, created friction. Dunham also took on the role of cultural development expert while living in Dakar, Senegal between 1965 and 1967. There, too, she faced pushback for her ideas and conflict over whether she was an "insider" or "outsider."

Dunham's difficulties in Dakar reinforced her sense that Haiti, not Africa, was the key to the future progress of the African diaspora. Beginning in the nineteenth century, Haitian intellectuals had posited that the Haitian Revolution paved the way for the liberation of all black people. Louis Joseph Janvier and Demesvar Delorme theorized that Haiti was the center of a new humanism, an "interconnected global intellectual tradition" that guided not only the Americas, but also Europe and Africa to eradicate racism.[4] Haitian anthropologists Anténor Firmin and Jean Price-Mars (whom Dunham had befriended in 1935) adopted similar positions. Dunham's writings in the 1950s and 1960s echoed this Haiti-centric humanist philosophy. While a valuable intellectual position, it displaced Africa from the center of diaspora.

It is not surprising that Dunham encountered problems when she resisted the drumbeat of nationalism in the mid-twentieth century. What is remarkable is what she *did* achieve in difficult situations. Ever the strategist, she shifted course when necessary. Throughout her time in Haiti, she continued to advocate for Vodou and the culture of the masses. She received at least nominal support from every presidential administration, a remarkable feat given Haiti's volatile political situation. And while it took some time, she eventually grasped a way to include Africa in her diasporic vision that did not devalue the continent's contributions to modernity.

From the beginning of her career Dunham saw herself, and was, an ambassador of Haitian culture to the world. Almost without exception, critics who reviewed her shows in the late 1930s had highlighted her Haitian dances as the best part of the programs.[5] Images of Haiti on the US stage and silver screen at the time were unabashedly sensationalist, misconstruing the Vodou religion as a "black magic" cult and the nation as a place populated by zombies and savages. Within Haiti itself, ruling elites maintained laws prohibiting Vodou worship. Even if the government did not enforce the laws very often, the potentiality of enforcement—and the threat of violence thus encoded—was a means to control the working masses.[6] Through performances, publications, and lectures, Dunham presented a more positive and dignified image of Haiti than the stereotyped notions of "voodoo" in circulation.

It was not only American dance critics who took notice. After attending Dunham's 1940 show *Tropics and Le Jazz "Hot"* in New York, Elie Lescot, the Haitian ambassador to the United States, praised her for paving the way for Vodou rituals to find "a permanent niche in the temple of Terpsichorean Art."[7] A year later, when he became the president of Haiti, Lescot insisted that a Haitian student group performing for the Eighth Annual National Folk Festival in Washington include dance in its production. To perform banned Haitian ritual dance onstage had been unthinkable only a few years earlier; *Tropics and Le Jazz "Hot"* had demonstrated that a reimagination of Haitian social and ritual dance as art was viable.[8] As Kate Ramsey has shown, however, the success of Dunham's shows may have also unintentionally circumscribed the limits of representation for that re-imagination. Instead of bringing working-class Haitians who actually danced such rituals to the festival, Lescot insisted on a "polished-off" troupe, one which mirrored the Dunham company in its layer of removal from ritual practice. In order to represent Haiti as a modern nation, the folkloric dances had to be "figured as transcended," and thus students from elite Port-au-Prince families took the stage in Washington.[9] At the exact same time, Lescot approved the Catholic Church's *anti-superstitieuse* campaign in rural Haiti. Church agents destroyed sacred drums and *houngfors* (temples).[10] Dunham aimed to raise the status of Haiti by valorizing its Vodou culture, but in mirroring her productions, the Haitian government decided that the cultural knowledge had to be desacralized and transferred to the elite.

Though she stayed connected to Haiti from afar, Dunham did not visit the island between June 1936 and July 1949. When she did come back after that thirteen-year absence, the then-Haitian president (who happened to be her former lover, Estimé) awarded her the Legion d'honneur for her years of service in promoting the island to the world. Such affirmation could not have come at a better time. In the midst of her grueling European tour, she received word that her brother, at age forty-two, had died in Saint Elizabeth's mental hospital in Washington; that her parents were ill; and that the Dunham School was in financial shambles.[11] She needed spiritual rejuvenation. She returned to New York to perform rituals, but Papa Augustin "insisted" that she return to Haiti and be "re-baptized" by one of the most important *mambos*, or high priestesses, in Port-au-Prince. On the whirlwind trip Dunham reconnected with Estimé, attended "five days of parties by army officers," and spent the nights sleeping on the beach, taking her first true vacation in years.[12] The Haitian poet Jean Brierre was her escort throughout the visit. Dunham's revived love for Haiti was so strong after this concentrated week that she discussed with psychologist Louis Price-Mars (son of Jean Price-Mars) the possibility of becoming an official "ambassadress" or "consul at large" for Haiti.[13]

The rejuvenation inspired Dunham to think of her career beyond the confines of her dance company. From Haiti, she wrote to her friend Dorothy, "I am again going to start working to try and make myself a more useful citizen in a more positive way, that way being for the first step to do something about permanent housing."[14] Dunham used "citizen" to mean citizen not of the United States, but of the world. For her, the center of the world was in Haiti. A few months later, she fulfilled her dream by purchasing Habitation Leclerc, a lush estate of roughly twenty wooded acres with multiple villas, pools, and sculptures, situated on the outskirts of Port-au-Prince. Leclerc had an ugly history beneath its physical beauty. It was purportedly the former home of Napoleon Bonaparte's sister Pauline and her husband General Charles Leclerc, sent to Haiti in 1801 to suppress the revolution. Archeological evidence supported local lore that General Rochambeau, the infamous Frenchman who gruesomely tortured and killed several Haitians during the last years of the Revolution, had also lived there.[15] Whether or not Leclerc and Rochambeau actually resided on the property did not matter as much as the belief that they did, for it shaped how Haitians understood the land.

Habitation Leclerc became Dunham's dream and nightmare. She asserted, "as soon as I set foot on Leclerc I felt its evil," and yet she felt compelled to buy it.[16] It was a financial albatross, purchased for $25,000 at a time when both she and her school in New York had already accumulated large debts.[17] From the beginning, Dunham's ownership of the historically fraught place sent a profoundly mixed message. She was only allowed to acquire the property because of the US occupation, during which the American government rewrote the Haitian Constitution to allow foreign land ownership. This legal change "empowered U.S. corporate interests and disrupted the already precarious existence of Haitian peasants."[18] Was Dunham's ownership a reproduction of foreign dominance, the transfer of French colonial power to American imperial power? Or, as a black woman, was she turning a formerly oppressive space into a site of liberation? Dunham attempted the latter, but arguably the transformation process was never completed during her lifetime. She reflected in 1969 that Leclerc "brought some deep, insoluble sadness into my life which even as yet I have not been able to unravel."[19] In some sense, it was the sadness of diaspora. The fact that she was "entranced" and inexorably drawn to a place of colonial horror revealed that one could not fully escape the tragedies of the past that had created the diaspora in the first place.

Dunham saw Haiti not only as her personal home, but also as the foundation for a more humanistic culture. Her deepening dismay about the Cold War led her to seek alternative solutions to the problems that had created World War II. The principles that inspired Haitians to "choose freedom rather than slavery," she stated, would be useful in preventing another descent into fascism or war. The language she used to promote Haiti echoed Senghor's discussion of *métissage*, the fusion of Africa and Europe as the foundation of the "civilization of the universal."[20] On January 1, 1950, in a radio address to Haiti from France, she announced a series of projects to make Haiti the center of scholarly and aesthetic investigations into modernity. Haiti, she wrote, synthesized the best of Renaissance thinking of eighteenth-century France and the best cultural ideas of Africa. This blend "makes of Haiti an atmosphere completely conducive to a reaffirmation of the goodness of things and the beauty of things and the reasonableness of man," which she felt "in practically every other country in the rest of the world has been destroyed" by the domination of "imperialist, industrialist, and capitalist societies."[21] Dunham harbored a particular dislike for the "evils of industrialism," which she equated with crass American consumerism and materialism. Haiti could be "a centre for provision of world peace, world citizenship, fundamental knowledge, resistance to political and social methods embracing violence and human antagonism."[22] This viewpoint echoed nineteenth-century Haitian intellectuals, who argued that Haiti could provide a purer foundation for the ideals of democracy and republicanism than the United States or Europe, which had been corrupted by slavery and imperialism.[23] Unlike others who developed an interest in Haiti based on a perception of what the country lacked, she saw what the country had to offer.

In an outline of her plans, Dunham proposed no less than twenty-four different projects to fulfill her vision. She called her proposal the "Haitian Projet," using the French word for "project," and wrote it in Italian. She listed the Projet's home address as UNESCO's library building on 48 Kerber Street in Paris.[24] Her ideas to establish a medical center, library, and a Museum of Cultural and Fine Arts in Port-au-Prince mirrored UNESCO's Fundamental Education program, which established health clinics, schools, libraries, and a museum in Haiti between 1948 and 1950.[25] Where Dunham's ideology differed from UNESCO's was in her emphasis on highlighting the achievements of black culture. She wanted a library to be housed in Paris "to facilitate knowledge of Haiti" and black civilization in general. She stated that she would establish two literary awards, one of which would go to a "young Haitian for work that will serve to forward the Haitian Projet." For the other, the "Touissant Louverture Prize," Dunham would give $1,000 for "the best literary work showing the contribution to world progress by the negro race." In Paris, she met with France's "outstanding literary minds," including André Maurois, André Breton, Fernand Gregh, and Marcel Achard, at the famed Maxim's café and convinced them to be the prize's jury.[26] Interestingly, all her selected jurors were white men. Dunham saw herself as part of a cosmopolitan elite class that transcended race, but her choice of jurors also reflected a failure to fully challenge white supremacist and masculinist notions of intellectualism. She also called for a modern art exhibit, staged in Paris and presented in Port-au-Prince, to facilitate artistic exchange between Haiti and Europe. She even wanted to enlist Garry Davis, who had famously renounced his US citizenship to become a "world citizen," to help in these efforts.[27] Because Dunham saw Haiti as the place where *métissage* had reached its apex, what better place could be the center for a new humanism founded on an idea of global citizenship? And what better person than Davis to be a symbol of this new humanistic culture?

The first sign that Dunham's ideals clashed with reality emerged in Jamaica in early 1951. There she reunited with Estimé, who had been deposed and gone into exile. He lived as a "hunted" and "haunted" man because of unpopular decisions he had made as president of Haiti, such as to dissolve the Senate. As Dunham recalled in *Island Possessed*, seeing her proud friend live with such fear and desperation "turned all the years that I had known Haiti into a mockery. I had dreamed of, written about, acquired property in, spread the good word far and wide about a country of which I really knew nothing."[28] Dunham's capacity for self-examination was one of the most important traits that allowed her to keep going with her dreams for Haiti. She acknowledged gaps in her knowledge and took steps to correct them, then pressed forward.

Dunham's return to Haiti after her trip to Jamaica also challenged her romanticized outlook. With Europe still recovering from World War II, the Caribbean—Haiti in particular—was exploding in popularity as a tourist destination. Both Haitian politicians and many African Americans saw tourism as a positive development that would bring foreign capital to Haiti and eliminate the negative stereotypes about the island.[29] Dunham disagreed. She felt that tourism destroyed Haiti's cultural integrity. She wrote to Berenson in June 1951, "I am pained to see the 'primitive' art exploited . . . . The voodoo temples that used to be sacred retreats for the initiated are now, at least in the environs of Port-au-Prince, decorated to the condescending tastes of tourists and exploited for a few dollars a visit."[30] She also felt she had fundamentally misjudged Haiti. She wrote, "Haiti is no place to find comfort in human-ness. The peasant in town combines French shrewdness with African traits of manipulation . . . . There is no truth and no system of morals or ethics here."[31] Dunham expressed negative stereotypes about French and African culture. The country she had lionized as a model of freedom and democracy she now saw as ridden with a lack of morality. She admitted to "a certain embarrassment & shame that things were so unclear, that my need was so great as to have attached my whole dream and career to an ideal that didn't exist."[32]

Despite her disillusionment, Dunham finalized the purchase of Habitation Leclerc during the extended 1951 visit. She often referred to herself as an "incurable optimist," unwilling to give up her ideals even in the face of seemingly impossible odds.[33] She hired a *mambo* to exorcise the evil on the property and asserted that it had worked.[34] Nonetheless, the demands of international touring took her away from Haiti and the implementation of her various projects. She visited the island only briefly in the next seven years. Throughout the 1950s she wrote of starting a research center, a museum, and a school at Leclerc, but nothing materialized.

Meanwhile, Dunham was still exerting an influence in Haiti, albeit indirectly. Her New York school, in operation from 1944 to 1954, was just as important as her dance company. As discussed in chapter 5, Haitian performers trained there during the late 1940s and brought their knowledge back to Haiti. Papa Augustin taught Haitian drumming at the school and maintained connections to his home country. The Dunham Technique and "primitive rhythms" classes offered a model for how to teach folkloric dance as an art form. Inspired by her example, Haitian president Paul Magloire determined in 1951 that creating a national school of folkloric dance would attract tourists and demonstrate "that the arts could enhance and create new possibilities for the modern project of economic and cultural development."[35] Instead of turning to one of the many successful Haitian dancers, his government recruited Lavinia Williams, who had danced in the Dunham company for years and had taught at the Dunham School. During Haiti Week in New York in the spring of 1951—when Dunham was on tour in Latin America—Papa Augustin invited Haitian officials to see Williams teach at her studio in Brooklyn. Impressed with Williams's approach to dance instruction, the Haitian government soon after invited her to establish the Haitian Academy of Folklore and Classic Dance.[36] Williams would run the institution for several years, training Viviane Gauthier, Lynn Williams Rouzier, Régine Montrosier-Trouillot, and others who would become leaders of Haitian folkloric dance.

Williams brought a "technical" and "disciplined" approach to dance training, words associated with American-style modern development. As Gauthier explained, "discipline" was about more than just learning the steps correctly. One also had to learn about the carriage of the torso, the way one dressed for class, and one's overall behavior in society. Gauthier, a member of the elite class who had learned to dance by mimicking the workers on her parents' sugar plantation, emphasized that folkloric dance was *not* Vodou. She asserted that she had almost no interaction with Dunham, whom she and others in the Haitian dance community of the mid-twentieth century perceived as fully immersed in the religious aspects of the dance and far removed from the concert dance scene. Other important folkloric dancers who trained with Williams declined to be interviewed, asserting that they, too, had little to do with Dunham.[37]

Williams, of course, based her technique on Dunham Technique, which itself was based on Haitian dances Dunham had learned during her 1935–1936 visit. Williams's arrival on the island meant that Haitian dance had come full circle. The government embarked on a "calculated transformation" of Vodou dance into folkloric dance, creating a "classified, disciplined and packaged" art that "could be shared with the modern world via formal dance instruction, African-based cultural awareness programs, and tourist entertainment."[38]

Dunham was jealous of Williams's position, but as someone who was constantly on tour with a dance company, she had neither the time nor resources to do what her former student could. At one point she asked Williams to start a dance school at Leclerc, but Williams refused, citing her loyalty to the Haitian Academy.[39] In Dunham's correspondence from Haiti in the subsequent years, she rarely mentioned Williams, the academy, or any attempts to form some type or relationship or partnership with the institution.

Instead of a school, Dunham tried another project at Leclerc: a health clinic. She returned to Haiti in November 1958 after running out of money and temporarily disbanding the company in Tokyo. She realized the degree to which her property had languished in her absence. In addition to the $25,000 purchase price, it now needed another $25,000 investment to rebuild crumbling buildings and landscape the grounds.[40] On February 24, 1959, the new president Francois "Papa Doc" Duvalier made Dunham an honorary citizen of Haiti and upgraded her Legion d'honneur ranking from Chevalier to Commander Grand Officier, "for services she has performed in the fields of art and culture to make Haitian folklore known throughout the world."[41] With Duvalier's blessing, she opened a free health clinic at Leclerc to serve the poor. *Ebony* ran a feature article on her effort in its September 1959 issue. The magazine testified that Dunham oversaw more than 225 patients whenever she arrived back in Haiti between tour stops, often attending to dozens of people a day to offer antibiotics, physiotherapy, and food.[42] Letters poured in from *Ebony* readers who wanted to help. One thirty-year-old man from Chicago wrote, "I must admit I know nothing about that kind of work, but I do love people (especially my people) that is black people wherever they are. I feel a longing to donate my life to suffering Humanity."[43] Dunham had to decline all such offers. By the time the article went to press, she had left the island again to tour with the company in Europe, and the clinic shuttered its doors after only a few months.

A longer-lasting project was the transformation of Habitation Leclerc into a tourist destination, a reversal of her position on tourism a decade earlier. In January 1960, Dunham again ran out of money while on tour, this time in Vienna, and once again disbanded the company. She told a group of Viennese students the following month that she had changed her opinion about presenting Haitian religious material. Earlier in her career, she stated, she refrained from exposing the secrets of Vodou. In the present moment, however, she felt that it was "important that the meaning of these ceremonies be disclosed" because "they have a universal feeling and meaning."[44]

It seems no mere coincidence that her change of mind coincided with her need to make an income from Leclerc. After the company's dissolution, Dunham, now fifty-one, went to Spain for three months with her new lover, Dick Frisell, a Swedish twenty-four-year-old with a substantial trust fund. During their travels, she convinced him to move with her to Haiti and become her business partner as she developed Leclerc. They called each other "dearly beloved husband" and "angel wife," and Frisell considered them to be "living in a marital state" even though technically Dunham was still married to Pratt.[45] She wrote in a letter to a friend that the two men had become "good friends," that there was "little conflict over what one would think," and that the three of them, along with Marie-Christine, lived in relative harmony together at Leclerc.[46]

Frisell's family wealth provided a lifeline to the estate. When Frisell Senior initially refused to take over the mortgage—suspicious that a woman more than twice his son's age was being manipulative—Dunham took it upon herself to convince him. She argued, in a February 1961 letter, that his son needed a sense of purpose and direction in life. Managing Leclerc would provide him with an opportunity. She urged Frisell Senior to stop withholding funds and said that his son's "excellent health" was marred only by "breaking out in a rash when he worries about money." Dunham smoothly transitioned from this emotional appeal into a business proposition to convince Frisell Senior that he was not merely throwing money away. She declared that Leclerc had an estimated value of over $100,000, which could "easily double" once "things are more normal."[47]

As Dunham obliquely referenced, Haiti's political problems stood in the way of creating the idyllic tourist haven that she imagined. Unfortunately, she had missed Haiti's heyday as a tourist destination. Tourism had increased five-fold between 1949 and 1954 and continued to rise until 1956. After President Magloire resigned that year, however, five provisional governments came into power over the course of nine months, creating political instability. Duvalier assumed the presidency in August 1957, and his regime soon began to perse-cute political rivals and adopt other antidemocratic policies. By August 1960, when Dunham began to develop her tourism project, Duvalier had established the Tonton Macoutes, a secret police force that terrorized political dissidents. The political turbulence and rumors of violence scared away tourists.[48] The assurance to Frisell Senior that things would soon become "more normal" was wishful thinking, for Duvalier would remain in power until his death in 1971.

Despite the financial and political problems, by June 1961, Dunham had Habitation Leclerc up and running as a tourist attraction, one that traded on notions of exoticism and colonial nostalgia. Indeed, Leclerc looked and felt like a colonial estate embedded in a tropical paradise. Lush, green plants cov-ered the crumbling ruins of magisterial stone living quarters. As visitors wan-dered through verdant flora, they stumbled upon a restored swimming pool, surrounded by statues of Pauline Leclerc and other French figures. They could continue wandering through a small forest and get lost in the copse of trees, as Pauline herself had purportedly done. An antique fountain poured water into a pond that had once held colorful species of fish. A press release declared that Dunham had "restored Leclerc in the same colonial style" of its original inhabitants and promised to recreate the "enchanting tropical evenings" of Pauline's era.[49] In selling the estate as a must-see destination for cruise ships,

Dunham argued, "Apart from the Citadelle in the north of Haiti, it is the only historic place which has been reconstructed and gives an impression of the colonial beauties of the Island."[50] This vision of "colonial beauties" ignored the fact that colonial Haiti was a brutal slavocracy.

But Leclerc was more than just a scenic place in which to wander and imagine a colonial past; it offered visitors embodied visions of a Haitian present. The *Los Angeles Times* called it the "newest gathering place for the Bohemian crowd."[51] The "Weekly Schedule of Entertainment" included nightly dinner in the Salon Guinee, drinks at the Bar Geisha, dancing until the wee hours to a live orchestra, and a "Vodun Ceremony" three evenings a week in an outdoor peristyle, with a cover charge of $1.50.[52] Fliers insisted that the performers offered audiences "enchantment." The advertisement characterized service workers as scenic props, stating, "The spell is woven as waiters and shadows flit through the foliage of Leclerc's hand tailored jungle." The promotional script concluded, "This is the evening in Haiti which is certain to include every civilized taste in entertainment."[53]

With the word "civilized," Dunham pushed back against notions that Vodou was primitive or savage. Without films, photographs, or descriptions of the ceremony, however, it is difficult to judge whether Dunham's rendition differed dramatically from the Vodou shows that catered to the "condescending tastes of tourists" she had decried a decade earlier. She attempted a type of high-culture tourism that educated audiences about Haitian cultural practices, but it is debatable whether the Leclerc performances escaped primitivist exoticism. Lorraine Mangonès, who saw the shows as a child, argues yes. In presenting a theatricalization of Vodou that captured the artistic beauty of the dances, Dunham succeeded in conveying a dignified cultural representation of Haitian culture to European and American tourists who would have otherwise remained ignorant. A claim of pure authenticity would have been a greater violation of Vodou and disrespectful to its practitioners.[54] Gauthier, who saw the show as a middle-aged adult, acknowledged the quality of the dancers but insisted that the show overall was "a mardi-gras," in the sense of cheap entertainment. The two women come from different positions. Mangonès has recently spearheaded the renovation of Leclerc into a park and has done important work to highlight Dunham's legacy for Haiti; Gauthier, as Williams's student, continues to insist that there is a separation between Vodou and folkloric dance.[55]

Advertisements and articles in the *Haitian Sun* newspaper offer challenges to both interpretations. On February 11, 1962, the paper ran advertisements for both Dunham's "Grand Spectacle" at Leclerc and Williams's "Bamboche Creole" at the Hotel Oloffson. The Leclerc ad promised a "True Vaudun Ceremony," which casts doubt on Mangonès's assertion that Dunham was not trying to cater to audience desires for authenticity. Gauthier's insistence that Dunham offered entertainment whereas Williams offered art also seems questionable. The ad for Williams' "Bamboche Creole" promised a "daring and dangerous fire dance" and a "spectacular variety program." A review of the performance in the same paper delighted in the "black light and fluorescent paint in a drum number" and called it a "popular" show.[56] If Williams truly had a more artistic aim than Dunham, the press did not notice.

Dunham attempted to align herself with local citizens in creating her new tourist spot. When writing letters to government officials to get support for Habitation Leclerc, she referred to Haiti as "our country" and "our land," implying common interest and shared goals.[57] The Duvalier government seemed to respond positively, first by granting her the new medal and then by supporting the clinic. Most tellingly, Leclerc was never robbed or targeted by Duvalier's Tonton Macoutes. Government support did not equal community support, however. In fact, it might have potentially worked against her. Given Duvalier's increasing unpopularity, Dunham theorized, "There must be until now some Haitians who, I suspect, regard this untouchedness as collaboration."[58] In December 1961, she suffered a major blow when the Pan American Festival canceled its plan to host a major event at Leclerc because a neighbor had told local newspapers that poisonous snakes lived on the property. The story was half-true: Dunham had imported snakes from around the world for Frisell's pet project, a zoological garden, but none were poisonous.[59]

The rumors soon exploded. Dunham recalled in *Island Possessed* that "victims of political feuds were reported to have been victims of serpents loosed from Habitation Leclerc, children on the way to school were reported to have been swallowed by the snakes now become dragon size, and a woman complete with donkey suffered the same fate . . . [there were] scurrilous announcements every five minutes on the local radio, around which, before the affair died down, portresses and peasants would gather to listen at every country store."[60] Marie-Christine's classmates at the Port-au-Prince private school she attended teasingly called her "python."[61] The news even made its way to the United States, where *Jet* magazine reported about the "hysterical" neighbor and quoted Dunham as saying, "Someone wants this propaganda to have an effect on my business. It's pretty convenient if you want to get rid of someone."[62]

Dunham blamed the "state of hysteria" on "mass hypnosis."[63] That the snake story could have such explanatory power as the cause of political troubles and physical violence, however, suggested that there was already a certain level of animosity toward Leclerc among the Haitian peasantry—the class with whom Dunham had said she wanted to identify the most, the keepers of the "true" Haitian spirit.[64] To finally quell the rumors, Dunham had to let "a large number of non-paying Haitians" onto the property.[65] Years after the snake scare receded, suspicion of Dunham remained. Children from the neighborhood who stood outside the forbidding gates and listened to the mysterious chanting coming from within thought of her as a "devil white woman," a designation that supports the theorization of whiteness as not about skin color, but about relative power and prestige.[66]

The snakes may have been the final straw for Dunham. Even though Frisell Senior had assumed a large part of Leclerc's mortgage and thus alleviated financial concerns, the political and social problems remained. She talked to officials at the US embassy in confidence about Duvalier. She disliked his entourage of *bocors*, practitioners of what she considered "black magic," and feared that he wanted to kill lighter-skinned Haitians and whites. She "wondered if some face-saving formula could be devised to permit the President to leave without censure," Charles William Thomas of the American embassy reported.[67] Dunham had decried American imperialism when she had first come to Haiti in the 1930s, but now she considered US intervention a possible necessity. Duvalier's anti-Americanism began to make it difficult for Dunham to deal with low-level government officials, who "in spite of my color, honorary decorations, honorary citizenship, and years as an adopted daughter of the country" treated her as an outsider.[68] With home no longer feeling like home, she cast her eyes across the ocean to Africa and new possibilities for diasporic engagement.

If Haiti was at the center of Dunham's diaspora, for most people Africa was the logical center. In 1962 a Dunham School scholarship-student-turned-Hollywood producer, Stephen Papich, encouraged her to visit the continent to research material for a new show. She told her friend Henry Polokow that she "hated the idea of Africa."[69] She never explicitly said why she felt such dis-identification in her letters or notes. Perhaps she felt that Africa lacked what engaged her intellectually and creatively: the coming together of cultures in the Western Hemisphere, from which she drew virtually all her choreographic inspiration. Dunham's 1962 trip to Senegal, Nigeria, and Morocco, which conveniently came at a time when she was looking for a way out of Duvalier's Haiti, changed her perspective, at least in part. Although few details of these trips exist in her archives or the biographies written about her, she told Polokow that the trip eventually made "sense for me through the broader scope."[70] She had begun to realize that her overall project of diaspora needed a connection to Africa. Dunham built new relationships with ambassadors, members of royal families, and European entertainment industry figures on this trip, but her most important connection was to Senghor, whom she had first befriended in 1949 in Paris and who had become the president of Senegal in 1960 (see Figure 7.1).[71]

Senghor had dreams for the entire continent of Africa. He continued to advocate *négritude* as the foundation of a humanistic, pan-African culture that would work together with Europe to forge the civilization of the universal. His version of African socialism combined black African culture with "the most

Figure 7.1 Katherine Dunham in conversation with Léopold Sédar Senghor at the Palais National in Dakar, Senegal, May 1962. Photographer unknown. Missouri History Museum, St. Louis.

advanced technological and organizational forms from the West."[72] He faced many critics for the seeming moderation of this plan, including Ghanaian president Kwame Nkrumah. Nkrumah advocated greater independence from Europe and the development of an "African Personality."[73] To promote *négritude*, Senghor planned a gathering of black artists and intellectuals, modeled on the 1956 International Congress of Negro Writers and Artists in Paris.[74] Senghor wanted Dunham to spearhead the United States' involvement in what he called the Festival mondial des arts nègres (in English the First World Festival of Negro Arts or, for short, the Dakar Festival). In February 1964, in coordination with Charles Delgado, head of the Senegalese mission to the UN, Ousman Soce Diop, Senegal's ambassador-at-large, and G. Mennen Williams, head of African affairs at the State Department, Dunham organized the Friends of the Dakar Festival committee.[75] In June 1964, however, the State Department announced that Virginia Inness-Brown, a member of ANTA, would head the festival committee, cutting Dunham out of the picture.

The Inness-Brown appointment caused controversy. Robert Pritchard, an African American classical pianist and chairman of the American Festival of Negro Arts, threatened to march on Washington. How could the State Department assign a white woman to head a committee that selected representative black American artists? He (and Dunham) had been in touch with Senegalese officials for years about organizing this festival. Dunham herself took a diplomatic approach. She wrote to Senghor and asked him to pressure the United States to add some "qualified Negro American people" to the committee.[76] Her efforts bore fruit. Soon afterward, John A. Davis, the African American president of the American Society of African Culture (AMSAC), was made co-chairman. It was later discovered, however, that the CIA had funded Davis and AMSAC as part of its attempt to control the political voices at the festival.[77] Thus even the appointment of a black co-chairman of the committee derived from cynical motives. Senghor then suggested that Dunham be appointed chair of the dance committee. Deliberately or not, the planning meetings occurred when she was in Italy and Sweden, so Arthur Mitchell, the former Dunham School student who was now a New York City Ballet star, became the chairman. Dunham was relegated to the position of sub-co-chairman, along with Alvin Ailey, who was twenty-two years her junior.[78]

Her leadership role now diminished, Dunham asked that her defunct company perform in Dakar. The State Department rehashed its racially coded political and artistic reasons when it refused. Officials mentioned Dunham's "difficult" personality and felt that her company was "too erotic," but they "did not want to tell her the reason" for turning her down. So along with the stick, the State Department offered a carrot: the possibility of sponsoring Dunham as an individual, as she "would be an excellent lecturer, a good representative of this country."[79] This option provoked mixed reactions from the members of the ANTA dance panel. All agreed that Dunham had "temperament" problems, but disagreed about how this would affect her if she were traveling alone as a lecturer. Some felt that Dunham's specialty in Caribbean dance meant that she would not represent the United States very well, but others felt that if she lectured on black dance in the Western Hemisphere it would be worthwhile.[80]

In a realigned world with independent African nations, the decision of whom to send abroad could not just be made by solely by the dance panel or the State Department. Dunham had strong allies in high places. She instructed Senghor and Dakar Festival co-organizer Alioune Diop (founder of *Presence Africaine*) to pressure the State Department and made similar overtures to the US ambassador to Senegal, Mercer Cook.[81] Eventually, the pressure worked. After repeated calls from Senghor, the panel capitulated. Although some members still protested the choice of Dunham, William Bales's response reflected the new power dynamics: "If I were being asked to recommend someone, I would think of someone else, but since they want her there, that is an important part of the consideration, because of the weight of these repeated requests." The State Department gave Dunham a grant and the title Special Ambassador.[82]

Without a dance company to run or a leadership role in organizing the US contribution to the festival, Dunham rebranded herself as a cultural development consultant. She had begun developing ideas along these lines even before the Dakar Festival committees solidified. In February 1964, she submitted a grant proposal to the Ford Foundation in which she suggested that the foundation and the State Department combine forces to develop the arts in Africa. Because she vehemently opposed industrialization, Dunham saw cultural resources as important tools for economic growth. She explained, "The most urgent need of newly emerging countries such as the African States ... is to find a system of exploitation of their own resources ... development of native arts into forms acceptable for world exploitation is one of the important resources in this day of cultural exchange."[83] Though Dunham used the word "exploitation" in a nonpejorative sense, it was a dubious choice at a time when several intellectuals were railing against the West's exploitation of Africa's material wealth and labor force. Her insistence that "native arts" needed transformation into "forms acceptable for world exploitation" revealed the potential problem of a fusion aesthetic. Was Dunham reproducing the dualism of Africa as supplier of raw materials, and the West—including herself—as the provider of refinement?

Dunham saw her project as important for political reasons as well. Cultural resources gave new African nations a seat at the table in international relations. She argued that the visual and performing arts in particular, which required no linguistic translation, were "among the most effective agents of contact, communication and persuasion."[84] She had spent three decades promoting the idea that her cross-cultural, educational performances would lessen racial prejudice. By showcasing their artistic resources, the new African nations could challenge negative images, command respect, and thus legitimize their right to belong to the international community of nations.

The Ford Foundation declined to sponsor Dunham's cultural development project, as did the State Department. So she amended the proposal for the United States Agency for International Development (USAID) and focused specifically on the island of Gorée (a part of Senegal), formerly a holding ground for captured Africans about to be sent to slavery in the Western Hemisphere. As with the Haitian Projet, the number and diversity of projects she proposed for Gorée seemed out of touch with financial and logistic realities. She called for developing a performing arts academy, constructing a permanent theater space, building geodesic domes to house students and hold classes, instituting an exchange program with other world universities, establishing an archive of West African performing arts, pursuing collaborative projects with musicologists and ethnologists, readying the island for commercial use in television and film, restoring the slave buildings for tourist purposes, and finally, building a casino and a nightclub on the island.[85]

Some of Dunham's ideas for Gorée would prove visionary. UNESCO would declare Gorée a World Heritage Site in 1978, and the island has become one of Senegal's largest tourist attractions. In particular, the restored slave-trade buildings—an idea Dunham suggested in 1964—have become symbolically important sites for African Americans and others who want to engage with the history of slavery.[86] At the time, however, her expansive plans overwhelmed her interlocutors. Ambassador Cook told her point blank that her proposals were too much and that she should "spend time following through" on her designated role as Special Ambassador for the Dakar Festival.[87] When she arrived in Senegal in 1965, tensions arose between Dunham and various Senegalese government officials, who viewed her multiple plans for Gorée as a distraction at a time when they were concerned with the "tough job" ahead of them in planning the festival. They saw the performing arts academy in particular as "competition [to] already existing cultural dance group."[88]

Nor did the Senegalese want to turn over the running of the festival dances to her. This was their moment to showcase national independence, not relinquish control to an American. Dunham did not see herself as representing American interests, but rather as a world citizen. Her insistence on being appointed as a cultural adviser to Senghor also caused concern. The US embassy in Dakar reported, "President Senghor, and Director and Members of the Senegalese Festival Art Committee have again made clear that GOS [Government of Senegal] does not know what to do with Miss Dunham before, during, or after the festival."[89] Dunham, who saw herself as promoting diasporic collaboration, instead came across as a paternalistic American interventionist. The State Department considered canceling her grant, but Senghor expressed reluctance, fearing it would cause a "public relations problem."[90]

During the festival, Dunham's ideas about cultural development continued to create friction. In a lecture before a colloquium of distinguished writers, she said that she was returning to a more anthropological definition of dance that "had been dormant during my performing years" but was now reawakened by her travels in Africa. She argued that "dance is not a technique, but is a social act" and that dance should "return to where it came from, which is the heart and soul of man, and man's social living."[91] To fully appreciate dance as a social act, aspiring dancers had to have an intimate knowledge of "the fundamentals of form and function, of roots and heritages." Otherwise, they would create "superficial" presentations.[92] She told her fellow colloquium members to turn to "the Old Ones for truth, more than the outside world," though, ironically, she also aggressively promoted herself—an outsider—as a guiding force in the cultural development of Senegal.[93] Historians Julia Foulkes and Penny Von Eschen assert that Dunham's emphasis on traditions placed her in conflict with her fellow colloquium members, who felt that such an injunction flew in the face of the desire of young Africans to be modern and cosmopolitan.[94] Foulkes further suggests that Dunham's speech "may have roused fears of continuing cultural imperialism and exploitative tourism."[95] This speculation is plausible, given that Dunham stressed the economic importance of dance for the fledgling nations.

Four years earlier, in fact throughout most of her career, Dunham had asserted the opposite point of view, favoring intercultural mixing and fusion over notions of authenticity.[96] Dunham's essentialist position at Dakar may have been influenced by her perception of Africa as the repository for culture that had either been lost or appropriated in the United States. Her ideas were rooted in romanticized notions of Africa's greater connection to nature and spirituality. Instead of seeing dynamic cultural exchange occurring within Africa itself, she viewed Africa as one of the primary sources for cultural creolization in places such as the Caribbean. She was far from alone in her perspective. Her view reflected a growing desire, shared by many in the African diaspora, for greater knowledge about and recognition of African culture in a world that had spent centuries denying or appropriating that culture. Often, that desire included a reification of African cultural practices as unchanging to rebuke to the consistent attempts to erase historical legacies and traditions. In the 1966 speech, Dunham mourned the absence of black history from American textbooks, which prevented young black students from taking pride in their heritage. Africa, she proclaimed, had "a profound knowledge of the rhythms by which every human organism lives, an unabused [sic] vitality and a beauty conforming with nature rather than fictionalized concepts" and thus had "an obligation to carefully examine the processes of education and expressions which will best forward . . . the 'image' of the entire race."[97]

Dunham also insisted that African nations had a duty not only to the race, but also to the rest of the world to export their cultural practices. "Africa is the custodian of rhythmic expressions essential to the rest of the world," she stated, in a virtual echo of Senghor's explication of *négritude*.[98] Whereas earlier in her career she had stressed sociological bases for difference, in 1966 she seemed to reinforce essentialist ideas about Africa. She did so, however, in the service of her understanding of dance as a social expression that could help people protect themselves from some of the difficulties of modernity. "I have personally witnessed the cathartic effect of rhythms," she told the colloquium audience, "and have participated in ceremonies where troubled spirits have been returned to equilibrium through the therapy of dance and drum and song. For this reason when I see only the exterior aspects, the meaningless form, I feel a great loss to the world and to Africa."[99]

African performers themselves resisted such ideas of purity. In 1957, Keïta Fodéba, who had asked Dunham for advice about founding a dance company back in 1950, wrote, "Authenticity is synonymous with reality . . . . If life is changing, there is no reason that folklore, which is a living expression, should not evolve . . . . Today's Africa, little by little, is imprinted with Western civilization. Indeed, it would be absurd to fasten our folklore solely to our country's past, for no folklore in the world is without mixture."[100] Even Senghor asked Dunham to shed her essentialism when he named her to the post of "conseil technique culturel" (technical cultural adviser) to the National Ballet of Senegal. He asked her to "turn out an Alvin Ailey type company" and bring what he called "formation et discipline" to the group.[101] Such a request echoed what the Haitian government had asked Williams to do. Alvin Ailey American

Dance Theater had been a huge hit at the Dakar Festival and represented the *métissage* that Senghor ultimately wanted, the bringing together of traditional Senegalese dance and "Western" technical training, staging, and theatricality. So instead of enforcing a rigid traditionalism on the troupe as her words suggested, Dunham began teaching daily Dunham Technique classes and pondering choreography for the group, her favorite one being a "baroque primitive" reinterpretation of Vaslav Nijinsky's famed ballet, *Apres Midi d'un Faun* (1912).[102]

Dunham's work was cut short because the State Department refused to renew her grant. Still hostile to her, officials gave the reason that other aid projects to Senegal "would be more important to overall US objectives."[103] Whereas in 1964 Senghor's pressure had overridden the State Department's objections, now his support for her was more lukewarm. Like most successful politicians, he modified his approach based on his audience. To Dunham, he stated a desire to have her stay in Senegal and train the company for at least another year; to the State Department, he expressed concern about her role and did not seem overly enthused about her work with the company. Furthermore, his nephew, the director of the National Theater where the ballet troupe was housed, disliked Dunham.[104] With the grant renewal dead and a personality conflict brewing with the nephew, Dunham quit as technical cultural advisor after a mere six weeks. She scraped by in Senegal for a few more months, "living on spit, chicken wire and charity" in order to remain outside of the United States for the eighteen months required to avoid paying income tax.[105]

During this final period in Dakar, Dunham began to write her ethnographic memoir of Haiti, *Island Possessed*, in which she also expressed her thoughts about Africa. Frustrated by her role with the festival and the National Ballet, she wrote, "I have been unable to feel emotional in Africa," revealing that she had failed to make the connections she desired.[106] *Island Possessed* also demonstrates how deeply Dunham attached herself to the idea of "acculturation," Herskovits's term for the coming together of European and African cultures. She noted that in Africa, "most of the acculturation is surface," for cultural practices on the continent were still "clearly marked off by tribal, clan, and national grouping."[107] Dunham held fast to the idea that the fusion of Europe and Africa in Haiti, as embodied by Touissant L'Ouverture, was ideal. She claimed that L'Ouverture was a "man of culture" who understood French principles, and "did not revert to the primitivism that keeps Africa from being a body of united nations today."[108] She also bemoaned what she saw as the corruption of *négritude*, a philosophy she had admired in the past as a "plea for humanism," which now was "so easily bordering on nationalism."[109]

She also wrote about Haiti as being more African than Africa. She described Téoline, one of the Haitian women who had presided over her *lavé tête* initiation in 1936, as "the large, earth-mother benevolence of the authentic African woman, undefiled by colonialism, untouched by the inroads of Western civilization in her own country, and enriched by the experience of slavery in the New World."[110] To describe slavery as "enrich[ing]" seems unconscionable. Dunham failed to recognize that her youth and inexperience when she met Teoline contributed to her nostalgic image, as contrasted to her experience in Senegal as a middle-aged world traveler. She continued, "In the New World, however, this earth mother, instead of remaining in the background, has been given her just due, perhaps because she fought for it, perhaps because there was so often opportunity for her to prove a selflessness and courage that is not typical of the Africa that I know."[111]

The gendered nature of Dunham's experience in Senegal also influenced her perspective. In dealing with the Ford Foundation, USAID, the State Department, and government of Senegal over the past four years, Dunham constantly found herself in rooms full of men who dismissed her ideas. Mitchell was the person tapped to lead the US dance committee for the Dakar Festival, and the Alvin Ailey American Dance Theater received all the accolades. She could not even attend the Ailey performances because she was busy preparing dinner for the company to eat afterward.[112] Instead of participating in the festival as an artistic director, she was fulfilling a stereotypical woman's role as domestic. Her conflict with the male head of the National Theater had led her to quit her consultant position after a few weeks. It seems that these conflicts reaffirmed Dunham's vision that Haiti, where she reigned as queen over Leclerc, was the heart and soul of global black culture.

For the rest of her life, Dunham continued to dream big for Haiti. In 1969, she wrote a proposal to the Rockefeller Foundation to make Habitation Leclerc a "center for research and confrontation," a place to investigate "cross-cultural communication" in the "Black World."[113] The center never materialized. Instead, financial need compelled Dunham, in 1972, to lease the majority of Habitation Leclerc to Olivier Coquelin, a French real estate developer who transformed the estate into a resort playground for wealthy European and American celebrities, including Mick Jagger, Prince Egon von Furstenberg, Jackie and Ari Onassis, and Baron Edmund de Rothschild. One journalist described the resort as a "dazzling new fleshpot" and "a haven for the hedonist who exchanges inhibitions for desire." Coquelin called it a place for guests to "enjoy a lascivious and decadent life."[114] For $150 a night, when the average yearly income for a Haitian person was less than $80, guests could eat, drink, and lounge to their hearts' content (see Figure 7.2). Williams, who had joined elite circles, called the opening night festivities "the most beautiful party in Haiti in years." Meanwhile, over 2,000 Haitians stood outside the gates, watching the wealthy and powerful enter.[115]

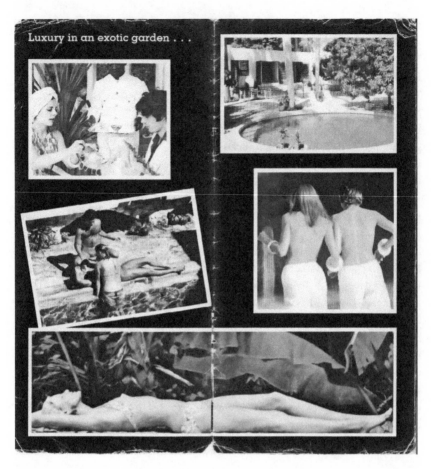

Figure 7.2 Brochure about Habitation Leclerc, mid-1970s. Photographer unknown. Courtesy of Ray Carrier.

Dunham started a smaller-scale, boutique hotel of her own on an adjoining piece of property called Residence Katherine Dunham. She enlisted an Israeli woman, Rosie Rubenstein, to run it. With most of her activist efforts now centered on East St. Louis and nearing retirement age, Dunham more and more considered Haiti a personal and spiritual retreat. She continued initiation into Vodou, undergoing the *canzo* ceremony and eventually becoming a *mambo*. She conducted her own ceremonies at a peristyle on her property, and like her Leclerc neighbor Coquelin, primarily invited well-heeled foreigners to attend.[116] For many Haitians today, this is the Dunham they remember: mysterious, closed off, and catering exclusively to Europeans and Americans.

Coquelin's pleasure palace was shut down in the early 1980s as the chronically unstable political conditions in Haiti worsened even further. Impoverished Haitians moved into the abandoned bungalows and villas, and eventually took over Residence Katherine Dunham as well when she started to spend less time there. While Dunham and others called the inhabitants "squatters" and "vandals,"[117] one could argue that citizens were finally inhabiting a space that had been taken from them 150 years earlier and reoccupied by foreigners since 1949. Some of the new Haitian residents also claimed to be former workers at Leclerc who had not been paid for their labor when Coquelin left.[118] Dunham often talked of turning Leclerc into a botanic garden, but she never fully followed through, for reasons that are up for debate.[119]

Later in life as in earlier, Dunham was best as an advocate for Haiti outside of Haiti. In 1992, a military coup ousted democratically elected president Jean-Bertrand Aristide, causing many Haitians to flee the country. The US Coast Guard turned back all refugees it found trying to enter the United States. Dunham staged a hunger strike in protest. Eighty-two-year-olds do not often go on hunger strikes, and her actions thrust the plight of the refugees into the national spotlight. Director Jonathan Demme (of *Silence of the Lambs* fame) held a vigil in New York in support of her actions; Louis Farrakhan, Dick Gregory, and Jesse Jackson visited her bedside. Black newspapers commended her work on behalf of "Haitian sisters and brothers," and pointed out that she was a model for black leadership, as someone who fought for "the Freedom of all."[120] The NAACP, American Jewish Committee, American Bar Association, AFL-CIO, and American Indian Movement showed support, as did school children in China and Japan. For forty-seven days, she subsisted on cranberry juice, hard candy, and water, remarkable for anyone but extraordinary given her age. Finally, after a final press conference that included Aristide himself, she ended it, feeling that the momentum had stalled.[121] Unfortunately, the strike did not have an effect on the government's refugee policy toward Haitians, and when President Clinton came into office in 1993, he continued the policy of his predecessor, George H. W. Bush.

Even though Dunham's efforts failed to produce tangible results, her insistence that Haitians be treated with the same dignity as Americans inspired many people across the nation. Her transnational solidarity stood forth as a model for how to become an ally to causes when one is not necessarily an insider. Ultimately, however, her greatest achievements in social justice through the arts happened not in Haiti or Senegal, but in her home state of Illinois. There, in the city of East St. Louis, she joined the Black Power revolution and put her radical humanist ideas into practice.

CHAPTER 8

The Radical Humanist Meets the Black Power Revolution

Dunham in East St. Louis

After returning to the United States from Senegal in the spring of 1967, Dunham was feeling unsure about her decision to settle in East St. Louis, Illinois. In coordination with Southern Illinois University (SIU), Dunham had developed a plan to improve East St. Louis through arts education, but she dreaded the thought of living there permanently. On April 25, she wrote to her friend Giovanella Zannoni, an Italian film producer, "I have come today to a conclusion which I think is firm": she would withdraw from the project to spend six months in Paris and six months in Haiti, rather than "panicking in th[e] isolation" of a declining, postindustrial midwestern city.[1] Four days later, she changed her mind. "The misery of East St. Louis is a terrible pull and I know that the president of the University ... expects me ... to confer and maybe do something about it," she admitted to Erich Fromm, with whom she had kept in touch since the Chicago days.[2] Feeling an obligation to use her decades of experience as an arts educator to help the city, she opened the Performing Arts Training Center (PATC) in June 1967 in a converted high school building.

Within a few years, Dunham had turned the troubled city of East St. Louis into an important hub of the Black Arts Movement, an artistic movement that shared Black Power's political goal of taking a more assertive stance to reject white supremacy in all areas of society, including culture. By 1972, she had enrolled over one thousand students in PATC, offered courses for college credit, founded a student dance company, opened a museum dedicated to African art, and secured hundreds of thousands of dollars of funding from government programs and private foundations. She routinely spoke of cultural "revolution," a term she had not used prior to 1965.[3] Dunham's efforts had ramifications beyond the city's limits. The PATC Performing Company performed at schools, rallies, and black cultural organizations across the nation, inspiring black pride. Dunham forged crucial links to black artists and intellectuals in Kansas City, Chicago, San Francisco, and New York, and overseas in Haiti, Nigeria, and Senegal. She became a board member for the Institute of the Black World in Atlanta and a co-organizer of the First International Congress of Black Dancers and Choreographers.

Even as she adopted the language of revolution and worked with students who invoked black nationalism, Dunham never abandoned her commitment to integrationist liberalism. In the 1960s, she gave herself a new epigraph—"radical humanist"—semantically combining the two intellectual foundations of her work.[4] She worked closely with university administrators, government officials, and private funders, assuring them that her goal was the "socialization and humanization" of East St. Louis youth.[5] At the PATC, ballet was taught alongside West African drumming, an echo of the curriculum at her New York school in the 1940s. She remained married to her white husband. In the 1970s, she turned her attention to a new endeavor, the Institute for Intercultural Communication, which de-emphasized black nationalism. She served on the board of the Kennedy Center for the Performing Arts, advised the National Council of the Arts in Education, and reviewed applications for the National Endowment for the Arts. Her embrace of liberal ideas was seemingly anathema to leaders of the Black Power movement, who were calling for a radical break with both European-American aesthetic standards and integrationist ideals.

Nevertheless, East St. Louis youth embraced Dunham, not the least because her cooperation with white liberal organizations in many ways ensured the success of the Black Arts Movement principles. With the funding from these organizations, PATC students created art by, for, and about black people. The PATC and Dunham's other institutions gave East St. Louis residents and African Americans throughout the Midwest a strong sense of individual and collective identity. Furthermore, Dunham's presence on the boards of "mainstream" arts organizations meant that she was able to be an advocate for the inclusion of black history and culture in nation-wide arts curricula. Though not of the 1960s youth generation most commonly considered the vanguard of the Black Power revolution, Dunham nonetheless nurtured the radical youth under her purview and supported their goals.[6] East St. Louis also changed Dunham, who had spent the majority of the 1950s and early 1960s abroad. As a result of her work in the Illinois city, she successfully rejoined the debate about the arts as a force in political and social movements of black America.

Dunham's journey to East St. Louis had begun five years prior to the opening of PATC. After the failure of her final revue, *Bamboche!*, in November 1962, she decided to stay in New York rather than return to Haiti. She wrote to a friend that she would now focus on "what has been essentially my purpose since 1938 ... that of bringing about inter-cultural exchanges in the most immediate sense" through a school.[7] In April 1963, she developed an arts outreach plan to serve the young people of Harlem, under the auspices of HARYOU (Harlem Youth Opportunities Unlimited Program), a new initiative by the Kennedy administration. In addition to classes and lecture-demonstrations, Dunham wanted HARYOU to include a performing group and eventually a professional dance company. She believed that a professional troupe would inspire students who "otherwise might be inclined to doubt a career in the performing arts, particularly in the social structure existing in America."[8] When the HARYOU program was still in the planning stages, Dunham also began to work with the Harlem Freedom Schools on Negro Art and Culture, serving as a consultant in developing a curriculum on "Afro American and African cultural contributions."[9] Years before the generally accepted advent of the Black Arts Movement, Dunham was laying the groundwork for African diasporic arts and education programs. Eventually, President Lyndon B. Johnson would incorporate HARYOU into the War on Poverty, placing the initiative under the Office of Economic Opportunity (OEO). Amiri Baraka would receive HARYOU funding for his Black Arts Repertory Theater in 1965, one of the founding institutions of the Black Arts Movement.[10]

By a twist of fate, Dunham's involvement in these arts initiatives ended up taking place in East St. Louis, not New York City. Dunham had withdrawn from the Harlem projects just weeks before President Kennedy's assassination on November 22, 1963, to focus on choreographing *Aida* for the Metropolitan Opera. She was the first African American hired to choreograph for the Met. She struggled, however, to make ends meet. Her brother-in-law Davis Pratt, a professor of design at the SIU main campus in Carbondale, offered a new possibility. He brought an SIU administrator, Burnett Shryock, to New York to see *Aida*. After an evening of Dunham's "wonderful chicken" and charming company, Shryock hired her to choreograph a production of *Faust* for SIU's theater department in the winter of 1964.[11] Though he voiced the hope that her appointment would lead to the creation of a dance department at the Carbondale campus, Dunham instead turned her attention to East St. Louis, a predominantly African American city a hundred miles to the northwest.

Located just across the Mississippi River from St. Louis, East St. Louis seemed ripe for an intervention. It had enjoyed a vibrant economy in the first half of the twentieth century because of its numerous industries and status as the second-busiest railway terminal in the country, but deindustrialization after World War II devastated the city. Dozens of factories closed, leaving many residents unemployed. The development of the federal highway system in the mid-1950s drastically reduced rail usage and further weakened the local economy. Financing for schools, sanitation, and other public services declined throughout the 1950s. In 1959, the only movie theater in town closed. In addition to the economic turmoil, federal housing policies that supported discriminatory mortgage lending contributed to the flight of the city's white, middle-class residents.[12] In 1950, the population of East St. Louis was 33 percent African American and 66 percent white. In 1970, it was 69 percent African American and 31 percent white, and the overall population had dropped by 16 percent.[13] The police force and City Hall, however, remained almost completely white. City government was notoriously corrupt, and the black community had been traumatized by the lingering memory of a brutal race riot in 1917.[14] Older black residents focused on church and family as sources of community strength, but by the 1960s, a younger generation began to protest against the entrenched racism and lack of opportunity in the city.

SIU saw itself as a part of the answer to East St. Louis's problems, even though its main campus was located far away. The regional state university was at the vanguard of a revolution in higher education that emphasized democratic access to post-secondary education and greater connectivity to local communities. SIU president Delyte Morris declared as early as 1944, "Only as a school grows out of a definite social need and as it prepares students to meet this social need will the school be truly filling its real function."[15] In 1962, he began to consider programs that would bring higher education to lower-income students and improve the region. Dunham became a part of that conversation when she arrived on campus. With SIU a willing partner, she developed a proposal for a "Cultural Enrichment Center" in East St. Louis, which she submitted, in July 1965, to the Community Action Program (CAP) of the OEO.

In the proposal, Dunham combined two different understandings of "culture" to make her case that an arts program could solve urban problems. The first approach defined culture as a set of attitudes or behaviors. Anthropologist Oscar Lewis had argued, in 1959, that the poor passed down a "culture of poverty" from generation to generation.[16] Lewis's ideas influenced the architects of Johnson's War on Poverty, including Daniel Patrick Moynihan. In 1965, Moynihan produced a report, *The Black Family: A Case for Action*, that suggested a correlation between black family structure, which he called a "tangle of pathology," and poverty. The report was leaked to the press and immediately received harsh criticism from civil rights activists.[17] Although the Johnson administration subsequently distanced itself from the "culture of poverty" thesis, several historians argue that the urban antipoverty efforts of the 1960s problematically continued to focus on behavior modification (or "culture"), rather than on solving the underlying structural issues of deindustrialization and racial discrimination.[18] Dunham deliberately used language that aimed at persuading government officials that her program could help solve the culture of poverty.

Dunham also spoke to the federal government's growing support for "culture" in the sense of elite arts. In 1959, philanthropist John D. Rockefeller III declared that business and political leaders had a "responsibility" to satisfy man's "spirit" and "humanness" through support of high culture. At a time of increasing complexity (especially for those living in urban environments), Americans needed "creative fulfillment" to "lighten the anxieties that darken our age."[19] The United States was the only major industrial country providing virtually no government support for the arts domestically. Presidents Kennedy and Johnson, in starting the conversation about federal funding for the arts, argued that elite culture would reflect American ideals of freedom, elevate citizens' quality of life, and combat the nation's growing materialism. Institutions such as Lincoln Center in New York City would make America's cities beacons of modernity for the rest of the world.[20] Dunham was aware of these new sentiments. In 1963, she had traveled to Washington at the behest of Senator Claiborne Pell to testify before Congress in favor of creating a National Endowment for the Arts, which was established in September 1965.[21]

Dunham tied together the behavioral and artistic definitions of culture in her OEO proposal on July 27, 1965. Her Cultural Enrichment Center, she wrote, could "be expected to provide support and groundwork for other parts of the War on Poverty by providing the means of breaking down psychological barriers to individual self-improvement."[22] Exposure to culture, meaning the arts, was the first steppingstone out of poverty because it made community members more psychologically open to changing their culture, meaning their attitudes and behaviors. Dunham returned to the understanding of dance she had pursued as an anthropologist in the Caribbean in the 1930s. Dance, she wrote, was essentially a social expression, useful "in group or individual catharsis, for the release of emotions, exhilaration, gratification of psychological & kinesthetic needs."[23] Through dance, community members could release tensions and find new means of communication and expression. In particular, the urban poor, once freed of psychological and emotional barriers, could break out of their dead-end situations. "If there is to be any progress at all towards the elimination of poverty," she wrote, "it is essential that certain undesirable elements in the community environment be eliminated by breaking the cycle of indifference and apathy which attends the limited horizons of the majority of the poor in the East St. Louis Area."[24]

By invoking "cycle" imagery, Dunham unwittingly reinforced the position of those who disavowed structural problems facing America's urban poor. She offered similar sentiments in a letter to OEO official Ralph Capprio, writing, "The apathy [of East St. Louis] is incredible and contagious and I firmly believe that a properly worked out program will inspire a desire to be relieved of the

Welfare situation rather than becoming addicted to it."[25] Dunham implied that a change in attitude would motivate the poor to pull themselves out of poverty. While she approached this issue with the aim of empowering local citizens, such language would eventually be co-opted by political conservatives who claimed that the biggest impediment facing the poor was the poor themselves.[26]

Despite several encouraging communications between Dunham and OEO officers, the OEO ultimately declined to fund the Cultural Enrichment Center. Sanford Kravitz, director of the Program Development Division of CAP, expressed a number of reservations about the project in his rejection letter in December 1965. Kravitz noted that the OEO, a relatively new part of the federal government, still felt uncertain about the connection between the arts and the alleviation of poverty, though they considered "culture" in the sense of behaviors and attitudes to be crucial to the fight. They were intrigued by Dunham's statements about dance as an antipoverty tool, but felt less certain about the other components of the center, such as theater and music. Kravitz was also doubtful about replicating the center in other areas of the country, an ostensible goal of all CAP-funded initiatives. Dunham had a "commanding and impressive personality," and Kravitz feared that "the success of the program might well rest on that, rather than on the inherent value of the service rendered." Finally, he voiced concern that "there does not appear to be significant involvement of the poor themselves" in planning or running the center. Dunham's application had listed SIU administrators in all the key positions. CAP faced mounting criticism that local citizens were not involved enough in designing or implementing projects, so funding Dunham's center would potentially reinforce such criticism.[27]

Another, unstated concern likely worried the OEO. Earlier that month, a firestorm of controversy had erupted over the funding of Amiri Baraka's Black Arts Repertory Theater in Harlem. Baraka's plays challenged white supremacy using what many white politicians considered extremist and offensive language. Over a hundred members of Congress wrote to the OEO demanding an explanation as to why the federal government should fund what they called a "racial-hate school."[28] Although the OEO defended its funding process, in the wake of the Baraka controversy it likely felt more hesitant about giving money to performing arts programs in predominantly black urban areas.

Even if the OEO grant had gone through, the project might have fallen apart in 1965. Dunham had always seen herself as a cosmopolitan without local roots. She had little desire to run the center herself; she felt isolated in southern Illinois and preferred to serve as a consultant from afar.[29] It was in July 1965 that she received State Department funding to attend the First World Festival of Negro Arts in Dakar, Senegal, and she subsequently left the country for almost two years. When news came of the OEO's rejection in

December 1965, Dunham was already gone and busy pressing SIU with proposals to develop international cultural-exchange projects with Senegal.[30]

Dunham's time in Dakar, explored more fully in Chapter 7, was crucial
to the development of her East St. Louis programs for multiple reasons. It
gave her new ties to Africa, which enhanced her ability to connect with youth
thirsty for knowledge of African culture. The experience also allowed her to
continue experimenting in the new direction she wanted to take dance. She
wrote to a friend, "I find that Senegal has done something important for me.
I have been forced to teach again from the very rudimentary analytical basis
which was the beginning of my career."[31] She wanted to return to the idea of
dance as one element in the matrix of a whole social complex.

Because of dance's social potential, she became even more convinced of its
utility in addressing the concerns of East St. Louis. She wrote to SIU administrator Ralph Ruffner in August 1966, "I feel well placed to proceed on studies
which should not only be documented but which might in some not so remote
way lead to a better understanding of some of our unsolved problems" and
described with excitement new efforts by Senegalese psychiatrists to treat
patients through dance and music.[32] The trip gave Dunham a new perspective
on the southern Illinois city. "I look on East St. Louis as a sort of outpost in
the world," she stated to the *St. Louis Post-Dispatch* a few months after returning from Senegal in 1967. "I've been all over the world and I've never known
an area with so much apathy and less reason to hope."[33] Even though Senegal
faced formidable obstacles in overcoming the legacy of colonialism, at least it
had cultural resources. Dunham had listened to Senghor proclaim in his opening address at the Dakar Festival in April 1966, "This Negro art sustains us
in our effort toward economic and social development, in our *determination
to live*."[34] Dunham aspired to bring this promise of black art to East St. Louis
when she returned to the United States in April 1967.

The national mood had changed during Dunham's two-year absence. The Watts
Rebellion, the rise of Black Power, and the founding of the Black Panther Party
had all occurred while she was abroad. The Black Arts Movement, the "aesthetic and spiritual sister" of Black Power, had also gained momentum. In a
manifesto for *Drama Review*, Black Arts Movement leader Larry Neal declared
that there were "two Americas—one black, and one white."[35] To liberate mind,
body, and spirit from white supremacy, young black artists had to create revolutionary new art inspired solely by the black experience. Neal wrote, "The
Western aesthetic has run its course: it is impossible to construct anything
meaningful within its decaying structure. We advocate a cultural revolution
in art and ideas."[36]

Not only had the United States changed, but so had Dunham herself. Nearly
sixty years old, she no longer wanted to perform. She finally felt ready to focus

on "that other thing of public service in my own peculiar way."[37] SIU and the St. Clair County branch of the Economic Opportunity Commission gave her $43,000 to open her cultural enrichment center, now called the PATC.[38] SIU president Morris still believed strongly in the cause of developing programs to help East St. Louis youth. In 1966, for example, he founded the Experiment in Higher Education, a school for low-income students who wanted to attend college but lacked adequate preparation. He compared the school and other SIU programs to Johnson's Great Society efforts, boasting that his own "community-oriented state university" provided the best antipoverty initiatives in the country.[39] Dunham added a cultural component to SIU's mission. In June 1967, PATC offered its first free classes: Primitive Rhythms, Dunham Technique, Introductory Percussion, Advanced Percussion, Music Evaluation, Film Evaluation, and Anatomy of Motion. She convinced several of her former company members to come teach.

Progress, initially, was slow. East St. Louis teenagers viewed anyone over the age of twenty-five with suspicion. They shied away from associating with Dunham's homosexual male dancers, for the masculinist rhetoric of Black Power was saturated with homophobia. Dunham also encountered resistance from the older generation. Though East St. Louis had a national reputation as a "wide-open" town, meaning, a place where prostitution, gambling, and drinking were practiced freely, a large segment of the African American community espoused conservative, Christian values. Her cosmopolitan ways and affiliation with Haitian Vodou did not impress the churchgoers. Rumors swirled that she practiced black magic and bit the heads off snakes. Her gay dancers did not appeal to the older generation either. Parents forbade their children to visit the hotbed of homosexuality that Dunham's center seemed to represent.[40]

To gain support for the program, Dunham began conducting lecture-demonstrations at various SIU campuses. Cleverly, she called these events "drumming demonstrations" in order to attract male students, even though dance was her primary focus. To young East St. Louis men, dance seemed feminine and soft. Drums, in contrast, felt directly connected to the pulsing, masculine energy of Black Power.[41] One night, in July 1967, a friend convinced nineteen-year-old Darryl Braddix to go see "this lady and her drums" in Edwardsville, Illinois. Braddix recalled that in a crowd of hundreds, she zeroed in on him and commanded him to take the stage. He complied, decked out in Levis and a black sweater, looking, as he later recalled, "like a Black Panther or something," and followed her lead in doing Progressions.[42] The experience captivated Braddix, who now wanted to learn more.

Gaining Braddix's allegiance proved invaluable to Dunham's goal of reaching local youth. Though the perception of Dunham probably changed slowly over time, one apocryphal event stands out East St. Louisans' minds as decisively turning the tide in favor of her program: her arrest. On July 29, 1967,

Braddix took Dunham to a meeting of the Imperial War Lords, a Black Power organization. After the meeting, the group went to a local bar, where Braddix and three others were arrested. Dunham followed the police car to the station to ask what the charges were against her youthful guide. She refused to give her name and continued to insist on knowing the charges, since Braddix had been arrested without any clear provocation. According to Dunham, the police officers grabbed her arms roughly and threw her into a "dirty cell with no water." Three hours later, when the officers discovered her identity, they released her with an official apology. She later returned to the jail, accompanied by a lawyer, to assist Braddix. In exchange, Braddix agreed to drum up support for the PATC.[43]

The arrest earned Dunham respect of East St. Louis youths, especially because she had helped get Braddix released and refused to reveal her name.[44] It also put the program in the national spotlight. Newspapers across the country, including the *New York Times, Los Angeles Sentinel*, and Baltimore *Afro-American* reported on Dunham's activities. Her picture made the front page of the Nation of Islam's newspaper, *Muhammad Speaks!*, under the headline, "The Devil and East St. Louis: The Worst Hell-Hole in America."[45] Local journalists, too, wanted to find out more about Dunham and her experimental new program.

In interviews with the East St. Louis press, Dunham shared her thoughts about the importance of the arts in building stronger communities. As in her grant application to the OEO, she avoided discussing larger structural problems. She told the *East St. Louis Monitor* that the "causes of poverty" stemmed from a "breakdown in communications" that had "strangle[d] a climate of harmony and good will necessary in a democratic society." Americans had lost the ability to understand one another, especially across racial lines. Dance, and the performing arts in general, had a "vital function in meeting man's natural needs to communicate" and thus could serve to remedy the problem.[46] Learning to express emotions through movement, drumbeats, or singing would teach students a new way to communicate to others, and intercultural communication would diminish racial prejudice.

Dunham's philosophy went against that of many Black Power activists, who saw white supremacy and institutionalized inequality, not a "breakdown in communications," as the primary causes of poverty in urban black communities. Nor did Black Power activists necessarily believe that intercultural communication would help end racism. In fact, many believed that white Americans' involvement in civil rights hindered progress, which is why SNCC (Student Nonviolent Coordinating Committee) voted to ban white members in December 1966. Yet Dunham's emphasis on African diasporic arts, her willingness to go to jail, and her commitment to living in East St. Louis outweighed her non-black-nationalist stances on poverty and integration, at least for the East St. Louis youth who began to flow into her programs.

By January 1968, the PATC was operating on a full schedule, offering classes for college credit through the Experiment in Higher Education and noncredit classes that were open to the public. Again, all classes were free. The winter quarter schedule listed twenty-eight classes a week, which included: Ballet, Dunham Technique, Percussion, Design for Theatre, Judo as Sport, Primitive Rhythms, and even Sewing. The teachers included Dunham, Pratt, former Dunham company dancer Camille Yarbrough, and even Braddix, who only six months earlier had had no interest in dance.[47] For the spring quarter, class offerings increased even further. Dunham pushed Africa-focused students to expand their horizons and take courses such as the Japanese Tea Ceremony, which she believed would teach ritual and discipline.[48]

Dunham soon organized a performing group, the PATC Performing Company, recognizing that opportunities to perform gave students concrete goals. She developed new repertory to reflect the issues and social needs of her students. In March 1968, she put together a public program for the East St. Louis community that included demonstrations of song, dance, and drumming by the instructors. Two pieces, *Psychadelia* and *The Lesson*, included students only a few months into their training.[49] She also created *Ode to Taylor Jones*, a dance drama that eulogized a young East St. Louis native and regional leader of CORE (Congress on Racial Equality) who had recently died in a car accident. In *Taylor Jones*, the chorus sang lines, such as "Ol' white power's given out / While Black has just begun" and "Taylor Jones was never bought / In life or after never caught / All they could find in that last hour / Was one small button / 'Black Power.'"[50] By penning these lyrics, Dunham demonstrated that she understood and respected the concerns of black youth.

Taylor Jones also connected the Black Power struggle to the wider African diaspora. The opening speech commented on Jones's importance for "human rights," linking his political activities to revolutionary movements across the globe. At one point, the musicians began playing Haitian rhythms that invoked the *loas* who signify death. In response, the dancers expressed grief through ritualized movements. One performer portrayed *Papa Guede*, a *loa* who stands at the crossroads between life and death to guide souls to the afterlife.[51] *Taylor Jones* both addressed a topic of deep personal relevance and introduced audiences to other African diasporic cultural traditions surrounding death, implicitly reminding East St. Louisans of their connection to a wider world.

Overall, Dunham's new choreography broached the topics of drugs, violence, youth education, and political activism, topics almost nonexistent in her company repertoire from the 1930s through 1950s. Unfettered by Cold War politics or the need to fill the seats of a music hall, Dunham was finally able to marry her political and aesthetic commitments onstage. She never mentioned activist Ron Karenga, but it is clear that she believed in the principles that Karenga outlined for what black arts needed to be: "*functional, collective* and *committing.*"[52] Dunham had specific goals with her choreography (functional);

she worked with youth and adults in the community to create the program (collective), and she committed herself wholeheartedly (committing).

Though aligned with the spirit of the Black Arts Movement, Dunham also impressed liberal funders. In 1968, the Arts and Education Council of Greater St. Louis submitted a proposal to the Rockefeller Foundation to support both PATC and an artists-in-residence program in St. Louis. Three main arguments convinced the Rockefeller Foundation to fund the proposal: the fact that community members themselves wanted cultural programs, the programs' emphasis on community empowerment, and Dunham's assurance that the ultimate goal would be to enhance communication across the racial divide. Norman Lloyd of the foundation came to tour East St. Louis in January 1968. Although almost every aspect of the city needed improvement, East St. Louis citizens expressed to him that building places of "recreation and culture" was among their top priorities.[53] Michael Newton of the Arts and Education Council convinced Lloyd that the arts represented a unique opportunity for intervention because black communities in the St. Louis area (and across the nation) had grown hostile to programs in housing and public health, which were seen as "Establishment" and paternalistic. By supporting black artists like Dunham who emphasized African diasporic cultural education, public-private initiatives in urban renewal could get an "in" into these communities.[54]

Not only did the Newton/Dunham proposal have community support, but also it seemed to offer more opportunities for local involvement than other urban renewal efforts. Apparently Dunham had learned from her OEO rejection in 1965. According to the proposal, PATC explicitly prioritized participation and "respect for the distinctive characteristics of the cultural life of the people to be served." By educating city residents about the rich heritage of African diasporic culture, the program would "give voice to the largely 'voiceless' residents of the inner city."[55] PATC also included a "teacher-trainee" program, in which students would learn to teach and eventually take over the instructor positions. The emphasis on black aesthetics and community autonomy, however, did not mean that Dunham and Newton would embrace separatism. Rather, they assured the Rockefeller Foundation that their main goal was to "help build communication across the white/black, rich/poor divisions of our society."[56] This formulation translated Black Arts Movement imperatives into a digestible, liberal democratic form.

On this point of racial reconciliation and cooperation, Dunham had to assuage the fears of the Rockefeller Foundation about her work with black militant groups and her focus on African diasporic arts. She insisted that funders had to let black youth feel in control of determining their future, for the students would eventually come around to better interracial communication after their "socialization through the arts." She argued that it did not matter if the instruments or dances learned were "primitive" rather than "high culture," for "what counts" in arts education "is incentive to the learning process."[57] Such a statement was curious, given that throughout her career, Dunham had challenged the distinction between "primitive" and "high culture," arguing that so-called primitive dance was "as highly developed" as ballet or European-American modern dance.[58] Regardless, her point was that through education about African-diasporic expressive culture, youth learned how they fit into the broader social complex. With confidence in their own identities and knowledge about the wider world, they would have the social skills needed to integrate into mainstream society.

By the end of his visit to East St. Louis, Lloyd was convinced. He wrote in his notes, "instead of believing that the Negro needed only to discover himself in African art, [Dunham] is coming around to where she feels . . . that he must think of himself primarily as an American."[59] Again, Dunham must have stifled some of her own beliefs to placate Lloyd, as she had never emphasized national American identity. After receiving assurance that the federal government's Model Cities Program would take on the burden of funding after the first year, the Rockefeller Foundation approved a $100,000 grant, which the St. Louis–based Danforth Foundation quickly matched.[60] Dunham was tapped as director of the funds for East St. Louis, most of which would go to the PATC.[61]

What probably further assured the liberal funders was that nothing in Dunham and Newton's proposal fundamentally challenged the economic and political structures that had caused poverty in the first place. In a letter to the Rockefeller Foundation in support of PATC, A. Donald Bourgeois of the East St. Louis Model City Agency wrote, "In an area where so many people are unemployed, it is imperative that we get into operation a strong arts and recreation program . . . . The need to feel productive, to be creative is a need which I feel the Model City Program must work to satisfy."[62] Dunham echoed such sentiments by pointing out that her programs helped East St. Louis youth spend their free time creatively, not destructively.[63] This reasoning revealed a fundamental problem with the cultural approach: the proposed arts program would solve a symptom of unemployment—excess leisure time—but not the problem of unemployment itself. Although Dunham also argued that she was providing job training, the teacher-trainees never numbered more than forty out of a city population of more than 50,000.[64] Intellectuals and policy makers of the 1960s emphasized changes in the social sphere but often stopped short of fighting for broad economic changes that could address the root causes of urban poverty.[65]

Foundation support for PATC had symbolic resonance beyond its local impact in East St. Louis. The Rockefeller Foundation called the program "an important experiment in determining the extent to which the arts can help to solve the social problems of the urban ghettos."[66] Although the federal government did not provide financial support at this stage, the assistant director of HUD (Department of Housing and Urban Development) did offer praise, stating, "This collective effort by national private foundations and government and private organizations in a metropolitan area is an excellent example of the co-operation the Model Cities Program is striving to obtain."[67] PATC was a test case for the viability of cultural (meaning artistic) solutions to what were perceived as the cultural (meaning way of life) problems of poverty.

Although the grant applications to Rockefeller and Danforth emphasized interracial cooperation, the volatile situation of East St. Louis caused Dunham to focus more immediately on the local black community's need for survival. The death of Dr. Martin Luther King in April 1968 triggered a wave of riots across the country, and the unrest spread to East St. Louis. Dunham made urgent appeals to Illinois governor Otto Kerner Jr. and East St. Louis mayor Alvin G. Fields to close the schools until the situation was defused, as she knew personally of "young militants" who had set bombs. Instead the mayor and government called in a thousand state troopers, but teachers walked out and school was canceled anyway. Violence spread to the middle-school level. One of Dunham's students, age thirteen, purchased two .22 rifles. Shootings and the launching of hand grenades occurred routinely on the streets outside her house. Interestingly enough, the prospect of facing imminent death inspired Dunham. She wrote to her friend Giovanella, "It is interesting how feeling certain now of the date of my death I find I have something to live for!"[68]

The situation in East St. Louis continued to deteriorate over the summer. Dunham found it increasingly difficult to keep the PATC Performing Company going when teenage dancers considered it too dangerous to walk home at night from rehearsals.[69] In an effort to stop the violence, she became directly involved with militant groups, trying to channel their energies into the arts, and redirected PATC funds to support them. She asked, for example, that a $3,000 fee paid to the Performing Company be sent to a bail bond fund for a group called the Black Liberators.[70] She also arranged for the Performing Company to put on a benefit performance at the Gateway Theater in St. Louis to help needy families of East St. Louis. Emory Link, professor of urban studies at SIU, told Lloyd, "'Thank God for Katherine Dunham—she has been the one who so far staved off disaster."[71] Marie-Christine Dunham Pratt recalled, "I cannot tell you how many times young men came up to me to say, 'If your mother hadn't come [to East St. Louis], I'd be dead.'"[72]

Although many were grateful for Dunham's efforts, her inability to operate within a budget and the Rockefeller and Danforth Foundations' unwillingness to become permanent funders soon led to financial problems. The foundations had agreed to support PATC for eighteen months; Dunham spent all the money in twelve months. Luckily, the state-financed Illinois Arts Council gave her a stopgap $25,000.[73] Another problem was the failure of the East St. Louis Model City Agency to follow through on its assurance to fund the program in the fall of 1969. Despite receiving $3.5 million from HUD, the East

St. Louis Model City Agency was decimated by political corruption to the point where almost no project got off the ground. As an additional problem, the local EOC office noted that Dunham had "offended some of the local politicos who try to utilize Federal grants for their own purposes."[74] By January 1970, Dunham had placated the Agency enough that it agreed to give the paltry sum of $13,000 with the condition that PATC aim for even "greater citizen involvement."[75]

A Model City Agency report from 1970 reveals another reason why it did not offer Dunham more support. It stated that while programs such as PATC "can give voice to increased awareness, self-pride, and confidence and build communications across the White/Black, rich/poor divisions of our society," the "larger range of characteristics that constitute Black Culture, derived from the Ghetto, from slave days and southern traditions, from the reaction to urbanization, and from poverty and deprivation may be hindrances to the goals of most Blacks for upward mobility."[76] The report linked black culture to a culture of poverty, implying that African American cultural traditions, far from being rich and vibrant, were entangled with experiences of abjection that had the potential to transfer that abjection to the next generation. Beyond political ineptitude, the Model City officials adopted a conservative, even racist philosophy that boded poorly for their future support of the PATC. In contrast to these officials, Dunham saw education in black culture as the key to upward social mobility for East St. Louis youth. Crucially, she saw this cultural education as diasporic. Dunham had long attributed many of East St. Louis' problems to the city's isolation, so she brought the world to her students. Between 1968 and 1970, she hired drummers Zakarya Diouf and Mor Thiam of Senegal, sculptor Paul Osifo of Nigeria, dramatist Muthal Naidoo of South Africa, and anthropologist Ena Campbell of Jamaica. She opened what she called the Dynamic Museum, filled with artifacts from her travels in Africa that visitors could touch.

Most importantly, Dunham attempted to make PATC a degree-granting institution of higher education, tapping into the nationwide movement to establish black studies programs. Beginning in the late 1960s, black students on college campuses demanded new courses with greater relevance to their lives and the modification of existing courses to reflect black contributions to American history. Dunham filled an entire scrapbook with newspaper articles on these student efforts, suggesting that she saw her work as aligned with their mission to reorient higher education.[77] African diasporic performing arts, she argued in an essay from 1970, were a way for disaffected or apathetic students in the area to tap into higher education. Students would start with areas of direct interest—a drumming class, an African dance class—and eventually add other courses that PATC offered, leading to an associate's degree. Once socialized to higher education and with a degree in hand, they could then pursue a bachelor's degree at more "conventional" institutions and integrate successfully into mainstream public life.[78]

For the PATC degree program Dunham insisted on alternative admissions criteria, another radical component that aligned with the nationwide black student movement. She did not count test scores, high school rank, or GPA but relied on recommendation letters, evidence of leadership ability, and career aspirations. This alternative model made it difficult to get funding. In an April 1971 report to SIU, she insisted that the chaotic and crisis-ridden conditions of life in East St. Louis mandated flexibility and adaptability, and that it was therefore hard to judge concrete progress. Furthermore, there were no precedents to guide PATC's development. The Rockefeller Foundation, SIU, and State of Illinois wanted to evaluate students and the program using traditional criteria, but Dunham argued that East St. Louis youth were "excluded by the very nature of the traditional requirements."[79]

Dunham expressed frustration with the inability of funders to understand her methods and objectives for the degree program. In 1971, the consultant she hired to evaluate PATC, Bill Brennan, suggested that she abandon her efforts in higher education. "The academic world is simply not free enough or flexible enough," Brennan wrote, "to supervise in any way a program which is avant-garde and grass-roots oriented, and which is implicitly critical of the educational establishment."[80] Dunham ignored the advice, and the academic program continued. Students could take classes for credit (transferable to other branches of SIU and potentially elsewhere) throughout the late 1960s and 1970s, but were not assured of an associate's degree at the end.[81]

Dunham also ignored Brennan's advice about restructuring the administration and finances of the program. She insisted on maintaining personal control over all decisions and refused to delegate authority. Brennan wrote that the staff functioned "as extensions of her body." He continued, "This means that no one can devote himself systematically to doing one fixed portion of the total work . . . without being ready to drop everything to respond to Katherine's immediate need."[82] Accustomed to reigning supreme as the artistic director of her dance company, Dunham seemed to enjoy having those under her respond to her beck and call. She placed personal friends in administrative positions to which they were highly unsuited, building an organizational culture where loyalty trumped competency. The misallocation of funds was another significant problem. For example, Dunham had spent $2,000 in grant money on art acquisitions for the Dynamic Museum, at a time when the Museum did not have enough funds to stay open, let alone to store or display the already existing objects.[83]

In contrast to his skepticism about the degree program and concerns about administrative dysfunction, Brennan saw the community classes and Performing Company as the "key to everything."[84] By 1970, between 200 and 300 students took PATC classes at the main building, and another 1,400 took classes at neighborhood community centers or public schools; 1,000 (pre-schoolers) took classes through Head Start, and 200 adults through the Concentrated Employment Program.[85] The free and open classes, not the degree program, created the greatest sense of community in the area. Ruby Streate remembers the late 1960s and early 1970s as a time when "everyone" in East St. Louis was taking a drumming or dancing class at PATC. Streate herself had undergone a remarkable personal transformation because of the institution. One of ten children, she began taking classes that PATC offered at her high school and soon joined the Performing Company. She was a rebellious teen-ager, and by her own account, headed for trouble. She would miss rehearsals and start fights with fellow dancers, which led to a warning that she would not be allowed to tour. The warning had an effect. Filled with a desire to perform, she developed self-discipline and traveled with the Performing Company to Atlanta and Washington, DC.[86]

Brennan felt even more strongly about the Performing Company's role in revitalizing East St. Louis and potentially urban communities across the nation. "The performing group is the *proof* of the merit of the whole program," he stated. "If you can transfer ghetto kids into real, proud performers, you have a living embodiment of everything you are trying to do."[87] Apparently, the Rockefeller Foundation agreed. Having denied Dunham's funding request of $311,948 for 1970–71, it did give her $23,000 specifically for the Performing Company.[88]

Brennan's faith was not misplaced. The Performing Company was flooded with performance requests from K-12 schools, historically black colleges and universities, black student and cultural organizations, and other groups throughout the Midwest during the late 1960s and early 1970s.[89] They traveled extensively to accommodate as many of these invitations as possible. Dunham was famed for her fearlessness. Wherever there seemed to be violence or controversy, she would take the Performing Company. Former members recall dancing in Kansas City in front of Ku Klux Klan protesters and in Cairo, Illinois, amid gun violence. They provided the spiritual uplift, the rallying energy, for Black Power.[90] They also took part in symbolically important events for the Black Arts Movement. In January 1970, for example, the company performed at the gala opening for the Institute of the Black World in Atlanta. Dunham created the dance "Chaka—Zulu" for these performances, a number that would remain in the repertory for years. The dance told the story of "a great folk hero of South Africa" who "succeeded in re-uniting many warring tribes and finally created a Zulu empire."[91] Whereas previously her career had focused on the Caribbean, in this new era Dunham drew on her more recent experience in Africa and tapped into growing youth demand for knowledge of African roots and cultural traditions.

Community response was overwhelmingly positive. Youth, teachers, and administrators wrote enthusiastic thank-you letters after the performances.

"You pricked our consciences, stirred our complacencies and lifted our spirits in a single evening," a woman from Marillac College of St. Louis wrote. "I learned a lot about African culture that I didn't know before," wrote a high school student. "Your organization has brought so much happiness, cultural training and education as well as entertainment to St. Louis, East St. Louis and our entire area ... I often wonder what it was like before Mrs. Dunham came here and developed the center," mused a member of the Berea Presbyterian Church.[92] Through its inspiring and exhilarating performances, the Performing Company left an indelible imprint on the collective well-being of African Americans throughout the Midwest.

In the fall of 1970, Dunham began planning an even more ambitious project: to take forty-two school-age students to perform in Washington, DC, for the White House Conference on Children. Many of them had never left the city before, let alone flown on an airplane. At the conference on December 15, 1970, at the White House, the delegates were "astounded" at the musical strengths of the children's groups that performed at the Conference. In particular, they were roused by the finale that included "a percussion orchestra, interpretive dancers, a karate dance team, and a rock band," all from the PATC. This finale "managed to draw in the entire cast spontaneously" and punctuated the end of the evening with a vigorous exclamation mark.[93] PATC students had achieved far more than most people had thought possible.

Achievement also lay in the local community-building aspect of the event. In the weeks and months leading up to the White House performance fundraising was necessary to pay for rehearsals, teachers and consultants, transportation to and from rehearsals, and costumes. Though most of the funding came from PATC's regular budget, East St. Louis families formed a steering committee to garner additional monies. Conservative parents who had been suspicious of Dunham now supported her work, as they were excited for their children to perform at the White House.[94] Mayor Alvin Fields took the unusual step of writing a letter to the city's businesses and government offices to ask them to support Dunham's efforts. The police force agreed to help transport the children, the local Economic Opportunity Commission office donated sandwiches, and other local businesses helped with raising monies and providing snacks. The Black Egyptians, a Black Power organization, provided crucial nonmonetary help. They transported students to rehearsals if the police could not and drove to each parent's home to get signatures on permission slips and other necessary paperwork. Although Dunham felt slightly bitter that the community did not offer more financial support, this level of involvement was unprecedented for East St. Louis.[95]

A second triumph occurred a little over a year later, when Dunham would again see the fruits of her East St. Louis efforts on a national stage. In January 1972, Morehouse College decided to stage the world premiere of Scott Joplin's long-lost opera, *Treemonisha*, composed in 1908 and discovered in 1970 by scholar Joshua Rifkin. The producers invited Dunham to a music rehearsal, hoping to woo her to do the choreography. As she told reporters later about that day, "By the time I heard the rehearsal, someone else would have had to do it over my dead body."[96] She brought twenty-five students from the PATC to form the dance chorus. In 1972, the opera was performed twice, first at Morehouse to a majority-black audience and then at Wolf Trap, an outdoor theater in the Virginia suburbs of Washington, DC, to a predominantly white audience.

The performances of *Treemonisha* were successful, but not because of Joplin's story or the orchestration. According to the local Atlanta and Washington newspapers, the *New York Times, Christian Science Monitor, Chicago Tribune,* and the academic journal *Phylon,* Dunham's dancers stole the show. One reviewer commented that "the lion's share of the credit for making the piece a tolerable entertainment goes to Katherine Dunham ... [her] touch is magical, and she did wonders with the big production pieces." Another wrote, "The production as a whole has been galvanized into a compelling drama by the singular genius of Katherine Dunham."[97] Joplin's opera called for many dance numbers, including a traditional ring-shout, the "Frolic of the Bears," "Aunt Dinah Has Blowed de Horn," and a finale, "A Real Slow Drag." These dances gave the show the final push toward favorable reviews, making it possible for investors to support further productions of *Treemonisha.* More importantly for East St. Louis, the opera became a unifying project in which the whole community took pride. Elementary school students, teenagers, adults, and even the elderly participated in organizing, rehearsing, traveling, and dancing in the production. The White House and *Treemonisha* performances are only two examples of many that demonstrate how PATC simultaneously influenced both East St. Louis and a broader community during its heyday in the late 1960s and early 1970s.

Dunham's approach also gained national recognition as a model for cultural initiatives. Between 1968 and 1975, she served as a consultant to the Institute of American Indian Arts in New Mexico on developing an American Indian Theater and intercultural education program. She traveled to Gainesville, Florida, to help set up a similar program at a local community college. She served on the Multi-Racial Steering Committee of the National Council of the Arts in Education, and when the Kennedy Center opened its doors in 1971, she was appointed to serve as a technical adviser in intercultural communication. Other groups came to East St. Louis to learn the model firsthand, including the Walla Walla Basics youth group from Chicago and Topper Carew, president of the New Thing Art and Architecture Center in Washington, DC. She served on the board of the Institute for the Black World in Atlanta, run by Vincent Harding. Along with Carole Johnson, founder of M.O.D.E. (Modern Organization for Dance Evolvement), she put the wheels in motion to organize

Figure 8.1 PATC students Linda McKinley and Darryl Braddix on train tracks in East St. Louis, 1970. Photographer unknown. Missouri History Museum, St. Louis.

the First International Congress of Black Dancers and Choreographers, which occurred in 1973 as the First National Congress on Blacks in Dance.[98]

All of this activity took place during an FBI inquiry into Dunham. During the late 1960s, the FBI began a massive investigation of Black Power groups, as part of its COINTELPRO (Counterintelligence Program). The St. Louis office was particularly interested in the Black Liberators. Dunham supported this group and attended its meetings, offering to provide members with "international contacts."[99] Several documents from the investigation remain redacted, since most of the reports came from an informant who infiltrated Black Liberators meetings. At one point, the FBI tried to foment division by circulating a false newspaper article purportedly written by younger Black Power activists that ridiculed Dunham, but based on the evidence in Dunham's archives, it seems that the article had little effect.[100]

PATC, the PATC Performing Company, Institute for Intercultural Communication, and Dynamic Museum continued to operate throughout the 1970s with success. Decreased funding and the entrenched corruption in East St. Louis's political system, however, made it difficult to extend the achievements in the cultural arena to the broader community.[101] Dunham also became increasingly dissatisfied with the SIU partnership, feeling that a major university could not be flexible or responsive enough to community needs. After retiring from SIU in 1982, Dunham opened the Katherine Dunham Children's Workshop and turned her focus to elementary and secondary school youth. The Children's Workshop continues to operate to this day.

During a time of tremendous violence and political unrest, in a place with few opportunities for recreation or public gathering, the PATC gave East St. Louis residents an identity that contradicted their national image as abject and violent ghetto dwellers. Dunham successfully engaged with both Black Power activists and liberal funders to create a thriving institution in which children, adults, and the elderly could weave a new fabric of community life. Students of the PATC transformed their lives. Braddix, a former drug dealer and high school dropout, went on to have a career as a firefighter and dance instructor. Eugene Redmond became a renowned poet. Warrington Hudlin received a scholarship to Yale and became a successful filmmaker based in New York. Since 1995, Marcia Robinson has been the director of the West Las Vegas Arts Center, which she models after the community-engagement ethos of the PATC. The list of examples could go on and on.

Finally, through the PATC, Dunham reestablished herself as a political activist and important voice in the dance world. Instead of disappearing from the arts mainstream, she became a national-level arts policy adviser. She nurtured the Black Arts Movement and built an international, diasporic network. Her tenacity, her intelligence, and her adaptability guided her as she adjusted to the new cultural and political landscape and found a place for her vision.

Epilogue

Dunham's Legacy

Dunham's combination of intellectual, artist, celebrity, educator, institution-builder, and activist has almost never been matched. Trying to communicate her multifaceted legacy thus presents a challenge, as contemporary parallels never quite align. Beyoncé has the celebrity, mesmerizing performance ability, artistic innovation, and increasingly after 2016, the activist orientation, but not the intellectual or pedagogical influence. Many dancer-choreographers in the twenty-first century are obtaining Master of Fine Arts (MFA) or Doctor of Philosophy (PhD) degrees, but few come close to matching Dunham's stature as an artist, let alone as a celebrity. She is uniquely inspirational as a model for how to live holistically: how to merge ideas and action, artistry and activism, mind and body. Because she applied her ideas primarily through dance, it is in the dance world that the efforts to promote her legacy are the most visible, efforts that have faced challenges over the years.

Maintaining any choreographer's legacy is difficult. Because dance is inherently an ephemeral art form, its greatest power and beauty lie in the moment of live performance. Balanchine famously argued that choreography should not attempt to live past its expiration date. He claimed that he expected his own work to die naturally as new choreographers, who spoke to new social contexts, came to the fore.[1] Ironically, of course, the company he co-founded with Lincoln Kirstein, New York City Ballet, still thrives and performs his work regularly. The Balanchine Foundation has become a major institution that licenses Balanchine repertory to ballet companies across the globe. The legal dispute over Martha Graham's school, company, and choreography caused deep divisions from which it was difficult to recover.[2] Merce Cunningham, not wanting to repeat the Graham debacle, instructed his board of directors to dissolve the Merce Cunningham Dance Company two years after his death, which it did in 2011. Dunham differs from these other artistic titans of the twentieth century for two reasons. First, African American culture generally places more emphasis on venerating ancestors than does European-American culture; therefore, remembering Dunham becomes not only an aesthetic imperative, but also a political one. The act of honoring Dunham simultaneously honors an Africanist orientation to the world. Second, while all the aforementioned figures had a cultural influence beyond their choreography, Dunham's political and intellectual impact was more explicit. She profoundly shaped the diasporic consciousness of the black freedom struggle and broadened how people viewed the political and social potential of dance in general.

As a testament to the importance of her legacy to black dance, in 1986 Alvin Ailey invited Dunham to set fourteen works on his company. Although Ailey had never trained with Dunham, he had often said that seeing *Tropical Revue* as a teenager in Los Angeles was his primary inspiration to dance.[3] He knew that her tenacity and talent had made it possible for Americans to accept black dance as an art form, which made his success possible. In return, he wanted to honor her by having a new generation of professional dancers learn and perform her choreography. He received a $100,000 grant from the Ford Foundation to bring Dunham and several of her former dancers to New York to teach his dancers.[4] After six weeks of rehearsal, Alvin Ailey American Dance Theater premiered *The Magic of Katherine Dunham* on the opening night of its 1987–1988 New York City Center season. Ailey later told the *Amsterdam News* that the show was a "dream come true."[5]

The process of creating *The Magic of Katherine Dunham* revealed both the challenges and importance of maintaining Dunham's legacy. With only six weeks to teach fourteen dances to a group with no background in Dunham Technique, the task was overwhelming from the outset. Ailey dancers, trained in ballet, Graham, and Horton techniques, had trouble grasping Dunham's emphasis on the pelvis and on the subtle isolations of various parts of the body.[6] They also had a difficult time with the expressiveness Dunham's choreography required. In general, modern dance performers in the 1980s showed minimal facial expressions or theatrical flair. In Dunham's revues of the 1930s through the 1950s, in contrast, dancers embraced dramatic facial expressions and performed with explicit enthusiasm. Ailey noted that his dancers felt uncomfortable with the idea of "sell[ing] the dance" in the way Dunham demanded.[7] Both emotionally and physically, most of the Ailey dancers were a mismatch for the choreography, at least when given only six weeks of training. Dunham felt that April Berry, who filled her lead roles in *L'Ag'Ya* and other dances, was a notable exception.[8]

Despite the difficult rehearsal process, the historic and symbolic importance of this transfer of black dance knowledge from one generation to another generated excitement on opening night. Former Dunham dancer Destiné called the atmosphere in the theater "electrifying."[9] Although Destiné admired the show overall, he felt that L'Ag'Ya had "failed to come across as it once did, in spite of the tremendous effort of the dancers." The problem was that the Ailey dancers "could not convey the Caribbean mystic of such a dramatic work."[10] Other Dunham affiliates felt the same. Albirda Rose was "very dissatisfied" with the show and felt that there was "a whole quality missing, an inner spirit."[11] Dunham's dancers had trained together and toured the world together, experiences that produced a communal performance quality onstage. They had worked with her daily for months, more often years, absorbing not only the movement, but also the spiritual and cultural meanings of the dances she taught them. After only six weeks of training, the Ailey Company could not reproduce the same results.

Audiences, too, had changed in the decades since the Dunham company's last show in New York. Dance critics had a positive response to *The Magic of Katherine Dunham* but seemed not to grasp Dunham's artistry. They instead embraced the theatricality of her style, which for them provided a refreshing contrast to the work being done in dance in the 1980s. Marcia Siegel, a respected dance critic, wrote in the *Christian Science Monitor*, "for dancing, visual splash, and high-energy entertainment, I'd take it any day over the current Broadway scene. More important, it galvanizes the Ailey dancers out of their mechanical glossiness and reveals some hidden talents."[12] Siegel, however, downplayed Dunham's choreographic abilities, writing, "Dunham seems less a choreographer than an expert constructor of showcases for regional dances. She doesn't develop steps or phrases as composed large forms but rather makes them into theatrical showpieces with lavish framing."[13] Allan Kriegsman of the *Washington Post* similarly focused his glowing praise on Dunham's "mastery of stagecraft" and "entertainment value."[14] According to *New York Times* dance critic Anna Kisselgoff, the "unabashed revue flavor" of Dunham's productions, forged from the blending of "show business, art and anthropology," was "so different from what we see today in modern dance and ballet that it is startling to have dancers sing and seduce us with their theatrical presence."[15]

Scholar VèVè Clark felt that the responses to *The Magic of Katherine Dunham* missed the point. According to Clark, critics like Kisselgoff and the others who focused on Dunham's theatricality failed to recognize the history and memory layered into the choreography. The deeper structures of meaning had been overlooked.[16] Audiences, too, had failed to see the larger significance. After realizing that "American audiences have not been trained to see black dance historically," Clark wrote "Performing the Memory of Difference in Afro-Caribbean Dance: Katherine Dunham's Choreography, 1938–87," a key article that challenged scholars to adopt a more sophisticated analytical lens for interpreting Dunham's oeuvre.[17] Clark's charge to scholars makes sense, but asking audience members to watch a live performance of any dance genre through a historical lens is difficult. Live performance must resonate with the contemporary moment. It is up to the dancers and *regisseurs* reconstructing the works to find ways to make those connections.

Despite the limitations of critical and audience reception, *The Magic of Katherine Dunham* enabled the filmed preservation of Dunham's choreography and succeeded in reviving interest in her career. Major newspapers conducted interviews with her that documented important pieces of her history, such as the discrimination she faced while on tour in the United States, the controversial performances of *Southland*, and the work she accomplished with Black Power youth in East St. Louis.[18] Clark's article was only the first of several written in the 1990s as scholarly interest in Dunham's life and career grew. At the same time, the show ultimately did little to change her presence in the dance world. Despite the enormous sums it had spent on *The Magic of Katherine Dunham*, the Ailey Company did not revive the show after its 1988 national tour. The film recording was never produced for commercial release, and so only archival copies exist, in a handful of libraries. Furthermore, the film is of a dress rehearsal, not a live performance or a performance specifically for video documentation. Without copies available to view at educational institutions or through digital distribution services, very few people have the opportunity to see these works.

Even more limiting to legacy efforts is the fact that since Dunham's passing in 2006, her choreography has not been regularly performed. Marie-Christine Dunham Pratt, who licenses the work, feels that there have been too many mediocre performances in recent years, which in her mind diminishes the Dunham legacy. The lack of accuracy in reconstructing her father's costumes and sets also disappoints her.[19] As a general rule, she outright rejects requests for choreography that starred her mother. When asked why, Dunham Pratt responded, "You cannot imagine what she was."[20] Dunham Pratt spent her childhood watching her mother seduce, entrance, and astonish audiences around the globe. During Dunham's heyday, critics called her the "the best dancer in America."[21] She did not leap, kick, or pirouette with perfection, but her genius ability to communicate with an audience was unsurpassed. Dunham Pratt feels the dances that featured her mother will fall flat without a dancer who can match that mesmerizing quality.[22]

Others involved in the legacy efforts feel differently. When Dunham's choreography is performed, awareness of her grows, and it provides proof of her continued relevance. Current generations may not perform the movements in the same way or with the same costumes, but if they can find parallel meaning to motivate their performances, then their emotional integrity will resonate with audiences.[23] Several certified Dunham Technique instructors point to the Cleo Parker Robinson Dance Company's 2012 restaging of *Southland* as proof. In 2010, Robinson won a $100,000 grant from the National Endowment for the Arts to set *Southland* on her company. Julie Robinson Belafonte, who originated the role of the white accuser, and former PATC student Theo Jamison, a Master Instructor, reconstructed the dance drama from music scores, photographs, Belafonte's memory, and film of "Field Hands" and "Plantation Dances" from Ailey's *The Magic of Katherine Dunham*.[24] Considerable portions required new choreography by Jamison. Belafonte, in a manner reminiscent of Dunham, took time to tell the dancers about the historical context for the original production, sharing stories of rehearsing *Southland* in Argentina and performing it in Chile and France.[25]

In September 2012, the piece premiered in Denver, Colorado, receiving rave reviews from the *Denver Post* critic, who called it "wrenching, vexing, raw. . . . something that must be revered, and needed to be danced again."[26] The Robinson Company repeated the performance in Gainesville, Florida in July 2013. Donna Bryson, writing for *Dance Magazine*, thought the movement "felt dated at times," but nonetheless "portrayed an intensity of emotion that brought some in the racially mixed audience to tears and brought them to their feet."[27] One year later, the Black Lives Matter movement gained national prominence in the wake of the shooting of Michael Brown in Ferguson, Missouri, making *Southland's* critique of racialized violence seemingly even more relevant. As of 2017, however, it has not been performed again.

In the absence of regularly performed choreography, Dunham's legacy more noticeably lives on through the Dunham Technique. During the 1960s and 1970s, the technique developed a "bad rap" for causing injury, which Rose attributes to poorly trained teachers who misunderstood the movement.[28] When Dunham created the technique, she emphasized rigor and discipline to combat the stereotype that black dancers just moved naturally. Some teachers took that emphasis on rigor to an unhealthy extreme. One former student remembers taking a Dunham class in New York in the 1970s in which the teacher commanded students to do thirty-two repetitions of a difficult leg lift and threatened to start the exercise over again if anyone faltered.[29] At the urging of Rose and others, the first Dunham Technique Seminar was held in East St. Louis in 1984, which the Katherine Dunham Centers for Arts and Humanities (KDCAH) continues to run every summer. A certification workshop began in 1993. The Institute for Dunham Technique Certification (IDTC) currently runs the certification process. By the 1990s, the technique included breathing exercises that Dunham derived from her growing interest in Buddhism, as well as other modifications based on new knowledge about anatomy and injury prevention. Rose and Halifu Osumare helped Dunham concretize the theoretical and philosophical precepts of the Dunham Technique—namely, Form and Function, Intercultural Communication, Socialization through the Arts, Self-Knowledge, Self-Examination, Discrimination, and Detachment.[30]

Some of these changes have led to friction among the generations of Dunham dancers.[31] Generational conflicts are inevitable when a creative mind continues to develop and change over time. Dunham wanted her technique to be a living art. She never stopped exploring new ideas about movement and the relationship of mind, body, and spirit. At the same time, codification eases the transmission of knowledge to new generations and ensures a standardization of quality. Finding the correct balance between precise standards and creative growth is a tricky endeavor, and the Dunham community of certified instructors holds a range of opinions on where exactly that balance lies. Despite the efforts of KDCAH and IDTC to promote the technique, the number of certified instructors remains small, and Dunham Technique is not widely taught, either in schools or in private studios.

Despite these struggles for recognition, Dunham's impact on dance is ironically so universal as to be practically invisible. One dancer who grew up in southern Illinois stated that she was trained directly by teachers who had worked with Dunham, yet she had no idea that the jazz dance she learned was based on the Dunham Technique.[32] Isolations, the fluid use of the pelvis and spine, the emphasis on percussion, and the incorporation of Africanist aesthetics are Dunham trademarks that one sees most strongly in jazz dance today, but also in modern dance and musical theater. The technique prepares students for West African and Afro-Caribbean dance as well. Multiple Afro-Caribbean dance classes in the United States, for example, use a Dunham Technique–based warm-up.[33]

Just as importantly, Dunham's focus on dance as a mechanism for creating positive social change has lived on in the work of dozens of choreographers, educators, and nonprofit organizations. Schools across the country and globe, such as the West Las Vegas Arts Center mentioned in chapter 8 and the Lula Washington Dance School in Los Angeles, are modeled on Dunham's pedagogy of community engagement. In Haiti, the non-profit organization FOKAL (Fondasyon konesans ak libète, or Foundation for Knowledge and Liberty), has renovated Habitation Leclerc and adjoining properties to create the Parc de Martissant, a green haven in one of Port-au-Prince's poorest and most crime-ridden neighborhoods. A central component of the Parc is the Centre Culturel Katherine Dunham (CCKD), which was completed in January 2014. With a library, reading rooms, multimedia center, medicinal garden, permanent outdoor exhibit on her performing career, and wending path inspired by Damballa, the CCKD not only honors Dunham through memorialization, but also through institutions to improve the lives of the area's residents.[34]

Dunham's life and work also offer a model for internationalism based on interculturalism, sorely needed in the post-9/11 world. From the political right, nationalist, ethnocentric, and xenophobic discourses have continued to gain currency. From the political left, intellectuals have criticized multiculturalism and interculturalism as naïve philosophies that ignore unequal power relations.[35] While valid, these latter criticisms sometimes fail to address the unavoidable truth that ideas are always being exchanged and that no cultural form emerges purely from one isolated group of people. The rigid policing of cultural boundaries can reproduce pernicious and essentialist ideas about racial and ethnic identity. At the same time, cultural innovators from nondominant groups often do not get the money or credit they deserve. Embracing interculturalism without reproducing cultural hierarchies or inequalities is a challenge Dunham leaves for us today. Throughout her career, she insisted on the idea that cultural exchange was a central component of creating world peace. By gaining respect and understanding for others' cultures, as well as for their own, individuals would be better equipped to live in a diverse and globally connected society. The Institute for Intercultural Communication, one of the last organizations she founded before her passing, was dedicated to this effort to arrive at "a true humanism for mankind."[36]

Given that "humanism for mankind" was Dunham's ultimate aim, to frame her work as being within the African diaspora (as the title of this book does) might seem limiting. Throughout her career, however, exposing her dancers, students, and audience members to dances of the African diaspora was how she most effectively promoted humanism. The foundations of her philosophy lie in her 1935–36 research trip to Haiti, where she discovered dance as a means of empowerment and met intellectuals who articulated Haiti's historical role in forging a more humanistic world. Her institutions put blackness at the center, one way in which she distinguished herself from other models of interculturalism.

Dunham's aesthetic innovations, institutions, and pedagogy were all a part of how she built a life of meaning. As a celebrity, she used her public stature to take concrete steps against discrimination and injustice, both in the United States and abroad. Through self-knowledge and a perpetual willingness to learn from others, she modeled how to be a socially conscious artist over the course of a lifetime. She never gave up on trying to live holistically. When one avenue closed, she broke ground on another. Onstage and off, Dunham choreographed the change she wished to see in the world, and we are better for it.

LIST OF ABBREVIATIONS USED IN NOTES

Amsterdam News	*New York Amsterdam News*
BECA	Bureau of Educational and Cultural Affairs Historical Collection, Special Collections, University of Arkansas Libraries, Fayetteville, Arkansas
BMBP	Bernard and Mary Berenson Papers, Series IV: Correspondence, Biblioteca Berenson, Villa I Tatti, Florence, Italy
JRDD	Jerome Robbins Dance Division, New York Public Library for the Performing Arts
JRP	Julius Rosenwald Papers, Special Collections, Fisk University Franklin Library, Nashville, Tennessee
LHC	Langston Hughes Collection, Beinecke Rare Book and Manuscript Library, Yale University, New Haven, Connecticut
LOC	Katherine Dunham Collection, Music Division, Library of Congress, Washington, DC
MHS	Katherine Dunham Papers, Missouri Historical Society Library and Research Center, St. Louis
LWP	Lavinia Williams Papers, Schomburg Center for Research in Black Culture, New York
MHP	Melville Herskovits Papers, University Archives, Northwestern University, Evanston, Illinois
NARA	National Archives and Records Administration, College Park, Maryland
NYT	*New York Times*
OEO/CAP	Office of Economic Opportunity, Community Action Program
RFR	Rockefeller Foundation Records, Rockefeller Archive Center, Sleepy Hollow, New York.
RG59	State Department Central Decimal File, Record Group 59, National Archives and Records Administration, College Park, Maryland
SIUC	Katherine Dunham Papers, Special Collections Research Center, Southern Illinois University Carbondale

NOTES

PREFACE AND ACKNOWLEDGMENTS

1. Personal conversations with Lee Nolting; Kenya Vaughn, "Stewards, Nolting, Win Arts Awards," *St. Louis American*, January 22, 2014, http://www.stlamerican.com/entertainment/living_it/ article_e5b6a516-83da-11e3-a636-001a4bcf887a.html.
2. Katherine Dunham, *Island Possessed* (Chicago: University of Chicago Press, 1969), 106.
3. Thomas F. DeFrantz, "Foreword: Black Bodies Dancing Black Culture; Black Atlantic Transformations," in *EmBODYing Liberation: The Black Body in American Dance*, ed. Dorothea Fischer-Hornung and Alison D. Goeller (Hamburg, Germany: LIT, 2001), 11.

INTRODUCTION

1. Multiple Dunham biographies recount this part of the story. See Joyce Aschenbrenner, *Katherine Dunham: Dancing a Life* (Urbana: University of Illinois Press, 2002), 134; James Haskins, *Katherine Dunham* (New York: Coward, McCann & Geoghegan, 1982), 75; Ruth Beckford, *Katherine Dunham: A Biography* (New York: M. Dekker, 1979), 69. Beckford mistakes Lexington for Louisville.
2. Beckford, *Katherine Dunham*, 69; Vanoye Aikens, interview by author, March 1, 2011, Los Angeles. Aikens remembers that the sign read "For Colored Only."
3. Richard Burns, "A Dancer's Swan Song," *Negro Digest*, December 1944, 42; Seymour Peck, "Dunham Troupes to Conquer," *PM*, December 20, 1944, 16, Dunham Scrapbooks, vol. 4, JRDD; fan letters are in box 4, folder 7, and box 5, folders 1 and 2, SIUC.
4. Barefield Gordon, "God Created Everybody Equal in His Own Image," *PM*, November 3, 1944, box 5, folder 1, SIUC. In the Haskins biography, Dunham claimed that Louisville was the only city where the company played to a segregated audience, but this was revisionist history. Haskins, *Katherine Dunham*, 75.
5. Dunham to Barefield Gordon, October 23, 1944, box 4, folder 7, SIUC.
6. There is a growing literature about women performing artists and the black freedom struggle. See Farah Jasmine Griffin, *Harlem Nocturne: Women Artists and Progressive Politics during World War II* (New York: Basic Civitas Books, 2013); Ruth Feldstein, *How It Feels to Be Free: Black Women Entertainers and the Civil Rights Movement* (New York: Oxford University Press, 2013). There is substantial scholarship on Dunham in dance studies and increased attention in anthropology. For a compilation of important work, see VèVè A. Clark and Sara E. Johnson, eds., *Kaiso! Writings by and about Katherine Dunham* (Madison: University of Wisconsin

Press, 2005). See also Elizabeth Chin, ed., *Katherine Dunham: Recovering an Anthropological Legacy, Choreographing Ethnographic Futures* (Santa Fe, NM: SAR Press, 2014).

7. Randy Martin, *Critical Moves: Dance Studies in Theory and Politics* (Durham, NC: Duke University Press, 1998); Rebekah J. Kowal, *How to Do Things with Dance: Performing Change in Postwar America* (Middletown, CT: Wesleyan University Press, 2010).

8. Carlton Wilson, "Conceptualizing the African Diaspora," *Comparative Studies of South Asia, Africa and the Middle East* 17, no. 2 (1997): 118. Other helpful works are Kim Butler, "Defining Diaspora, Refining a Discourse," *Diaspora* 10, no. 2 (2001): 189–219; Brent Hayes Edwards, "The Uses of Diaspora," *Social Text* 19, no. 1 (2001): 45–73; Tiffany Ruby Patterson and Robin D. G. Kelley, "Unfinished Migrations: Reflections on the African Diaspora and the Making of the Modern World," *African Studies Review* 43, no. 1 (2000): 11–45. Black dance studies has also turned to diaspora. See Thomas DeFrantz and Anita Gonzalez, eds., *Black Performance Theory* (Durham, NC: Duke University Press, 2014).

9. My ideas of diaspora are largely indebted to Brent Edwards, *The Practice of Diaspora: Literature, Translation, and the Rise of Black Internationalism* (Cambridge, MA: Harvard University Press, 2003); and Stuart Hall, "Cultural Identity and Diaspora," in *Identity: Community, Culture, Difference*, ed. Jonathan Rutherford (London: Lawrence & Wishart, 1990), 222–37.

10. Michelle M. Wright, *Becoming Black: Creating Identity in the African Diaspora* (Durham, NC: Duke University Press, 2004), 3.

11. Wilson, "Conceptualizing the African Diaspora," 121.

12. John O. Perpener, *African-American Concert Dance: The Harlem Renaissance and Beyond* (Urbana: University of Illinois Press, 2001), 1–127.

13. On literature, see Houston A. Baker, *Modernism and the Harlem Renaissance* (Chicago: University of Chicago Press, 1987). On music, see Paul Gilroy, *The Black Atlantic: Modernity and Double Consciousness* (Cambridge, MA: Harvard University Press, 1993), 72–110.

14. Melville J. Herskovits, *The Myth of the Negro Past* (New York: Harper, 1941). While Herskovits's ideas predate those of Dunham, *The Myth of the Negro Past* was published after Dunham's articles were. Zora Neale Hurston also considered dance in her formulation of diaspora, but her dance production *One Fine Day* had far less impact than her writing. She also lacked the dance training that Dunham had. For more on Hurston and dance, see Anthea Kraut, *Choreographing the Folk: The Dance Stagings of Zora Neale Hurston* (Minneapolis: University of Minnesota Press, 2008).

15. Although several black choreographers before Dunham had attempted to gain recognition for their art, she was the first to receive widespread affirmation from audiences and critics. See Perpener, *African-American Concert Dance*, 128–29. A note about Dunham's company: the name changed multiple times over the course of its existence. In 1937, it was "Katherine Dunham and Her Group." Under Sol Hurok, from 1943 to 1945, the company was billed as "Sol Hurok Presents Katherine Dunham and Her Company in a Tropical Revue" or, simply, "Sol Hurok Presents Katherine Dunham in a Tropical Revue." After Dunham fired Hurok, she continued to give herself sole billing, until the mid-1950s, when she settled on "Katherine Dunham and Her Dancers – Singers – Musicians." During the company's final performing years in the 1960s, the official name again excluded everyone

but Dunham: "Katherine Dunham in *Bamboche!*" and "Katherine Dunham and Her Revue." I will not capitalize "Company," as the name "Dunham Company" was never used. Instead, I will generally refer to it as the Dunham company.

16. See André Lepecki, *Exhausting Dance: Performance and the Politics of Movement* (New York: Routledge, 2006); Martin, *Critical Moves*.

17. Audre Lorde, "The Uses of the Erotic: The Erotic as Power," in *Sister Outsider: Essays and Speeches by Audre Lorde* (Berkeley, CA: Crossing Press, 1984), 53–59.

18. André Lepecki, "Choreopolice and Choreopolitics: Or, the Task of the Dancer," *TDR: The Drama Review* 57, no. 4 (2013): 14.

19. bell hooks, *Black Looks: Race and Representation* (Boston: South End Press, 1992), 4.

20. Ramona Lowe, "Being a Closeup on Miss Dunham: Noted Danseuse Concerned with Prejudices Affecting the Theatre," *Amsterdam News*, September 18, 1943, 22; and Aikens interview.

21. I offer a modification of VèVè Clark's argument about the "memory of difference" in Dunham's work in that I stress Dunham's presentation of the Caribbean's modernity in addition to its historicity. See Clark, "Performing the Memory of Difference in Afro-Caribbean Dance: Katherine Dunham's Choreography, 1938–1987," in Clark and Johnson, *Kaiso!*, 320–40.

22. I will not always put the word *primitive* in scare quotes, not because I support the uncritical use of the term, but rather for ease of reading.

23. Dunham, field notes, ca. 1936, box 79, folder 5, SIUC.

24. Dunham, Application for Fellowship, Julius Rosenwald Fund, November 19, 1934, box 409, folder 10, JRP.

25. This truth complicates what Clark and Halifu Osumare have called Dunham's "research-to-performance" model. See Halifu Osumare, "Dancing the Black Atlantic: Katherine Dunham's Research-to-Performance Method," *Ameriquest* 7, no. 2 (2010): 1–10.

26. "Dunham Annual 27th International Seminar," flier, July 24–August 1, 2010, personal collection.

27. Susan Hiller, *The Myth of Primitivism: Perspectives on Art* (New York: Routledge, 1991).

28. 2015 Dunham Certification Workshop, June 30, 2015, University of South Florida, Tampa.

29. Dunham to Gerald Goode, ca. August 1943, box 3, folder 7, SIUC.

30. Ruth Ann Taylor, acting coordinator of the PATC, to Dr. Emil Johnson, president of Southern Illinois University, February 11, 1977, box 10, folder 10, MHS.

31. Anna Kisselgoff, "Katherine Dunham's Timeless Legacy, Visible in Youth and Age," *NYT*, September 16, 2003, E1.

32. Search "matriarch of black dance" on Google and Dunham's name comes up. For examples of her being invoked as a divine ancestor, see the preface.

33. Discussion following paper presentation of "Dancing Diaspora; Katherine Dunham's International Tours during the Cold War," Collegium of African Diaspora Dance, February 8, 2014, Duke University.

34. Brenda Dixon Gottschild, *Digging the Africanist Presence in American Performance: Dance and Other Contexts* (Westport, CT: Greenwood Press, 1996), xiii–xiv. Throughout this book, I borrow Gottschild's term "Africanist" to denote cultural practices in the Americas that derive at least in part from African sources.

35. DeFrantz and Gonzalez, introduction to *Black Performance Theory*, 1–2.

36. Takiyah Nur Amin, "A Terminology of Difference: Making the Case for Black Dance in the 21st Century and Beyond," *Journal of Pan African Studies* 4, no. 6 (2011): 13.

37. One important exception is Elgie Gaynell Sherrod, "The Dance Griots: An Examination of the Dance Pedagogy of Katherine Dunham and Black Pioneering Dancers in Chicago and New York City, from 1931–1946," (PhD diss., Temple University, 1998).

38. William Hawkins, "Star of 'Bal Negre' Runs a Unique Dancing School," *New York World-Telegram*, December 6, 1946, box 102, folder 14, SIUC; Dunham, "A Funding Proposal for the Center for Intercultural Communication," May 1, 1971, box 18, folder 1, MHS.

39. Dunham, *Island Possessed*, 79.

40. Ibid., 4.

41. Dorathi Bock Pierre, "Katherine Dunham," *Dance: Screen*Stage*, May 1947, 11.

42. Dunham, *Island Possessed*, 4.

43. Aschenbrenner, *Katherine Dunham*, 134; Beckford, *Katherine Dunham*, 69; Haskins, *Katherine Dunham*, 75; Susan Manning, "Modern Dance, Negro Dance, and Katherine Dunham," *Textual Practice* 15, no. 3 (2001): 501–2.

44. Dunham to Margot Johnson, December 18, 1957, box 23, folder 7, SIUC. For the sake of preserving Dunham's reputation, several of her dancers kept their complaints private. See Lavinia Williams to Rex Nettleford, February 27, ca. mid-1970s, box 12, folder 2, LWP.

45. *Tropics and Le Jazz "Hot"* program, February 18, 1940, Windsor Theatre, Gumby Scrapbooks, box 53, folder 23, Rare Books and Manuscript Library, Columbia University; *Bal Negre* advertisement, *Amsterdam News*, November 2, 1946, 21.

46. "A Conversation with Katherine Dunham," March 29, 2004, Barnard College, New York. DVD, private collection.

47. W. E. B. Du Bois, *The Souls of Black Folk*, 3rd ed. (Chicago: A. C. McClurg & Co., 1903), 3.

CHAPTER 1

1. William Raney to Margot Johnson, February 4, 1958, box 23, folder 8, SIUC.

2. Langston Hughes, back jacket of Katherine Dunham, *A Touch of Innocence* (New York: Harcourt, 1959).

3. The 1900 census lists Fanny June's birth year as 1865; her death certificate states that she was born in 1868. Albert Millard Dunham's World War I draft card states that he was born in 1880. Dunham claims that Fanny was twenty years older than Albert, but that was most likely an exaggeration.

4. Cook County, Illinois, Birth Certificates Index, 1871–1922; Dunham, *Touch of Innocence*, 14.

5. Dunham, *Touch of Innocence*, 25.

6. Fanny Taylor Dunham, death certificate, Cook County Vital Records, Illinois.

7. Dunham, *Touch of Innocence*, 294.

8. Ibid., 51–53.

9. Ibid., 59–60.

10. Ibid., 54.

11. Ibid., 178. In the memoir Dunham refers to Chouteau Avenue as "Chouteau Street."

12. Ibid., 179.

13. R. H. Hagan, "The Lively Arts: Katherine Dunham Tells of Debt to Berenson," *San Francisco Chronicle*, September 30, 1955, 20.

14. Dunham, *Island Possessed*, 4.

15. Beckford, *Katherine Dunham*, 20–21.

16. For more on Dalcroze, see Ana Keilson, "The *Méthode Jaques-Dalcroze* and a Sentimental (Musical) Education," in "Making Dance Knowledge: Politics and German Modern Dance, 1890–1972," (PhD diss., Columbia University, 2017).

17. For more on Laban's aesthetic philosophy, see Keilson, "Rudolf Laban and the End of Politics," in "Making Dance Knowledge."

18. Dunham, *Touch of Innocence*, 188.

19. Dunham, n. 2, 187–88, 259.

20. Ibid., 191.

21. For more on St. Denis, see Jane Desmond, "Dancing Out the Difference: Cultural Imperialism and Ruth St. Denis's 'Radha' of 1906," *Signs: Journal of Women in Culture and Society* 17, no. 1 (1991): 28–49; Priya Srinivasan, *Sweating Saris: Indian Dance as Transnational Labor* (Philadelphia: Temple University Press, 2011), 67–82.

22. David Krasner, "Black *Salome*: Exoticism, Dance, and Racial Myths," in *African American Performance and Theater History: A Critical Reader*, ed. Harry J. Elam Jr. and David Krasner (New York: Oxford University Press, 2001), 192–211.

23. Dunham, *Touch of Innocence*, 194. For more on the Talented Tenth and dance, see Brenda Dixon Gottschild, *Joan Myers Brown & the Audacious Hope of the Black Ballerina: A Biohistory of American Performance* (New York: Palgrave Macmillan, 2012), 1–32.

24. Dunham, *Touch of Innocence*, 283; Aschenbrenner, *Katherine Dunham*, 7–18.

25. Dunham, *Touch of Innocence*, 16; Aschenbrenner, *Katherine Dunham*, 15.

26. Dunham gave the press and her students the impression that her mother was white. See Holland Festival 1949 Souvenir Programme, July 15–16, 1949, box 85, folder 14, SIUC; Albirda Rose, interview by author, July 26, 2011, Edwardsville, IL. For more on Dunham's maternal heritage, see Dunham, *Touch of Innocence*, 19–20; and Aschenbrenner, *Katherine Dunham*, 7.

27. Twelfth Census of the United States, Hyde Park Township, Cook County, Illinois; Thirteenth Census of the United States, Glen Ellyn Village, Milton Township, DuPage County, Illinois.

28. Aschenbrenner, *Katherine Dunham*, 8.

29. Dunham, *Touch of Innocence*, 196–97.

30. Ibid., 287–88.

31. Aikens interview; Beckford, *Katherine Dunham*, 20.

32. Albirda Rose, *Dunham Technique: A Way of Life* (Dubuque, IA: Kendall Hunt, 1990), 26.

33. For the foundational expressions of New Negro ideology, see Alain Locke, ed., *The New Negro* (New York: A. and C. Boni, 1925). Recent works on Chicago's New Negro Movement/Black Renaissance include Davarian L. Baldwin, *Chicago's New Negroes: Modernity, the Great Migration, and Black Urban Life* (Chapel Hill: University of North Carolina Press, 2007); Davarian L. Baldwin and Minkah Makalani, eds., *Escape from New York: The New Negro Renaissance beyond Harlem* (Minneapolis: University of Minnesota Press, 2013); Robert Bone and Richard A. Courage, *The Muse in Bronzeville: African American Creative Expression in Chicago, 1932–1950* (Piscataway, NJ: Rutgers University Press, 2011); Darlene Clark Hine

and John McClusky Jr., ed., *The Black Chicago Renaissance* (Urbana: University of Illinois Press, 2012).

34. Albert J. Dunham to Annette Dunham, ca. February 1928, box 38, folder 2, SIUC.
35. W. E. B. Du Bois, "'Krigwa Players Little Negro Theatre': The Story of a Little Theatre Movement," *The Crisis* 32, no. 3 (1926): 134.
36. The Cube program, January 1929, box 85, folder 1, SIUC.
37. Ibid.
38. Dunham, "The Minefield," book I (unpublished manuscript, ca. 1980–1989), 10, box 20, MHS. Although portions of "The Minefield" are excerpted with the title "Minefields" in Clark and Johnson, *Kaiso!*, this quotation only appears in the original manuscript.
39. Dunham, "Minefield," bk. I, 20; Katherine "Kitty" de la Chapelle, "Colored Culture in Chicago: Theatre Continued," November 12, 1937, Negro in Illinois, Illinois Writers Project, box 47, folder 7, Vivian G. Harsh Research Collection, Woodson Regional Branch of the Chicago Public Library, Illinois. For more about Lewis, see Anne Meis Knupfer, *The Chicago Black Renaissance and Women's Activism* (Urbana: University of Illinois Press, 2006), 55–56.
40. Dunham, "Minefield," bk. I, 44.
41. A. Dunham to K. Dunham, ca. 1930, box 38, folder 2, SIUC.
42. Dunham, "Survival: Chicago after the Caribbean: Excerpt from 'Minefields,'" in Clark and Johnson, *Kaiso!*, 85.
43. A. Dunham to K. Dunham, ca. 1930, box 38, folder 2, SIUC.
44. For more on Albert, see Dunham, "Prologue: Excerpt from 'Minefields,'" in Clark and Johnson, *Kaiso!*, 75–83.
45. George Dorris, "Dance and the New York Opera War, 1906–1912," *Dance Chronicle* 32, no. 2 (2009): 195–262; Jessica Zeller, "Shapes of American Ballet: Classical Traditions, Teachers, and Training in New York City, 1909–1934" (PhD diss., Ohio State University, 2012). San Francisco Ballet calls itself the "first professional ballet company in America"; it was founded in 1933 with the name San Francisco Opera Ballet. See the San Francisco Ballet website, accessed May 6, 2015, https://www.sfballet.org/about/history.
46. James C. Scott, *Domination and the Arts of Resistance: Hidden Transcripts* (New Haven, CT: Yale University Press, 1990); Jayna Brown, *Babylon Girls: Black Women Performers and the Shaping of the Modern* (Durham, NC: Duke University Press, 2008), 5–6.
47. For more on Guy and Winfield, see Perpener, *African-American Concert Dance*, 25–77.
48. Mark Turbyfill, "Shall We Present to the World a New Ballet?" *Abbott's Monthly*, November 1930, 63.
49. Mark Turbyfill, "Autobiography," copy 1, unpublished manuscript, n.d., box 1, folder 8, Mark Turbyfill Papers, Roger and Julie Baskes Department of Special Collections, Newberry Library, Chicago.
50. Turbyfill, "Autobiography."
51. Ibid.
52. Ibid.
53. *Abbott's Monthly* covers, 1930–1933, Black Press Research Collective, accessed April 21, 2015, http://blackpressresearchcollective.org/?attachment_id=646.
54. Turbyfill, "Autobiography."
55. Ibid.
56. Turbyfill, "Shall We Present," 63.

57. Locke, *New Negro*, 4.
58. Dunham, quoted in Turbyfill, "Shall We Present," 64.
59. Turbyfill, "Autobiography."
60. Lawrence Schenbeck, *Racial Uplift and American Music, 1878–1943* (Jackson: University Press of Mississippi, 2012), 139–70.
61. Samuel A. Floyd Jr., "The Negro Renaissance: Harlem and Chicago Flowerings," in Hine and McCluskey, *Black Chicago Renaissance*, 39–40. See also Bone and Courage, *Muse in Bronzeville*, 94–97; Schenbeck, *Racial Uplift*, 7.
62. Baldwin, *Chicago's New Negroes*, 28–29.
63. K. Dunham to A. Dunham, November 17, 1931, box 38, folder 2, SIUC.
64. Ibid.
65. Arthur Schomburg, "The Negro Digs up His Past," in Locke, *New Negro*, 231.
66. K. Dunham to A. Dunham, November 17, 1931.
67. Rosalind Rosenberg, *Divided Lives: American Women in the Twentieth Century* (New York: Hill and Wang, 1992); Victoria W. Wolcott, *Remaking Respectability: African American Women in Interwar Detroit* (Chapel Hill: University of North Carolina Press, 2001).
68. K. Dunham to A. Dunham, November 17, 1931.
69. "'Run, Little Chillun' Comes to Chicago's Loop October 29," *Chicago Defender*, October 13, 1934, 9; Associated Negro Press, "'O, Sing a New Song' Draws 40,000 People," *Philadelphia Tribune*, August 30, 1934, 2.
70. Dunham to Turbyfill, August 24, 1933, box 1, folder 8, Mark Turbyfill Papers, Special Collections Research Center, Southern Illinois University, Carbondale.
71. "Moscow 'Bat Theatre' Coming to New York," *NYT*, January 5, 1922, 13.
72. Susan Manning, *Ecstasy and the Demon: Feminism and Nationalism in the Dances of Mary Wigman* (Berkeley: University of California Press, 1993), 43–44, 89–96.
73. Dunham interview by Constance Valis Hill, November 18, 1999, box 13, folder 3, LOC.
74. Frank L. Hayes, "First Negro Ballet Ever Danced to Be Feature[d] at Artists' Ball," *Chicago Daily News*, December 5, 1932, vol. 1, Scrapbooks, MHS.
75. "Chicago Folk to See First Negro Ballet: Type Never Attempted by Dancers of Black Race," *Daily Boston Globe*, December 7, 1932, 23.
76. "Modern Dancers Praised at Stevens," *Chicago Defender*, national edition, December 24, 1932, 12.
77. Joellen A. Meglin, "Choreographing Identities beyond Boundaries: *La Guiablesse* and Ruth Page's Excursions into World Dance (1926–1934)," *Dance Chronicle* 30, no. 3 (2007): 457; Elinor H. Rogosin, "Vera Mirova: Portrait of a Forgotten Artist," *Arabesque* 9, no. 1 (1983): 10–11; Aschenbrenner, *Katherine Dunham*, 27.
78. As an example, see Gottschild's discussion of Essie Marie Dorsey's dance recitals in *Joan Myers Brown*, 12–18.
79. Meglin, "Choreographing Identities," 439.
80. "Negro Dance Group" program, Abraham Lincoln Center, Chicago, March 2–4, 1934, vol. 107, folder 5, SIUC.
81. Stephanie Leigh Batiste, *Darkening Mirrors: Imperial Representation in Depression-Era African American Performance* (Durham, NC: Duke University Press, 2011), 117, 144.
82. Program notes for *La Guiablesse*, June 23, 1933, box 17, Ruth Page Collection, JRDD.
83. Meglin, "Choreographing Identities," 447.
84. Program notes for *La Guiablesse*.

85. *Birth of a Nation*, directed by D. W. Griffith, 1915, Kino International, accessed via Amazon Video, October 1, 2016; program notes for *La Guiablesse*.

86. Edward Moore, "Critic Praises Innovation of Ballet Night," *Chicago Daily Tribune*, December 1, 1934, 13.

87. "Joliet Girl Wins Praise as Dancer in Opera Ballet," *Joliet Spectator*, December 6, 1934, box 102, folder 1, SIUC.

88. "Composer Here for Showing of *La Guiablesse*: Katherine Dunham in Main Dance Role," *Chicago Defender*, December 8, 1934, 5.

89. Chapelle, "Colored Culture in Chicago."

90. "Duke Kwensi Kuntu and His Ceremonial Tribesmen," Illinois Digital Archives, accessed August 18, 2016, http://www.idaillinois.org/cdm/singleitem/collection/lakecou02z/id/2985/rec/4.

91. Dunham to Herskovits, June 18, 1933, box 7, folder 12, MHP. Unless otherwise noted, all cited correspondence between Dunham and Herskovits in the MHP is in box 7, folder 12.

92. Harold Courlander, "Caribbean Folk Music," Liner Notes, Ethnic Folkways Library, 1960, Music Online: Smithsonian Global Sound for Libraries, accessed August 18, 2016, http://glmu.alexanderstreet.com.ezproxy.cul.columbia.edu/View/71901.

93. Herskovits to Dunham, June 20, 1933, MHP.

94. Ronald E. Martin, *The Languages of Difference: American Writers and Anthropologists Reconfigure the Primitive, 1878–1940* (Newark: University of Delaware Press, 2005), 165–66.

95. Daphne Mary Lamothe, *Inventing the New Negro: Narrative, Culture, and Ethnography* (Philadelphia: University of Pennsylvania Press, 2008), 1–2.

96. Aschenbrenner, *Katherine Dunham*, 28–37.

97. A. Lynn Bolles, "Katherine Dunham's First Journey in Anthropology," in Chin, *Katherine Dunham*, 32–34.

98. Aschenbrenner, *Katherine Dunham*, 31.

99. Clifford Wilcox, *Robert Redfield and the Development of American Anthropology* (Lanham, MD: Lexington Books, 2004), 3.

100. Herskovits, *Myth of the Negro Past*, 1.

101. Jerry Gershenhorn, *Melville J. Herskovits and the Racial Politics of Knowledge* (Lincoln: University of Nebraska Press, 2004), 5.

102. George E. Marcus and Michael M. J. Fischer, *Anthropology as Cultural Critique: An Experimental Moment in the Human Sciences* (Chicago: University of Chicago Press, 1986); Richard Handler, *Critics against Culture: Anthropological Observers of Mass Society* (Madison: University of Wisconsin Press, 2005).

103. Dunham to Herskovits, March 9, 1932, MHP.

104. David Luis-Brown, "Cuban *Negrismo*, Mexican *Indigenismo*: Contesting Neo-colonialism in the New Negro Movement," in Baldwin and Makalani, *Escape from New York*, 54–56.

105. Aschenbrenner, *Katherine Dunham*, 44; Lawrence J. Friedman, *The Lives of Erich Fromm: Love's Prophet* (New York: Columbia University Press, 2013), 82–96.

106. Iris Schmeisser, "'Ethiopia Shall Soon Stretch Forth Her Hands': Ethiopianism, Egyptomania, and the Arts of the Harlem Renaissance," in *African Diasporas in the New and Old Worlds: Consciousness and Imagination,* ed. Genevieve Fabre and Klaus Benesch (Amsterdam: Rodopi, 2004), 263–70.

107. Dunham, Application for Fellowship.

108. Ibid.

109. Martin, *Languages of Difference*, 24, 213; Batiste, *Darkening Mirrors*, 173.

110. The literature on primitivism in modern art is extensive. See Jody Blake, *Le Tumulte Noir: Modernist Art and Popular Entertainment in Jazz-Age Paris, 1900–1930* (University Park: Pennsylvania State University Press, 1999); Hiller, *Myth of Primitivism*; Sieglinde Lemke, *Primitivist Modernism: Black Culture and the Origins of Transatlantic Modernism* (New York: Oxford University Press, 1998); Marianna Torgovnick, *Gone Primitive: Savage Intellects, Modern Lives* (Chicago: University of Chicago Press, 1990).

111. Dunham, Application for Fellowship.

112. Melville Herskovits to Edwin Embree, May 2, 1935, box 20, folder 21, MHP.

CHAPTER 2

1. Dunham, *Island Possessed*, 65, 79. There are many variations on the spelling of Vodou. Dunham spelled it "vaudun"; I use the more widely accepted spelling Vodou. I also capitalize the word. The use of the lower case is another way in which the religion has been delegitimized.

2. Katherine Dunham, *Dances of Haiti* (1947; Los Angeles: Center for Afro-American Studies, University of California, Los Angeles, 1983), xxiv. The phrase is also written as *Nan Guinin*.

3. Dunham to Herskovits, January 13, 1936, MHP.

4. Clark, "Performing the Memory of Difference," 321.

5. Butler, "Defining Diaspora," 207.

6. Aimé Césaire, *The Original 1939 Notebook of a Return to the Native Land*, bilingual ed., trans. and ed. A. James Arnold and Layton Eshleman (Middletown, CT: Wesleyan University Press, 2013), 19. This translation states, "where negritude rose for the first time," but most texts use the "stood up" translation. See Michael J. Dash, *The Other America: Caribbean Literature in a New World Context* (Charlottesville: University Press of Virginia, 1998), 62.

7. Schomburg, "Negro Digs up His Past"; Herskovits, *Myth of the Negro Past*, 1.

8. Katherine Dunham, "The Anthropological Approach to the Dance" (1942), reprinted in Clark and Johnson, *Kaiso!*, 508.

9. Katherine Dunham, *Journey to Accompong* (New York: H. Holt, 1946), 90.

10. Dunham to Herskovits, ca. October 1935, MHP.

11. Katherine Dunham, "The Negro Dance," in *The Negro Caravan: Writings by American Negroes*, ed. Sterling Allen Brown, Arthur Paul Davis, and Ulysses Lee (New York: Dryden Press, 1941), 991.

12. Patterson and Kelley, "Unfinished Migrations"; Terence Ranger, "The Invention of Tradition in Colonial Africa," in *The Invention of Tradition*, ed. Eric Hobsbawm and Terence Ranger (Cambridge: Cambridge University Press, 1983), 211–262; V. Y. Mudimbe, *The Invention of Africa: Gnosis, Philosophy, and the Order of Knowledge* (Bloomington: Indiana University Press, 1988).

13. Dunham, "The Negro Dance," 991.

14. Ibid., 1000.

15. Dunham, *Dances of Haiti*, xix.

16. Ibid., 25.

17. Patricia Ticineto Clough, introduction to *The Affective Turn: Theorizing the Social*, ed. Patricia Ticineto Clough and Jean O'Malley Halley (Durham, NC: Duke University Press, 2007), 2–3.

18. Dunham to Herskovits, June 23, 1935, MHP.

19. Alain Locke, "Reason and Race: A Review of the Literature of the Negro for 1946," *Phylon* 8, no. 1 (1947): 23.

20. Dunham, *Island Possessed*, 74.
21. Amy Porter, "Anthropological Katie," *Negro Digest*, April 1945, 38.
22. Dunham to Herksovits, November 15, 1935, MHP.
23. Dunham to Herskovits, December 28, 1935, MHP.
24. Dunham to Herskovits, November 15, 1935, MHP.
25. Erving Goffman, *The Presentation of Self in Everyday Life* (Garden City, NY: Doubleday, 1959). Kowal launches a similar critique when examining the writings of Pearl Primus. See Kowal, *How to Do Things with Dance*, 145.
26. Herskovits to Dunham, January 6, 1936, MHP.
27. Dunham to Herskovits, January 13, 1936, MHP.
28. Dunham, notes, ca. 1935–38, box 79, folder 4, SIUC. Her notes are also found in folders 5 and 6. It is unclear exactly when Dunham wrote these notes; some seem to have been composed when she was doing her research; others, after she returned to Chicago.
29. Dunham to Herskovits, December 10, 1935, MHP.
30. Dunham, *Island Possessed*, 109, 131–32.
31. Gwendolyn Mikell, "When Horses Talk: Reflections on Zora Neale Hurston's Haitian Anthropology," *Phylon* 43 (September 1982): 221; Martin, *Languages of Difference*, 234–35.
32. Zora Neale Hurston, *Tell My Horse* (Philadelphia: J. B. Lippincott Co., 1938); Lamothe, *Inventing the New Negro*, 142.
33. Hurston to Herskovits, July 30, 1936, box 9, folder 32, MHP.
34. Herskovits to Hurston, September 28, 1936, box 9, folder 32, MHP.
35. Hurston to Herskovits, April 6, 1937, box 9, folder 32, MHP.
36. For more on this production see Kraut, *Choreographing the Folk*.
37. Hurston to Herskovits, April 6, 1937, box 9, folder 32, MHP.
38. Zora Neale Hurston, "Thirty Days among Maroons," in Clark and Johnson, *Kaiso!*, 272.
39. Herskovits to Dunham, December 19, 1935, MHP.
40. Dunham, *Dances of Haiti*, 31; Dunham to Herskovits, December 10, 1935, MHP.
41. Dunham to Herskovits, January 13, 1936, MHP. Dunham discusses Reiser's presence at the ceremonies she attended in Haiti and considered him one of her "closest friends" there. See *Island Possessed*, 18–20, 235.
42. Dorathi Bock Pierre, "A Talk with Katherine Dunham," *Educational Dance Magazine* 4, no. 3 (1941): 7; *Bal Negre* program biography, December 16, 1946, box 85, folder 11, SIUC. This misinformation has been repeated in most of the scholarly work on Dunham. See Durkin, "Dance Anthropology," 124–25; Osumare, "Dancing the Black Atlantic," 8; Perpener, *African-American Concert Dance*, 139.
43. Dunham, n. 28.
44. The history of Haiti, the Haitian Revolution, and the Haitian class/color/caste system has a vast literature. To start, see C. L. R. James, *The Black Jacobins: Toussaint L'Ouverture and the San Domingo Revolution* (1938; New York: Vintage, 1963); Laurent Dubois, *Avengers of the New World: The Story of the Haitian Revolution* (Cambridge, MA: Belknap Press of Harvard University Press, 2004). For more on the relationship between the state and Vodou throughout the nineteenth and twentieth centuries, see Kate Ramsey, *The Spirits and the Law: Vodou and Power in Haiti* (Chicago: University of Chicago Press, 2011).
45. Brenda Gayle Plummer, "The Afro-American Response to the Occupation of Haiti, 1915–1934," *Phylon* 43 (1982): 131; J. Michael Dash, *Haiti and the*

United States: National Stereotypes and the Literary Imagination (Basingstoke, UK: Macmillan, 1988), 45–46.

46. James Weldon Johnson, "The Truth about Haiti: An N.A.A.C.P. Investigation," *The Crisis* 20, no. 5 (1920): 217–24.

47. Dash, *Haiti and the United States*, 51.

48. Mary A. Renda, *Taking Haiti: Military Occupation and the Culture of U.S. Imperialism, 1915–1940* (Chapel Hill: University of North Carolina Press, 2001), 185.

49. The literature criticizing the colonialism of anthropology is vast. See Talal Asad, ed., *Anthropology and the Colonial Encounter* (New York: Humanities Press, 1973); for a more recent overview, see Paul A. Erickson and Liam D. Murphy, *A History of Anthropological Theory*, 4th ed. (North York, Ontario: University of Toronto Press, 2013).

50. Dunham, notes, ca. 1935–38.

51. Dunham, *Dances of Haiti*, 5, 6, 9–10.

52. Dunham, notes, ca. 1935–38.

53. Isadora Duncan, *My Life*, rev. ed. (1927; repr., New York: Liveright, 2013), 61.

54. Dunham to Turbyfill, December 29, 1935, box 1, folder 8, Mark Turbyfill Papers.

55. Dunham, notes, ca. 1935–38.

56. Dunham, *Dances of Haiti*, 17.

57. See Marc McLeod, "Undesirable Aliens: Race, Ethnicity, and Nationalism in the Comparison of Haitian and British West Indian Immigrant Workers in Cuba, 1912-1939," *Journal of Social History* 31, no. 3 (1998): 599–623.

58. Dunham, notes, ca. 1935–38.

59. Yvonne Daniel (with Catherine Evleshin), *Caribbean and Atlantic Diaspora Dance: Igniting Citizenship* (Urbana: University of Illinois Press, 2011), 110.

60. Dunham, notes, ca. 1935–38.

61. Ibid.

62. Ibid.

63. Dash, *Haiti and the United States*, 38, 57.

64. Dunham, notes, ca. 1935–38.

65. Ibid.

66. Ibid.

67. Ibid.

68. Vladmir Lenin, "Imperialism, the Highest State of Capitalism" (1916), Marxists Internet Archive, accessed May 16, 2015, https://www.marxists.org/archive/lenin/works/1916/imp-hsc/.

69. Dunham, notes, ca. 1935–38.

70. See chapter 7.

71. Dunham, notes, ca. 1935–38.

72. Typed note, addressed to Dr. Johnson, n.d., box 79, folder 5, SIUC.

73. Dunham, *Island Possessed*, 42, 46.

74. Jean Price-Mars, *So Spoke the Uncle* [*Ainsi parla l'oncle*], trans. Magdaline W. Shannon (1928; Washington, DC: Three Continents Press, 1983); Magdaline W. Shannon, *Jean Price-Mars, the Haitian Elite and the American Occupation, 1915–1935* (New York: St. Martin's Press, 1996), 8.

75. The system of child slavery still exists today in Haiti under the name "*restavèk.*" See "The Plight of Restavèk (Child Domestic Servants)," Report to the United Nations Human Rights Committee, September 12, 2014, http://www.ijdh.org/wp-content/uploads/2014/09/HRC_Restavek-Sept-12.pdf.

76. Dunham, notes, ca. 1935–38.

77. Dunham, "Haiti," *Chicago Sunday Times*, July 10, 1938, box 102, folder 4, SIUC.

78. For more on black radicalism in the interwar period, see Robin D. G. Kelley, *Hammer and Hoe: Alabama Communists during the Great Depression* (Chapel Hill: University of North Carolina Press, 1990); Mark I. Solomon, *The Cry Was Unity: Communists and African Americans, 1917–36* (Jackson: University Press of Mississippi, 1998); Glenda Elizabeth Gilmore, *Defying Dixie: The Radical Roots of Civil Rights, 1919–1950* (New York: W. W. Norton, 2008); Minkah Makalani, *In the Cause of Freedom: Radical Black Internationalism from Harlem to London, 1917–1939* (Chapel Hill: University of North Carolina Press, 2011).

79. In the twenty-first century, choreographers use "ballet" to refer to a genre of dance based on the so-called *danse d'école*. In the first half of the twentieth century, Dunham and other choreographers used the term "ballet" to denote a serious, artistic, and lengthy piece of choreography, not necessarily based on the *danse d'école*.

80. Dunham, "Christophe: A Ballet in Five Scenes," June 16, 1938, box 442, folder 10319, LHC.

81. Dunham, *Dances of Haiti*, 42–43.

82. Dunham, "Christophe."

83. Ibid.

84. Ibid.

85. Ibid.

86. Ibid.

87. Dunham to Herskovits, December 28, 1935, MHP.

88. Dunham to Hughes, July 16, 1938, box 57, folder 1085, LHC; John J. Trounstine to Dunham, June 13, 1936; Still to Dunham, June 20, 1936, box 1, folder 4, SIUC.

89. Still to Dunham, ca. May 1936. Courtesy of Judith Anne Still and William Grant Still Music.

90. Still to Dunham, June 20, 1936; Dunham to Still, July 30, 1936; Still to Dunham, August 19, 1936; Dunham to Still, February 20, 1937. Courtesy of Judith Anne Still and William Grant Still Music.

91. Jordis McCoo to Dunham, July 17, 1935, box 38, folder 2, SIUC.

CHAPTER 3

1. Herskovits to Edwin Embree, May 27, 1936, box 20, folder 21, MHP. Offering a second grant was "exceptional." See Embree to Dunham, August 21, 1936, box 1, folder 4, SIUC.

2. Herskovits to Embree.

3. Herskovits to Jackson Davis, November 11, 1936, box 20, folder 15, MHP.

4. Dunham, *Island Possessed*, 66; Dunham to Herskovits, January 1, 1937, MHP.

5. Robert Redfield, ca. 1939, Rosenwald Fund Application, box 409, folder 10, JRP. Though this letter is from 1939, not 1937, it is likely that he had felt similarly two years before.

6. Dunham to Herskovits, May 5, 1937, MHP.

7. Susan Manning, *Modern Dance, Negro Dance: Race in Motion* (Minneapolis: University of Minnesota Press, 2004), 143; Penny M. Von Eschen, "Made on Stage: Transnational Performance and the Worlds of Katherine Dunham from London to Dakar," in *Transnational Lives: Biographies of Global Modernity, 1700–Present*, ed. Desley Deacon, Penny Russel, and Angela Woollacott (New York: Palgrave Macmillan, 2010), 157. Other terms used are "synthesis" and "creole"; see Perpener, *African-American Concert Dance*, 141. Although these scholars and others have

written about Dunham's aesthetic, there has been less discussion of how she arrived at that aesthetic or the options she discarded along the way.

8. For the idea of diaspora as a web, see Nadine George-Graves, "Diasporic Spidering," in DeFrantz and Gonzalez, *Black Performance Theory*, 33–34; for rhizome, see Gilroy, *Black Atlantic*, 4.

9. Jasmine Johnson argues that West African dance allows practitioners to "travel" without the means to physically go to Africa. I argue that viewing Dunham's shows had the same effect. See Johnson, *Rhythm Nation: West African Dance and the Politics of Diaspora* (New York: Oxford University Press, forthcoming).

10. I understand "kinesthetic empathy" to mean that viewers can have a physiological, not just mental or emotional, reaction to watching dance and thus form an empathetic bond with the performer. On the origins of the term, see Deidre Sklar, "Can Bodylore Be Brought to Its Senses?," *Journal of American Folklore* 107, no. 423 (1994): 14. See also Susan Foster, *Choreographing Empathy: Kinesthesia in Performance* (New York: Routledge, 2010).

11. Manning, *Modern Dance, Negro Dance*, 143.

12. For more on the idea of Dunham's performed ethnography or "performative anthropology," see Osumare, "Dancing the Black Atlantic," and Elizabeth Chin, "Dunham Technique: Anthropological Politics of Dancing through Ethnography," in Chin, *Katherine Dunham*, 81, 87–88.

13. *Tropics: Impressions and Realities* program, January 29 and 31, 1937, box 85, folder 2, SIUC.

14. Ibid.

15. Michael Denning, *The Cultural Front: The Laboring of American Culture in the Twentieth Century* (New York: Verso, 1996).

16. Denning, *Cultural Front*, xv, 50; Bill Mullen, *Popular Fronts: Chicago and African-American Cultural Politics, 1935–46* (Urbana: University of Illinois Press, 1999), 3.

17. Denning, *Cultural Front*, 125; Mullen, *Popular Fronts*, 3.

18. Mullen, *Popular Fronts*, 6.

19. Dunham, "Survival," 104.

20. The Abraham Lincoln Center later appeared on the Attorney General's list of Communist front organizations. See "Red Fronts on—and off—Dept. of Justice List," *New York World-Telegram*, January 29, 1948, 16.

21. Dunham, "Survival," 105.

22. Program, "Dance Concert: Proceeds to Children in Spanish War Area," June 2, 1937, and Program, "Dance Recital and Concert, for the Wounded Veterans of the Abraham Lincoln Brigade of Spain," December 16, 1938, both in box 85, folder 2, 3, SIUC.

23. Dunham, "Survival," 104–5.

24. Denning, *Cultural Front*, 5–7; Mary Jane Brown, *Eradicating This Evil: Women in the American Anti-Lynching Movement, 1892–1940* (New York: Garland, 2000).

25. *Tropics: Impressions and Realities* program.

26. Dunham, "Survival," 117.

27. Louis Mitchell, "Panorama of Negro Dances," *Daily Worker*, March 16, 1937, 7. I am indebted to Susan Manning for bringing this review to my attention.

28. "Katherine Dunham in Haitian Dances," *Amsterdam News*, June 12, 1937, 20.

29. "Joliet Colored Dancer Scores Hit at Chicago," *Chicago Daily News*, June 3, 1937, box 102, folder 3, SIUC.

30. Edward Barry, "Miss Dunham Is Sensation in Haitian Dances," *Chicago Daily Tribune*, June 3, 1937, 27.

31. Olin Downes to Dunham, January 19, 1937, box 1, folder 5, SIUC; Alan Lomax to Dunham, July 16, 1937, box 1, folder 5, SIUC.

32. "Noted Dance Interpreter to Make Fall Tour," *Chicago Defender*, July 24, 1937, 15. For more on the terminology of "ballet" in the 1930s, see chapter 2, note 79.

33. Dunham to Still, August 17, 1937. Courtesy of Judith Grant Still.

34. Fellowship Cards, General Education Board-N Dunham, Katherine, Series 10.2, RFR.

35. Dunham, Anthropology Notes, box 79, folders 1, 2, and 3, SIUC.

36. Dunham, untitled essay, ca. 1937, box 79, folder 4, SIUC.

37. Ibid.

38. Dunham, interview by Constance Valis Hill, November 18, 1999, box 13, folder 3, LOC.

39. Susan Quinn, *Furious Improvisation: How the WPA and a Cast of Thousands Made High Art out of Desperate Times* (New York: Walker & Co., 2008), 11, 96, 99. See also A. Joan Saab, *For the Millions: American Art and Culture between the Wars* (Philadelphia: University of Pennsylvania Press, 2004).

40. Frederick Orme, "The Negro in the Dance, as Katherine Dunham Sees Him," *American Dancer*, March 1938, 46.

41. Dunham writing as Kaye Dunn, "L'ag'ya of Martinique," *Esquire* 12, no. 5 (1939), reprinted in Clark and Johnson, *Kaiso!*, 201; Explanatory Notes on Calendar of Events for American Museum of Natural History, April 1947, box 85, folder 12, SIUC.

42. Dunham, "L'ag'ya of Martinique," 201–7. Characteristics of the *ag'ya* also come from personal observations after viewing Dunham's *ag'ya* film clips. See "Selections from the Katherine Dunham Collection: Ag'ya, Martinique Fieldwork, 1936," Library of Congress, accessed July 30, 2016, https://www.loc.gov/collections/katherine-dunham/.

43. *Ballet Fedré* program, Great Northern Theatre, Chicago, January 27, 1937, box 85, folder 3, SIUC; Program Notes, July 25, 1954, box 17, folder 3, SIUC.

44. "Selections from the Katherine Dunham Collection: Ag'ya, Martinique Fieldwork, 1936."

45. Ibid.

46. "Selections from the Katherine Dunham Collection: *Ag'ya* Fight from 'L'Ag'Ya,'" Library of Congress, accessed July 30, 2016, https://www.loc.gov/collections/katherine-dunham/.

47. Orme, "Negro in the Dance," 46.

48. Rachel Carrico, "Un/Natural Disaster and Dancing: Hurricane Katrina and Second Lining in New Orleans," *Black Scholar* 46, no. 1 (2016): 1, 3, 7–8.

49. For more on the transition of African diasporic social/vernacular practices to concert dance, including hip-hop, see DeFrantz, "Foreword: Black Bodies Dancing Black Culture," 14–16, and DeFrantz, "Hip-Hop Habitus v.2.0," in DeFrantz and Gonzalez, *Black Performance Theory*, 230–39.

50. *Ballet Fedré* photographs, box 979, WPA Records, Music Division, Library of Congress.

51. Saab, *For the Millions*, 1–9.

52. Martha Graham, "Seeking an American Art of the Dance," in *Revolt in the Arts: A Survey of the Creation, Distribution and Appreciation of Art in America*, ed. Oliver M. Sayler (New York: Brentano's, 1930), 249–51.

53. Lincoln Kirstein, quoted in Isabel Morse Jones, "Ballet Caravan Uses All-American Themes," *Los Angeles Times*, November 13, 1938, C5. For more see Lynn Garafola,

"Lincoln Kirstein, Modern Dance, and the Left: The Genesis of an American Ballet," *Dance Research: The Journal of the Society for Dance Research* 23, no. 1 (2005): 18–35.

54. For more on the dance world's segregation in the 1930s, see Manning, *Modern Dance, Negro Dance*.

55. Richard Newman, "'The Brightest Star': Aida Overton Walker in the Age of Ragtime and Cakewalk," *Prospects* 18 (1993): 476.

56. Cecil Smith, "Federal Dance Project Gives First Program," *Chicago Daily Tribune*, January 28, 1938, box 102, folder 4, SIUC. See also "Cecil Smith" in *The Oxford Companion to American Theatre*, ed. Gerald Bordman and Thomas S. Hischak, 3rd ed., online edition, 2004, http://www.oxfordreference.com/view/10.1093/acref/9780195169867.001.0001/.

57. Robert Pollak, "All-Negro Folk Ballet Steals Federal Show," *Chicago Daily Times*, January 28, 1938, 43.

58. "Ballet Fedre Is Fine WPA Theatre Production," *Chicago Defender*, February 5, 1938, 4.

59. Ann Barzel, "Dance in Review: BALLET FEDRE," *Dance*, April 1938, 33.

60. See chapter 4.

61. Dunham, "Survival," 92.

62. Ibid.

63. Dunham to Arthur W. Mitchell, July 8, 1938, box 1, folder 7, SIUC. Knupfer argues that Dunham's support of director Shirley Graham caused Dunham's dismissal. As evidence, Knupfer mistakenly attributes a quote to Dunham that actually is from FTP director Hallie Flanagan. I have found nothing in the archives that expresses Dunham's opinion on Graham. Knupfer, *Chicago Black Renaissance*, 60. Actual letter is Hallie Flanagan to Edwin Embree, July 20, 1938, box 1, folder 7, SIUC.

64. Dunham to Mitchell; emphasis added.

65. Cecil Smith, "Miss Dunham Is Effective in Exotic Dances," *Chicago Daily Tribune*, October 27, 1938, box 107, folder 5, SIUC.

66. Cecil Smith, "Dunham Dance Group Puts on a Dandy Show," *Chicago Daily Tribune*, November 23, 1939, box 102, folder 5, SIUC.

67. "Katherine Dunham and group..." *Chicago Dancer*, December–January, 1939–1940, box 102, folder 5, SIUC.

68. Dunham, application for fellowship.

69. Dunham, "Early New York Collaborations," in Clark and Johnson, *Kaiso!*, 126; "A Concert in Primitive Rhythms Program," Panther Room, Hotel Sherman, Chicago, ca. July 1940, box 85, folder 3, SIUC.

70. "Negro Dancer Studied Long," *Oregonian*, April 12, 1943, vol. 1, Dunham Scrapbooks, JRDD.

71. "BATUCADA (also known as BAHIANA)," production notes, box 18, folder 4, LOC; *Carnival of Rhythm*, directed by Stanley Martin, (1941; New York: Dance Film Associates, 1989), VHS.

72. Dunham called it "one of the most celebrated and world known of the Dunham repertoire" in the BATUCADA production notes; negative reflections from students at Stanford University, February 2015, and Williams College, October 2015.

73. Smith, "Dunham Is Effective."

74. "Notes of Music and Musicians," *Chicago Tribune*, November 19, 1939; Dunham, "Survival," 119.

75. Dunham, "Survival," 119.

76. Dan Burley, "Chicago Danseuse Scores on Broadway," *Amsterdam News*, February 24, 1940, 21.

77. John Martin, "Negro Dance Art Shown in Recital," *NYT*, February 19, 1940, 23.

78. Advertisement for *Tropics and Le Jazz "Hot,"* *NYT*, May 8, 1940, 30.

79. John Martin, "The Dance: A Negro Art," *NYT*, February 25, 1940, 114.

80. Orme, "Negro in the Dance," 46.

81. Martin, "Dance: A Negro Art."

82. Burley, "Chicago Danseuse Scores on Broadway."

83. Windsor Theater Program, February 18, 1940, box 53, folder 23, Gumby Scrapbooks, Columbia Rare Book and Manuscript Library, New York.

84. Dunham, "Negro Dance," 999.

85. Margery Dana, "The Dance," *Daily Worker*, February 21, 1940, 7.

86. Windsor Theater Program, February 18, 1940, Gumby; Windsor Theater Program, March 7, 1940, Dunham programs, box 28, folder 7, JRDD.

87. Burley, "Chicago Danseuse Scores on Broadway."

88. Dan Burley, "Backdoor Stuff," *Amsterdam News*, February 24, 1940, 20.

89. Publicity Flyer and Program, Negro Dance Evening, March 7, 1937, Young Men's Hebrew Association, JRDD. Manning and Kraut equate the performance of diaspora in the Negro Dance Evening with Dunham's *Tropics and Le Jazz "Hot,"* but there were important differences. See Manning, "Modern Dance, Negro Dance, and Katherine Dunham," 495; Anthea Kraut, "Between Primitivism and Diaspora: The Dance Performances of Josephine Baker, Zora Neale Hurston, and Katherine Dunham," *Theatre Journal* 55, no. 3 (2003): 447.

90. Associated Negro Press, "O, Sing a New Song" Draws 40,000 People," *Philadelphia Tribune*, August 30, 1934, 2.

91. Dunham, interview by James Briggs Murray, August 27, 1987, VHS, Schomburg Center for Research in Black Culture, New York.

92. Clark, "On Stage with the Dunham Company: An Interview with Vanoye Aikens," in Clark and Johnson, *Kaiso!*, 282.

93. *Carnival of Rhythm.*

94. Dunham, quoted in "Negro Dancer Studied Long."

95. For more on Dunham and Balanchine's collaboration, see Joanna Dee Das, "Choreographing a New World: Katherine Dunham and the Politics of Dance" (PhD diss., Columbia University, 2014), 98–105.

96. Emily Herzog, "Katherine Dunham," *WHO*, May 1941, vol. 104, folder 2, SIUC.

97. Herzog, "Katherine Dunham."

CHAPTER 4

1. Helen Vail to Katherine Dunham, December 28, 1944, box 5, folder 2, SIUC. Vail's observation offers proof of Susan Manning's argument that Dunham's shows enabled "cross-viewing." See Manning, *Modern Dance, Negro Dance*, xvi.

2. Eric Foner, *The Story of American Freedom* (New York: W. W. Norton, 1998), 239.

3. The "Double V" logo first appeared on the front page of the *Pittsburgh Courier* on February 7, 1942, exactly two months after the United States had declared war on Japan. It quickly became a symbol of the Civil Rights Movement.

4. Thomas J. Sugrue, *Sweet Land of Liberty: The Forgotten Struggle for Civil Rights in the North* (New York: Random House, 2008), 62–84; Lauren Rebecca Sklaroff, *Black Culture and the New Deal: The Quest for Civil Rights in the Roosevelt Era* (Chapel Hill: University of North Carolina Press, 2009), 193–96.

5. Dunham is not generally included in the historical literature on this period of the black freedom struggle. See Martha Biondi, *To Stand and Fight: The Struggle for Civil Rights in Postwar New York City* (Cambridge, MA: Harvard University Press, 2003), 187; Sugrue, *Sweet Land of Liberty*; Penny M. Von Eschen, *Race against Empire: Black Americans and Anticolonialism, 1937–1957* (Ithaca, NY: Cornell University Press, 1997).

6. Evelyn Brooks Higginbotham, "African-American Women's History and the Metalanguage of Race," *Signs* 17, no. 2 (1992): 251–74.

7. Dunham, "Minefield," bk. III, 84; Lorde, "Uses of the Erotic."

8. Frantz Fanon, *Black Skin, White Masks* (1952; New York: Grove Press, 1967), 118–32.

9. See Aisha Durham, Brittney C. Cooper, and Susana M. Morris, "The Stage Hip-Hop Feminism Built: A New Directions Essay," *Signs* 38, no. 3 (2013): 721–37.

10. Katherine Dunham to Annette Dunham, June 31, 1942, box 38, folder 3, SIUC.

11. Dunham to Martin Sobelman, May 17, 1941; Sobelman to Dunham, May 20, 1941; box 2, folder 3, SIUC.

12. Darlene J. Sadlier, *Americans All: Good Neighbor Cultural Diplomacy in World War II* (Austin: University of Texas Press, 2012), 37–44.

13. Dunham, "Minefield," bk. II, 61–62.

14. Hannah Durkin, "The Black Female Dancing Body in the Films and Writings of Josephine Baker and Katherine Dunham" (PhD diss., University of Nottingham, 2011), 210–11.

15. *Carnival of Rhythm*, directed by Stanley Martin (1941; New York: Dance Film Associates, 1989), VHS.

16. Durkin, "Black Female Dancing Body," 221, 219.

17. Dunham to Sobelman, May 17, 1941.

18. "Dunham Troupe Short Scores," *Los Angeles Times*, February 20, 1942, Dunham Scrapbooks, vol. 5, JRDD.

19. John Martin, "The Dance: In the Films: First Festival Program at Fifth Avenue Playhouse—June Folk Calendar," *NYT*, May 31, 1942, X8.

20. For more on Maya Deren, see VèVè Clark, Millicent Hodson, and Catrina Neiman, eds., *The Legend of Maya Deren: A Documentary Biography and Collected Works* (New York: Anthology Film Archives/Film Culture, 1984).

21. Lawrence F. LaMar, "'Stormy Weather' to Immortalize Bill Robinson," *Amsterdam News*, January 23, 1943, 17.

22. Arthur Knight, *Disintegrating the Musical: Black Performance and American Musical Film* (Durham: Duke University Press, 2002), 124–25, 155.

23. Megan E. Williams, "The 'Crisis' Cover Girl: Lena Horne, the NAACP, and Representations of African American Femininity, 1941–1945," *American Periodicals* 16, no. 2 (2006): 200.

24. Fred Stanley, "Hollywood Takes a Hint from Washington: Two Big Negro Musicals Are Underway," *NYT*, February 7, 1943, X3. For more, see Donald Bogle, *Toms, Coons, Mulattoes, Mammies, and Bucks: An Interpretive History of Blacks in American Films* (New York: Continuum, 2001), 132–42; Sklaroff, *Black Culture and the New Deal*, 196–208.

25. Shane Vogel, "Performing 'Stormy Weather': Ethel Waters, Lena Horne, and Katherine Dunham," *South Central Review* 25, no. 1 (2008): 93.

26. *Stormy Weather*, directed by Andrew Stone (1943, Los Angeles: 20th Century Fox, 2006), DVD.

27. Dunham, "Minefield," bk. III, 38.
28. Herman Hill, "Coast Fans Applaud Lena Horne at 'Stormy Weather' Opening," *Pittsburgh Courier*, August 7, 1943, 20.
29. Peter Suskind, "Two Artists Not So Well Known to Race," *Norfolk Journal and Guide*, December 19, 1942, B23.
30. Letter to Dunham, September 17, 1943, box 3, folder 5, SIUC.
31. In May 1945, the *Amsterdam News* also reported that Dunham was the "unanimous" selection of the 574th Quartermaster Railhead Company as pinup girl of 1945. See "Chosen Pacific Pin Up Girl of 1945," *Amsterdam News*, May 5, 1945, 8B.
32. Dunham, "Minefield," bk. II, 46.
33. Ibid., 77, 80.
34. Ibid., 84.
35. Ibid., 96, 122.
36. Ibid., 122, 124–137, 144. Dunham gives Gray's age as seventeen, but Gray's official IMDB entry lists her birth date as October 23, 1922, making her at least nineteen by the time Dunham arrived in Los Angeles in 1941.
37. Dunham, "Minefield," bk. III, 84.
38. Honore Weld, "Katherine Dunham Dances for French Prisoners," *People's World*, July 31, 1942, Dunham Scrapbooks, vol. 5, JRDD.
39. For more on "freedom" as the political potential of dance, see Lepecki, "Choreopolice and Choreopolitics." On freedom as the fundamental political concept of the American experience, see Foner, *Story of American Freedom*.
40. Weld, "Katherine Dunham Dances for French Prisoners."
41. Katherine Dunham to Annette Dunham, June 31, 1942, box 38, folder 3, SIUC.
42. Ibid.
43. Lavinia Williams, interview by James Briggs Murray, VHS, 1983, Schomburg Center for Research in Black Culture, New York.
44. Dunham compared her company to the Ballet Russe de Monte Carlo on several occasions. For an example, see Lowe, "Being a Closeup on Miss Dunham."
45. Telegram, Gerald Goode to Dunham, April 26, 1943, box 3, folder 3, SIUC; Dunham to Goode, ca. May 1943, box 3, folder 7, SIUC.
46. Dunham to Goode, ca. May 1943.
47. Ibid.
48. Lowe, "Being a Closeup on Miss Dunham."
49. Thomas F. DeFrantz, Mellon Summer Seminar in Dance Studies, June 24, 2014, Stanford University; Rosemarie A. Roberts, "Research-to-Performance Methodology: Embodying Knowledge and Power from the Field to the Concert Stage," in Chin, *Katherine Dunham*, 18.
50. See Dunham, "Thesis Turned Broadway," 1941, in Clark and Johnson, *Kaiso!*, 214–15; Dunham, "Notes on the Dance," 1954, in Clark and Johnson, *Kaiso!*, 519; Dunham, transcript of interview by Viennese student, February 1960, box 26, folder 6, SIUC; Dunham, "Dance as a Cultural Art and its Role in Development," 1976, in Clark and Johnson, *Kaiso!*, 543.
51. Dunham, "Minefield," bk. II, 114.
52. This idea is explored in greater depth in chapter 2.
53. *Tropical Revue* program notes, September 19, 1943, Givens Collection Playbills/Programs, box 1, University of Minnesota.
54. *Divine Drumbeats: Katherine Dunham and Her People*, directed by Merril Brockway, telecast April 16, 1980, PBS *Dance in America*. Series, personal collection.
55. Donald Horton to Dunham, January 22, 1941, box 2, folder 1, SIUC.

56. Geoffrey Gorer to Dunham, January 20, 1941, box 2, folder 1, SIUC.

57. *Tropical Revue* program notes.

58. "Sex-Conscious Hub Ices Hot Dunham Terps," *Billboard* 56, no. 5 (1944): 1.

59. Margaret Lloyd, "Primitive Dances Featured in New Show at Opera House," *Christian Science Monitor*, January 18, 1944, 4.

60. Lloyd, "Primitive Dances Featured in New Show at Opera House," 4.

61. Joyce Aschenbrenner first suggested this argument in *Katherine Dunham: Reflections on the Social and Political Contexts of Afro-American Dance* (New York: CORD, 1981), 19. Ramsay Burt also makes this argument in "Katherine Dunham's *Rites De Passage*: Censorship and Sexuality," in Firscher-Hornung and Goeller, *EmBODYing Liberation*, 88.

62. I thank Lynn Garafola for this insight.

63. John D'Emilio and Estelle B. Freedman. *Intimate Matters: A History of Sexuality in America* (Chicago: University of Chicago Press, 1997), 233–73.

64. Marilyn E. Hegarty, "Patriot or Prostitute? Sexual Discourses, Print Media, and American Women during World War II," *Journal of Women's History* 10, no. 2 (1998): 112.

65. Hegarty, "Patriot or Prostitute," 113; Joanne J. Meyerowitz, "Women, Cheesecake, and Borderline Material: Responses to Girlie Pictures in the Mid-Twentieth Century U.S.," *Journal of Women's History* 8, no. 3 (1996): 20; Williams, "'Crisis' Cover Girl," 210.

66. For more on this subject, see earlier chapters and Torgovnick, *Gone Primitive*.

67. John Livingston, Letter to the Editors of the *Boston Daily Globe*, January 19, 1944, box 4, folder 1, SIUC.

68. Elinor Hughes, "The Dunham Dance Revue and the New Saroyan Play," *Boston Herald*, January 23, 1944, Dunham, Katherine [clippings], JRDD.

69. Dunham, "Minefield," bk. 3, 103.

70. Jack Balch, "Katherine Dunham Dancers at American," *St. Louis Post-Dispatch*, February 22, 1944; Herbert L. Monk, "Katherine Dunham Torrid in Dances at American," *St. Louis Globe-Democrat*, February 22, 1944, both in box 102, folder 12, SIUC.

71. Dunham Scrapbooks, vol. 2, April–May, 1944, JRDD.

72. "Summary of Gross Receipts—1943-44-45: 'Tropical Revue,'" box 9, folder 6, SIUC.

73. John Martin, "Katherine Dunham Gives Dance Revue," *NYT*, September 20, 1943, 24.

74. Martin, "New Voodoo Dance in Dunham Revue," *NYT*, December 27, 1944, 15.

75. Edwin Denby, "The Dance: Dunham in Full Bloom," *New York Herald Tribune*, December 27, 1944, 10.

76. For more on mythic abstraction, see Manning, *Modern Dance, Negro Dance*, 118–22.

77. Julia Foulkes, *Modern Bodies: Dance and American Modernism from Martha Graham to Alvin Ailey* (Chapel Hill: University of North Carolina Press, 2002), 72; Gay Morris, *A Game for Dancers: Performing Modernism in the Postwar Years, 1945–1960* (Middletown, CT: Wesleyan University Press, 2006), 128.

78. For more on Primus, see Griffin, *Harlem Nocturne*, 19–78; Peggy Schwartz and Murray Schwartz, *The Dance Claimed Me: A Biography of Pearl Primus* (New Haven, CT: Yale University Press, 2011).

79. Ellen Graff, *Stepping Left: Dance and Politics in New York City, 1928–1942* (Durham, NC: Duke University Press, 1997), 51–55; Victoria Phillips Geduld, "Performing

Communism in the American Dance: Culture, Politics and the New Dance Group," *American Communist History* 7, no. 1 (2008): 60.

80. Quoted in David Margolick, *Strange Fruit: Billie Holiday, Café Society, and an Early Cry for Civil Rights* (Philadelphia: Running Press, 2000), 17.

81. For more, see Amanda Vaill, *Somewhere: The Life of Jerome Robbins* (New York: Broadway Books, 2006), 52–54.

82. Schwartz and Schwartz, *Dance Claimed Me*, 35–36.

83. Peter Suskind, "Her Dancing Was Really Superb," *New Journal and Guide*, February 27, 1943, B22.

84. Don Deleighbur, "Katherine Dunham vs. Pearl Primus: Style and Purposes in Negro Folk Dancing Are Compared," *Amsterdam News*, February 12, 1944, 11A.

85. Deleighbur, "Katherine Dunham vs. Pearl Primus."

86. Schwartz and Schwartz, *Dance Claimed Me*, 55, 63–64.

87. L. D. Reddick to Dunham, February 24, 1944, box 4, folder 1, SIUC.

88. See boxes 4, 7, and 9, SIUC.

89. Oliver Trolson to Dunham, telegram, May 21, 1946, box 8, folder 5, SIUC.

90. Manning, "Modern Dance, Negro Dance," 502.

91. Amy Porter, "Anthropological Katie," condensed from *Colliers*, *Negro Digest*, April 1945, 39.

92. Albert Gins to Dunham, May 4, 1945, box 6, folder 1, SIUC; *Carib Song* souvenir program, September 1945, JRDD.

93. Dunham to Herskovits, November 15, 1935, MHP.

94. *The Magic of Katherine Dunham*, dress rehearsal, Alvin Ailey American Dance Theater, 1987, VHS, JRDD.

95. Dunham, interview by WEEI Radio Boston, September 14, 1945, box 6, folder 5, SIUC.

96. Alfred Berger to Dunham, September 29, 1945, box 6, folder 5, SIUC.

97. Lewis Nichols, "The Play: 'Carib Song,' with Katherine Dunham and Avon Long, Makes Its Bow at the Adelphi Theatre," *NYT*, September 28, 1945, 17.

98. "The Theater: New Musical in Manhattan," *Time*, October 8, 1945, http://www.time.com/time/magazine/article/0,9171,776284,00.html#ixzz19cTVmJZx.

99. Carl Diton, "Avon Long Outstanding in Katherine Dunham Vehicle," *Baltimore Afro-American*, October 13, 1945, 10; Abe Hill, "Carib Song Not Too Fascinating to Critic Hill," *Amsterdam News*, October 20, 1945, 15.

100. Lou Swartz, "In Spite of K. Dunham Beauty, Artistry, Says 'Carib Song' Closed As Broadway Venture because of Poor Race Picturization," *Cleveland Call and Post*, November 10, 1945, 9A.

101. Associated Negro Press, "Lena Horne Refuses Lead Role in MGM's 'St. Louis Woman,'" *Chicago Defender* (national ed.), September 29, 1945, 14.

102. "Minefield," bk. III, 18–20.

103. Biondi, *To Stand and Fight*, 187.

104. Dunham had an apartment for herself, John Pratt, and Dorothy Gray, but she needed hotel rooms for the company members. Evelyn Seeley, "Hotels OK Reservation: A Negro? 'All Filled Up,'" *PM*, September 1, 1943, 9.

105. "Katherine Dunham Weary of Hotel Trek," *PM*, September 5, 1943, Dunham Scrapbooks, vol. 1, JRDD.

106. Dunham, "Minefield," bk. II, 44.

107. Associated Negro Press, "Discrimination Bane of Miss Dunham's Existence," *Journal and Guide*, September 18, 1943, 14; "Kay Dunham Is Fed Up on Race Discrimination," *Atlanta Daily World*, September 20, 1943, 2; "Dancer Is 'Fed Up' with Discrimination," *Philadelphia Tribune*, September 18, 1943, 18.

108. "Katherine Dunham Weary of Hotel Trek."
109. Alexander Sterne to Dunham, September 6, 1943, box 3, folder 5, SIUC.
110. Williams interview.
111. Earl B. Dickerson and Mindley C. Cyrus, Attorneys for Miss Katherine Dunham, to Blackstone Hotel Corp., June 6, 1944. box 4, folder 4, SIUC.
112. Dunham, "Comment to a Louisville Audience," October 19, 1944, reprinted in Clark and Johnson, *Kaiso!*, 255.
113. Dunham to Gerald Goode, October 20, 1944, box 4, folder 7, SIUC. For an example of positive press, see Dwight Anderson, "Dunham Troupe Offers Colorful, Exciting Revue," *Courier-Journal*, Louisville, KY, October 20, 1944, Dunham Scrapbooks, vol. 4, JRDD.
114. Richard Burns, "A Dancer's Swan Song," *Negro Digest*, December 1944, 42; Seymour Peck, "Dunham Troupes to Conquer," *PM*, December 20, 1944, 16, Dunham Scrapbooks, vol. 4, JRDD.
115. Norman Johnson to Dunham, December 31, 1944, box 5, folder 2, SIUC. Other examples: Naomi Lattimore to Dunham, November 18, 1944, box 5, folder 2, SIUC; Mr. and Mrs. Kenton Atwood to Dunham, October 22, 1944, Box 4, Folder 7, SIUC.
116. Talley Beatty, *Speaking of Dance: Conversations with Contemporary Masters of American Modern Dance*, produced by Charles Reinhart and Stephanie Reinhart, American Dance Festival (Oregon, WI: American Dance Festival Video, 1993), VHS, JRDD; Aschenbrenner, *Katherine Dunham*, 133.
117. Beatty, *Speaking of Dance*.
118. Dunham, "Minefield," bk. 3, 51.
119. Dunham, "Minefield," bk. 2, 50. The Clark County register has no record of such a marriage taking place in Las Vegas.
120. Langston Hughes, "Ballad in Black and White," *Chicago Defender*, September 1, 1945, 12.
121. Hughes, "Ballad in Black and White."
122. Unsigned note, June 1944, box 4, folder 4, SIUC.
123. Giuseppe Antonio Borgese, "A Bedroom Approach to Racism," *Negro Digest*, December 1944, 31.
124. John H. Johnson to Dunham, January 11, 1945, box 5, folder 4, SIUC.
125. Johnson to Dunham, March 7, 1945, box 5, folder 5, SIUC.
126. Dunham to Johnson, May 9, 1945, box 6, folder 1, SIUC.
127. Dunham, "Minefield," bk. 2, 124–25.
128. Dunham to Johnson, May 9, 1945, box 6, folder 1, SIUC.
129. Ibid.
130. Johnson to Dunham, May 22, 1945, box 6, folder 1, SIUC.
131. Adam Green, *Selling the Race: Culture, Community, and Black Chicago, 1940–1955* (Chicago: University of Chicago Press, 2007), 139.
132. Dunham, "Minefield," bk. 3, 40.
133. Dunham, "Minefield," bk. 3, 39–46, 67–70; John Pratt to Dunham, May 26, 1944, box 38, folder 4, SIUC.
134. Tim Durant to Dunham, April 28, 1945, box 5, folder 7, SIUC; Durant to Dunham, January 19, 1946, box 7, folder 3, SIUC; Durant to Dunham, April 17, 1947, box 10, folder 1, SIUC.
135. David Robinson, *Chaplin, His Life and Art* (London: Collins, 1985), 580.
136. Durant to Dunham, May 1944, box 4, folder 3, SIUC; Special Inquiry, February 1, 1967, FBI File 100-334975 reproduces Durant's May 15, 1944 testimony in front of Federal Judge J. F. T. O'Connor about his relationship with Dunham.

137. For example, the FBI detained Dunham at the Mexican border in 1944 when she returned from a vacation, and noted that she had relationships with several Communist groups. October 23, 1944, FBI file 100-334795.

138. Boxes 3-11, SIUC; Report to State Department, March 18, 1953, FBI File 100-334795.

139. See chapter 2, n. 78.

140. "Dancing Star Says Soldiers Best Audience, One of Hollywood Pictures Made by Katherine Dunham among Eight Shown in Russia," *Evening Telegram*, Toronto, January 4, 1944, Dunham Scrapbooks, vol. 1, JRDD.

141. Barbara S. Prigmore, "Talented Negroes Given Raw Deal in Hollywood; Must Look to Russia, Latin Countries Says Katherine Dunham," *Philadelphia Tribune*, February 5, 1944, Dunham Scrapbooks, vol. 1, JRDD.

142. Mark Marvin to Anatol[y] Gromov, press secretary, Embassy of the USSR, ca. 1946, box 7, folder 2, SIUC.

143. Dunham, interview for unnamed Russian magazine, ca. May 1945, box 7, folder 2, SIUC.

CHAPTER 5

1. "The Following Guests Attended Rehearsal on Sunday, January 20, 1946," box 7, folder 3, SIUC.

2. Aikens interview.

3. Discussions of the school are often relegated to a few pages in larger treatments of Dunham's life. See Aschenbrenner, *Katherine Dunham*, 136–39; Beckford, *Katherine Dunham*, 55–57. One exception is Gaynell Sherrod's unpublished dissertation, which examines the philosophical and theoretical aspects of Dunham's pedagogy and covers 1931 to 1946. This chapter builds upon Sherrod's work by examining the socio-historical impact of the school and considering how it operated until its closing in 1954. See Sherrod, "Dance Griots."

4. Boas to Dunham, October 1, 1941, box 2, folder 5, SIUC; Dunham to Boas, August 21, 1944, box 75, folder 9, Franziska Boas Papers, Music Division, Library of Congress; Allana C. Lindgren, "Civil Rights Strategies in the United States: Franziska Boas's Activist Use of Dance, 1933–1965," *Dance Research Journal* 45, no. 2 (2013): 4.

5. Dale Wasserman to Eileen Hamilton, September 30, 1944, box 4, folder 7, SIUC; Dunham to Boas, February 14, 1945, box 75, folder 9, Boas Papers.

6. Franziska Boas, "The Negro and the Dance as an Art," *Phylon* 10, no. 1 (1949): 40; Lindgren, "Civil Rights Strategies," 40–41.

7. That is $2.6 million in 2015 dollars. Inflation calculations come from the United States Bureau of Labor Statistics, accessed August 18, 2016, www.bls.gov/data/inflation_calculator.htm/.

8. Katherine Dunham School of Dance, press release, January 23, 1945, box 5, folder 4, SIUC.

9. "Katherine Dunham Buys House in East 71st St. for Her Troupe," *New York Herald Tribune*, January 23, 1945, box 5, folder 4, SIUC.

10. "People: Ladies of Fashion," *Time*, January 29, 1945, http://www.time.com/time/magazine/article/0,9171,933974,00.html.

11. Dan Burley, writing as Don Deleighbur, "Katherine Dunham Buys Mansion, Purchase Price Reported $280,000 for Residence, Dancing School," *Cleveland Call and Post*, February 10, 1945, 10A.

12. Delighbur, "Katherine Dunham Buys Mansion," and "New York Show Front," *Philadelphia Tribune*, February 10, 1945, 14.

13. Fitelson and Mayers to Dunham, February 6, 1945, box 5, folder 5, SIUC.

14. Abe Hill, "N.Y.C. Silk Stocking 400 Attack Katherine Dunham," *Amsterdam News*, February 24, 1945, 1A.

15. The story was reported in all of New York's main newspapers. See "Dancer Wins in Court: Katherine Dunham's Right to Buy House Is Upheld," *NYT*, February 17, 1945, 11.

16. "Katherine Dunham Yields East 71st Street House," *New York Herald Tribune*, March 8, 1945, Dunham, Katherine [clippings], JRDD; "Famed Dancer Calls Off Deal to Take Place," *Amsterdam News*, March 17, 1945, A1.

17. Mrs. Herbert H. Lehman to Dunham, February 13, 1945; Dunham to Lehman, February 21, 1945, box 5, folder 5, SIUC.

18. Sherrod, "Dance Griots," 190.

19. Advertisement for Katherine Dunham School of Dance, *Amsterdam News*, September 15, 1945, 21.

20. There are numerous letters in box 6, folders 1–7 at SIUC.

21. See Doris Schiff to Dunham, October 9, 1945, Charles Pratt Young to Dunham, October 10, 1945, box 6, folder 6, and several letters from January 1946 in box 7, folder 3, SIUC.

22. Julie Robinson Belafonte, interview by author, July 26, 2013, New York.

23. David Vaughan, interview by author, January 23, 2013, New York.

24. Dunham School of Dance and Theatre Summer Quarter, 1946, box 6, folder 3, SIUC.

25. "Large Student Crowds Register at Dunham's," *Amsterdam News*, July 6, 1946, 18.

26. Bureau of Labor Statistics inflation calculator, http://www.bls.gov/data/infla-tion_calculator.htm/. In comparison, in October 2016, drop-in class rates at two of New York's biggest dance studios, Steps on Broadway and Broadway Dance Center, were $20, and virtually all classes lasted one-and-a-half hours. If one signed up for a session of ten classes, roughly equivalent to the Dunham School's sessions, rates were $18 or $17 per class, respectively. Those studios are considered on the more expensive end, and Dunham's classes cost 50 per cent more for fewer hours of contact. See http://www.stepsnyc.com/classes/rates-regulations/; http://www.broadwaydancecenter.com/studioinfo/rates.shtml.

27. Dunham School of Dance and Theatre, "Statement of Income and Disbursements for the week ending September 21, 1946," box 9, folder 1, SIUC.

28. See boxes 44–46, SIUC.

29. "Statement of Income and Disbursements."

30. Dunham to Edwin R. Embree, February 28, 1946, box 7, folder 6, SIUC; Dunham to Laura Jane Musser, June 15, 1946, box 8, folder 6, SIUC.

31. Sherrod, "Dance Griots," 194.

32. Janice Ross, *Moving Lessons: Margaret H'Doubler and the Beginning of Dance in American Education* (Madison: University of Wisconsin Press, 2000), 3–8.

33. Dunham to Embree, February 28, 1946.

34. Dunham School of Dance and Theatre, prospectus, ca. 1946, box 5, folder 3, SIUC.

35. Dunham School of Arts and Research, 1946–1947 Schedule, box 47, folder 34, SIUC.

36. Dunham, interview by Katharine Wolfe, December 14, 1945, box 15, folder 7, Katharine Wolfe Papers, JRDD; William Hawkins, "Star of 'Bal Negre' Runs A Unique Dancing School," *New York World-Telegram*, December 6, 1946, box 102,

folder 14, SIUC; Dunham to Lavinia Williams, January 17, 1946, box 12, folder 2, LWP.

37. Hawkins, "Star of 'Bal Negre.'"
38. Dunham to Embree, February 28, 1946.
39. See David Tyack, *Seeking Common Ground: Public Schools in a Diverse Society* (Cambridge, MA: Harvard University Press, 2003).
40. Sherrod, "Dance Griots," 222.
41. Margaret Morrison is currently conducting research on the topic of interracial dance education and has documented the existence of many interracial dance schools in the mid-1950s, but few in the 1940s. E-mail communication with Margaret Morrison, January 13, 2014. Sherrod discusses the difficulties black students faced when traveling downtown to white-dominant studios in mid-century New York in "Dance Griots," 338–39.
42. Chin, "Dunham Technique," 98–99.
43. Lavinia Williams, Notes on Dunham Technique class, box 3, folder 3, LWP.
44. Rose, *Dunham Technique*, and Sherrod, "Dance Griots," 214–24.
45. Constance Valis Hill, "From Bharata Natyam to Bop: Jack Cole's Modern Jazz Dance," *Dance Research Journal* 33, no. 2 (2001): 29–39; Larry Stempel, *Showtime: A History of the Broadway Musical Theater* (New York: W. W. Norton, 2010), 573.
46. Dunham School of Dance and Theatre Summer Quarter, 1946; Dunham School of Arts and Research, 1946–1947 Schedule.
47. *West Side Story*, directed by Robert Wise and Jerome Robbins (1961; Los Angeles: MGM Home Entertainment, 2003), DVD. For more on Dunham's contributions to jazz dance, see Saroya Corbett, "Katherine Dunham's Mark on Jazz Dance," in *Jazz Dance: A History of the Roots and Branches*, ed. Lindsay Guarino and Wendy Oliver (Gainesville: University Press of Florida, 2014), 89–96.
48. Aikens interview; Marie-Christine Dunham Pratt, telephone interview by author, August 10, 2016.
49. Dunham interview by Wolfe.
50. Ibid.
51. "Prospectus: Katherine Dunham and Company," ca. February 1946, box 7, folder 2, SIUC.
52. Nancy Reynolds and Malcolm McCormick, "Ballet in America Comes of Age," in *No Fixed Points: Dance in the Twentieth Century* (New Haven, CT: Yale University Press, 2003), 265–318; Gay Morris, "Bourdieu, the Body, and Graham's Post-War Dance," *Dance Research: The Journal of the Society for Dance Research* 19, no. 2 (2001): 61–64.
53. Mark Marvin to Galaxy Music Company, December 12, 1945, box 7, folder 1, SIUC.
54. Eunice Brown, "An Experiment in Negro Modern Dance," *Dance Observer* 13, no. 1 (1946): 4.
55. Todd Bolender to Editor of *Dance Observer*, January 9, 1946, box 7, folder 3, SIUC.
56. See chapter 1.
57. Dunham to Embree, February 28, 1946.
58. George Abbott to Dunham, March 9, 1946, box 7, folder 7, SIUC.
59. Dunham to Daniel Rybb, April 9, April 13, 1946, box 8, folder 2, SIUC.
60. Dunham to Albert B. Gins, May 7, 1946, box 8, folder 9, SIUC.
61. Although the first *e* in the French word "Nègre" has a grave accent mark, the programs and publicity materials for Dunham's show do not include it.

62. *Bal Negre* advertisement, *Daily Worker*, November 3, 1946, 22.

63. Dunham to Mary Titus, January 14, 1947, box 9, folder 7, SIUC.

64. Jesse L. Rosenberg to Dunham, May 23, 1946, box 8, folder 5, SIUC.

65. Dunham to Nicolás Guillén, June 18, 1946, box 8, folder 6, SIUC.

66. Josephine Powell, *Tito Puente: When the Drums Are Dreaming* (Bloomington, IN: AuthorHouse, 2007), 159.

67. For more on the Cuban influence on Dunham and Dunham's influence on the flourishing of Cuban culture in New York, see Marta Moreno Vega, "The Yoruba Orisha Tradition Comes to New York City," *African American Review* 29, no. 2 (1995): 201–6.

68. Robert Sylvester, "Dunham at Her Best in Fine 'Bal Negre' Revue at Belasco," *New York Daily News*, November 8, 1946, box 102, folder 14, SIUC; John Martin, "Dunham Dancers Star in New Revue," *NYT*, November 8, 1946, 20.

69. Ezra Goodman, "Afterthoughts on Katherine Dunham's *Bal Negre*," *Dance Magazine*, January 1947, 35.

70. Emerante de Pradines, interview by author, January 10, 2016, Port-au-Prince, Haiti.

71. For more on the Experimental Group's performances and repertoire, see box 7, folders 1–2, box 9, folders 6–9, and box 14, folder 7, SIUC.

72. Antoine Brevin of the Pan American Union, June 27, 1947, box 10, folder 3, SIUC.

73. Dunham, "Haiti," ca. October–December 1951, box 15, folder 9, SIUC.

74. Ibid.

75. For more on Destiné, see Millery Polyné, *From Douglass to Duvalier: U.S. African Americans, Haiti and Pan Americanism, 1870–1964* (Gainesville: University Press of Florida, 2010), 154–79; Kate Ramsey, "Vodou and Nationalism: The Staging of Folklore in Mid-Twentieth Century Haiti," *Women and Performance: A Journal of Feminist Theory* 7, no. 2 (1995): 187–218.

76. Photographs from *Chicago Defender*, November 22, 1947, 20.

77. "Mixed Couple, Kat' Dunham Dancers, Stir Television Rap," *Afro-American*, November 1, 1947, 6. Other African American newspapers also reported on the incident.

78. "Mixed Couple, Kat' Dunham Dancers."

79. Katherine Dunham School of Dance, press release, December 13, 1945, box 7, folder 2, SIUC.

80. "The Dunham Dancers," *New York World*, July 1946, Dunham Scrapbooks, JRDD.

81. Angelica Welldon, "A New Kind of School," *Glamour*, August 1946, box 102, folder 14, SIUC.

82. See chapter 1.

83. "Katherine Dunham School of Cultural Arts, Inc., School of Dance, "Application for: Full Scholarship, Half Scholarship, Student Aid," box 47, folder 34, SIUC.

84. Advertisement for the Dunham School of Dance and Theatre, *Daily Worker*, November 3, 1946, 22.

85. Dunham School of Dance and Theatre, prospectus, ca. 1946, box 5, folder 3, SIUC.

86. Hawkins, "Star of 'Bal Negre' Runs a Unique Dancing School"; Associated Negro Press, "Dunham Dance School Lures Swiss Dancer," *Philadelphia Tribune*, August 27, 1946, 7.

87. Dunham to William C. Haygood, November 22, 1946, box 409, folder 10, JRP; Dunham School of Dance and Theatre, Summer Quarter, box 6, folder 3, SIUC; "Dunham Schools, Students, and Faculty," boxes 44–47, SIUC.

88. "Red Fronts on—and off—Dept. of Justice List"; Report to State Department, March 18, 1953, Katherine Dunham FBI file 100-334795. Dunham also describes the constant surveillance of the FBI and CIA in "Minefield," bk. 3, 67–68.

89. Franklin D. Roosevelt, State of the Union Address, January 6, 1941, Franklin D. Roosevelt Presidential Library and Museum, Hyde Park, NY, http://docs.fdrli-brary.marist.edu/od4frees.html.

90. Von Eschen, *Race against Empire*, 17–20.

91. Associated Negro Press, "Dunham's $2000 for Scholarship," *Afro-American*, September 15, 1945, 15.

92. Paul Robeson to Dunham and notes on dictated reply, October 12, 1945, box 6, folder 6, SIUC.

93. Max Yergan to Dunham, October 25, 1945, box 4, folder 7, SIUC; "Principals in N.Y. Freedom for Africa Rally," *Afro-American*, July 6, 1946, 9.

94. Dunham, interview for unnamed Russian magazine, ca. May 1945, box 7, folder 2, SIUC.

95. Thelma Thurston Gorham, "Katherine Dunham's Cocktailer among Swank Conference Socials," *Afro-American*, June 16, 1945, 12; P. I. Prattis, "Conference Confetti," *Pittsburgh Courier*, May 26, 1945, 12.

96. Ralph Matthews, "Sidelights on UNICO," *Afro-American*, June 2, 1945, 3.

97. Elaine Tyler May, *Homeward Bound: American Families in the Cold War Era* (New York: Basic Books, 1988), 95.

98. Arthur Mitchell, telephone interview by author, October 13, 2016.

99. Memo to J.E.H., unsigned, April 13, 1948, FBI file 100-334795.

100. Katherine Dunham School of Cultural Arts, Inc. Loans Payable–May 20, 1948, box 11, folder 6, SIUC.

101. Dunham to Dorothy Gray, September 27, 1948, box 12, folder 1, SIUC.

102. Dunham to Bernard Berenson, July 15, 1949, BMBP.

103. Elise DuTreuille to Dunham, May 13, 1950, box 15, folder 4, SIUC.

104. See student files, boxes 44–46, SIUC.

105. Dunham to Gray, October 29, 1948, box 12, folder 2, SIUC.

106. Dunham to Gray, December 17, 1948, box 12, folder 3, SIUC.

107. Mitchell interview.

108. Michelle Newton student file, box 46, folder 6, SIUC.

109. Glory Van Scott, interview by author, July 15, 2011, New York.

110. Pradines interview; "New York Beat," *Jet*, January 14, 1954, 64.

111. Dunham to Gray, May 5, 1949, box 13, folder 2, SIUC.

CHAPTER 6

1. There are no original program notes from *Southland*'s Chile world premiere. See *Southland* program notes, Palais de Chaillot Theatre, Paris, January 9, 1953, box 49, folder 7, SIUC. Though Dunham called *Southland* a ballet, Belafonte calls it a dance drama because of its heavy emphasis on plot and acting. Julie Belafonte interview, June 25, 2002, Cultural Traditions Tape 14, Jacob's Pillow Archives, Beckett, MA.

2. *Southland* program notes.

3. See chapter 4.

4. Du Bois, *Souls of Black Folk*, 3.

5. Walter L. Hixson, *Parting the Curtain: Propaganda, Culture, and the Cold War, 1945–1961* (New York: St. Martin's Press, 1998), 8, 129. For more on civil rights and the Cold War, see Mary L. Dudziak, *Cold War Civil Rights: Race*

and the Image of American Democracy (Princeton, NJ: Princeton University Press, 2000); Kevin Gaines, African Americans in Ghana: Black Expatriates and the Civil Rights Era (Chapel Hill: University of North Carolina Press, 2006); Von Eschen, Race against Empire. For more on Cold War cultural diplomacy, see David Caute, The Dancer Defects: The Struggle for Cultural Supremacy during the Cold War (New York: Oxford University Press, 2003); Frances Stonor Saunders, The Cultural Cold War: The CIA and the World of Arts and Letters (New York: New Press, 2000); Penny M. Von Eschen, Satchmo Blows up the World: Jazz Ambassadors Play the Cold War (Cambridge, MA: Harvard University Press, 2004).

6. Most of the scholarship on Dunham's international tours focuses on the repression she faced as a result of Southland. Although that narrative is important, it threatens to overshadow what she did accomplish as an unofficial ambassador of diaspora. See Aschenbrenner, Katherine Dunham, 149–51; Clare Croft, Dancers as Diplomats: American Choreography in Cultural Exchange (New York: Oxford University Press, 2015), 112, 114–16; Constance Valis Hill, "Katherine Dunham's Southland: Protest in the Face of Repression," Dance Research Journal 26, no. 2 (1994): 1–10; Von Eschen, "Made on Stage."

7. For the rave reviews and accolades that Dunham received in Mexico, see box 10, folders 2–8, and box 102, folder 15, SIUC.

8. Antonio Luna Arroyo, Ana Merida en la historia de la Danza Mexicana Moderna (Mexico City: Publicaciones de Danza Moderna, 1959), 29–32; "Academia de la Danza Mexicana," Subdirección General de Educación e Investigación Artisticas, Government of Mexico, March 16, 2015, http://www.sgeia.bellasartes.gob.mx/.

9. Aikens interview; Katherine Dunham, "Love Letters from I Tatti" (unpublished manuscript, 1980), vol. 3, box 15, folder 3, LOC; VèVè Clark, "On Stage with the Dunham Company: An Interview with Vanoye Aikens," in Clark and Johnson, Kaiso!, 285.

10. Anita Gonzalez, Afro-Mexico: Dancing between Myth and Reality (Austin: University of Texas Press, 2010), 1, 32.

11. Val Parnell to Dunham, June 4, 1948, box 11, folder 7, SIUC.

12. Gordon Bickles, "Some Portraits in Print," Tatler, June 16, 1948, box 102, folder 16, SIUC; "Profile: Katherine Dunham," The Observer, September 12, 1948, box 102, folder 7, SIUC; "Dunham Dancing While Rome Pays," Chicago Daily News, ca. March 1949, box 107, SIUC.

13. Dunham discusses trying to get support for her school from Astor in her letter to Gray, September 27, 1948.

14. Aschenbrenner, Katherine Dunham, 153; Dunham to Annette Dunham, January 27, 1950, box 39, folder 1, SIUC; Billy Rowe, "'Aly Khan Not Romancing Me'— Katherine Dunham," Pittsburgh Courier, May 13, 1950, 1; Aikens interview.

15. Hagan, "Lively Arts."

16. Antonio Sant'Angelo to Dunham, May 6, 1949, box 13, folder 2, SIUC.

17. A. Wolters to Dunham, July 23, 1949, box 13, folder 7, SIUC.

18. Susan Manning has written about this effect of Dunham's shows in America in the early 1940s. See "Modern Dance, Negro Dance, and Katherine Dunham," 503.

19. Scholars generally attribute négritude to the convergence in the thought of Aimé Césaire, Léopold Sédar Senghor, and Léon Damas. Brent Hayes Edwards and T. Denean Sharpley-Whiting have argued that négritude owes as much to Paulette and Jane Nardal, Martinican-born sisters who ran a salon out of their Parisian home, and Suzanne Césaire, Aimé's wife. See Edwards, Practice of Diaspora;

T. Denean Sharpley-Whiting, *Negritude Women* (Minneapolis: University of Minnesota Press, 2002).

20. Léopold Sédar Senghor, "What the Black Man Contributes" (1939), trans. Mary Beth Mader, in *Race and Racism in Continental Philosophy*, ed. Robert Bernasconi and Sybol Cook (Bloomington: Indiana University Press, 2003), 288.

21. See Barbara Ischinger, "Negritude: Some Dissident Voices," *Journal of Opinion* 4, no. 4 (1975): 23–25.

22. Bennetta Jules-Rosette, *Josephine Baker in Art and Life: The Icon and the Image* (Urbana: University of Illinois Press, 2007), 48–49, 61.

23. Dunham to Gray, November 29, 1948, box 12, folder 3, SIUC.

24. "Personalités de la premiere representation Theatre de Paris, ercredi 19 octobre 1949," box 14, folder 2, SIUC.

25. René Dumesnil, "Katherine Dunham: ses danseurs et ses musiciens," *Le Monde*, November 28 and 29, 1948, Bibliotheque National de France, Arts du spectacle R Supp 2387.

26. Dina Abragam, "Musique, danse, magie: les Ballets de Katherine Dunham," *Combat*, November 29, 1948, Bibliotheque National de France, Arts du spectacle R Supp 2387.

27. Pal Ahluwalia, *Politics and Post-colonial Theory: African Inflections* (London: Routledge, 2001), 23; Abiola Irele, "Negritude or Black Cultural Nationalism," *Journal of Modern African Studies* 3, no. 3 (1965): 346.

28. Jacques Howlett, "Presence Africaine 1947–1958," *Journal of Negro History* 43, no. 2 (1958): 140. For more on Senghor and universalism, see Janet Vaillant, *Black, French, and African: A Life of Léopold Sédar Senghor* (Cambridge, MA: Harvard University Press, 1990), 266.

29. All quotes are from Paul Niger, "Rhapsodie Caraïbe de Katherine Dunham," *Présence Africaine* 6 (1949): 153. I thank Brent Edwards for bringing this review to my attention.

30. Niger, "Rhapsodie Caraïbe," 151.

31. All quotes are from Niger, "Rhapsodie Caraïbe," 152.

32. Dunham, "Address Delivered at the Dakar Festival of Negro Arts," 1966, in Clark and Johnson, *Kaiso!*, 414.

33. T. R. Makonnen to Dunham, January 28, 1949, box 12, folder 7, SIUC.

34. Beckford, *Katherine Dunham*, 60–61.

35. "Show: All Exotic," *Leader Magazine*, June 26, 1948, box 102, folder 16, SIUC.

36. Transcript of recording for "For Your Leisure," November 14, 1948, North of England Home Service, BBC, box 12, folder 3, SIUC.

37. Transcript, "For Your Leisure."

38. Jennifer Dunning, "Alvin Ailey Dancers Follow the Steps of a Trailblazer," *NYT*, November 22, 1987, H21.

39. "Katherine Dunham and Her Company" program, April 24, 1950, box 15, folder 7, Katharine Wolfe Collection, JRDD.

40. Program for 1959 European tour, April 20, 1959, box 24, folder 8, SIUC.

41. Program, Wolfe Collection; program for 1959 European tour.

42. Productions notes for *Afrique*, n.d., box 18, folder 4, LOC; *The Magic of Katherine Dunham*, Alvin Ailey Dance Company, 1987, videocassette, JRDD.

43. Production notes for *Afrique*.

44. Dunham, interviewed by R. Goupillieres of Radiodiffusion Français, ca. 1949, box 14, folder 5, SIUC.

45. Production notes for *Afrique*.

46. Dunning, "Alvin Ailey Dancers."

47. Van Scott interview.

48. Dinah Maggie, "La Rentrée de Katherine Dunham," *Combat*, October 24, 1949, n.p.

49. In some sources, Fodéba's name is switched: Fodéba Keita. Pierre Fromentin, interview with Keita Fodéba, "Gala de l'Afrique Noire" program, November 28, 1949. I thank Joshua Cohen for his transcription.

50. Keita Fodéba to Dunham, January 10, 1950, box 14, folder 7, SIUC.

51. Keita Fodéba, "La danse africaine et la scène," *Presence Africaine* 14–15 (1957): 202–209.

52. For more see Joshua Cohen, "Stages in Transition: Les Ballets Africains and Independence, 1959 to 1960," *Black Studies* 43, no. 11 (2012): 11–48.

53. Edith Colombier to Dunham, December 24, 1948, box 38, folder 6, SIUC.

54. Edith Colombier to Dunham, January 15, 1950, box 39, folder 1, SIUC; "Declaration de Volonte D'Adoption," May 4, 1950, box 39, folder 2, SIUC.

55. American Embassy, Paris, to State Department, Washington, DC, Despatch 995, November 15, 1949, RG59.

56. American Embassy, Rome, to Department of State, Washington, DC, Despatch 831, March 20, 1950, RG59.

57. Despatch 995; Despatch 831.

58. *Stoneman's* January Mailer No. 1, Paris, January 3, 1950, box 14, folder 6, SIUC; Katherine Dunham to Annette Dunham, January 31, 1949, box 38, folder 7, SIUC.

59. Dunham, Statement, March 16, 1950, box 15, folder 2, SIUC; Dunham to Bernard Berenson, May 2, 1950, box 40, folder 9, SIUC.

60. Dunham Statement; Dunham to Berenson, May 2, 1950.

61. Dunham, *Island Possessed*, 4, 74.

62. For more on the importance of Emmett Till to the Civil Rights Movement, see Charles M. Payne, *I've Got the Light of Freedom: The Organizing Tradition and the Mississippi Freedom Struggle* (Berkeley: University of California Press, 1995), 53–54.

63. Dunning, "Alvin Ailey Dancers," H21.

64. See chapter 1.

65. Hill, "Katherine Dunham's *Southland*," 2.

66. Dunham, "Love Letters from I Tatti," vol. 1.

67. See "Revoltante Incidente Com Uma Artist Americana," *Correio Paulistano*, July 13, 1950, box 104, vol. 4, SIUC; "Conserva o Esplanada Preconceitos de Côr: Negaram Hospedagem a Uma Famosa Bailarina Negra Norte-Americana," *O Tempo*, July 12, 1950, enclosure to US Embassy, São Paulo, to Department of State, Washington, DC, Despatch 26, July 18, 1950, RG59.

68. "Brazil: Jaime Crow," *Time*, July 31, 1950, box 104, vol. 4, SIUC; "Dunham Ban Stirs Brazil; Exclusion of Dancer by Hotel Brings Action by Deputies," *NYT*, July 19, 1950, 22; "Ban on Katherine Dunham Stirs Brazil Chamber of Commerce; Urges Civil Rights Law with Fine, Jail," *Chicago Defender*, July 29, 1950, 21.

69. "Anti-Racial Discrimination Law," US Embassy, Rio de Janeiro, to Department of State, Washington, DC, Despatch 77, July 13, 1951, RG59.

70. Dunham to Berenson, August 17, 1950, BMBP.

71. Dunham, "Love Letters from I Tatti," vol. 1.

72. Dunham to Berenson, August 17, 1950.

73. Gilberto Freyre, *The Masters and the Slaves: A Study in the Development of Brazilian Civilization*, trans. Samuel Putnam (1946; New York: Alfred A. Knopf, 1956), 322.

74. Dunham, "Love Letters from I Tatti," vol. 1; Aikens interview.

75. Hill, "Katherine Dunham's *Southland*," 2.
76. "Mañana Cambia Programa La Cia. Katherine Dunham," *El Diario Ilustrado* (Chile), December 1, 1950, 19.
77. "Katherine Dunham Estrenara Mañana Dos Ballets de su Creacion," *El Mercurio* (Chile), December 5, 1950, 13.
78. "Un programa extraordinario ofrece hoy Katherine Dunham," *El Mercurio*, December 6, 1950, 46.
79. US Embassy, Santiago, to Department of State, Washington, DC, Despatch 550, December 12, 1950, RG59.
80. Despatch 550.
81. "Hoy, programa extraordinario de la Cía. Katherine Dunham," *El Diario*, December 7, 1950, 19.
82. Belafonte interview; *Southland* program notes. Hill's article and other sources erroneously report that Dunham was kicked out of the country and that the company's visas were revoked. They performed *Southland* on the last two days of the run and left, as planned, for a vacation in Argentina the day after.
83. "'Southland' Rehearsal–K. Dunham," May 24, 1981, East St. Louis, IL, videocassette, VRA 0849–0851, LOC.
84. Hill, "Katherine Dunham's *Southland*," 3.
85. Robert F. Thompson, *Tango: The Art History of Love* (New York: Vintage, 2006), 112.
86. W. C. Handy, "Wyer Was Wrong," *Downbeat*, May 21, 1952, 9.
87. See Margolick, *Strange Fruit*.
88. *Southland* program notes, 1953.
89. Despatch 550.
90. Manuel Solano, "El Bailarin Debe Saber Lo Que Expresa Su Cuerpo," *Pro Arte*, December 7, 1950, translation by US Embassy official, corroborated by author, enclosure to Despatch 550.
91. Despatch 550. In a letter to Berenson dated June 17, 1953, Dunham talks of the "fear-ridden, materialistic conscious, greed driven, young, immature average American," box 48, SIUC.
92. Despatch 550.
93. See *El Mercurio*, *El Diario*, and *La Nacion* (Chile), November 7, 1950–December 11, 1950.
94. Hill, "Katherine Dunham's *Southland*," 5.
95. "Katherine Dunham desmiente haber firmado manifiesto de Estocolmo," *El Diario*, December 14, 1950; "Desmentido de Katherine Dunham, artista americana," *El Mercurio*, December 14, 1950; "No firmo el Manifiesto de Estocolmo K. Dunham," *La Nacion*, December, 14, 1950; all translations by author, enclosures to Despatch 550.
96. Despatch 550.
97. The State Department has records of several interviews Dunham gave to Communist newspapers in France, Italy, and Chile in 1949 and 1950, but none after December 1950.
98. Dunham to Berenson, January 24, 1951, BMBP.
99. Dunham, "Love Letters from I Tatti," vol. 1.
100. Dunning, "Alvin Ailey Dancers."
101. Kenneth Osgood, *Total Cold War: Eisenhower's Secret Propaganda Battle at Home and Abroad* (Lawrence: University Press of Kansas, 2006), 77, 107.
102. US Embassy, Lima, to Department of State, Washington, DC, Despatch 804, February 2, 1951, RG59.

103. US Embassy, Port-au-Prince, to Department of State, Washington, DC, Despatch 98, August 21, 1951, RG59.
104. Diary of Annette Dunham, July 25, 1951, box 105, vol. 3, SIUC.
105. Despatch 804.
106. Heidi Carolyn Feldman, *Black Rhythms of Peru: Reviving African Musical Heritage in the Black Pacific* (Middletown, CT: Wesleyan University Press, 2006), 49, 55.
107. Rex Nettleford, "Katherine Dunham: The Jamaican Connexion (or *Journey from Accompong*)" (1981), in Clark and Johnson, *Kaiso!*, 599.
108. Polyné, *From Douglass to Duvalier*, 173.
109. For more on this institution, see chapter 7.
110. Dunham, "Love Letters from I Tatti," London section.
111. Ibid.
112. Dunham to Berenson, February 7, 1952, box 15, folder 1, LOC.
113. Dunham to Berenson, November 1, 1952, BMBP.
114. Julie Belafonte, conversation with author, August 27, 2014, New York.
115. Dunham to Berenson, November 1, 1952.
116. Dunham to Berenson, February 1, 1953, BMBP.
117. Berenson to Dunham, January 6, 1953, box 40, folder 9, SIUC.
118. Dunham, "Love Letters from I Tatti," vol. 1.
119. Hill, "Katherine Dunham's *Southland*," 6.
120. *Southland* program notes.
121. Nazir _____ to Julie Robinson, January 1953, Belafonte personal collection.
122. Newspaper clippings in Belefonte personal collection.
123. Gilbert Bloch, "Une oeuvre bouleversante contre le lynchage: Southland de Katherine Dunham," *L'Humanité*, January 12, 1953, 2; Jean Durkheim, "Katherine Dunham Monte 'Southland,'" *Ce Soir*, January 12, 1953, 2; Dunham to Berenson, February 1, 1953.
124. Hill, "Katherine Dunham's *Southland*," 7.
125. Hill, "Katherine Dunham's *Southland*," 6; Belafonte interview.
126. Aikens interview; Hill, "Katherine Dunham's *Southland*," 6.
127. Belafonte interview.
128. Dunham to Berenson, February 1, 1953.
129. Report on Katherine Dunham, January 29, 1953, FBI File 100-334795.
130. George McTurnan Kahin, *The Asian-African Conference: Bandung, Indonesia, April 1955* (Ithaca, NY: Cornell University Press, 1956).
131. Vijay Prashad, *The Darker Nations: A People's History of the Third World* (New York: New Press, 2007), 82.
132. Gaines, *African Americans in Ghana*, 2.
133. Sarah Maldoror, Pour le Comité de Patronage, Theatre Popualire Africain, November 27, 1959, box 26, folder 1, SIUC.
134. Dunham, *Island Possessed*, 194; Eugenia Cadús, "Katherine Dunham and Peronism: An Analysis of Dunham's *Tango* (1954)" (unpublished manuscript, 2015), 18.
135. Dunham, quoted in Clark, "Performing the Memory of Difference," 334; Production notes on *Tango*, ca. 1954, box 18, folder 4, LOC.
136. Dunham, "Love Letters from I Tatti," vol. 2.
137. Cadús, "Katherine Dunham and Peronism," 8.
138. Quoted in Cadús, "Katherine Dunham and Peronism," 25.
139. Dunham to Berenson, April 16, 1955, BMBP; Dunham to Tim Durant, January 10, 1956, box 20, folder 1, SIUC.

140. Dance Advisory Panel meeting minutes, September 14, 1955, box 101, folder 13, BECA.
141. Dunham to Durant, January 10, 1956; Naima Prevots *Dance for Export: Cultural Diplomacy and the Cold War* (Middletown, CT: Wesleyan University Press, 1998), 104.
142. Calvin Swanson to Dunham, April 1, 1958. box 23, folder 9, SIUC.
143. Von Eschen, "Made on Stage," 164; Croft, *Dancers as Diplomats*, 66–67.
144. Dunham, "Thesis Turned Broadway," 215.
145. "Passport Particulars," February 21, 1960, box 43, folder 4, SIUC.
146. Dance Panel minutes, August 28, 1958, box 101, folder 15, BECA.
147. Dance Panel minutes, May 21, 1959, box 101, folder 15, BECA.
148. American Embassy, Canberra, Australia, to United States Information Agency and Tousi Consulate, October 23, 1956, RG59; Department of State to American Embassy, Manila, and American Consulate, Hong Kong, June 18, 1957, RG59.
149. Doug Lackersteen, "The Negro Problem as Miss Dunham Sees It," *Sunday Times* (Singapore), June 23, 1957, box 103, folder 8, SIUC.
150. American Embassy in Vienna to the Secretary of State, Washington, DC, Despatch 2132, March 21, 1960, RG59.
151. Joint State Department–USIA Message to the American Embassy in Vienna, March 30, 1960, RG59 (emphasis added).
152. Anthony Shay, *Choreographic Politics: State Folk Dance Companies, Representation and Power* (Middletown, CT: Wesleyan University Press, 2002), 10.
153. Allen Hughes, "Dance: Revue by Katherine Dunham," *NYT*, October 23, 1962, 42.
154. Cohen, "Stages in Transition," 13, 21.
155. Chestyn Everette, "Bamboche Has Fire—Appeal," *Los Angeles Sentinel*, August 23, 1962, A18; Jesse H. Walker, "Katherine Dunham and 'Bamboche,'" *Amsterdam News*, October 27, 1962, 19.
156. The Dunham company performed once more, in 1964, at the Apollo Theater, but for all intents and purposes the troupe ended after the close of *Bamboche!*
157. Dunham to Mrs. Keane, November 1, 1962, box 30, folder 1, SIUC.

CHAPTER 7

1. Dunham to Dorothy Gray, July 11, 1949, box 13, folder 6, SIUC.
2. Dash, *Haiti and the United States*; Paul Farmer, *The Uses of Haiti*, 3rd ed. (New York: Common Courage Press, 2005); Brenda Gayle Plummer, *Haiti and the United States: The Psychological Moment* (Athens: University of Georgia Press, 1992).
3. In 1963, the cultural theorist Frantz Fanon declared, "Every culture is first and foremost national." Frantz Fanon, *The Wretched of the Earth* (1963; repr. New York: Grove Press, 1968), 216.
4. Marlene L. Daut, "Caribbean 'Race Men': Louis Joseph Janvier, Demesvar Delorme, and the Haitian Atlantic." *L'Esprit Createur* 56, no. 1 (2016): 9–23.
5. See chapter 3.
6. Ramsey, *Spirits and the Law*, 3.
7. E. Lescot, "In Appreciation," *Tropics and Le Jazz "Hot"* program, April 28, 1940, JRDD.
8. Kate Ramsey, "Katherine Dunham and the Folklore Performance Movement in Post-US Occupation Haiti," in Chin, *Katherine Dunham*, 65–66; Polyné, *From Douglass to Duvalier*, 174.
9. Ramsey, *Spirits and the Law*, 231, 236.

10. Ibid.

11. Dunham to Serge Tolstoy, June 1, 1949, box 13, folder 4, SIUC.

12. Dunham, "Love Letters from I Tatti," vol. 1.

13. Recounted in Dunham to Francois Duvalier, August 11, 1960, box 27, folder 6, SIUC.

14. Dunham to Gray, July 11, 1949, box 13, folder 6, SIUC.

15. Dunham, *Island Possessed*, 242.

16. Ibid.

17. Tonton Nord to Dunham, December 10, 1953, box 16, folder 9, SIUC.

18. Ramsey, *Spirits and the Law*, 119.

19. Dunham, *Island Possessed*, 239.

20. Souleymane Bachir Diagne, "Rhythms: L. S. Senghor's Negritude as a Philosophy of African Art," *Critical Interventions* 1, no. 1 (2007): 56.

21. Dunham, "Haiti," memo, ca. 1951, box 15, folder 9, SIUC.

22. Dunham, "Haiti" memo.

23. Daut, "Caribbean 'Race Men,'" 14.

24. Dunham, "Haitian Projet," March 12, 1950, box 15, folder 1, SIUC. Translation by author.

25. For more on UNESCO's Fundamental Education Program in Haiti, see Mulugeta Wodajo, "An Analysis of UNESCO's Concept and Program of Fundamental Education," (Ed.D diss., Teacher's College of Columbia University, 1963).

26. Dunham, "Haitian Projet"; Homer Gayne, "Visit of Miss Katherine Dunham to Haiti," US Embassy Port-au-Prince to Department of State, Washington, DC, Despatch 98, August 21, 1951, RG59; Biographical material written by Budd Fielding White, ca. 1953, 1948–49, box 1, folder 1, SIUC.

27. Dunham, "Haiti" memo.

28. Dunham, *Island Possessed*, 53.

29. Polyné, *From Douglass to Duvalier*, 117, 33.

30. Dunham to Berenson, June 13, 1951, BMBP.

31. Ibid.

32. Ibid.

33. Dunham to Berenson, January 24, 1952, box 15, folder 1, LOC; Aschenbrenner, *Katherine Dunham*, 48.

34. Dunham, *Island Possessed*, 244, 250–56.

35. Polyné, *From Douglass to Duvalier*, 158.

36. Ibid., 175–76. After marrying Shannon Yarborough in 1949, Lavinia Williams briefly went by her married name, Lavinia Williams Yarborough, but returned to using her maiden name after her divorce. For simplicity's sake, she will be referred to as Lavinia Williams in the text.

37. Vivianne Gauthier, interview by author, trans. Claude Martin, January 12, 2016, Port-au-Prince; communication with Lynn Williams Rouzier, trans. Claude Martin, January 12, 2016, Port-au-Prince. For more, see Polyné, *From Douglass to Duvalier*, 169.

38. Polyné, *From Douglass to Duvalier*, 173.

39. Williams interview by Murray.

40. Dunham to Julie and Harry Belafonte, February 2, 1959, box 24, folder 5, SIUC.

41. "Haiti Honors Miss Dunham," *NYT*, February 25, 1959, 36.

42. "Haiti's Good Samaritan: Katherine Dunham Builds Island Clinic for Needy," *Ebony*, September 1959, 54.

43. Jack Taylor to Dunham, August 21, 1959, box 25, folder 5, SIUC. There are numerous such letters in box 25.

44. Interview with Dunham, February 1960, box 26, folder 6, SIUC.
45. Dunham to Dick Frisell, January 3, 1961, box 28, folder 2, SIUC; Frisell to Dunham, January 27, 1961, box 28, folder 2, SIUC; Dick Frisell to Sven Frisell, March 5, 1961, box 28, folder 3, SIUC.
46. Dunham to Margery Scott, August 3, 1961, box 28, folder 6, SIUC.
47. Dunham to father of Dick Frisell, February 24, 1961, box 28, folder 2, SIUC.
48. For more on Haitian politics and economics during the mid-twentieth century, see Polyné, *From Douglass to Duvalier*; and Michel-Rolph Trouillot, *Haiti: State against Nation: Origins and Legacy of Duvalierism* (New York: Monthly Review Press, 2000).
49. "Visit Katherine Dunham at Leclerc," ca. June 1961, box 86, folder 8, SIUC; "Some Facts about Katherine Dunham's Fabulous Habitation Leclerc," undated, box 86, folder 9, SIUC.
50. Dunham to Director of the Tour Department of American Export Lines, January 24, 1962, box 29, folder 1, SIUC.
51. "Haiti Has Napoleon Kin Shrine," *Los Angeles Times*, November 26, 1961, 18.
52. "Habitation Leclerc: Weekly Schedule of Entertainment," ca. June 1961, box 86, folder 8, SIUC.
53. "Habitation Leclerc for Your Wednesday and Friday Entertainment," ca. 1961, box 86, folder 18, SIUC.
54. Lorraine Mangonès, interview by author, January 9, 2016, Port-au-Prince.
55. Gauthier interview.
56. Advertisements for Katherine Dunham's "Grand Spectacle" and Lavinia Williams's "Bamboche Creole," *Haitian Sun*, February 11, 1962, 3, 12; "Ambassadors at Oloffson Enjoy 'Bamboche Creole,'" *Haitian Sun*, February 11, 1962, 3.
57. Dunham to Duvalier, August 11, 1960; Dunham to Duvalier, August 5, 1961, box 28, folder 6, SIUC; Dunham to Windsor Day, February 7, 1962, box 29, folder 2, SIUC.
58. Dunham, *Island Possessed*, 197.
59. Ibid., 183; Dunham Pratt interview.
60. Dunham, *Island Possessed*, 183.
61. Dunham Pratt interview.
62. "Snakes Bring Problems for Katherine Dunham," *Jet*, January 18, 1962, 59.
63. Dunham, *Island Possessed*, 182.
64. Ibid., 3.
65. Dunham to Editor of *Journal le Nouvelliste*, December 15, 1961, box 28, folder 8, SIUC; Dunham to Frisell, December 10, 1961, box 28, folder 8, SIUC.
66. Erol Josué, interview by author, January 13, 2016, Port-au-Prince; See Cheryl I. Harris, "Whiteness as Property," *Harvard Law Review* 106, no. 8 (1993): 1710–91.
67. "The Role of Voodoo in Haitian Politics," US Embassy, Port-au-Prince, to Department of State, Washington, DC, Despatch #261, January 17, 1962, RG59.
68. Dunham, *Island Possessed*, 171.
69. Dunham to Henry Polokow, June 3, 1962, box 29, folder 5, SIUC.
70. Ibid.
71. "List of People Met on the African Trip," ca. June 1962, box 29, folder 5, SIUC.
72. Vaillant, *Black, French, and African*, 268.
73. Gaines, *African Americans in Ghana*, 251–53.
74. Ibid., 252; Léopold Sédar Senghor, "The Function and Meaning of the World Festival of Negro Arts," Speech given at the Colloquium on Negro Art in the Life of the People, box 10, folder 1, LWP.

75. Charles Delgado of the Permanent Mission of the Republic of Senegal to Dunham, February 21, 1964, box 33, folder 2, SIUC; Dunham to Delgado, March 16, 1964, box 33, folder 3, SIUC; Dunham to Mrs. Virginia Inness-Brown, April 6, 1964, box 33, folder 4, SIUC; Dunham to G. Mennen Williams, African Affairs, the State Department, April 8, 1964, box 33, folder 4, SIUC.

76. Senghor to Dunham, July 27, 1964, box 33, folder 7, SIUC.

77. Gaines, *American Africans in Ghana*, 254.

78. "Minutes of Meeting of the United States Committee for the First World Festival of Negro Arts," November 6, 1964, Box 582, Folder 13860, LHC.

79. US Government Memorandum, February 19, 1964, FBI File 100-334795.

80. US Government Memorandum To: CU/CP–Mr. Glenn Wolfe, from CU/ECS:AA— John Pressly Kennedy. Subject: Katherine Dunham, February 11, 1964, Box 144, Folder 4, BECA.

81. Dunham to Alioune Diop, January 1965, box 35, folder 4, SIUC; Dunham to Mercer Cook, January 18, 1965, box 12, folder 5, LOC.

82. US Government Memorandum to: Dance Panel from: Beverly Gerstein. Subject: Katherine Dunham for Specialists grant to open a school in Dakar. April 29, 1965, box 144, folder 4, BECA; Department of State United States Government Grant Authorization, July 9, 1965, box 99, folder 1, SIUC.

83. Dunham, "Recommendation for Program of Cultural Expansion in Three Areas of the World by Private Foundation Aid Preferably in Collaboration with State Department," Notes for the Ford Foundation, January 3, 1964, box 50, folder 9, SIUC.

84. Dunham, "Recommendation for Program of Cultural Expansion."

85. Untitled document, July 1965, box 53, folder 12, SIUC; Dunham to Senghor, June 16, 1965, box 36, folder 5, SIUC.

86. Saidiya Hartman, "The Time of Slavery," *South Atlantic Quarterly* 101, no. 4 (2002): 757–77.

87. Memo between Erin Hubbert, Office of African Programs, and Dunham, May 19, 1965, box 36, folder 3, SIUC.

88. US Embassy, Dakar, to State Department, Washington, January 5, 1966, box 12, folder 5, LOC.

89. US Embassy, Dakar, to State Department, Washington, December 23, 1965, box 12, folder 5, LOC.

90. Ibid.

91. Dunham, "The Performing Arts of Africa: Preface to the Future," Draft of speech given at the First World Festival of Negro Arts, April 1966, box 52, folder 1, SIUC.

92. Dunham, n. 91.

93. Ibid.

94. Julia L. Foulkes, "Ambassadors with Hips: Katherine Dunham, Pearl Primus, and the Allure of Africa in the Black Arts Movement," in *Impossible to Hold: Women and Culture in the 1960s*, ed. Avital H. Bloch and Lauri Umansky (New York: New York University Press, 2005), 89; Von Eschen, "Made on Stage," 164.

95. Foulkes, "Ambassadors with Hips," 90.

96. Dunham to Mrs. Keane, November 1, 1962, box 30, folder 1, SIUC.

97. Dunham, n. 91.

98. Ibid.

99. Ibid.

100. Fodéba, "La danse africaine et la scène," 206.

101. Dunham to Giovanella Zannoni, May 13, 1966, box 40, folder 6, SIUC.

102. Ibid.; Dunham to John Pratt, ca. April 1966, box 40, folder 6, SIUC.

103. US Embassy, Dakar, to State Department, Washington, "Education Cultural Exchange: Request for Extension of Grant to Miss Katherine Dunham," August 2, 1966, box 12, folder 5, LOC.

104. US Embassy, Dakar, to State Department, Washington, January 5, 1966; US Embassy, Dakar, to State Department, Washington, August 2, 1966.

105. Dunham to Bill Gaston, November 15, 1966, box 37, folder 1, SIUC.

106. Dunham, *Island Possessed*, 83.

107. Ibid.

108. Ibid., 163.

109. Ibid., 46–47.

110. Ibid., 128.

111. Ibid.

112. Dunham to Pratt, ca. April 1966.

113. Dunham to Rubin Gorewitz, July 27, 1969, box 12, folder 2, SIUC; Dunham, "Proposal for One Year Research and Travel Grant," October 25, 1969, box 13, folder 4, STL.

114. Jerry Hulse, "In Hot Pursuit of Happiness in Haiti," *Los Angeles Times*, July 14, 1974, 11.

115. Judy Klemesrud, "A New Retreat for the Rich—Surrounded by Tumbledown Shacks," *NYT*, January 6, 1974.

116. Sharona El-Saieh, interview by author, January 11, 2016, Port-au-Prince; when Dunham was still running Leclerc, gossip columnist Sara Slack wrote that Dunham only "permit[s] carefully selected guests" and that "screening is necessary" because of the valuable objects Dunham owned. See Sara Slack, "Sara Speaking: It's a Woman's World!," *Amsterdam News*, October 16, 1971, B1.

117. David Gonzalez, "Port-au-Prince Journal: In Katherine Dunham's Eden, Invaders from Hell," *NYT*, August 6, 2002, A4.

118. El-Saieh interview.

119. Mangonès interview. For more details about the botanic garden, see Gregory Alan Beckett, "The End of Haiti: History under Conditions of Impossibility" (PhD diss., University of Chicago, 2008).

120. Benjamin F. Chavis Jr., "Helping Haitians: The Inspiration of a Katherine Dunham," *New Pittsburgh Courier* and *Los Angeles Sentinel*, March 21, 1992, 4, A7.

121. Martha Sherrill, "The Dance with Death: Katherine Dunham and Her Fast for the Troubled Masses from Haiti," *Washington Post*, March 16, 1992, C1; William Moore, "Pres. Aristide's Visit Ends Dunham's Hunger Strike," *Amsterdam News*, March 28, 1992, 23; Patricia Wilson, conversation with author, January 23, 2016.

CHAPTER 8

Sections of Chapter 8 previously appeared in "Between the 'Culture of Poverty' and the Cultural Revolution: Katherine Dunham's Performing Arts Training Center in East St. Louis, 1965–1973," *The Journal of Urban History*, Vol. 41, no. 6 (November 2015): 981–998, doi:10.1177/0096144215602007, copyright Joanna Dee Das, published by SAGE Publishing, all rights reserved.

1. Dunham to Giovanella Zannoni, April 25, 1967, box 40, folder 4, SIUC.

2. Dunham to Erich Fromm, April 29, 1967, box 40, folder 11, SIUC.

3. Though the archival record is of course incomplete, the first time that Dunham seems to use the word "revolution" when speaking about her work is in a June 3, 1965 speech at Southern Illinois University, box 53, folder 11, SIUC.

4. Joan Foster Dames, "'Professor' in SIU Program for Ghetto Youth," *St. Louis Post-Dispatch*, October 4, 1967, Miscellaneous Clippings, vol. 7, MHS.

5. Dunham, "A Funding Proposal for the Center for Intercultural Communication," May 1, 1971, box 18, Folder 1, MHS.

6. Dunham is not often mentioned in texts about the Black Arts Movement because of this generational difference. Two exceptions are Foulkes, "Ambassadors with Hips," and James Smethurst, *The Black Arts Movement: Literary Nationalism in the 1960s and 1970s* (Chapel Hill: University of North Carolina Press, 2005), 370–71.

7. Dunham to Mrs. Keane, November 1, 1962, box 30, folder 1, SIUC.

8. "Community Performing Arts—Experimental Plan for Haryou," July 18, 1963, box 31, folder 3, SIUC.

9. Milton Yale to Dunham, October 3, 1963, box 31, folder 6, SIUC.

10. Iain Anderson, *This Is Our Music: Free Jazz, the Sixties, and American Culture* (Philadelphia: University of Pennsylvania Press, 2007), 108–9.

11. Burnett H. Shryock to Dunham, November 21, 1963, box 32, folder 1; April 27, 1964, box 33, folder 4, SIUC.

12. Kenneth T. Jackson, *Crabgrass Frontier: The Suburbanization of the United States* (New York: Oxford University Press, 1985), 198–201.

13. Illinois Capital Development Board, *The East St. Louis Area: An Overview of State Capital Projects and Policies* (Springfield: the Board, 1977), n.p. For more on East St. Louis history, see Andrew J. Theising, *Made in USA: East St. Louis, the Rise and Fall of an Industrial River Town* (St. Louis, MO: Virginia Publishing, 2003).

14. For more on the East St. Louis riot, see Harper Barnes, *Never Been a Time: The 1917 Race Riot That Sparked the Civil Rights Movement* (New York: Walker & Company, 2008); Charles L. Lumpkins, *American Pogrom: The East St. Louis Race Riot and Black Politics* (Athens: Ohio University Press, 2008).

15. Betty Mitchell, *Delyte Morris of SIU* (Carbondale: Southern Illinois University Press, 1988), xix.

16. Oscar Lewis, *Five Families: Mexican Case Studies in the Culture of Poverty* (New York: Basic Books, 1959).

17. Daniel P. Moynihan, *The Negro Family: The Case for National Action* (Washington, DC: Office of Policy Planning and Research, US Department of Labor, 1965); William Julius Wilson, *The Truly Disadvantaged: The Inner City, the Underclass, and Public Policy*, 2nd ed. (Chicago: University of Chicago Press, 2012), 4–6.

18. Howard Brick, *Age of Contradiction: American Thought and Culture in the 1960s* (Ithaca, NY: Cornell University Press, 2000), 103; Colin Gordon, *Mapping Decline: St. Louis and the Fate of the American City* (Philadelphia: University of Pennsylvania Press, 2008), 13; Ira Katznelson, "Was the Great Society a Lost Opportunity?" in *The Rise and Fall of the New Deal Order*, ed. Steve Fraser and Gary Gerstle (Princeton, NJ: Princeton University Press, 1988), 201–3; Sugrue, *The Origins of the Urban Crisis*, 264; Sugrue, *Sweet Land of Liberty*, 508–9, 540.

19. John D. Rockefeller III, "The Arts and American Business," *Music Journal*, February 1959: 11, 64.

20. Donna Binkiewicz, *Federalizing the Muse: United States Arts Policy and The National Endowment for the Arts, 1965–1980* (Chapel Hill: University of North Carolina Press, 2004), 62–72; Samuel Zipp, *Manhattan Projects: The Rise and Fall of Urban Renewal in Cold War New York* (New York: Oxford University Press, 2010), 159–61.

21. Senator Claiborne Pell to Dunham, October 23, 1963, box 31, folder 6, SIUC; Congressional Record–Daily Digest, 109th Congress, October 30, 1963, D524.

22. Dunham, "A Proposal for the Development of a Cultural Enrichment Center under the Provisions of the Economic Opportunity Act," July 27, 1965, OEO/CAP, Executive Correspondence, 1965–1969, box 1, RG 381, NARA.

23. Dunham, n. 22.

24. Ibid.

25. Dunham to Ralph Capprio, June 10, 1965, box 36, folder 4, SIUC.

26. Wilson, *Truly Disadvantaged*, 4–5.

27. Sanford Kravitz to J. Philip Waring, Executive Director, Opportunity Commission, East St. Louis, December 29, 1965, OEO/CAP, Executive Correspondence, 1964–1969, box 1, RG 381, NARA; William P. Kelly and Henry Bass, "Request from Civil Rights Organizations," November 19, 1965, OEO/CAP, Executive Correspondence, 1964–1969, box 2, RG 381, NARA.

28. Memo, Harold C. Marlowe to Sargent Shriver, December 17, 1965, OEO/CAP, Subject Files 1965–1969, box 4, RG 381, NARA.

29. Memo: Telephone conversation between Ralph Capprio and Dunham, May 25, 1965, box 36, folder 3, SIUC; Dunham to Irving Maidman, August 27, 1965, box 36, folder 6, SIUC.

30. Dunham began creating such proposals months earlier, simultaneous to the East St. Louis project, and became increasingly invested in them as she spent more time in Senegal. See chapter 7.

31. Dunham to N. Bammatte, ca. June 1966, box 37, folder 4, SIUC.

32. Dunham to Ruffner, August 31, 1966, box 37, folder 4, SIUC.

33. Dames, "'Professor' in SIU Program for Ghetto Youth."

34. Senghor, "Function and Meaning"; emphasis in original.

35. Larry Neal, "The Black Arts Movement," *Drama Review* 12 (1968): 29. For more on the Black Arts Movement, see Takiyah Nur Amin, "Dancing Black Power? Joan Miller, Carole Johnson and the Black Aesthetic, 1960–1975," (PhD diss., Temple University, 2011); James L. Conyers, ed., *Engines of the Black Power Movement: Essays on the Influence of Civil Rights Actions, Arts, and Islam* (Jefferson, NC: McFarland & Co., 2007); Lisa Gail Collins and Margo Natalie Crawford, eds., *New Thoughts on the Black Arts Movement.* (New Brunswick, NJ: Rutgers University Press, 2006), Waldo E. Martin, *No Coward Soldiers: Black Cultural Politics and Postwar America* (Cambridge, MA: Harvard University Press, 2005); Amy Abugo Ongiri, *Spectacular Blackness: The Cultural Politics of the Black Power Movement and the Search for a Black Aesthetic* (Charlottesville: University of Virginia Press, 2010); Smethurst, *Black Arts Movement*; William L. Van Deburg, *New Day in Babylon: The Black Power Movement and American Culture, 1965–1975* (Chicago: University of Chicago Press, 1992).

36. Neal, "Black Arts Movement," 29.

37. Dunham to Zannoni, February 26, 1967, box 40, folder 7, SIUC.

38. Michael Newton to Norman Lloyd, August 13, 1969, box 289, folder 2722, RG1.2, Series 200R, RFR.

39. Mitchell, *Delyte Morris of SIU*, 110.

40. Darryl Braddix, interview by author, St. Louis, February 12, 2009; Ruby Streate, interview by author, Edwardsville, IL, July 27, 2011; Aschenbrenner, *Katherine Dunham*, 184.

41. Warrington Hudlin, interview by author, July 11, 2013, New York; Braddix interview.

42. Braddix interview. On Progressions, see chapter 5; and Albirda Rose, "Dunham Technique: Barre Work and Center Progressions," in Clark and Johnson, *Kaiso!*, 488–94.

43. Braddix interview; "Katherine Dunham Threatens False Arrest Suit against Police," *Afro-American*, August 5, 1967, 3. John Brooks recounts a different version of the story in Aschenbrenner, *Katherine Dunham*, 179–80. He claims that the arrest came after an H. Rap Brown speech. Brown did not come to East

St. Louis until September 1967, however, so Brooks most likely conflated two different events.

44. Braddix interview; Aschenbrenner, *Katherine Dunham*, 180.
45. Braddix interview; "Katherine Dunham Is Jailed 3 ½ Hours Following Protest," *NYT*, July 30, 1967, 54; "'At Bat for Kids,' Dunham Jailed, Freed," *Los Angeles Sentinel*, August 10, 1967, A2; "The Devil and East St. Louis: The Worst Hell-Hole in America," *Muhammad Speaks!*, September 15, 1967, n.p., courtesy of Darryl Braddix.
46. "Famed Negro Dance Artist Seen in Candid Portrait," *East St. Louis Monitor*, August 31, 1967, Press books, vol. 7, MHS.
47. Performing Arts Training Center and Dynamic Museum, Cultural Arts Program-Class Schedule, January 18, 1968, box 37, folder 6, SIU.
48. Ibid.
49. Draft of program for March 3, 1968 performance; box 37, folder 6, SIUC.
50. "Script: Ode to Taylor Jones," ca. March 1968, box 7, folder 4, MHS.
51. Ibid.
52. Ron Karenga, "Us, Kawaida and the Black Liberation Movement in the 1960s: Culture, Knowledge, and Struggle," in Conyers, *Engines of the Black Power Movement*, 112.
53. Norman Lloyd, Notes on conversation with Dunham, January 19, 1968, box 289, folder 2720, RFR.
54. Notes on conversation with Dunham, Arthur Custer and Michael Newton, March 21, 1968, box 289, folder 2720, RFR.
55. Ibid.
56. Michael Newton to Norman Lloyd, February 29, 1968, box 13, folder 22, MHS.
57. Notes on discussion with Dunham, Custer and Newton.
58. "For Your Leisure."
59. Norman Lloyd, notes on East St. Louis, February 8, 1968, box 289, folder 2720, RFR.
60. Newton to Lloyd, February 29, 1968; "RESOLUTION RF 68036," Rockefeller Foundation Arts Program, April 3, 1968, box 289, folder 2720, RFR.
61. "Illinois Agencies to Aid East St. Louis," *St. Louis Post-Dispatch*, March 3, 1968; "East St. Louis Shares with St. Louis in $200,000 Grant," *Metro-East Journal*, May 14, 1968; Press books, vol. 8, MHS.
62. A. Donald Bourgeois to Norman Lloyd, April 1, 1968, box 289, folder 2720, RFR.
63. "Famed Negro Dance Artist Seen in Candid Portrait."
64. Population statistic from Illinois Capital Development Board, in Board, *East St. Louis Area*, n.p.
65. Brick, *Age of Contradiction*, xii–xiii.
66. "RESOLUTION RF 68036."
67. Press Release, "Grant Supports Arts Program in St. Louis Model Cities Areas," May 14, 1968, box 289, folder 2721, RFR.
68. Dunham to Gionvanella Zannoni, April 27, 1968, box 40, folder 11, SIUC.
69. Dunham to Ralph Ruffner, November 5, 1968, box 12, folder 1, MHS.
70. Dunham to James E. Tisdale, January 13, 1969, box 6, folder 5, MHS.
71. Norman Lloyd, Notes, February 14, 1969, box 289, folder 2722, RFR.
72. Dunham Pratt interview.
73. Dunham to George Irwin, chairman, Illinois Arts Council, June 9, 1969, box 12, folder 2, MHS.
74. Norman Lloyd, notes on visit to St. Louis, July 16–17, 1969, box 289, folder 2722, RFR.

75. George Washnis, assistant to the Mayor of East St. Louis, to Norman Lloyd, January 8, 1970, box 289, folder 2722, RFR.
76. "Program Summary–Cultural Component Model City Program," April 6, 1970, box 420, folder 3620, RFR.
77. For an example of the kind of article Dunham was reading, see "Black and Other Studies," *St. Louis Post-Dispatch*, January 31, 1969, Press books, vol. 12, MHS. For more on this student movement, see Martha Biondi, *Black Revolution on Campus* (Berkeley: University of California Press, 2012).
78. Dunham to Norman Lloyd, September 3, 1967, box 12, folder 22, MHS; Dunham, "Performing Arts Training Center as a Focal Point for a New and Unique College or School" (1970), in Clark and Johnson, *Kaiso!*, 551.
79. Dunham, "Evaluation Criteria," April 12, 1971, box 420, folder 3620, RFR.
80. William Brennan, "A Funding Proposal for the Center for Intercultural Communication," May 1, 1971, box 18, folder 1, MHS.
81. Dunham, "Evaluation Criteria."
82. William Brennan, "Some Reflections on the Development of the Performing Arts Training Center," ca. May 1971, box 3, folder 2, MHS.
83. Brennan, "Some Reflections."
84. Ibid.
85. Michael Newton to Norman Lloyd, August 13, 1969, box 289, folder 2722, RFR.
86. Streate interview.
87. Brennan, "Some Reflections."
88. Norman Lloyd, Notes on interview with Dunham, June 4, 1970; Grant-in-Aid from Rockefeller Foundation, July 13, 1970, box 420, folder 3620, RFR.
89. See Performance Requests, box 6, folders 12–16, MHS.
90. Streate interview; Hudlin interview.
91. PATC Program Notes, December 13–17, 1970, box 7, folder 16, MHS.
92. See box 6, folder 22, MHS.
93. MENC: The National Association for Music Education, "The Sounds of Children," *Music Educators Journal* 57, no. 7 (1971): 47, 50.
94. Ruby Streate, conversation with author, October 26, 2016, St. Louis.
95. Alvin G. Fields, mayor of East St. Louis, to city businesses and government offices, September 14, 1970, box 7, folder 15, MHS; "Background Information on Preparation for White House Conference on Children," ca. January 1971, box 7, folder 13, MHS.
96. Quoted in Donald Sanders, "Dunham to Direct Scott Joplin Opera," *Los Angeles Times*, August 12, 1972, B9.
97. Robert Evett, "Dunham Touch Is Dance Magic," *Evening Star and Daily News* (Washington, DC), August 11, 1972, C6; Richard Fletcher, "Scott Joplin's 'Treemonisha': From Ragtime to Grand Opera," *Christian Science Monitor*, August 19, 1972, Press books, vol. 15, MHS.
98. Dunham's involvement with these initiatives is documented in box 7, box 15, and box 34, MHS.
99. Dunham, FBI File 157-6050.
100. Benjamin Looker, *BAG: "The Point from Which Creation Begins": The Black Artists' Group of St. Louis* (St. Louis: Missouri Historical Society Press, 2004), 51.
101. Dunham to Mr. Tom Cooney of the Ford Foundation, June 16, 1973, box 12, folder 21, MHS.

EPILOGUE

1. Beth Genné, "Creating a Canon, Creating the 'Classics' in Twentieth-Century British Ballet," *Dance Research* 18, no. 2 (2000): 152.
2. For more on this court case, see Anthea Kraut, *Choreographing Copyright: Race, Gender, and Intellectual Property Rights in American Dance* (New York: Oxford, 2015), 219–25, 246–62.
3. Thomas F. DeFrantz, *Dancing Revelations: Alvin Ailey's Embodiment of African American Culture* (New York: Oxford University Press, 2004), 28.
4. Jennifer Dunning, "Ailey Dancers to Stage Past Works by Dunham," *NYT*, December 27, 1986, 12. Julie Belafonte spearheaded a committee to raise another $200,000. The production went far over budget and cost close to $500,000, money that Ailey did not have. As a result, the following year the company came close to bankruptcy. See Alan M. Kriegsman, "Dance's Dynamic Duo: Alvin Ailey, in Collaboration with Katherine Dunham," *Washington Post*, May 8, 1988, G1; Louis Sweeney, "Alvin Ailey: Honored, but on the Brink of Financial Ruin," *Christian Science Monitor*, December 5, 1988, 21.
5. Elois L. Hibbert, "Alvin Ailey Recreates 'The Magic of Katherine Dunham,'" *NYT*, December 12, 1987, 30.
6. Dunning, "Alvin Ailey Dancers Follow the Steps of a Trailblazer."
7. Kriegsman, "Dance's Dynamic Duo."
8. Dunham, interview by James Briggs Murray, August 27, 1987, VHS, Schomburg Center for Research in Black Culture, New York.
9. Jean-Léon Destiné to Lavinia Williams, December 9, 1987, box 2, folder 1, LWP.
10. Destiné to Williams.
11. Aschenbrenner, *Katherine Dunham,* 220.
12. Marcia Siegel, "Dance That Rivals Broadway's Color, Theatricality: Ailey Troupe Revives Works of Katherine Dunham," *Christian Science Monitor*, December 31, 1987, 19.
13. Siegel, "Dance That Rivals Broadway's Color."
14. Alan M. Kriegsman, "Ailey Does Dunham," *Washington Post*, May 12, 1988, D4.
15. Anna Kisselgoff, "Dance: Alvin Ailey Company Salutes Dunham," December 4, 1987, *NYT*, C3.
16. Clark, "Performing the Memory of Difference," 323.
17. Ibid., 324.
18. Mel Tapley, "'Magic of Katherine Dunham' Spans 5 Decades," *Amsterdam News*, September 12, 1987, 23.
19. Dunham Pratt, interview. One need only read the hundreds of newspaper reviews over the decades of the Dunham company's performances, or listen to Dunham herself proclaim that Pratt was an equal partner in the success of the company, to confirm this perception. See Dunham interview at Barnard College, 2004.
20. Dunham Pratt interview.
21. Sylvester, "Dunham at Her Best."
22. Dunham Pratt interview.
23. A major proponent of this viewpoint is Keith Tyrone Williams, who trained with Dunham at SIU in Edwardsville. Personal conversations, July and August, 2016.
24. Donna Bryson, "A Lost Protest: Reviving Katherine Dunham's Controversial *Southland*," *Dance Magazine*, December 2012, http://www.dancemagazine.com/issues/December-2012/A-Lost-Protest.

25. Belafonte interview.

26. Ray Mark Rinaldi, "Katherine Dunham's Long Lost 'Southland' Revived With Spirit by Denver's Cleo Parker Robinson Dance," September 15, 2012, http://blogs.denverpost.com/artmosphere/2012/09/15/katherine-dunhams-long-lost-southland-revived-spirit-denvers-cleo-parker-robinson-dance/6869/.

27. Bryson, "A Lost Protest."

28. Albirda Rose, Katherine Dunham International Technique Seminar, July 27, 2010, SIU, Edwardsville. Dunham Pratt also mentions the Dunham Technique's bad reputation during those decades.

29. Mary-Jean Cowell, personal conversation with author, July 22, 2016, St. Louis.

30. For more on the theories and philosophies of Dunham Technique, see Molly E. Christie Gonzalez, "Katherine Dunham Technique and Philosophy: A Holistic Dance Pedagogy," (master's thesis, College at Brockport: State University of New York, 2015).

31. Aikens interview; Braddix interview; Ruby Streate, pers. communication, July 2013; Rose interview.

32. Personal conversation with Jessica Ray Herzogenrath, August 10, 2016.

33. For example, Jean Apollon's Haitian dance classes at the Dance Complex in Cambridge, MA use a Dunham warmup.

34. Author visit to Parc de Martissant and Centre Culturel Katherine Dunham, Port-au-Prince, Haiti, January 11–12, 2016; Mangonès interview.

35. Pallabi Chakravorty, "From Interculturalism to Historicism: Reflections on Classical Indian Dance," *Dance Research Journal* 32, no. 2 (2000): 108–19; Royona Mitra, *Akram Khan: Dancing New Interculturalism* (Houndmills, UK: Palgrave Macmillan, 2015), 11–28.

36. Jeanelle Stovall to Earl Lazerson, Memorandum about the Institute for Intercultural Communications, September 21, 1976, box 18, folder 1, MHS.

BIBLIOGRAPHY

ARCHIVAL COLLECTIONS

Biblioteca Berenson, Villa I Tatti, Florence, Italy:
Bernard and Mary Berenson Papers
Chicago Public Library, Woodson Regional Branch:
Vivian G. Harsh Research Collection
Columbia University Rare Book and Manuscript Library, New York City, New York:
Givens Collection
Jerome Robbins Dance Division, New York Public Library for the Performing Arts:
Dunham, Katherine Clippings File
Jerome Robbins Archive of the Recorded Moving Image
Katharine Wolfe Papers
Katherine Dunham Scrapbooks
Popular Balanchine Collection
Ruth Page Collection
Missouri Historical Society Library and Research Center, St. Louis:
Katherine Dunham Papers
Katherine Dunham Collection, Photographs and Prints Division
Music Division, Library of Congress, Washington, DC:
Franziska Boas Papers
Katherine Dunham Collection
Works Progress Administration Records
National Archives and Records Administration, College Park, Maryland:
Katherine Dunham FBI File 100-334795
Katherine Dunham FBI File 157-6050
Records of the Department of State, Record Group 59
Office of Economic Opportunity, Record Group 381
Rockefeller Archive Center, Sleepy Hollow, New York:
Rockefeller Foundation Records
Roger and Julie Baskes Department of Special Collections, Newberry Library, Chicago,
Illinois:
Mark Turbyfill Papers
Schomburg Center for Research in Black Culture, New York City, New York:
Lavinia Williams Papers
Special Collections, Fisk University Franklin Library, Nashville, Tennessee:
Julius Rosenwald Papers
Special Collections, University of Arkansas Libraries, Fayetteville:
Bureau of Educational and Cultural Affairs Historical Collection

Special Collections Research Center, Southern Illinois University, Carbondale:
    Katherine Dunham Papers
    Katherine Dunham Photograph Collection
    Selected Mark Turbyfill Letters
University Archives, Northwestern University, Evanston, Illinois:
    Melville Herskovits Papers
Yale University, New Haven, Connecticut:
    Langston Hughes Collection (Beinecke Rare Book and Manuscript Library)

NEWSPAPER AND MAGAZINE COLLECTIONS

Amsterdam News (also *New York Amsterdam News*)
Atlanta Daily World
Ballet (London)
Afro-American (also *Baltimore Afro-American*)
Ce Soir (Paris)
Chicago Daily News
Chicago Daily Tribune
Chicago Defender
Cleveland Call & Post
Christian Science Monitor
Combat (Paris)
Daily Boston Globe
Daily Worker (New York)
Dance Observer
El Diario Ilustrado (Santiago, Chile)
East St. Louis Monitor
L'Humanité (France)
Los Angeles Sentinel
Los Angeles Times
El Mercurio (Santiago, Chile)
Le Monde (Paris)
La Nación (Santiago, Chile)
Metro-East Journal (East St. Louis, IL)
Muhammad Speaks!
Negro Digest
New York Herald-Tribune
New York Times
New York World-Telegram
The Observer (London)
Philadelphia Tribune
Phylon
Pittsburgh Courier
PM (New York)
Presence Africaine (Paris)
St. Louis Post-Dispatch
San Francisco Chronicle
Time
Washington Post

INTERVIEWS CONDUCTED BY JOANNA DEE DAS

Aikens, Vanoye. Digital recording. Los Angeles, CA, March 1–3, 2011.
Belafonte, Julie. Digital recording. New York, NY, July 26, 2013.

Braddix, Darryl. Digital recording. St. Louis, MO, February 12, 2009.
Carrier, Ray. Telephone. December 4, 2015.
Corbett, Saroya. Digital recording. Philadelphia, PA, February 2, 2014.
de Pradines, Emerante. Digital recording. Port-au-Prince, Haiti. January 10, 2016.
Dunham Pratt, Marie-Christine. Telephone. August 10, 2016.
El-Saieh, Sharona. Digital recording. Port-au-Prince, Haiti. January 11, 2016.
Gauthier, Viviane. Digital recording. Port-au-Prince, Haiti. January 12, 2016.
Gennaro, Jean. Telephone. May 31, 2012.
Hudlin, Warrington. Digital recording. New York, NY, July 11, 2013.
Jamison, Theodore. Digital recording. Edwardsville, IL, July 29, 2011.
Josué, Erol. Port-au-Prince, Haiti. January 13, 2016.
Mangonès, Lorraine. Digital recording. Port-au-Prince, Haiti. January 9, 2016.
Mitchell, Arthur. Telephone. October 13, 2016.
Osumare, Halifu. Digital recording. Edwardsville, IL, July 28, 2011.
Rose, Albirda. Digital recording. Edwardsville, IL, July 26, 2011.
Streate, Ruby. Digital recording. Edwardsville, IL, July 27, 2011.
Tavernier, Rachel. Digital recording. Edwardsville, IL, July 25, 2011.
Van Scott, Glory. Digital recording. New York, NY, July 15, 2011.
Vaughan, David. New York, NY, January 23, 2013.
Wilson, Patricia. Digital recording. Edwardsville, IL, July 25, 2011.

SELECT BOOKS, ARTICLES, DISSERTATIONS, AND FILMS

Amin, Takiyah Nur. "A Terminology of Difference: Making the Case for Black Dance in the 21st Century and Beyond." *Journal of Pan African Studies* 4, no. 6 (2011): 7–15.

Amin, Takiyah Nur. "Dancing Black Power? Joan Miller, Carole Johnson and the Black Aesthetic, 1960–1975." PhD diss., Temple University, 2011.

Aschenbrenner, Joyce. *Katherine Dunham: Reflections on the Social and Political Contexts of Afro-American Dance*. Dance Research Annual. New York: CORD, 1981.

Aschenbrenner, Joyce. *Katherine Dunham: Dancing a Life*. Urbana: University of Illinois Press, 2002.

Baker, Houston A. *Modernism and the Harlem Renaissance*. Chicago: University of Chicago Press, 1987.

Baldwin, Davarian L. *Chicago's New Negroes: Modernity, the Great Migration, and Black Urban Life*. Chapel Hill: University of North Carolina Press, 2007.

Baldwin, Davarian L., and Minkah Makalani, eds. *Escape from New York: The New Negro Renaissance Beyond Harlem*. Minneapolis: University of Minnesota Press, 2013.

Barnes, Harper. *Never Been a Time: The 1917 Race Riot That Sparked the Civil Rights Movement*. New York: Walker & Company, 2008.

Batiste, Stephanie Leigh. *Darkening Mirrors: Imperial Representation in Depression-Era African American Performance*. Durham, NC: Duke University Press, 2011.

Beckett, Gregory Alan. "The End of Haiti: History under Conditions of Impossibility." PhD diss., University of Chicago, 2008.

Beckford, Ruth. *Katherine Dunham: A Biography*. New York: M. Dekker, 1979.

Binkiewicz, Donna M. *Federalizing the Muse: United States Arts Policy and the National Endowment for the Arts, 1965–1980*. Chapel Hill: University of North Carolina Press, 2004.

Biondi, Martha. *To Stand and Fight: The Struggle for Civil Rights in Postwar New York City*. Cambridge, MA: Harvard University Press, 2003.

Biondi, Martha. *Black Revolution on Campus*. Berkeley: University of California Press, 2012.

Blake, Jody. *Le Tumulte Noir: Modernist Art and Popular Entertainment in Jazz-Age Paris, 1900–1930*. University Park: Pennsylvania State University Press, 1999.

Bogle, Donald. *Toms, Coons, Mulattoes, Mammies, and Bucks: An Interpretive History of Blacks in American Films*. New York: Continuum, 2001.

Bone, Robert, and Richard A. Courage. *The Muse in Bronzeville: African American Creative Expression in Chicago, 1932–1950*. Piscataway, NJ: Rutgers University Press, 2011.

Brick, Howard. *Age of Contradiction: American Thought and Culture in the 1960s*. Ithaca, NY: Cornell University Press, 2000.

Brown, Jayna. *Babylon Girls: Black Women Performers and the Shaping of the Modern*. Durham, NC: Duke University Press, 2008.

Burt, Ramsay. "Katherine Dunham's *Rites de Passage*: Censorship and Sexuality." In *EmBODYing Liberation: The Black Body in American Dance*, edited by Dorothea Fischer-Hornung and Alison D. Goeller. Hamburg, Germany: LIT, 2001.

Butler, Kim. "Defining Diaspora, Refining a Discourse." *Diaspora* 10, no. 2 (2001): 189–219.

Carnival of Rhythm. Directed by Stanley Martin. 1941. New York: Dance Film Associates, 1989. VHS.

Caute, David. *The Dancer Defects: The Struggle for Cultural Supremacy During the Cold War*. New York: Oxford University Press, 2003.

Césaire, Aimé. *The Original 1939 Notebook of a Return to the Native Land*. Translated by A. James Arnold and Layton Eshleman. Middletown, CT: Wesleyan University Press, 2013.

Chin, Elizabeth, ed. *Katherine Dunham: Recovering an Anthropological Legacy, Choreographing Ethnographic Futures*. Santa Fe, NM: SAR Press, 2014.

Clark, VéVé. "Performing the Memory of Difference in Afro-Caribbean Dance: Katherine Dunham's Choreography, 1938–1987." In *History and Memory in African-American Culture*, edited by Geneviève Fabre and Robert O'Meally, 188–204. New York: Oxford University Press, 1994.

Clark, VèVè, Millicent Hodson, and Catrina Neiman, eds. *The Legend of Maya Deren: A Documentary Biography and Collected Works*. New York: Anthology Film Archives/Film Culture, 1984.

Clark, VèVè A., and Sara E. Johnson, eds. *Kaiso! Writings by and about Katherine Dunham*. Madison: University of Wisconsin Press, 2005.

Cohen, Joshua. "Stages in Transition: Les Ballets Africains and Independence, 1959 to 1960." *Black Studies* 43, no. 11 (2012): 11–48.

Collins, Lisa Gail, and Margo Natalie Crawford, eds. *New Thoughts on the Black Arts Movement*. New Brunswick, NJ: Rutgers University Press, 2006.

Conyers, James L., ed. *Engines of the Black Power Movement: Essays on the Influence of Civil Rights Actions, Arts, and Islam*. Jefferson, NC: McFarland & Co., 2007.

Corbett, Saroya. "Katherine Dunham's Mark on Jazz Dance." In *Jazz Dance: A History of the Roots and Branches*, edited by Lindsay Guarino and Wendy Oliver, 89–96. Gainesville: University Press of Florida, 2014.

Croft, Clare. *Dancers as Diplomats: American Choreography in Cultural Exchange*. New York: Oxford University Press, 2015.

Daniel, Yvonne. *Caribbean and Atlantic Diaspora Dance: Igniting Citizenship*. Urbana: University of Illinois Press, 2011.

Dash, J. Michael. *Haiti and the United States: National Stereotypes and the Literary Imagination*. Basingstoke, UK: Macmillan, 1988.

DeFrantz, Thomas. "Foreword: Black Bodies Dancing Black Culture—Black Atlantic Transformations." In *EmBODYing Liberation: The Black Body in American Dance*, edited by Dorothea Fischer-Hornung and Alison D. Goeller, 11–16. Hamburg, Germany: LIT, 2001.

DeFrantz, Thomas, ed. *Dancing Many Drums: Excavations in African American Dance.* Madison: University of Wisconsin Press, 2002.

DeFrantz, Thomas. *Dancing Revelations: Alvin Ailey's Embodiment of African American Culture.* New York: Oxford University Press, 2004.

DeFrantz, Thomas, and Anita Gonzalez, eds. *Black Performance Theory.* Durham, NC: Duke University Press, 2014.

Denning, Michael. *The Cultural Front: The Laboring of American Culture in the Twentieth Century.* New York: Verso, 1996.

Desmond, Jane. "Dancing Out the Difference: Cultural Imperialism and Ruth St. Denis's 'Radha' of 1906." *Signs: Journal of Women in Culture and Society* 17, no. 1 (1991): 28–49.

Diagne, Souleymane Bachir. "Rhythms: L. S. Senghor's Negritude as a Philosophy of African Art." *Critical Interventions* 1, no. 1 (2007): 51–68.

Divine Drumbeats: Katherine Dunham and Her People. Directed by Merril Brockway, produced by Merril Brockway and Catherine Tatge. Telecast April 16, 1980, WNET-TV, PBS *Dance in America* Series.

Du Bois, W. E. B. "Criteria of Negro Art." *The Crisis* 32, no. 6 (1926): 290–97.

Du Bois, W. E. B. "Krigwa Players Little Negro Theatre." *The Crisis* 32, no. 3 (1926): 134–35.

Du Bois, W. E. B. *The Souls of Black Folk: Essays and Sketches.* Chicago: A. C. McClurg & Co., 1903.

Dubois, Laurent. *Avengers of the New World: The Story of the Haitian Revolution.* Cambridge, MA: Belknap Press of Harvard University Press, 2004.

Dudziak, Mary L. *Cold War Civil Rights: Race and the Image of American Democracy.* Princeton, NJ: Princeton University Press, 2000.

Dunham, Katherine. "The Negro Dance." In *The Negro Caravan: Writings by American Negroes,* edited by Sterling Allen Brown, Arthur Paul Davis, and Ulysses Lee, 990–1000. New York: Dryden Press, 1941.

Dunham, Katherine. *Journey to Accompong.* New York: H. Holt, 1946.

Dunham, Katherine. *A Touch of Innocence.* New York: Harcourt, 1959.

Dunham, Katherine. *Island Possessed.* Chicago: University of Chicago Press, 1969.

Dunham, Katherine. *Dances of Haiti.* Los Angeles: Center for Afro-American Studies, University of California, Los Angeles, 1983. Originally published in 1947.

Durkin, Hannah. "The Black Female Dancing Body in the Films and Writings of Josephine Baker and Katherine Dunham." PhD diss., University of Nottingham, 2011.

Edwards, Brent Hayes. "The Uses of *Diaspora.*" *Social Text* 19, no. 1 (Spring 2001): 45–73.

Edwards, Brent Hayes. *The Practice of Diaspora: Literature, Translation, and the Rise of Black Internationalism.* Cambridge, MA: Harvard University Press, 2003.

Fanon, Frantz. *Black Skin, White Masks.* New York: Grove Press, 1967.

Fanon, Frantz. *The Wretched of the Earth.* New York: Grove Press, 1963.

Feldman, Heidi Carolyn. *Black Rhythms of Peru: Reviving African Musical Heritage in the Black Pacific.* Middletown, CT: Wesleyan University Press, 2006.

Feldstein, Ruth. *How It Feels to Be Free: Black Women Entertainers and the Civil Rights Movement.* New York: Oxford University Press, 2013.

Fodéba, Keita. "La Danse Africaine et la scène." *Presence Africaine* 14–15 (1957): 202–9.

Foner, Eric. *The Story of American Freedom.* New York: W. W. Norton, 1998.

Foster, Susan. *Choreographing Empathy: Kinesthesia in Performance.* New York: Routledge, 2010.

Foulkes, Julia L. "Ambassadors with Hips: Katherine Dunham, Pearl Primus, and the Allure of Africa in the Black Arts Movement." In *Impossible to Hold: Women and Culture in the 1960s*, edited by Avital H. Bloch and Lauri Umansky, 81–97. New York: New York University Press, 2005.

Foulkes, Julia L. *Modern Bodies: Dance and American Modernism from Martha Graham to Alvin Ailey*. Chapel Hill: University of North Carolina Press, 2002.

Freyre, Gilberto. *The Masters and the Slaves: A Study in the Development of Brazilian Civilization*. Translated by Samuel Putnam. New York: Alfred A. Knopf, 1956. Originally published in 1946.

Friedman, Lawrence J. *The Lives of Erich Fromm: Love's Prophet*. New York: Columbia University Press, 2013.

Gaines, Kevin Kelly. *American Africans in Ghana: Black Expatriates and the Civil Rights Era*. Chapel Hill: University of North Carolina Press, 2006.

Garafola, Lynn. "Lincoln Kirstein, Modern Dance, and the Left: The Genesis of an American Ballet." *Dance Research: The Journal of the Society for Dance Research* 23, no. 1 (Summer 2005): 18–35.

Geduld, Victoria Phillips. "Performing Communism in the American Dance: Culture, Politics and the New Dance Group." *American Communist History* 7, no. 1 (2008): 39–65.

Gershenhorn, Jerry. *Melville J. Herskovits and the Racial Politics of Knowledge*. Lincoln: University of Nebraska Press, 2004.

Gilmore, Glenda Elizabeth. *Defying Dixie: The Radical Roots of Civil Rights, 1919–1950*. New York: W. W. Norton, 2008.

Gilroy, Paul. *The Black Atlantic: Modernity and Double Consciousness*. Cambridge, MA: Harvard University Press, 1993.

Gordon, Colin. *Mapping Decline: St. Louis and the Fate of the American City*. Philadelphia: University of Pennsylvania Press, 2008.

Gottschild, Brenda Dixon. *Digging the Africanist Presence in American Performance: Dance and Other Contexts*. Westport, CT: Greenwood Press, 1996.

Gottschild, Brenda Dixon. *Joan Myers Brown & the Audacious Hope of the Black Ballerina: A Biohistory of American Performance*. New York: Palgrave Macmillan, 2012.

Graff, Ellen. *Stepping Left: Dance and Politics in New York City, 1928–1942*. Durham, NC: Duke University Press, 1997.

Graham, Martha. "Seeking an American Art of the Dance." In *Revolt in the Arts: A Survey of the Creation, Distribution and Appreciation of Art in America*, edited by Oliver M. Sayler, 249–51. New York: Brentano's, 1930.

Green, Adam. *Selling the Race: Culture, Community, and Black Chicago, 1940–1955*. Chicago: University of Chicago Press, 2007.

Griffin, Farah Jasmine. *Harlem Nocturne: Women Artists and Progressive Politics during World War II*. New York: Basic Civitas Books, 2013.

Hall, Stuart. "Cultural Identity and Diaspora." In *Identity: Community, Culture, Difference*, edited by Jonathan Rutherford, 222–37. London: Lawrence & Wishart, 1990.

Haskins, James. *Katherine Dunham*. New York: Coward, McCann & Geoghegan, 1982.

Herskovits, Melville J. *The Myth of the Negro Past*. New York: Harper, 1941.

Higginbotham, Evelyn Brooks. "African-American Women's History and the Metalanguage of Race." *Signs* 17, no. 2 (1992): 251–74.

Hill, Constance Valis. "Katherine Dunham's *Southland*: Protest in the Face of Repression." *Dance Research Journal* 26, no. 2 (Fall 1994): 1–10.

Hill, Constance Valis. "From Bharata Natyam to Bop: Jack Cole's Modern Jazz Dance." *Dance Research Journal* 33, no. 2 (2001): 29–39.

Hiller, Susan. *The Myth of Primitivism: Perspectives on Art.* New York: Routledge, 1991.

Hine, Darlene Clark, and John McClusky Jr., eds. *The Black Chicago Renaissance.* Urbana: University of Illinois Press, 2012.

Hixson, Walter L. *Parting the Curtain: Propaganda, Culture, and the Cold War, 1945–1961.* New York: St. Martin's Press, 1998.

hooks, bell. *Black Looks: Race and Representation.* Boston: South End Press, 1992.

Howlett, Jacques. "Presence Africaine 1947–1958." *Journal of Negro History* 43, no. 2 (1958): 140–50.

Hurston, Zora Neale. *Tell My Horse.* Philadelphia: J. B. Lippincott, 1938.

Irele, Abiola. "Negritude or Black Cultural Nationalism." *Journal of Modern African Studies* 3, no. 3 (1965): 321–48.

Ischinger, Barbara. "Negritude: Some Dissident Voices." *Journal of Opinion* 4, no. 4 (1975): 23–25.

James, C. L. R. *The Black Jacobins: Toussaint L'Ouverture and the San Domingo Revolution.* New York: Vintage, 1963. Originally published in 1938.

Johnson, Jasmine E. *Rhythm Nation: West African Dance and the Politics of Diaspora.* New York: Oxford University Press, forthcoming.

Jules-Rosette, Bennetta. *Josephine Baker in Art and Life: The Icon and the Image.* Urbana: University of Illinois Press, 2007.

Kahin, George McTurnan. *The Asian-African Conference: Bandung, Indonesia, April 1955.* Ithaca, NY: Cornell University Press, 1956.

Katznelson, Ira. "Was the Great Society a Lost Opportunity?" In *The Rise and Fall of the New Deal Order,* edited by Steve Fraser and Gary Gerstle, 185–211. Princeton, NJ: Princeton University Press, 1988.

Kelley, Robin D. G. *Hammer and Hoe: Alabama Communists during the Great Depression.* Chapel Hill: University of North Carolina Press, 1990.

Knight, Arthur. *Disintegrating the Musical: Black Performance and American Musical Film.* Durham, NC: Duke University Press, 2002.

Knupfer, Anne Meis. *The Chicago Black Renaissance and Women's Activism.* Urbana: University of Illinois Press, 2006.

Kowal, Rebekah J. *How to Do Things with Dance: Performing Change in Postwar America.* Middletown, CT: Wesleyan University Press, 2010.

Krasner, David. "Black *Salome*: Exoticism, Dance, and Racial Myths." In *African American Performance and Theater History: A Critical Reader,* edited by Harry J. Elam Jr. and David Krasner, 192–211. New York: Oxford University Press, 2001.

Kraut, Anthea. "Between Primitivism and Diaspora: The Dance Performances of Josephine Baker, Zora Neale Hurston, and Katherine Dunham." *Theatre Journal* 55, no. 3 (2003): 433–50.

Kraut, Anthea. *Choreographing the Folk: The Dance Stagings of Zora Neale Hurston.* Minneapolis: University of Minnesota Press, 2008.

Lamothe, Daphne Mary. *Inventing the New Negro: Narrative, Culture, and Ethnography.* Philadelphia: University of Pennsylvania Press, 2008.

Lemke, Sieglinde. *Primitivist Modernism: Black Culture and the Origins of Transatlantic Modernism.* New York: Oxford University Press, 1998.

Lepecki, André. "Choreopolice and Choreopolitics: Or, the Task of the Dancer." *TDR: The Drama Review* 57, no. 4 (2013): 13–27.

Lepecki, André. *Exhausting Dance: Performance and the Politics of Movement.* New York: Routledge, 2006.

Lindgren, Allana C. "Civil Rights Strategies in the United States: Franziska Boas's Activist Use of Dance, 1933–1965." *Dance Research Journal* 45, no. 2 (2013): 25–62.

Locke, Alain, ed. *The New Negro.* New York: A. and C. Boni, 1925.

Looker, Benjamin. *Bag: "Point from Which Creation Begins": The Black Artists' Group of St. Louis.* St. Louis: Missouri Historical Society Press, 2004.

Lorde, Audre. "The Uses of the Erotic: The Erotic as Power." In *Sister Outsider: Essays and Speeches by Audre Lorde*, edited by Audre Lorde, 53–59. Berkeley, CA: Crossing Press, 1984.

Lumpkins, Charles L. *American Pogrom: The East St. Louis Race Riot and Black Politics.* Athens: Ohio University Press, 2008.

Makalani, Minkah. *In the Cause of Freedom: Radical Black Internationalism from Harlem to London, 1917–1939.* Chapel Hill: University of North Carolina Press, 2011.

Manning, Susan. "Modern Dance, Negro Dance, and Katherine Dunham." *Textual Practice* 15, no. 3 (2001): 487–505.

Manning, Susan. *Modern Dance, Negro Dance: Race in Motion.* Minneapolis: University of Minnesota Press, 2004.

Marcus, George E., and Michael M. J. Fischer. *Anthropology as Cultural Critique: An Experimental Moment in the Human Sciences.* Chicago: University of Chicago Press, 1986.

Margolick, David. *Strange Fruit: Billie Holiday, Café Society, and an Early Cry for Civil Rights.* Philadelphia: Running Press, 2000.

Martin, Randy. *Critical Moves: Dance Studies in Theory and Politics.* Durham, NC: Duke University Press, 1998.

Martin, Ronald E. *The Languages of Difference: American Writers and Anthropologists Reconfigure the Primitive, 1878–1940.* Newark: University of Delaware Press, 2005.

Martin, Waldo E. *No Coward Soldiers: Black Cultural Politics and Postwar America.* Cambridge, MA: Harvard University Press, 2005.

May, Elaine Tyler. *Homeward Bound: American Families in the Cold War Era.* New York: Basic Books, 1988.

Meglin, Joellen A. "Choreographing Identities beyond Boundaries: *La Guiablesse* and Ruth Page's Excursions into World Dance (1926–1934)." *Dance Chronicle* 30, no. 3 (2007): 439–69.

Mikell, Gwendolyn. "When Horses Talk: Reflections on Zora Neale Hurston's Haitian Anthropology." *Phylon* 43 (September 1982): 218–30.

Morris, Gay. "Bourdieu, the Body, and Graham's Post-War Dance." *Dance Research: The Journal of the Society for Dance Research* 19, no. 2 (2001): 52–82.

Morris, Gay. *A Game for Dancers: Performing Modernism in the Postwar Years, 1945–1960.* Middletown, CT: Wesleyan University Press, 2006.

Mullen, Bill. *Popular Fronts: Chicago and African-American Cultural Politics, 1935–46.* Urbana: University of Illinois Press, 1999.

Neal, Larry. "The Social Background of the Black Arts Movement." *Black Scholar* 18, no. 1 (1987): 11–30.

Ongiri, Amy Abugo. *Spectacular Blackness: The Cultural Politics of the Black Power Movement and the Search for a Black Aesthetic.* Charlottesville: University of Virginia Press, 2010.

Osgood, Kenneth. *Total Cold War: Eisenhower's Secret Propaganda Battle at Home and Abroad.* Lawrence: University Press of Kansas, 2006.

Osumare, Halifu. "Dancing the Black Atlantic: Katherine Dunham's Research-to-Performance Method." *Ameriquest* 7, no. 2 (2010): 1–12.

Patterson, Tiffany Ruby, and Robin D. G. Kelley. "Unfinished Migrations: Reflections on the African Diaspora and the Making of the Modern World." *African Studies Review* 43, no. 1 (2000): 11–45.

Perpener, John O. *African-American Concert Dance: The Harlem Renaissance and Beyond.* Urbana: University of Illinois Press, 2001.

Plummer, Brenda Gayle. "The Afro-American Response to the Occupation of Haiti, 1915–1934." *Phylon* 43 (June 1982): 125–43.

Plummer, Brenda Gayle. *Haiti and the United States: The Psychological Moment.* Athens: University of Georgia Press, 1992.

Polyné, Millery. *From Douglass to Duvalier: U.S. African Americans, Haiti and Pan Americanism, 1870–1964.* Gainesville: University Press of Florida, 2010.

Prashad, Vijay. *The Darker Nations: A People's History of the Third World.* New York: New Press, 2007.

Prevots, Naima. *Dance for Export: Cultural Diplomacy and the Cold War.* Middletown, CT: Wesleyan University Press, 1998.

Price-Mars, Jean. *So Spoke the Uncle [Ainsi parla l'oncle].* Translated by Magdaline W. Shannon. Washington, DC: Three Continents Press, 1983. Originally published in 1928.

Quinn, Susan. *Furious Improvisation: How the WPA and a Cast of Thousands Made High Art out of Desperate Times.* New York: Walker & Co., 2008.

Ramsey, Kate. "Vodou and Nationalism: The Staging of Folklore in Mid-Twentieth Century Haiti." *Women and Performance: A Journal of Feminist Theory* 7, no. 2 (1995): 187–218.

Ramsey, Kate. *The Spirits and the Law: Vodou and Power in Haiti.* Chicago: University of Chicago Press, 2011.

Renda, Mary A. *Taking Haiti: Military Occupation and the Culture of U.S. Imperialism, 1915–1940.* Chapel Hill: University of North Carolina Press, 2001.

Reynolds, Nancy, and Malcolm McCormick. *No Fixed Points: Dance in the Twentieth Century.* New Haven, CT: Yale University Press, 2003.

Rose, Albirda. *Dunham Technique: A Way of Life.* Dubuque, IA: Kendall Hunt, 1990.

Rosenberg, Rosalind. *Divided Lives: American Women in the Twentieth Century.* New York: Hill and Wang, 1992.

Ross, Janice. *Moving Lessons: Margaret H'Doubler and the Beginning of Dance in American Education.* Madison: University of Wisconsin Press, 2000.

Saab, A. Joan. *For the Millions: American Art and Culture between the Wars.* Philadelphia: University of Pennsylvania Press, 2004.

Sadlier, Darlene J. *Americans All: Good Neighbor Cultural Diplomacy in World War II.* Austin: University of Texas Press, 2012.

Saunders, Frances Stonor. *The Cultural Cold War: The CIA and the World of Arts and Letters.* New York: New Press, 2000.

Schenbeck, Lawrence. *Racial Uplift and American Music, 1878–1943.* Jackson: University Press of Mississippi, 2012.

Schwartz, Peggy, and Murray Schwartz. *The Dance Claimed Me: A Biography of Pearl Primus.* New Haven, CT: Yale University Press, 2011.

Scott, James C. *Domination and the Arts of Resistance: Hidden Transcripts.* New Haven, CT: Yale University Press, 1990.

Senghor, Léopold Sédar. "What the Black Man Contributes." In *Race and Racism in Continental Philosophy*, edited by Robert Bernasconi and Sybol Cook, 287–302. Bloomington: Indiana University Press, 2003. Originally published in 1939.

Shannon, Magdaline W. *Jean Price-Mars, the Haitian Elite and the American Occupation, 1915–1935*. New York: St. Martin's Press, 1996.

Sharpley-Whiting, T. Denean. *Negritude Women*. Minneapolis: University of Minnesota Press, 2002.

Shay, Anthony. *Choreographic Politics: State Folk Dance Companies, Representation and Power*. Middletown, CT: Wesleyan University Press, 2002.

Sherrod, Elgie Gaynell. "The Dance Griots: An Examination of the Dance Pedagogy of Katherine Dunham and Black Pioneering Dancers in Chicago and New York City, from 1931–1946." PhD diss., Temple University, 1998.

Sklar, Deidre. "Can Bodylore Be Brought to Its Senses?" *Journal of American Folklore* 107, no. 423 (1994): 9–22.

Sklaroff, Lauren Rebecca. *Black Culture and the New Deal: The Quest for Civil Rights in the Roosevelt Era*. Chapel Hill: University of North Carolina Press, 2009.

Smethurst, James Edward. *The Black Arts Movement: Literary Nationalism in the 1960s and 1970s*. Chapel Hill: University of North Carolina Press, 2005.

Solomon, Mark I. *The Cry Was Unity: Communists and African Americans, 1917–1936*. Jackson: University Press of Mississippi, 1998.

Srinivasan, Priya. *Sweating Saris: Indian Dance as Transnational Labor*. Philadelphia: Temple University Press, 2011.

Stormy Weather. Directed by Andrew Stone. 1943. Los Angeles: Twentieth Century Fox, 2006. DVD.

Sugrue, Thomas J. *The Origins of the Urban Crisis: Race and Inequality in Postwar Detroit*. Princeton, NJ: Princeton University Press, 1996.

Sugrue, Thomas J. *Sweet Land of Liberty: The Forgotten Struggle for Civil Rights in the North*. New York: Random House, 2008.

Theising, Andrew J. *Made in USA: East St. Louis, the Rise and Fall of an Industrial River Town*. St. Louis, MO: Virginia Publishing, 2003.

Torgovnick, Marianna. *Gone Primitive: Savage Intellects, Modern Lives*. Chicago: University of Chicago Press, 1990.

Trouillot, Michel-Rolph. *Haiti: State against Nation: The Origins and Legacy of Duvalierism*. New York: Monthly Review Press, 2000.

Vaillant, Janet G. *Black, French, and African: A Life of Léopold Sédar Senghor*. Cambridge, MA: Harvard University Press, 1990.

Van Deburg, William L. *New Day in Babylon: The Black Power Movement and American Culture, 1965–1975*. Chicago: University of Chicago Press, 1992.

Vogel, Shane. "Performing 'Stormy Weather': Ethel Waters, Lena Horne, and Katherine Dunham." *South Central Review* 25, no. 1 (Spring 2008): 93–113.

Von Eschen, Penny M. "Made on Stage: Transnational Performance and the Worlds of Katherine Dunham from London to Dakar." In *Transnational Lives: Biographies of Global Modernity, 1700–Present*, edited by Desley Deacon, Penny Russel, and Angela Woollacott, 156–70. New York: Palgrave Macmillan, 2010.

Von Eschen, Penny M. *Race against Empire: Black Americans and Anticolonialism, 1937–1957*. Ithaca, NY: Cornell University Press, 1997.

Von Eschen, Penny M. *Satchmo Blows up the World: Jazz Ambassadors Play the Cold War*. Cambridge, MA: Harvard University Press, 2004.

Williams, Megan E. "The 'Crisis' Cover Girl: Lena Horne, the NAACP, and Representations of African American Femininity, 1941–1945." *American Periodicals* 16, no. 2 (2006): 200–218.

Wilson, Carlton. "Conceptualizing the African Diaspora." *Comparative Studies of South Asia, Africa and the Middle East* 17, no. 2 (1997): 118–22.

Wilson, William Julius. *The Truly Disadvantaged: The Inner City, the Underclass, and Public Policy.* 2nd ed. Chicago: University of Chicago Press, 2012. First edition published in 1987.

Wright, Michelle. *Becoming Black: Creating Identity in the African Diaspora.* Durham, NC: Duke University Press, 2004.

Zipp, Samuel. *Manhattan Projects: The Rise and Fall of Urban Renewal in Cold War New York.* New York: Oxford University Press, 2010.

INDEX

France and West Africa, 3
Franco, Francisco, 58–59
French colonialism in Haiti, 43, 48
Freyre, Gilberto, 135
Frisell, Dick, 160–161, 163
Fromm, Erich, 15, 32, 175
Furstenberg, Egon von, 171

Garçon, Maurice, 127
Garvey, Marcus, 3, 44
Gateway Theater in St. Louis, 187
Gauguin, Paul, 32
Gauthier, Viviane, 159
Gennaro, Peter, 110, 114
Ghana, 132, 146
Goffman, Erving, 40
Gonzalez, Anita, 6–7
Goode, Gerald, 84
Goodman, Ezra, 114
Goodman Theatre, 66, 67, 69
Gorée, Senegal, 167–168
Gorer, Geoffrey, 88
Gottschild, Brenda Dixon, 6
Goupillières, R., 131
Graham, Martha, 9
   ballet and, 112
   dance company, 21, 26
   Dunham dance in style of, 66, 67
   legal dispute over work of, 195
   modern dance as American dance, 65
   Night Journey, 91
   State Department sponsorship
      of, 148
Graham School, 121
Graham Technique, 110
Gray, Dorothy, 82, 98, 153,
   156, 222*n*36
Great Day, The (Hurston), 42
Great Depression, 10, 24, 32, 56, 59–60
Great Dictator, The (film), 101
Great Migration, 14
Great Northern Theatre, 39–43, 60
Great Society, 182
Green, Adam, 101
Green, Paul, 19
Gregh, Fernand, 157
Gregory, Dick, 173
Gromov, Anatoly, 102
Gubelman, Walter S., 104, 105
Guiablesse, La (Page), 27–29, 30
Guillén, Nicolás, 113, 146

Guinea, 133, 151
Gusar, Alta, 107
Guy, Edna, 21

Habitation Leclerc, 156, 158–164,
   171–173, 172*f*, 240*n*116
Haiti
   Carnival (*Kanaval*) in, 46–47
   dance, 44–47, 57–59
   diaspora centered in, 3, 170–171
   Dunham School and, 114–115, 117
   Dunham's legacy in, 200
   Dunham's performing in, 141,
      142*f*, 151
   Dunham's research in, 35, 38, 39,
      40–41, 42–53
   Experimental Group and, 114–115
   ignorance about, 57
   military coup of 1992, 173
   political situation in, 44
   Pratt and Marie-Christine in, 13
   slave revolution in, 47
   tourism in, 158, 160–164,
      171–173, 172*f*
   United Nation's delegates, 118
   United States and, 36, 44, 47,
      49, 156
   See also Vodou
Haiti (DuBois, William), 3, 53
Haitian Ceremonial Dances
   (Dunham), 57, 70
Haitian Revolution, 49–53, 154, 156
Hamilton, Eileen, 104
Handy, W. C., 20, 138
Harding, Vincent, 192
Hard Time Blues (Primus), 92
Harlem and Dunham School, 104–105
Harlem Black Arts Repertory Theater,
   177, 180
Harlem Freedom Schools on Negro Art
   and Culture, 177
Harlem Renaissance, 18
Harlem's Cotton Club, 80
Harlem Youth Opportunities Unlimited
   Program (HARYOU), 177
Harper, Dolores, 145
Hayes, Frank, 25
Hays, Will, 78
Hayworth, Rita, 126
H'Doubler, Margaret, 108
Hearn, Lafcadio, 27

Herskovits, Melville
  on African retentions, 4, 37, 38, 46
  criticism of Dunham, 42
  Dunham influenced by, 31, 33, 39
  Dunham's correspondence with,
    29–30, 31, 37, 40, 41
  Dunham's graduate studies and, 55
  Haitian research, 44
  Hurston's correspondence with, 41–42
  Life in a Haitian Valley, 44
  Myth of the Negro Past, The, 31, 206n14
  recording equipment for Dunham
    and, 39–40
  theory of acculturation, 4, 31, 46, 170
  third-person voice, 39
Herzog, Emily, 73
Hill, Constance Valis, 134, 144–145
Hill, Herman, 81
"Histoire d'un Soldat" ("A Soldier's
  Tale"), 112
Holiday, Billie, 92, 138
Holly, Mathilde, 115
Hollywood, 4, 75–84, 91, 92, 99f, 102,
  110, 121, 164
Hollywood Ten, 119
homosexuality, 8, 63, 70, 118, 182
Honor Roll of Race Relations, 93
hopak dance (Ukraine), 16
Horne, Lena, 80–81, 95
House Un-American Activities
  Committee (HUAC), 119, 149
Howard University, 114
HUD (Department of Housing and
  Urban Development), 186–188
Hudlin, Warrington, 194
Huebert, Diana, 25
Hughes, Allen, 150
Hughes, Elinor, 90
Hughes, Langston
  black folk expression and, 23
  Christophe and, 52
  Cuban Evening and, 113
  Cube Theatre and, 20
  at Dunham School rehearsals, 103
  Emperor of Haiti/Troubled Island, 53
  in Haiti, 44
  on interracial marriage, 99
  on *Touch of Innocence, A*, 13
  Tropics and Le Jazz "Hot" and, 71
humanism
  Dunham's, 2–3, 86, 156–158, 201

global citizenship and, 158
Haiti and, 3, 154, 156–158
négritude and, 170
Senghor on, 164–165
Humphrey, Doris, 21
Hunter College/Hunter College High
  School, 91
Hunter, Mary, 20, 21, 45, 69, 93
Hurok, Sol, 1, 9, 77, 84, 85, 91,
  93, 96, 98
Hurston, Zora Neale, 41–42, 206n14
Hutchins, Robert, 15
Hyde Park, 21–22

IDTC (Institute for Dunham Technique
  Certification), 199–200
Illinois Arts Council, 187
Illinois Writers Project, 29
imperialism/capitalism/colonialism
  Afrique, 131–132
  anticolonial activism, 117, 128, 129
  artificial culture and capitalism, 31
  culture and new world order,
    145–146
  decolonization, 117–118, 123–124,
    133, 150, 153
  Dunham on, 3, 36, 48, 49, 108–109,
    140, 157
  Dunham's choreography and, 4–5, 52
  free state of Ghana, 132
  functionalism and, 30–31
  in Haiti, 36, 43, 47–48, 50–52,
    156–157, 161–162, 164, 171
  in Jamaica, 143
  Lenin on imperialism and
    capitalism, 48
  lynching and, 144
  in Martinique, 37
  minority oppression and, 108–109
  post–World War II, 124
  primitivism and, 31
  Rhapsodie Caraïbe, 127–129
  in Senegal, 168, 181
Imperial War Lords, 183
indigenous Americans and island
  peoples, 67
Inness-Brown, Virginia, 165–166
Institute for Dunham Technique
  Certification (IDTC), 199–200
Institute for Intercultural
  Communication, 7, 176

Lee, Canada, 20
Lehman, Herbert S., 104
Lehman, Herbert S., Mrs., 105
Lepecki, André, 5
Lescot, Elie, 155
Lesson, The (Dunham), 184
Lévi-Strauss, Claude, 103
Lewis, Bertha Moseley, 20
Lewis, Oscar, 178
Life in a Haitian Valley (Herskovits), 44
Limón, José, 107
Lincoln Center, 179
Lindy, 110
Lindy Hop, 31
Link, Emory, 187
Lloyd, Margaret, 89
Lloyd, Norman, 185–186, 187
loa (lwa, loi), 35, 45, 47, 57, 94, 184
Locke, Alain, 18, 20, 23, 39, 44
Lomax, Alan, 59
"Look Upon a Star" program, 115–116
Lorde, Audre, 77
Lotus Eaters, 57
Louisville, 1–2, 97–98
Louisville's Memorial Auditorium, 1–2
L'Ouverture, Toussaint, 50, 52, 170
Luis-Brown, David, 31
Lula Washington Dance School, 200
lynching
    Dunham's work against, 56, 59
    Man Has Just Been Lynched, A, 92
    Popular Front and, 59
    See also Southland (Dunham)

Maggie, Dinah, 132
Magic Island, The (Seabrook), 44
Magic of Katherine Dunham, The (Ailey),
    196–198, 199, 245n4
Magloire, Paul, 143, 159, 161
Makonnen, T. R., 129
Maldoror, Sarah, 146
Man Has Just Been Lynched, A
    (Primus), 92
Man Who Died at Twelve O'Clock, The
    (Green), 19
Marchant, Claude, 7
Mardi Gras, 45
Martha Graham Dance Company, 26
Martin Beck Theatre, 85, 96
Martin, Carlos, 78

Martin, John, 70, 79, 91, 114
Martinique, 27, 35, 37, 40, 61–63
Marvin, Mark, 102
Masque Players, 20
Masters and the Slaves, The (Freyre), 135
Matthews, Basil, 107
Matsoukas, Nicholas, 19
Maurois, André, 127, 157
McClendon, Rose, 20
McCoo, Jordis, 20, 24, 53, 66
McCracken, Joan, 103
McKinley, Linda, 193f
Mead, Margaret, 30, 60, 89
Medical Bureau to Aid Spanish
    Democracy, 58, 59
Meerpol, Abel (Lewis Allan), 92
Melanesian dance, 1, 113
Mendez, Julio, 130
Merce Cunningham Dance Company,
    195–196
Mérida, Ana, 124
Metropolitan Opera, 21, 103, 177
Mexican Dunham School teachers, 117
Mexico, Dunham tour in, 119,
    124–126, 125f
Mille, Agnes de, 22, 112
"Minefield, The"/"Minefields"
    (Dunham), 58, 59
Minnehaha, 14
Minstrelsy, 26, 70, 71
Miranda, Carmen, 78
Miranda, Luis, 114
Mirova, Vera, 27, 30
Mitchell, Arthur, 120, 121, 166, 171
Mitchell, Louis, 59
M.O.D.E. (Modern Organization for
    Dance Evolvement), 192
Model Cities Program, 186
Model City Agency (East St. Louis),
    187–188
modern dance
    as American, 65
    Dunham and, 10, 11, 25, 26, 32, 36,
        56, 65, 112, 113, 126, 186
    in early 20th century, 16–17, 21, 25
    in Mexico, 124
    in 1940s, 91
    in 1980s, 196–197
    primitivism and, 5–6, 32, 113
    racial stereotypes and, 33, 65, 66